THE TWO WITNESSES

Lance Johnson

COME & SEE Ministries
Books
Davis, California

THE TWO WITNESSES

All rights of this book are yielded to the Holy Spirit Whose chief purposes, the Bible teaches, are to guide believers into all truth and to further the Gospel of Jesus Christ. However, believing a measure of stewardship has been extended to him in this effort, Lance Johnson accepts the responsibility of providing the following guidelines for any duplications of the contents of this book:

(1) Use is encouraged; therefore, brief excerpts may be reproduced for Bible study discussions, etc., without written approval.

(2) To obtain express permission for major reproductions of the book, please contact the author and/or publisher, Lance Johnson, Director of COME & SEE Ministries, giving the details of the extent and manner in which usefulness is planned.

(3) No duplications, rewrites, etc., are permitted for resale without proper approval from the author or those he designates for this purpose.

Scripture quotations are from the King James Authorized Version or from the New King James Version of the Holy Bible. (NKJV used by permission from Thomas Nelson Publishers.)

Other quotations noted in the Bibliography in back of this book.

Revised Edition. (First edition copyrighted 1990; published Nov. 1991 under ISBN 0-9631328-0-6.)

Library of Congress Catalog Card Number: 91-93097
International Standard Book Number (ISBN) 0-9631328-1-4

Printed in the United States of America

DEDICATION

Every word in this book I have probably at some time spoken to someone. I suspect those who have received my repeated-expoundings — mostly family — needed to hear it the least. The Holy Spirit must have been responsible to cause them to *be still* while I verbally rehearsed my beliefs. The fact is, *I* needed them.

"Thanks to all of you!"

Martin Johnson (son)
Jane Johnson (daughter-in-law)
James Eilers (son-in-law)
Jennifer Eilers (daughter)
Shirley *(Cindy)* Johnson (my patient wife)

Also, I wish to thank my mother, Mildred Johnson, Daphine Ray (sister) and husband Philip, and Diane Clayton (sister), for a lifetime of their expressed love and confidence in me.

A special note of appreciation is due a good friend and pastor, Dr. Dennis Lloyd, for his spirit of discernment regarding the concepts found here and for his encouragement in the writing of this manuscript.

All of you have been a far greater blessing to me than you'll ever know. God bless you for your understanding, hearing hearts and prayers in support of me in this effort.

CONTENTS

INTRODUCTION

It is said among successful authors that *good writing is re-writing.* If this is true, the book you are holding should be a masterpiece! Kidding aside, I've lost count of the minor editions and this is the fourth complete revision of this manuscript, the time now spanning 15 years.

My theme centers around predictions. *God's* predictions. Bible prophecy. Scriptural eschatology. This subject is far-removed from optometry (my *tent-making* profession) nor I am an academically-prepared minister. However, I am encouraged by the fact that Isaiah, Amos, Jeremiah, Elijah, Daniel, Peter, John and other Bible personalities were also laymen. I'm not claiming spiritual equality with these men, just pointing out the fact that God did not use formal institutions to train them. God simply called and revealed Himself to them. Their response was to convey God's ways and His Word to all mankind. Thanks to them we have the Bible.

What, then, are my credentials and qualifications for writing this book? 1 — I believe God called me. 2 — I believe He has given me certain, pertinent insights into Biblical prophecy. I have decided to accept this as sufficient. I hope you do too.

It was late 1978 that I began my study of prophecy, completing the first edition of this work by mid-1979. Now, 15 years later, I'm more convinced than ever about the conclusions I reached at that time. I base this on becoming increasingly aware of prophecies already fulfilled (some ancient, some modern) which encourages me to share my observations with you.

The following introductory remarks will be longer than customary. However, in light of the intense nature of the subject matter, and because of my unusual background for such an undertaking as this, I feel it will be helpful for the reader to first know a few of my basic convictions concerning the Bible, in general, and about God's involvement with humanity.

THE BIBLE

God's Word is perfect. Now there are some differences among the various interpretations and modern translations but I'm convinced even most of these were under God's sovereign surveillance and protection. But on this we must not be mistaken: The original delivery recorded by those God chose to write the Bible was without error!

A modern Bible might be likened to an LP recording. In our day, when the Bible's purity and reliability is under such severe attack, I think it's worth the time it takes to explain what I mean.

With every handling of a record disc comes a few nicks and scratches that, when played, produce some pops and other unwanted sounds. However, you can also still hear clearly a duplicate of the original sounds that were put on the recording company's master disc.

I've been a sound-enthusiast for many years and in my earlier days learned about the process of record production. For example, let's suppose a conductor and orchestra get together to perform Beethoven's Fifth Symphony. Typically, the recording engineer records the session using several microphones and the sound output from those is put on several tracks of a multi-track tape recorder. Later, in the studio, that tape is played and the multi-tracks are mixed, balanced and combined into only two electronic signals (to create a stereo effect) and those are put on yet another tape recorder.

From this last two-track tape recording they make a round, hard-metal, master disc. The sound from the tape produces permanent 'wiggles' and 'squiggles' cut into the master disc. These tiny movements conform exactly to the electronic impulses from the tape recorder, which are 'carbon copies' of the original performance. In cookie-cutter fashion, this hard master disc is used to make impressions upon soft, plastic discs, the ones you and I (used to) buy. At home we place a phonograph needle onto the record and, 'miraculously', listen to beautiful music; in fact, a nigh-perfect replica of the original.

Although frequent playing has resulted in some imperfections, my 20-year-old LP copy of Beethoven's Fifth Symphony will always sound like the original master recording the record company has on file. Also noteworthy, when other orchestras play this same piece of music, producing shades of differences of course, every Beethoven fan will know that it is still his Fifth Symphony.

God's original *statement* to those who recorded the Bible is somewhat like that original, multi-track, master recording. When God first spoke to those who recorded what He said, there was no misunderstanding of His speech. Biblical authors (the recording 'engineers') wern't inspired as we ordinarily understand that term. The Bible was **God-breathed** into the minds of the writers. (See 2 Timothy 3:16.) They wrote down the exact words in the language (s) of God's choice (Hebrew, Aramaic or Greek), accurate in every detail like a master-tape records every nuance of sound made by an original orchestra performance. There were no mistakes.

Today, we do not have those original *recordings* from God. But we *do* have thousands of excellent, original-language, ancient copies, as well as meticulous translations from those ancient manuscripts written in hundreds of different languages. God has guarded His Word through the years. It may be that He has actually allowed several English translations to surface <u>specifically</u> to broaden some of the slightly-hidden meanings contained in the original languages. In other words, the translations don't necessarily contradict one another but each brings out certain shades of meaning others may miss. (Keep in mind, I'm not including here 'translations', so-called, introduced by certain non-Christian cults.)

The bottom line, even though there may be some 'nicks and scratches' in modern translations, the **Master's Voice**, and message, can still be heard loud and clear by anyone who cares to *listen.*

THE AUTHOR

So, God was both Author and Conductor of the original book (the 66 books recorded by 40+ writers) of what we call the Bible. It was a grand 'performance'. No scratches. No flaws. And during the Christian age, the Holy Spirit has watched over the 'musicians' (the translators) who made the original composition relevant to the readers of their day.

Later *performances* may not be exactly alike but, nevertheless, the *Master Leader* is still behind the scenes, and just as reachable as ever, through the reading and application found in today's versions of the Bible. On the whole, there is little, significant variation on the main themes and doctrines in the several English translations I use. Indeed, far more amazing is the tremendous agreement among translations rather than the few inconsistencies sometimes found.

Now I've said all that to instill in the reader's mind the value and credibility I place in the Bible as the authoritative and reliable source of wisdom and knowledge I believe it to be. And since the Bible is the only book which describes God and man and their inter-relationships with perfect accuracy, then it seems reasonable to assume it is also the only written resource we have which would predict, with absolute accuracy, the future of all mankind up to the end of time itself.

If this is true, then we must search out with all diligence, every "nook and cranny" of the Bible for all evidences which inform us of our day *and* what we can expect in the future. This has been my quest for the past 15 years and what I found is sufficiently-different from other prophetic writers that I think it is not too presumptuous to believe God would have me share it. Thus, I introduce you to my book, *THE TWO WITNESSES*.

"IN THE BEGINNING..."

As I said, before any Biblical commentary on any subject (but especially prophecy) is presentable, understandable, or deemed credible, the reader needs to know what the author believes about certain, foundational Biblical-truths. Here's mine.

From the onset of creation, God has purposed, and is now executing, a Master Plan which involves time, space and the material universe. Paradoxically, even scientists (largely an unbelieving group today) have helped prove that the earth is the apple-of-God's-eye, through the discovery that outer space holds no life as we know it here. The Bible agrees with this conclusion; but *why* it is so eludes us. For now it must be left in God's mind alone.

Basically, the book of Genesis explains all that God wanted us to know about how it all started. When there was yet nothing and God said, *"Let there be..."*, followed by words which reflected His creative desires, whatever was in His mind suddenly materialized! Thus, God used words to bring into being everything you and I can see. Now if you can believe that, you are well on your way to becoming a *believer* — in the Biblical sense. On the other hand, if this troubles you, so will most everything else written in this book. (But even if you can't 'digest' these facts just yet, stick around anyway; becoming a believer is usually progressive. Perhaps somewhere along the way, things will begin to 'jive' for you.)

Actually, all creation is summarized by the first verse in the Genesis account:

"In the beginning God created the heaven and the earth."

After that verse, Moses (the recorder) was inspired to tell us a few of the details: The first creative act we are told about has to do with *light.* God said, *"Let there be light, and there was light."* Incredible! Light followed in the path of His words! This was the first prediction and when it came true, the first prophecy was fulfilled. So, from Genesis through the Bible's 66 books, one can trace all prophecy (and its fulfillment), right up to the end of time as described in Revelation, the last book of the Bible. And fittingly, the Bible ends with a prophecy:

"And if any man shall take away from the words of the book of this prophecy, God shall take away his part out of the book of life, and out of the holy city, and from the things which are written in this book." Rev. 22:19.

This verse is quite sobering, assuming the speaker here is as reliable as the One Who spoke *light* into existence. Let's face it, the creative speech of the 'Genesis God' perfectly matches everything seeable. This alone is indicative that the 'Biblical God' means business; business worthy of being believed. Since the Genesis account is so self-evident today, the verse above ought to cause an unbeliever to cry out to this God for His mercy. History's reality is pretty convincing proof that what *God* says shall come to pass, will!

OKAY, THE 'GENESIS GOD' IS GOD. BUT WHO IS THE 'REVELATION GOD'?

In Revelation 1:8 we find these words:

"I am the Alpha and the Omega, the Beginning and the End," says the LORD, who is and who was and who is to come, the Almighty." And then in Rev. 22:13 we see:

"I am the Alpha and the Omega, the Beginning and the End, the First and the Last." Then comes the identifier:

"I, Jesus, have sent my angel to testify to you these things in the churches. I am the Root and the Offspring of David, and the Bright and Morning Star." Rev. 22:16.

An astounding discovery is made when these titles are linked. The 'Revelator' is said here to be *"the LORD"*, *"the Alpha and the Omega"*, *"the Beginning and the End"*, *"the First and the Last"*, *"the Root and the Offspring of David"* and *"the Bright and Morning Star"*. Then, the absolute clincher that *God* is talking, the speaker is referred to as *"the Almighty"*. Finally, in verse 22:16, this One who said all these titles belonged to Him, identified Himself by His common name---*"I, Jesus,...".*

There's no getting around the fact that the 'Revelation God', the One who made the statement of prophetic warning to those who attempt to alter Biblical prophecy, is Jesus of Nazareth. In fact, if one takes the time to trace it, this same Jesus is found to be the center-stage personality of all prophecy. Note, for example, the first verse of Revelation:

> *"The Revelation of <u>Jesus Christ</u>, which God gave unto him, to shew unto his servants things which must shortly come to pass, and he sent and signified it by his angel unto his servant John."*

Wait a minute! If Jesus, "the Almighty", has the authority to speak at the end of God's Revelation to man, why don't we find Him in the beginning? Actually, we can. But before going into that, there is another personality who ought to be discussed here: God's primary opposing force.

THE ADVERSARY

Unsaved-man's understanding of the devil is a caricature of the truth of the matter. But because the reliability of the Bible is so well-founded, we need to know what *it* has to say about God's primary adversary. Since we are trying to establish a solid footing for understanding prophecy, I think it's important to find out how God's opposition came into the picture in the first place. Let's go back to Genesis again. Ironically, the very first mention of any opposition to what God had said after He spoke the universe into existence was:

"...*Yea, hath God said,...?*" Gen. 3:1.

Note the speaker's strategy. He struck at the very heart of the issue: the validity of God's own spoken words. You see, the whole foundation of Biblical-belief hinges on whether or not we can trust the One Who declared Himself as *the* Book's Author; and whether He is the source of power behind creation. The 'person' who spoke above was obviously trying to cast doubt in the mind of the one he was talking to.

Without quoting the whole passage, let me summarize the scene: (See Gen. 3.) God had already created man and woman at this time, naming them Adam and Eve. We don't know exactly how long it was after their existence that the above incident happened. However, a creature called the serpent came to Eve, conversed with her and was obviously attempting to destroy her confidence in God. He achieved his goal. She did what God had specifically told her and Adam not to do: eat of a certain forbidden fruit. She then enticed Adam and he also ate. From this seemingly-trite action eminated all human rebellion and ultimately all sin! The first human transgression against God had been committed.

Later, God judged the serpent for his temptation to Eve, saying he would in the future crawl on his belly. (Obviously, prior to the temptation the serpent was quite different from a snake as we now know it.)

But Genesis 3:15 is the verse I want to underscore:

"*And I will put enmity between thee and the woman, and between thy seed and her seed; it shall bruise thy head, and thou shalt bruise his heel.*"

This is an example of one of those passages I referred to earlier which has deeper meanings that will be missed without careful scrutiny. Most Christian scholars agree on the following:

1. First of all, on the physical plane, God is obviously talking to the serpent.

2. The *"seed"* of the woman, to which God refers in the verse, alludes to the Messiah — Whom God would eventually send to the world to solve the sin problem which had been introduced there in the garden.

> Note: (a), this *"seed"* is in the singular tense; (b), it would come from a woman; and (c), it would eventually *"bruise"* the head of the serpent. But, the fact is, a woman does not produce seed! She produces eggs, which must be fertilized by the seed of a man in order to propagate life. And yet, the emphasis here is that this *seed* would be from a woman, not from a man! How can this be?

Is it not reasonable to conclude that this prediction is referring to a woman who, not impregnated by a man, would someday produce a son? Surely this Genesis account about the woman and her *seed* is a forecast of what has become known as **the incarnation:** God in man form. (Read Matt. 1 and Luke 1).

But we must also ask, what is meant by the seed "bruising" the serpent's head and the serpent "bruising" the seed's heel? Well, regarding how God would eventually take care of man's rebellion in the Garden of Eden, and it's consequences, all Scripture points to Jesus Christ, the *seed* of God, as the One Who shouldered that responsibility. How did Jesus do this? The Bible says He took upon Himself the wrath of God (Luke 22:44) and the wrath of man (Acts 2:23 & 24), for the benefit of all man's sin (John 3:16). Jesus' crucifixion was the fulfillment of the serpent's part in the "bruising" of the "seed's" heel. The serpent thought he had destroyed the Son of God. But actually, Jesus' resurrection proved to be the crushing-blow to the serpent's head! In light of all history, the crowning 'blue ribbon' for plots-that-backfired must go to the serpent.

In this passage, God is pronouncing judgement upon the serpent who, at that time, had a nature quite different than afterwards. But the serpent was not acting only out of his own mentality. A careful study shows conclusively that it was Lucifer who had entered the serpent, and under his inspiration, Eve was tempted. (The Bible identifies Lucifer by many names such as *devil, adversary, prince of the power of the air, prince of this world, god of this age, dragon,* and *serpent.* But the most common Biblical name is *Satan.)*

Scripture presents Satan as the primary leader of all spiritual wickedness. As Lucifer, before his fall, Satan thought he was equal with God; and till this day is still determined to try proving he is. (See Is. 14.) Even though his eventual doom was sealed by Jesus' work at Calvary, Satan still has certain freedoms and privileges in this age. He plots and plans to thwart God's Master plan of the ages. Of course, Christians alone presently have the victory over Satan, but even they must access this victory through faith in Jesus Christ and application of the principles he laid down for us to follow. (I can't take the time here to Biblically-prove all this but the reader needs to know what I believe about the Bible's central themes for the overall presentation of this book to have its intended thrust.)

SATAN'S 'MASTER' PLAN

Obviously God has a Master plan. And He is bringing it to pass in a methodical way. We see its commencement in the Garden of Eden. In Revelation, we see a picture of the end of this age and even a general perspective of eternity-future. My book is about the time in between those two extremes.

But also, all along the way, Satan has attempted to place obstacles in the way of God's plan. It must be admitted that he's sometimes effective at it. How does he do it? In the garden of Eden, Satan did his dirty work through deception. He entered the serpent and through him, misguided Eve; and through her, tempted Adam. Satan has never deviated from this tactic. He doesn't have to, because it seems we are still just as blind to his spiritual trickery as they were. But he can only achieve evil results in and around our lives as we allow him to. Mainly, this comes through denying Jesus, the *seed* Whom God sent to deliver us from the serpent's deceptions.

Make no mistake, Satan has a 'master' plan too. This will be discussed later in greater detail, but for now we need to know that his system is founded on two obsessions:

1. Satan wants man to worship him, and
2. he wants to convince man that he can solve his own problems without the acknowledgement and submission to the God of the Bible.

This plan has been on-going since the beginning of the Fall of mankind. The Bible and history show very clearly that Satan thought he just about had his plan completed when certain kingdoms prevailed which he had inspired. (I shall later touch on several of these attempts.) To not see the satanic evidences of specific threats against God's coming-Kingdom will insure blindness in the area of Biblical prophecy. A key to understanding Satan, although somewhat paradoxical, is the fact that he desires to keep people ignorant of his existence.

WHY DOES GOD GRANT SO MUCH TIME AND SPACE TO SATAN?

Even though Satan's doom was sealed at Calvary almost 2,000 years ago, he still has God's permission, within certain limitations, to operate in this present generation. Actually, the Bible doesn't give an easy answer as to why this is so. However, I think the following comments do not violate any of the Scriptures.

Today, God is weaving His Master Plan primarily through the fabric of the Church. He is preparing for eternity those who believe in His Son and His kingdom. For reasons we can't fully fathom just yet, God has determined that Christians function under conditions of pressure from our common enemy — Satan and all his *angelic brothers* (demons) who fell with him.

In his earthly mission, Jesus beat Satan's temptations through the use of Scripture. Today, Christians must do likewise. So, even though every act of Satan is for evil intents and purposes, from God's omnipotent (all-powerful) and omniscient (all-knowing) position, He will ultimately use it to His Own glory.

To fully comprehend this is beyond any of us. My hope, belief and conviction is that <u>nothing</u> is out of God's control. He knows exactly what's going on and I believe that one day He will make very clear to Christians the meaning of these *foggy* days through which we are now passing. That's what <u>trust</u> is and trust is what true Christianity is all about.

To put this on a personal level, even though sin sometimes still exists in my life, by faith I accept the promise that I am a child of God. Even though Satan is still free to tempt and *bite the heel*, by faith I know that his defeat was determined at Calvary. Just as I was spiritually-saved (though yet physically-unborn) by what Christ did for me 2,000 years ago, at the same time Satan's doom was sealed. I hadn't come on the scene yet but my life, in God's mind, was as sure to occur as light was certain to come forth when God first said, *"Let there be light..."*. Whether predicting good or evil, all God's promises became prophetic-reality the moment God spoke it!

Satan will eventually lose his *grace-space*. I'm just as certain of that as I am of my own salvation. I'm going to heaven. Satan is going to hell. Both were guaranteed by the obedience and work of Jesus Christ 2,000 years ago. The promise of God's *seed* in the garden of Eden was the word of prophecy which insured my eternal security. Just as surely, God made a statement that insured Satan's eventual, eternal separation from God and man.

The Bible says that hell was prepared for the devil and his angels. But people who reject God's Master Plan of the ages (i.e., the promise of the *seed* of God, Christ Jesus, Who would become the Redeemer of lost mankind), will also join Satan and all his cohorts in the same hell, for eternity. Now I realize that's hard, even frightening, negative talk. But the fact is, it's truth-talk. It's Biblical-talk. It's the kind of talk that can lead one to freedom. Jesus paid the price for us to avoid hell. If you never have, trust in Him now, and become eternally saved!

Next, let's see what Jesus Himself had to say about prophecy relative to our day.

JESUS ANSWERS A DIRECT QUESTION ABOUT THE END

Jesus Christ promised His disciples that He would some day return to earth to receive those who believe in Him and accept the gift of His salvation. Concerned about the establishment of His Kingdom, Jesus' disciples once asked Him:

"...*What shall be the sign of thy coming, and of the end of the world?...,* (Matt. 24:3), to which He later responded, *"But of that 'day and hour' knoweth no man, no, not the angels of heaven, but my Father only."* (Matt. 24:36)

Clearly, we will not know the exact day or hour of His return. However, in the next verse following the above text, Jesus further explained, "...*But as the days of Noah were...*". At this point Jesus goes on to give a long discourse of the signs and conditions which would prevail upon the earth just prior to His return, making it clear He expects Christians to be on the alert and cognizant of these specific occurrences.

THE PROPHECY PUZZLE

Prophecy, much like a cardboard puzzle, is difficult to figure out; especially at first. Imagine a large puzzle scattered on a table and your job is to put it together correctly. Although many pieces look similar, no two are exactly alike. Now you know the designer of the puzzle had a very specific *picture* in mind because you have already seen a completed sketch on the box cover. What do you do?

First, find a few pieces, the curves, colors, and lines of which look as though they might be a part of a section of the picture. You assess, turn, align, push, shove, and finally two pieces fit exactly into position. Voila, you have successfully begun the project! No one could ever persuade you that those two pieces don't go together, right? The lines are correct, a portion of the picture is unmistakeably there, the colors match, and so on. It's right and you know it's right! Next, you proceed to another section and continue until you complete the full picture.

Similar to some pieces of a puzzle, there are certain Scripture passages which may seem trivial as they stand alone, but when placed alongside other passages, a clearer, prophetic word-picture begins to emerge. (A WORD OF CAUTION HERE: Cults have a long track record of interpreting Scriptures so that they conform to their already-established beliefs. Unfortunately though, this fact has caused many knowledgeable Bible-researchers to shy away from even looking for the deeper Biblical truths of Scripture---particularly concerning prophecy. The right approach? Careful, balanced, prayerful search.)

Let me give you an example of what I mean by "deeper, Biblical truth": It is well-accepted that Isaiah 53 is a prophetic portrait of Jesus as the suffering Messiah. If we were to stick to the rule 'interpret-the-literal-sense-only', as some suggest, the spiritual significance of Jesus would never have been realized as the *greater* truth of this passage!

THE LAW OF DOUBLE REFERENCE

Thus, we see in Isaiah 53 an excellent example of Scripture which has two meanings, both equally true, but the second inference is spiritually-deeper, and obviously more important. This is known as **THE LAW OF DOUBLE REFERENCE**. There are numerous Old Testament portraits of the Messiah demonstrated in the lives of many individuals: e.g., Joseph, Moses, David, and others. These are well-known, thoroughly-established, factual fore-shadowings of Jesus Christ. Lesser known, it seems, is the fact that this same pattern is found in many prophetic passages that concern the entire Christian era. It is of utmost importance to understand this principle in order to comprehend my book. For brevity sake, I shall hereafter refer to the principle as the **LODR**.

VIEWS ON INTERPRETING THE BOOK OF REVELATION

According to Biblical commentators Jamieson, Fausset and Brown[1], there are three schools of interpreters on the book of Revelation.

1. **THE PRETERISTS**
   The Preterists believe that almost the entire book of Revelation was fulfilled very early in Church history.

2. **THE HISTORICAL**
   The Historical interpreters believe the book of Revelation comprises the history of the Church from John's time to the end of the world, the Seals being chronologically succeeded by the trumpets and the trumpets by the vials.

---

[1]"Commentary on the Whole Bible", by Jamieson, Fausset and Brown.

3. **THE FUTURISTS**
    The Futurists consider almost the whole of Revelation as
    yet future, to be fulfilled immediately before Christ's
    second coming.

Now let me quote Jamieson, Fausset and Brown's response to
the above schools:

*"The first theory (The Preterists) was not held by any of
the earliest Fathers and is only held now by Rationalists,
who limit John's vision to things within his own horizon,
pagan Rome's persecutions of Christians and its
consequently anticipated destruction. The Futurists
School, who believe that basically everything in
Revelation is yet future, is open to this great objection:
It would leave the Church of Christ unprovided with
prophetical guidance or support under her fiery trials for
almost 2,000 years! Now God has said, 'surely He will do
nothing but He revealeth His secrets unto His servants the
prophets.' The Jews had a succession of prophets who
guided them with the light of prophecy: What their
prophets were to them, that the apocalyptic scriptures
have been, and are, to us."*

Thus, it is obvious that Jamieson, Fausset and Brown support
the Historical view of the Book of Revelation; namely, the
continually-unfolding of the prophecies contained in the book
from John's day on. In their commentary, J F & B give their
view of a historical portrayal of the Seals, Trumpets and Vials.
In my book, I am not embracing the identifications they give
these prophecies. However, I do agree with them to this extent:
That the book of Revelation is not understandable without
seeing it as a prophetic picture of long-range events; not merely
an end-of-the-age seven-year-countdown-to-Armageddon as
proposed by most writers today.

A FOURTH WAY TO INTERPRET THE REVELATION

It is my opinion that none of these views (Preterist, Historical, or Futuristic), can singly provide full understanding of this prophecy puzzle. Upon completion of my commentary on the Seals, Trumpets and Vials (as well as other prophecies covered in this book), I came to the conclusion that <u>both</u> the Historical and the Futuristic concepts must be applied to cogently understand the Revelation. The question is, how can this be done? I'm convinced that the Law of Double Reference (LODR) is the only solution to this apparent dilemma.

Jumping a little ahead, take Seal # 1 as an example of my point. The words there describe a white horse, his rider and a brief explanation is given of the rider's accomplishments:

1. As of now (1994), the first meaning is already past, the long-range aspect having begun about the third century, and continued on for a long time after that (more fully explained later). This meets the requirements of the first of two meanings contained in the LODR---the Historical.
2. At some future date from now (i.e., after 1994), another white horse and rider will come upon the scene in the early days of the Tribulation (coming out of the same *white-horse-system* as occurred in the Historical) and will continue for the space of only a few years. When this occurs, the secondary part of the LODR, the Futuristic, will be fulfilled.

Neither of these fulfillments is more true than the other. Picture the Historical as a fore-shadowing of the Futuristic. In the same manner as prophecy has always occurred, the first was a long-range picture of a similar, yet-to-be, shorter-scaled occurrence, the latter actually growing out of the first. Thus, the same words of Seal # 1 are describing **both** the Historical and the Futuristic aspects of this prophecy. This is not some wild thought of mine. In fact, it is exactly the same method God used in Isaiah 53, as already discussed.

Actually, I'm soft-pedaling my beliefs here. I think the concept is used throughout Scripture and what I will present in this book is probably only the tip of the iceburg of what God has placed in His Word with double-reference meaning. I anticipate criticism on this, particularly from those who fear over-spiritualizing the Scriptures. However, I must say what I believe God has shown me. My purpose is not to impress (or degrade) anyone. My desire is to be obedient to the Lord Jesus Christ.

But let me be fair by asking: Why would God inspire Revelation to be written with the LODR strategy in mind?

1. It follows the same pattern as the Old Testament, thus showing God's consistency in His Word.

2. It allows scripturally-sensitive Christians to see God's prophetic time-table. You see, if there is a Historical side to Revelation, i.e., not altogether Futuristic, then it follows that we can determine approximately where we are right now on the prophetic calendar. (Later in this book is a longitudinal time chart which shows an outline of the Seals, Trumpets, and Vials, each of which will be discussed in the text.)

NOTE:

The Seals and Trumpets mainly represent conflicts among men, which results from sin brought upon themselves; these, we'll see, have an unmistakeable dual-meaning. But the Vials are seven judgements upon the ungodly and the anti-Christ regime. They represent the Wrath of God which has no double-reference application. One dispensation will be quite sufficient! (More on this later.)

One last word before I begin my commentary on Biblical prophecy. I do not want to convey that I think my prophetic scenario is infallible. We are all subject to error. But once again, the commonly-held view in the Church today is that the Seals and Trumpets have nothing to do with the past 2,000 years. Based on Scriptural guidelines, this position must be challenged.

In writing this book, it is very important to know that I did not set out to dispel the Futuristic, or any other, viewpoint. My purpose is to present what I believe God has shown me. And obviously I want to be believed. But I shall be encouraged if this presentation does no more than cause the reader to think on just how unsensible and Biblically-untypical the notion is that the bulk of the book of Revelation refers only to a brief seven-year period.

PREFACE

As already noted, the primary focus of this book is to show the historical highlights of the past 2,000 years believed to be predicted in Bible prophecy. The main content of those prophecies is found in Revelation chapters 6 - 20, where I will devote most of my attention. For convenience, I want the chapter numbers of this book to coincide with the chapter numbers of the book of Revelation. So, with only brief comments, I will include also the text of chapters 1 - 5 and 21 & 22. (It may come as a surprise to some to learn that Revelation 1:3 promises a blessing for the mere reading of this book of prophecy.)

REVELATION OUTLINED

I believe Revelation can be divided into seven distinct groups, which basically follow a sequential and chronological pattern. (There are exceptions to this rule and they will be noted appropriately in the book.)

CHAPTERS 1 - 3

Jesus Christ is presented as *Lord* and *Redeemer*. His relationship and authority over the seven churches is revealed.

CHAPTERS 4 & 5

John's view of the magnificence of heaven and Jesus' worthiness of being an exalted Savior.

CHAPTERS 6 - 11

The long-range historical forecast is revealed in these six chapters, commencing after Christ's first advent. The unfolding is described by the seven SEALS followed by the seven TRUMPETS. Each Seal and Trumpet explains a particular historical event which gives adequage information for us to see God's timetable as it progresses. Remember — the long-range prophecy does not negate the concept that these same Seals and Trumpets also describe the final seven year Tribulation period. As you read, don't forget the **LODR**.

CHAPTER 12

This chapter shows a broad overview of prophecy, beginning with the nation of Israel, and continues up through the entire Church age. It will be seen as a key chapter to the understanding of Biblical prophecy in general, and this book in particular.

CHAPTER 13

This is a past, present and future 'picture' of Satan and his demonic forces, in association with certain individuals and nations which he inspires to set up his kingdom on earth. The focus is broad in scope, yet not without very detailed specifics. A very revealing chapter.

CHAPTERS 14 - 18

After the Church is raptured, God will use 144,000 set-aside Israelites for world evangelization during the Tribulation. This is discussed in chapter 14. Chapters 15 and 16 present the seven VIALS which contain the **Wrath of God** to be dispensed against the anti-Christ forces and all ungodly, unrepentant mankind. Chapters 17 and 18 reveal the identity of *Mystery Babylon*.

CHAPTERS 19 - 22

This group of chapters present God's more direct ties with man:

(1)   Christ's personal, 1000-year reign as Lord and King over the earth. With Him will be His Bride (the Church) which consists of Christians from this present age. These will have new, immortalized bodies, similar to Jesus' body after His resurrection. The earth will be renewed and repopulated by ordinary people who survive the Tribulation. Israel will finally have 'their day' — i.e., 1000 years under the Lordship of Jesus as their King.

(2)   Satan will be bound and unable to tempt man during this 1000 years. Somewhat of a paradox is the fact that at the end of the 1000 years he will be loosed for a brief time and once again permitted to gather those people who willingly follow him instead of God.

(3)   After Satan, sin and even death itself have been removed from man, God will take up His reign among those He has drawn to Himself. Then, together they shall seek *"new heavens"* and *"a new earth"* where only righteousness prevails. (2 Peter 3:13) Hallelujah!

CHAPTER 23

This chapter includes certain key passages from the Book of Daniel which helps tie the whole prophetic picture together.

CHAPTER ONE

JESUS CAME! JESUS IS COMING!

This chapter makes clear that Jesus Christ is the originator of The Revelation. John was to write to the seven churches of Asia which are: Ephesus, Smyrna, Pergamos, Thyatira, Sardis, Philadelphia and Laodicia. He explains the things he saw in heaven, and tells of the things that were yet to come.

Some theologians believe these seven churches of Asia in the first century also represent seven Church Ages through which the whole Christian era has gone, and will continue to go, up to the return of the Lord Jesus. This seems reasonable. For example, the Laodician Church does indeed seem to accurately describe the general apostate condition of the Church as a whole in the world today. In fact, this was predicted in 2 Thessalonians 2:3 which says, *"Let no one deceive you by any means; for that Day will not come unless the falling away comes first, and the man of sin is revealed, the son of perdition,..."* In context, *"that Day"*, refers to the day of the return of Christ. I also call your attention to the words *"falling away"*. The translators have used these two English words to describe the Greek word, 'apostasia', from which we get 'apostasy'.

So, here in the very first chapter of Revelation we see the distinct probability of the **LODR** in effect. That is, the early Laodician Church in John's day typified and foreshadowed the same spirit of shallowness and lukewarmness so prevalent in the Church as a whole in our day. Therefore, it can indeed be appropriately said that we are currently living in the Laodician Church age. (It's significant also to note this is the <u>seventh</u> age, God's number for Biblical completeness, thus implying the <u>last</u> Church Age.)

1

Introduction and Benediction

1 "The Revelation of Jesus Christ, which God gave Him to show His servants, things which must shortly take place. And He sent and signified it by His angel to His servant John,
2 who bore witness to the word of God, and to the testimony of Jesus Christ, and to all things that he saw.
*3 **Blessed is he who reads**, and **those who hear** the words of this prophecy, and keep those things which are written in it; for the time is near.*

Greeting the Seven Churches

4 John, to the seven churches which are in Asia: Grace to you and peace from Him who is and who was and who is to come, and from the seven Spirits who are before His throne,
5 and from Jesus Christ who is the faithful witness, the firstborn from the dead, and the ruler over the kings of the earth. To Him who loved us and washed us from our sins in His own blood,
6 and has made us kings and priests to His God and Father, to Him be glory and dominion forever and ever. Amen.
7 Behold, He is coming with clouds, and every eye will see Him, and they also who pierced Him. And all the tribes of the earth will mourn because of Him. Even so, Amen.
8 I am the Alpha and the Omega, the Beginning and the End," says the Lord, who is and who was and who is to come, the Almighty."

Vision of the Son of Man

9 I, John, both your brother and companion in tribulation, and in the kingdom and patience of Jesus Christ, was on the island that is called Patmos for the word of God and for the testimony of Jesus Christ.

10 I was in the Spirit on the Lord's Day, and I heard behind me a loud voice, as of a trumpet,

11 saying, "I am the Alpha and the Omega, the First and the Last," and, "What you see, write in a book and send it to the seven churches which are in Asia: to Ephesus, to Smyrna, to Pergamos, to Thyratira, to Sardis, to Philadelphia, and to Laodicia."

12 And I turned to see the voice that spoke with me. And having turned I saw seven golden lampstands,

13 and in the midst of the seven lampstands One like the Son of Man, clothed with a garment down to the feet and girded about the chest with a golden belt.

14 His head and His hair were white like wool, as white as snow; His eyes were like a flame of fire.

15 His feet were like fine brass, as if refined in a furnace, and His voice as the sound of many waters.

16 He had in His right hand seven stars, out of His mouth went a sharp two-edged sword, and His countenance was like the sun shining in its strength.

17 And when I saw Him, I fell at His feet as dead. And He laid His right hand on me, saying to me, Do not be afraid; I am the First and the Last.

18 "I am He who lives, and was dead, and behold, I am alive for evermore. Amen. And I have the keys of Hades and of Death.

19 "Write the things which you have seen, and the things which are, and the things which will take place after this.

20 "The mystery of the seven stars which you saw in My right hand, and the seven golden lampstands: The seven stars are the angels of the seven churches, and the seven lampstands which you saw are the seven churches."

This beautiful passage and the upcoming four chapters deserve more attention than this but our main focus is further on so let's move quickly ahead.

CHAPTER TWO

This chapter deals with the first four churches of Asia mentioned in chapter one: Ephesus, Smyrna, Pergamos, and Thyatira. Jesus pointed out both their faults and their strengths, with recommendations for improvement. Presented here is a beautiful example of God's mercy and long-suffering as He endures the unfaithfulness of His followers by waiting patiently for His own to repent and return to greater loyalty. (Today's Church congregations may assume that each of these letters was written for us as well. If we find ourselves described herein, we are therefore called to work on the weaknesses described in the passages. I believe that's at least partly the explanation of the oft-repeated phrase in Revelation, "*He that hath an ear, let him hear what the Spirit says to the churches.*")

The Loveless Church

1 "To the angel of the church of Ephesus write, 'These things says He who holds the seven stars in His right hand, who walks in the midst of the seven golden lampstands:
2 'I know your works, your labor, your patience, and how you cannot bear those who are evil. And you have tested those who say they are apostles and are not, and have found them liars;
3 'and you have persevered and have patience, and have labored for My name's sake and have not become weary.
4 'Nevertheless I have this against you, that you have left your first love.
5 'Remember therefore from what you have fallen; repent and do the first works, or else I will come to you quickly and remove your lampstand from its place---unless you repent.
6 'But this you have, that you hate the deeds of the Nicolaitans, which I also hate.

7 *'He who has an ear, let him hear what the Spirit says to the churches. To him who overcomes I will give to eat of the tree of life, which is in the midst of the Paradise of God.'*

The Persecuted Church

8 *"And to the angel of the church in Smyrna write, 'These things says the First and the Last, who was dead, and came to life:*
9 *'I know your works, tribulation, and poverty (but you are rich); and I know the blasphemy of those who say they are Jews and are not, but are a synagogue of Satan.*
10 *'Do not fear any of those things which you are about to suffer. Indeed, the devil is about to throw some of you into prison, that you may be tested, and you will have tribulation ten days. Be faithful until death, and I will give you the crown of life.*
11 *'He who has an ear, let him hear what the Spirit says to the churches. He who overcomes shall not be hurt by the second death.'*

The Compromising Church

12 *"And to the angel of the church in Pergamos write, 'These things says He who has the sharp two-edged sword:*
13 *'I know your works, and where you dwell, where Satan's throne is. And you hold fast to My name, and have not denied My faith even in the days in which Antipas was My faithful martyr, who was killed among you, where Satan dwells.*
14 *'But I have a few things against you, because you have there those who hold the doctrine of Balaam, who taught Balak to put a stumbling block before the children of Israel, to eat things sacrificed to idols, and to commit sexual immorality.*

15 'Thus you also have those who hold the doctrine of the Nicolaitans, which thing I hate.
16 'Repent, or else I will come to you quickly and will fight against them with the sword of My mouth.
17 'He who has an ear, let him hear what the Spirit says to the churches. To him who overcomes I will give some of the hidden manna to eat. And I will give him a white stone, and on the stone a new name written which no one knows except him who receives it.'

The Corrupt Church

18 "And to the angel of the church in Thyatira write, 'These things says the Son of God, who has eyes like a flame of fire, and His feet like fine brass:
19 'I know your works, love, service, faith, and your patience; and as to your works, the last are more than the first.
20 'Nevertheless I have a few things against you, because you allow that woman Jezebel, who calls herself a prophetess, to teach and beguile My servants to commit sexual immorality and to eat things sacrificed to idols.
21 'And I gave her time to repent of her sexual immorality, and she did not repent.
22 "Indeed, I will cast her into a sickbed, and those who commit adultery with her into great tribulation, unless they repent of their deeds.
23 'And I will kill her children with death. And all the churches shall know that I am He who searches the minds and hearts. And I will give to each one of you according to your works.
24 'But to you I say, and to the rest in Thyatira, as many as do not have this doctrine, and who have not known the depths of Satan, as they call them, I will put on you no other burden.

25 'But hold fast what you have till I come.

26 'And he who overcomes, and keeps My works until the end, to him I will give power over the nations-

27 "And he shall rule them with a rod of iron; As the vessels of a potter they shall be broken to pieces" - as I also received from My Father.

28 'And I will give him the morning star.

29 'He who has an ear, let him hear what the Spirit says to the churches."

CHAPTER THREE

This chapter completes the messages to the seven churches in Asia. The format is the same as the previous chapter: the Lord Jesus describes the existing problems in the churches, mentions things of worthiness and gives them recommendations for improvement.

I love the chapter's closing statement. It ends in simplicity, yet greatness, as Jesus gives this invitation: "...*behold, I stand at the door and knock. If anyone hears My voice and opens the door, I will come in to him and dine with him, and he with Me.*" Jesus Christ is *the door* and *the way*. Entrance to heaven is provided only through Him as a result of His finished work at Calvary. Praise God! Our work is to believe in His work. This is not to say that Christians have no task to do other than intellectual assent to Jesus as Savior of the world. However, a Christian's work (obedience to God and ministry to others) will follow belief in Christ, not precede it. In other words, Christian work is an outgrowth of a believing heart. I emphasize this because man has a problem remembering that salvation originates in God, not himself.

Dead Church

1 "And to the angel of the church in Sardis write, 'These things says He who has the seven Spirits of God and the seven stars: I know your works, that you have a name that you are alive, and yet you are dead.
2 'Be watchful, and strengthen the things which remain, that are ready to die, for I have not found your works perfect before God.
3 'Remember therefore how you have received and heard; hold fast and repent. Therefore if you will not watch, I shall come upon you as a thief, and you shall not know what hour I shall come upon you.

4 'You have a few names even in Sardis who have not defiled their garments; and they shall walk with Me in white, for they are worthy.
5 'He who overcomes shall be clothed in white garments, and I will not blot out his name from the Book of Life; but I will confess his name before My Father and before His angels.
6 'He who has an ear, let him hear what the Spirit says to the churches.'

The Faithful Church

7 And to the angel of the church in Philadelphia write, 'These things says He who is holy, He who is true, "He who has the key of David, He who opens and no one shuts, and shuts and no one opens".
8 'I know your works. See, I have set before you an open door, and no one can shut it; for you have a little strength, have kept My word, and have not denied My name.
9 'Indeed I will make those of the synagogue of Satan, who say they are Jews and are not, but lie — indeed, I will make them come and worship before your feet, and to know that I have loved you.
10 'Because you have kept My command to persevere, I also will keep you from the hour of trial which shall come upon all the world, to test those who dwell on the earth.
11 'Behold, I come quickly! Hold fast what you have, that no one take your crown.
12 He who also overcomes, I will make him a pillar in the temple of My God, and he shall go out no more. And I will write on him the name of My God and the name of the city of My God, the New Jerusalem, which comes down out of heaven from My God. And I will write on him My new name.
13 'He who has an ear, let him hear what the Spirit says to the churches.'

9

The Lukewarm Church

14 "And to the angel of the church of the Laodiceans write, 'These things says the Amen, the Faithful and True Witness, the Beginning of the creation of God:
15 'I know your works, that you are neither cold nor hot. I wish you were cold or hot.
16 'So then, because you are lukewarm, and neither cold not hot, I will spew you out of My mouth.
17 'Because you say: I am rich, have become wealthy, and have need of nothing--and do not know that you are wretched, miserable, poor, blind, and naked--
18 'I counsel you to buy from Me gold refined in the fire, that you may be rich; and white garments, that you may be clothed, that the shame of your nakedness not be revealed; and anoint your eyes with eye salve, that you may see.
19 'As many as I love, I rebuke and chasten. Therefore be zealous and repent.
20 'Behold, I stand at the door and knock. If anyone hears My voice and opens the door, I will come in to him and dine with him, and he with Me.
21 'To him who overcomes I will grant to sit with Me on My throne, as I also overcame and sat down with My Father on His throne.
22 He who has an ear, let him hear what the Spirit says to the churches.'"

CHAPTER FOUR

The first verse of this chapter separates the Futurist and Historical viewpoints. When the apostle John was told to *"Come up here"*, the Futurists believe this to be a foreshadowing of the eventual call which will come to the Church; i.e., it supposedly represents the Rapture. And since everything from verse 1 onward is presumed to occur after the 'going up', the Futurists believe all of Revelation from here on must happen during or after the Tribulation. As you already know, I do not ascribe to the Futuristic-only scenario.

I believe the LODR is the only solution which allows ALL the book of Revelation to be understood. Once again, I recall your attention to what I mean: First, there is the Historical perspective of Revelation; then, the Futuristic aspect will follow.

In this chapter John saw God on a magnificent throne surrounded by four living creatures and twenty-four elders, all of whom fall before God and worship Him. Later on, we'll see that these 'persons' do the anouncing of events which are about to occur on earth, as directed from heaven. For example, they announce the Seals, the Trumpets and the Vials when the fulness-of-time has been completed according to God's perfect timetable.

John is reminded that God created all things for His own good pleasure. How reassuring it is to know this! Now the text:

The Throne Room of Heaven

1 After these things I looked, and behold, a door standing open in heaven. And the first voice which I heard was like a trumpet speaking with me, saying, "Come up here, and I will show you things which must take place after this."
2 And immediately I was in the Spirit, and behold, a throne set in heaven, and One sat on the throne.

3 And He who sat there was like a jasper and a sardius stone in appearance; and there was a rainbow around the throne, in appearance like an emerald.

4 And around the throne were twenty-four thrones, and on the thrones I saw twenty-four elders sitting, clothed in white robes; and they had crowns of gold on their heads.

5 And out of the throne proceeded lightnings, thunderings, and voices. And there were seven lamps of fire burning before the throne, which are the seven Spirits of God.

6 And before the throne there was a sea of glass like crystal. And in the midst of the throne, and around the throne, were four living creatures full of eyes in front and in back.

7 And the first living creature was like a lion, the second living creature like a calf, the third living creature had a face like a man, and the fourth living creature was like a flying eagle.

8 And the four living creatures, full of eyes around and within, each had six wings. And they do not rest day or night, saying: "Holy, holy, holy, Lord God Almighty, Who was and is and is to come!"

9 And whenever the living creatures give glory and honor and thanks to Him who sits on the throne, who lives forever and ever,

10 the twenty-four elders fall down before Him who sits on the throne and worship Him who lives forever and ever, and cast their crowns before the throne, saying:

11 "You are worthy, O Lord, To receive glory and honor and power; For You have created all things, And by Your will they exist and were created!"

CHAPTER FIVE

JESUS OPENS THE SEVEN SEAL BOOK

One of my favorite songs is called "Worthy Is The Lamb". It is based on a verse from this chapter. The "creatures" in heaven all agree that only Jesus is worthy to open the seven-sealed scroll whick contains prophetic mysteries. Isn't it wonderful that there is One who *is* worthy before God; the very same One who has redeemed us; the One who purchased us with His own precious blood. Yes indeed, worthy is the Lamb that taketh away the sins of the world. Praise His Holy Name!

The Lamb Takes The Scroll

1 And I saw in the right hand of Him who sat on the throne a scroll written inside and on the back, sealed with seven seals.
2 And I saw a strong angel proclaiming with a loud voice, "Who is worthy to open the scroll and to loose its seals?"
3 And no one in heaven or on the earth or under the earth was able to open the scroll, or to look at it.
4 And I wept greatly, because no one was found worthy to open and read the scroll, or to look at it.
5 And one of the elders said to me, "Do not weep. Behold, the Lion of the tribe of Judah, the Root of David, has prevailed to open the scroll and to loose its seven seals."
6 And I looked, and behold, in the midst of the throne and of the four living creatures, and in the midst of the elders, stood a Lamb as it had been slain, having seven horns and seven eyes, which are the seven Spirits of God sent out into all the earth.
7 And He came and took the scroll out of the right hand of Him who sat on the throne.

Worthy Is The Lamb

8   And when He had taken the scroll, the four living creatures and the twenty-four elders fell down before the Lamb, each having a harp, and golden bowls full of incense, which are the prayers of the saints.

9   And they sang a new song, saying: "You are worthy to take the scroll, And to open its seals; For You were slain, And have redeemed us to God by Your blood out of every tribe and tongue and people and nation,

10   And have made us kings and priests to our God; And we shall reign on the earth."

11   And I looked, and I heard the voice of many angels around the throne, the living creatures, and the elders; and the number of them was ten thousand times ten thousand, and thousands of thousands,

12   saying with a loud voice: "Worthy is the Lamb who was slain To receive power and riches and wisdom, And strength and honor and glory and blessing!"

13   And every creature which is in heaven, on the earth, under the earth, and such as are in them, I heard saying: "Blessing and honor and glory and power Be to Him who sits on the throne, And to the Lamb, forever and ever. Amen!"

14   And the four living creatures said, "Amen!" And the twenty-four elders fell down and worshiped Him who lives forever and ever.

If prophetic, Bible commentary was what was on your mind when you acquired this book, you can now relax because from here on that's the format. Some may think I have belabored this preparatory section but please understand that this book is intended for those not so acquainted with prophecy as well as the astute reader.

CHAPTER SIX

THE FIRST SIX SEALS

This chapter describes the first six Seals and their results. For some strange reason the seventh is omitted! We will not see it in the seventh chapter either. Surprisingly, it isn't opened until chapter 8, followed there by the Trumpets. This 'misplacement' seemed at first a little mysterious but actually later discovered to be of utmost importance, in fact, even key to seeing the LODR in operation.

Recalling the analogy relating prophecy to a puzzle, I suggested one way of assembling a puzzle is to first find a few pieces which appear similar in color, form, etc. Once those are put together, a small section is completed, correctness being assured because the pieces fit. Well, that's the way Revelation 'came together' for me. I didn't one day decide, *"O.K., I think I'll write a commentary on the book of Revelation,"* and then proceed to do it. No, it came about a 'few pieces' at the time.

As I recall, the first thing I saw which made sense to me was that Seal Six could be symbolic of modern warfare. After more careful scrutiny I decided it didn't seem to abuse the passage to identify it as World War One. But I admit that didn't stack up too well with what I had been taught by the Futuristic approach, which would say all the Seals are descriptive only of the first portion of the final seven year period called The Tribulation. But by the time I left off reading other commentaries and studied the Bible only for a change, I had made up my mind to be open to new thought, especially if it appeared to be the leading of the Holy Spirit.

It was about the same time I saw the Sixth Seal as WW1, I also interpreted the Fifth Trumpet as symbolic of WW2! These two discoveries led me to take a broader look at history of the past 2,000 years. Quite obviously, if I was right about the Sixth Seal and the Fifth Trumpet, then the other Seals and Trumpets should likewise represent other outstanding historical events of the Christian era. Folks, to me, that's exciting!

So, the sixth Seal (WW1) and the fifth Trumpet (WW2) turned out to be two key parts of the 'puzzle' which were instrumental to the eventual unlocking of other Seals and Trumpets. Once I was this far along, the book of Revelation became steadily more interesting with every reading, for I was seeing that it is a 'now' book, and not altogether futuristic, as most preachers teach.

Thus, I reasoned, if Seal #6 is WW1, and Trumpet #5 is WW2, the other Seals and Trumpets would likewise have historical significance. Therefore, it seemed reasonable to assume Seal One would have to represent some person, and/or event, early in the Church age. When these ideas were birthing, I wasn't thinking about whether my understanding would get beyond my desk. This, I guess, made me somewhat 'fearless' regarding the identification process. You see, some of the prophecies describe not only events but specific individuals. That means real people, with real names! And from here on I will be matching these names with certain persons the apostle John described.

(If you have not yet accepted the possibility of the historical side of Revelation, hence the LODR, please just keep reading, realizing at one time I too believed only the Futuristic approach to Revelation. At first, it wasn't easy for me to break away from that viewpoint either. But once I saw a portion of the 'puzzle' unfold right before my eyes, other parts began to fall into place, too. I'm convinced you will see this also if you'll give the idea a chance.)

Now let's observe what the Seals reveal:

16

SEAL ONE

1 And I saw when the Lamb opened one of the seals; and I heard, like the noise of thunder, one of the four living creatures saying, "Come and See."
2 And I looked and behold, a white horse. And he who sat on it had a bow; and a crown was given to him, and he went out conquering and to conquer."

First, get the overall picture — there is a white horse and rider with a bow and a crown, who went out to conquer the world. The white color of the horse is significant. It portrays the rider came in-the-name of Jesus. (See Revelation 19 where Jesus will return to earth on a white horse.) However, I do not believe this rider in the First Seal was truly anointed of God.

We often see in Scripture, before God's servants are sent, those who come as counterfeits pretending to represent God or Jesus, even wearing a form of godliness. As I searched early Church history for a person who would fit the model as portrayed in this First Seal, there was one who stood out like a 'sore thumb': Constantine the Great (280 - 337 A.D.)

Constantine attempted to "christianize" the world. History clearly shows that he tried to tie "religion" to the main political system of that day — the Roman Empire. Till this day, he has had no equal in this regard. I think it will be truly revealing for you to hear what a secular historian, Michael Hart[2] (not writing from a Biblical perspective) had to say about Constantine:

"He was the first Christian emperor of Rome and by his adoption of Christianity, and by his various policies

---

[2]**"The 100"**, by Michael H. Hart. A book about the author's selections of the 100 most influential people to have ever lived, without regard to whether they were good or bad. His perspective is mainly factual (non-spiritual) which I found very appropriate for my inclusion here.

17

encouraging its growth, he played a major role in transforming it from a persecuted sect into the dominant religion of Europe."

There are several points to note here:

(1)   Constantine was the FIRST "Christian" emperor of Rome. This places him strategically as the first and most influential perverter of Christianity, particularly as related to political regimes.

(2)   Mr. Hart emphasizes Constantine's "adoption" of Christianity. That is very aptly put. However, true Christians don't "adopt" the faith. On the contrary, we become adopted!

(3)   Constantine played a "major role in transforming it (Christianity) from a persecuted sect into the dominant religion of Europe." Now Jesus has said that true followers of Him would always have trouble in this world and would be persecuted as was He. Christ never instructed his disciples to attempt making Christianity the acceptable "religion" of the world. Mr. Hart continues:

"Constantine's father became the ruler of the western half of the Roman Empire in about 305 and when he died, Constantine was proclaimed emperor by his troops. However, his reign was questioned and a series of civil wars followed and ended in 312 when Constantine defeated his remaining rival, Maxentius. But, Constantine still only ruled the Western half of the Empire and he then attacked and defeated Licenius and then remained sole ruler of the Roman Empire until his death in 337 A.D."

"It is uncertain when Constantine became converted to Christianity. The most usual story is that on the eve of the Battle of the Melvian Bridge, Constantine saw a fiery cross in the sky, together with the words, 'By this sign shalt thou conquer.'"

Note here that Constantine was PROCLAIMED emperor by his troops. Now look back at the Scripture which says, "And a crown was <u>given</u> to him"! But even though his troops crowned him, the battle wasn't over. And how interesting that on the night before the Battle of The Melvian Bridge, he had a vision of his "conquering". Then on the next day, he "went forth conquering" (see verse 2) and defeated Licenius to become the "soul ruler" of the Roman Empire, remaining so until he died.

Another very important point here was what Constantine considered his 'call' to serve. He saw a fiery cross in the sky and by it the words emblazened, **"By this sign shalt thou conquer."** Note how Constantine's supernatural encounter exactly fits the Scripture, *"He went forth conquering and to conquer."* Let's hear more of what Mr. Hart says:

"One of his early actions was the Edict of Milan, under which Christianity became a legal and tolerated religion. The Edict also provided for the return of church property which had been confiscated during the preceding period of persecution and it established Sunday as a day of worship."

Here we see how effectively Constantine linked organized religion with the government he headed. He made "Christianity" legal and tolerated. Even though he was instrumental in establishing Sunday as a day of worship, it should be noted that he was not the first to initiate this step. Early Christians from Paul's day onward honored Sunday as the Lord's Day. Constantine obviously wanted to add to his fame by legalizing the day. Mr. Hart goes on:

19

"Constantine never established Christianity as the official state religion. Commenced under his reign was the Church of the Nativity in Bethlehem, and the Church of the Holy Sepulchre in Jerusalem. It was also under Constantine's reign that the Nicene Creed became orthodox Church doctrine. It is quite plain that with Constantine's encouragement, Christianity rapidly expanded in both numbers and influence. From the creed of a small minority it became within a century, the predominant and established religion of the largest empire on earth."

The above is but a brief sketch of the life of Constantine "the Great". In summary, I think it would be helpful to condense the accomplishments of this man, comparing them with John's description of Seal One's white horse rider:

John's picture of the rider:

1. He rode a white horse. (signifies he came in Jesus' name)
2. He had a bow. (alludes to military might)
3. A crown was given to him. (declared emperor by his troops)
4. He went forth conquering. (he was a war hero)
5. His purpose was "to conquer". (great at strategy).

Now compare Constantine's life to the Scriptural portrayal:

1. First "Christian" emperor of Rome.
2. "Adopted" Christianity.
3. Transformed "Christianity" into the major religion of Europe.
4. Was proclaimed emperor by his troops.

5. Defeated all his rivals to become emperor of Rome until his death.
6. Saw a fiery cross in the sky with words, "by this sign shalt thou conquer".
7. Made "Christianity" a legal religion.
8. Established Sunday as a day of worship.
9. Commenced the Church of the Nativity in Bethlehem.
10. Commenced the Church of the Holy Sepulchre.
11. Under him the Nicene Creed became orthodox doctrine.
12. "Christianity" expanded under his rule.
13. "Christianity" became the predominant religion of the largest empire on earth.

Taken together, I believe these historical facts regarding the life and activities of Constantine fully meets the requirements of the prophetic picture of Seal One.

It is said that Constantine wasn't baptized until he was on his deathbed. Is this not indicative of the man's real attitude towards Jesus Christ? It makes one wonder who sent his vision in the sky? Do you think perhaps his power wasn't really from the Holy Spirit at all? Surely any sensitive Christian can see Constantine's experiences are more like what we typically see when people fall prey to Satan's delusions. Satan is the "prince of this world", the "god of this age". He comes as an "angel of light", particularly, it seems, to those who are empire-prone.

It would be rather foolish to ignore the ties established between Constantine and the Roman Catholic Church since Constantine started the Church of the Nativity and the Holy Sepulchre as well as effectualizing "church" doctrine. Although these shrines were built in the name and honor of the Lord Jesus Christ, I cannot accept that the Holy Spirit guided Constantine in these endeavors. As we move on, you will see just how severely these organizations distort the real Church of Jesus Christ. Indeed, they have become the very haven of Satan's kingdom, the one he will use to establish his throne in what is known as the anti-Christ system.

SUMMARY OF SEAL ONE

This segment is the first of many examples of the Law of Double Reference. Constantine the Great represented the Historical perspective, foreshadowing the Futuristic. Another will come who will be linked with the same organizations Constantine commenced. The ancient Roman Empire went down in defeat but it will rise again, the forerunner today being Europe's Common Market. Of course, the Roman Catholic Church still exists and will likely merge with the state. When together, the Holy Roman Empire will once again be established. (The EEC is attempting to merge now.)

So, Constantine typified and set the stage for the final conqueror who will, I believe, soon be "on stage" for his final act. This last-days, magnificent man will be none other than the one known as the anti-Christ.

(A word of explanation here: "Anti" implies AGAINST. The great leader who is yet to come on the scene will probably not first speak against Christ. That will come later. In the beginning, he will probably come, like Constantine, in the name of Jesus in order to win the allegiance of the people. I'm jumping a little ahead of myself but felt it timely for you to see the LODR concept here at this most critical point in our study.)

MISPLACED ALLEGIANCE

All too often Christians give their allegiance to wrong institutions. I hold no ill-will towards born-again people no matter what organization they are attached to. There are true, Christian Catholics, people I shall spend eternity with. However, I feel impelled to share what I believe God has shown me concerning some of the gross errors surrounding Roman Catholicism. More on this later.

22

SEAL TWO

Noting how accurately Constantine's life fits the qualifications of the rider on the white horse was a remarkable discovery to me. This being the case, combined with my on-going studies of other prophecies, I became increasingly aware that God is truly not the author of prophetic confusion (as I find the Futuristic-only bias). Indeed, I have learned that God allows comprehension of things about His Word which can be related to real life situations of both today and the past. Revelation is not merely an outline of the yet-future Tribulation, most of which, according to the Futurists, occurs after the Church will be gone from the earth! However, if one is 'locked in' to this interpretation of prophecy, accepting new thought is difficult.

However, seeing **just one** prophetic fulfillment helps prepare the mind to be sensitive to other significant historical evidence. In other words, if Constantine truly represents Seal One, then we would logically expect Seal Two to be just as identifiable and should fall right in line after Seal One. I found this to be exactly the case.

SEAL TWO, Verses 3 & 4

3 "And when He opened the second seal, I heard the second living creature saying, "Come and see."
*4 And another horse that was fiery red went out. And power was given to him who sat on it to take peace from the earth, and that they should kill one another; and there was given to him a **great sword**."*

From the beginning of time, there have been oft-repeated patterns of conflict between those trying to reach high goals. Sometimes this was between persons, sometimes between nations, sometimes between religions, etc. For example, among individuals, it was demonstrated with Abel and Cain, Jacob and

23

Esau, etc.; nationally, between Israel and Egypt, and so on. In earlier days (A.D.), the most notable conflict was between European 'Christianity' and Islam. (I put Christianity in quotes to differentiate between Constantine's Holy Roman Empire and true Christianity. I'm convinced that whole organizational structure was, and is, mainly cultural, thus man-conceived and man-oriented. Churchianity would be a more appropriate name. However, because the world perceives that which comes out of Rome as Christianity, I'll use this term — but in quotes to signify that I'm not referring to true Christianity.)

The power and influence of Roman Catholicism has been undeniably great and this form of 'Christianity' was always in great conflict with the Muslim religion, Islam. For these and other reasons to follow, I identify the red horse rider as Mohammad (570 - 632 A.D.), the founder and first leader of Islam. Now, for a brief historical look at Mohammad's life, I shall again quote from Michael Hart's book.

"Islam tradition tells us Mohammad was illiterate and that he was raised in a backward area away from the centers of trade, art and learning. At the age of 25 though he married a wealthy widow. Most Arabs in Mohammad's day were paganistic who believed in many gods. There were in Mecca where he lived, a small number of Jews and Christians and it was probably from them that Mohammad first learned of a single, omnipotent God. When he was forty years old Mohammad became convinced that God (Allah) was speaking to him and had chosen him to spread the true faith. For about three years he preached to close friends and associates and in about 613 he started preaching in public. As he started getting converts, the Meccan authorities came to consider him a dangerous nuisance. In 622, fearing for his safety, Mohammad fled to Medina. This was the turning point in Mohammad's life."

"In Medina he got more followers and soon acquired an influence that made him a virtual dictator. During the next few years, while Mohammad's following grew rapidly, a series of battles were fought between Medina and Mecca. This war ended in 630 with Mohammad's triumphant return to Mecca as conqueror."

"Unified by Mohammad, the inspired Arabs, though small then, embarked upon one of the most astonishing series of conquests in human history. They soon conquered all of Mesopotamia, Syria and Palestine. By 642, Egypt had been taken from the Byzantine Empire and the Persian armies defeated in 637, and Nahavend in 642."

"For a while, it must have seemed that the Moslems would overwhelm all of Christian Europe. However, in 732 at the Battle of Tours, a Moslem army, which had advanced into the center of France, was at last defeated by the Franks. Nevertheless, in a scant century of fighting, these Bedouin tribesmen, inspired by the word of Mohammad had CARVED OUT (interesting choice of words for this swordsman in light of the Seal 2 description above) *an empire stretching from the borders of India to the Atlantic Ocean---the largest empire that the world had yet seen."*

From the above, it can readily be seen that Mohammad was indeed given a "great sword", one with which he took "peace from the earth". (Go back and read verse 4.) He also, like Constantine, achieved success in two different ways: as a military conqueror and as a religious leader. (There are an estimated 1,000,000,000 followers of Mohammad today and, ironically, about the same number of Catholics.)

Reader, taken together, this is almost 2/5ths of the population on the planet! I ask you, is it reasonable that God would be Biblically-silent about these tremendous, religious (although perverted) fronts, both claiming to be linked to Abraham? To me, it is foolhardy to take such a position.

25

But, even if he was prophesied to come (as the rider of the red horse), this does not make him a true prophet of God. Mohammad wrote that Jesus, while a prophet, was just a man, not incarnate Deity (still believed by Muslims today). Mohammad believed *he* was a messenger from God (Allah), and according to him, the last.

Ironically, just recently I saw in a Christian magazine that Islam is the fastest growing religion in America today. The author had photographed a bumper sticker which said, "Prophets of Islam: Adam, Noah, Abraham, Moses, Jesus and Mohammad". But all this contradicts Holy Scripture. In 1 John 4:3 we find:

"...and every spirit that does not confess that Jesus Christ has come in the flesh is not of God. And this is the spirit of Antichrist, which you have heard was coming, and even now it is already in the world."

And perhaps even clearer yet, 1 John 2: 22 & 23 says:

"Who is a LIAR but he who denies that Jesus is the Christ? He is antichrist who denies the Father and the Son. Whoever denies the Son (as did Mohammad) *does not have the Father either; he who acknowledges the Son also has the Father."* (Allah is not God!)

These Scriptures plainly show that it is impossible to know God unless manifested through the Lord Jesus Christ. Thus, his denial that Jesus was the Christ unquestionably proves Mohammad could not have been a true prophet from God.

However, Mohammad's sincerity and power of leadership seems undoubtably super-natural. Therefore, we need to ask where his power came from. I'm convinced he was under the direct influence of Satan himself, who the Bible says comes as an "angel of light" (i.e., a communicator of information).

Now, all of us are capable of being tempted by Satan. But at various times and sundry ways, Satan has come to certain individuals who would first give mental assent to his deceptions, later their entire being, at last becoming subject to all the authority and power he has at his disposal to give them. I believe Mohammad and Constantine were perhaps two of the most significant of these in all history.

When Jesus was tempted by Satan, one of the temptations was that he would give Jesus all the kingdoms of this earth if He would but fall down and worship him. Jesus rebuked Satan, and refused to do it. However, Jesus never denied Satan's authority over these earthly kingdoms. Therefore, based on this Biblical account of Satan's ways, and on the historical evidence surrounding their lives, I'm convinced Constantine and Mohammad were chiefly motivated by satanic delusion. What each of them began, would later flourish and in finality become the world's greatest threats to the real Church of God, up to and including this very hour.

Let's look at the Biblical account showing how pride entered the picture leading to the Muslim religion. Mohammad was a proclaimed descendant of Ishmael (Abraham's son by Hagar). Obviously, the descendants of Ishmael would want their lives to be specially blessed of God and they probably think they have this right since Ishmael was a son of Abraham. But notice what God actually said about this situation in Genesis 17:20 & 21:

"And as for Ishmael, I have heard you. Behold, I have blessed him, and will make him fruitful, and will multiply him exceedingly. He shall beget twelve princes, and I will make him a great nation.
"But My covenant I will establish with Isaac, whom Sarah shall bear to you at this set time next year."

This forever establishes that God's covenanted people would be the descendants of Isaac, later to become the nation of Israel. Clearly, the Bible leaves Ishmael out of this Covenant.

He would be "blessed" with many descendants and nations (the Arabic) but he would NOT receive the anointing to be God's messenger. If Ishmael, Mohammad or any of their followers want to know God, it will have to be the same as for other Gentiles, namely faith placed in the Lord Jesus Christ. But unbelief and pride entered into the Arabic world, subsequently their false religion. And again we have it prophesied for us right in God's Word. Genesis 16:12 gives a clear statement of the character of Ishmael:

"He shall be a wild man; His hand shall be against every man, And every man's hand against him. And he shall dwell in the presence of all his brethren."

Satan knew of Mohammad's point of vulnerability and how to appeal to his pride, convincing him that he had been chosen to declare God's final message to the world. But because Mohammad's teachings were so contrary to the Bible, we can be sure he and his followers know nothing of the true, revealed God of Holy Scriptures. In fact, because of their rebellion, they have bowed (perhaps unawares) to the "god of this world" (Satan), who inspired their false doctrines. Thus, one can only conclude that the Koran, Islam's 'holy book', are the words planted into the mind of Mohammad directly under 'inspiration' from the devil himself.

DOUBLE-SIDED EVIL

Up to this point in Revelation chapter six, we see two riders on two horses, the first white; the second red. There is a very significant point to grasp here. Constantine (the white horse rider) started working on the inside of the Church structure of the Christian era. Clearly, the true Gospel became extremely perverted beginning chiefly at that point in time. And because there is a "form of godliness" associated with the "Holy Roman

Empire", the proclamation of the true Gospel would thereafter be conveyed only through greater difficulty. This is a common trick of Satan. It is based upon the Biblical principle---"a small amount of leaven, leavens the whole lump".

On the other hand, we see the rider of the red horse, Mohammad, starting a movement on the <u>outside</u> of the Church. Not only did Mohammad's teachings pervert the truth of the Gospel, he started a religion making no pretenses of a relationship to Christianity, (other than the recognition that Mohammad is traceable to Abraham).

Now if you have followed my reasoning up to this point you can see Satan had engineered a very clever pair of potentially opposing forces — perverted 'Christianity' versus the Islamic religion. It is my belief that neither of these movements were under God's Divine inspiration, even though by His sovereign wisdom and control, He allowed it to happen, working through them in spite of themselves.

There have been numerous false religions and perverted 'Christian' movements throughout the Christian age but Islam and the Holy Roman Empire stand head-and-shoulders above all others (together comprising, we have noted, about 2/5ths of the world's population). And, at the end of the age, I believe these two power structures will once again rise to oppose one another. They will be the stars of the 'show' as the final curtain rises. It was so in the Historical Seals and, if I'm right, the pattern will be repeated again, futuristically.

SEAL THREE: Scarcity on Earth

5 "And when He opened the third seal, I heard the third living creature say, 'Come and see.' And I looked, and behold, a black horse, and he who sat on it had a pair of scales in his hand.
6 And I heard a voice in the midst of the four living creatures saying, 'A measure of wheat for a denarius, and three measures of barley for a denarius; and do not harm the oil and the wine.'"

The Futurists (those who see Revelation as all-yet-future from Rev. 4:1 onward) regard the above passage as only portraying the hard times of the last half of the coming Tribulation. But what about historical hard times? I am amazed that 20th-century Christians, even Church leaders, have such difficulty relating the extremely tough living conditions of the past to Biblical prophecy. Could it be that soft and easy living has made us (particularly Americans and Canadians) so insensitive that we forget the intense survival problems mankind has already faced?

I am convinced the above prophecy is specifically descriptive of "The Dark Ages". Modern historians say our knowledge of the era is somewhat limited because even the writers of the day were so strongly affected by the awful conditions of the period that little record is available to us. One encyclopedia said civilization almost completely disappeared in much of western Europe during this period and that only a few places, such as monasteries, preserved Latin learning. Greek learning almost vanished and few persons received any schooling. Authors of the period had little sense of style. One might well conclude that it was the desperate poverty which ruined the western provinces of the Roman Empire and may well have caused the Dark Ages.

Now honestly, were you aware of the extent of these horrible conditions? I was not, until the study of Bible prophecy drove me to search out this information. It seems very obvious to me that the "black horse" rider who said "a measure of wheat for a denarius" was prophesying that which both logically and chronologically followed the Constantine and Mohammadan empires, namely the Dark Ages. I suspect the "oil and wine" not being hurt means that the very wealthy still had their luxuries, even in the days of world-wide poverty.

I could go on with a description of the severity of the Dark Ages and perhaps reading and learning of the depth and extent and the long duration of the period might make us more acutely aware of the era. And with that background it might finally impress on our minds sufficiently just how reasonable is this identification of the "black horse" and its "rider". However, if I did that with all the prophecies I plan to touch on in this book, it would end up being a three-inch-thick history book which few would read. My purpose is to make the identifications, sprinkled with just enough historical evidence to show the soundness of the perspective.

What I'm trying to say is that even though God sometimes camouflages, He is not a God Who hides things forever. In fact, He has given us His Word in The Revelation, which symbolically sets forth the whole of the Christian age. The main highlights are here for us to see and understand. The commentary on these first three Seals should provide you with enough information to get a gist of how I approached the prophecies of the Bible. Let me illustrate even further the straight-forward approach I've used in studying prophecy.

A "PRETEND TRIP" FROM SAN FRANCISCO TO ATLANTA

Revelation is a book containing prophetic highlights. Suppose I were to tell you how to drive from San Francisco to Atlanta. Now I could explain every single detail of the journey between the two major cities. But that isn't necessary or reasonable. All you really need is enough information so that you don't get lost. Thus, I hit the high points, listing only the names of major cities, identifying the main highway routes and connections, mentioning where to be especially watchful to make sure you get on that highway, saying "turn left" or "turn right" at such-and-such a place, etc.

So, with only a few sentences it is possible to provide you with instructions on how to get from San Francisco to Atlanta even though the cities are separated by 2,600 miles. Now along the way you would see thousands of places and things which I wouldn't have mentioned at all, and yet, you would learn that you didn't need to know all that information to be sure that you were still on the right road. Occasionally, you would see a highway number or a particular city which I had told you about, confirming and increasing your confidence in the correctness of my instructions to you.

Now, that little scenario parallels the way I see prophecy. My approach is just that simple! As I said, God is not the author of confusion. For God to leave out long-range predictions in the Scriptures would be like me telling you, *"Oh, don't worry, Atlanta is south-east. Drive in that general direction and you'll get there. Just trust me. You don't need to know anything about any major obstacles or anything like that. It would only worry you."* Get the idea?

I've taken my point to this extreme to demonstrate how illogical the Futuristic-only concept really is when you think about it. It may seem that I'm being too cynical as well as belaboring the point but this view is so prevalent, I feel that repeated "blows" will be necessary to jar some readers from adhering to the reasoning of the Futuristic-only principle. Thus, I emphasize clarification of my interpretation principles (i.e., Historical <u>and</u> Futuristic), not so much to insist on acceptance of my specific prophetic identifications, but because I believe so strongly that the <u>approach</u> I've taken is both logically and Biblically correct — namely, following the Law of Double Reference.

THE FOURTH SEAL: Widespread Death on Earth

7 "And when He opened the fourth seal, I heard the voice of the fourth living creature saying, "Come and See."
8 "And I looked, and behold, a pale horse. And the name of him who sat on it was Death, and Hades followed with him. And power was given to them over a fourth of the earth, to kill with sword, with hunger, with death, and by the beasts of the earth."

Ironically, as I was in the process of editing this section, I just 'happened' to tune in a television special program about the Roman Empire, the central focus of which was on Constantine. The story graphically confirmed what has already been presented about him in this book, showing conclusively that his prominence in that era was unequalled in terms of 'conquering'. The show also emphasized the ties he brought about between the Roman government and the Catholic Church. (Incidentally, the program was completely secular, therefore with no Biblical connotations. But I found it really interesting that the narrator 'just happened' to include the basic historical facts concerning Constantine's accomplishments in the very same areas I've just been discussing! God's timing is always right on and his sovereign influence in the lives of even unbelievers is truly an amazing thing to observe.)

Recapping events up to this point, remember that Constantine represents Seal One. By the 1100s his endeavors and great influence resulted in many European nations becoming "Christianized". (As a side note, the narrator of the T.V. show referred to Constantine as the "13th Apostle!" They meant that in a positive sense. I see it a little differently but perhaps it was an inadvertently-appropriate title, since it is the "13th" chapter of Revelation which describes the anti-Christ and the False Prophet.)

Then, the Second Seal signified Mohammad and his sword-slashing sweep throughout the Middle East, developing the largest empire ever in that region. At first it seemed there would be no stopping him.

Thus, that which began with only two individuals, Constantine and Mohammad, finally erupted into the greatest European - Middle Eastern conflict of all times, which history calls the Crusades.

THE CRUSADES

The word "crusade" comes from the Latin word "crux", meaning cross. The "Christianized", European nations joined forces and carried a cross and marched toward the Holy Land to take it back from the Muslims, feeling it was rightfully theirs. The Muslims defended their hold on the "land" (especially the "Holy Land", Israel) and the battles went on for at least two centuries! There are recorded at least four Crusades and some historians write of a fifth Crusade. The loss of life was large as a result of these conflicts, the Land shifting hands, back and forth, the Moslems finally winning out. Surely God was not the force behind the European Crusaders. After all, wouldn't one expect the "Christian" Crusaders to have won if God was back of it? Clearly, these Crusaders, like Constantine, although coming in the name of Christ, were really just demonstrating the pride they had for the Land, which they believed to be their inheritance.

34

THE BLACK PLAGUE

Another death-causing phenomena was happening at the same time as the Crusades. It was called "The Black Plague". History reveals that in the 1300s a form of Bubonic Plague called the Black Death destroyed **a fourth** of the population of Europe...The Crusaders carried the disease to Europe. From 1334 to 1351, it swept over Russia, Germany, Italy, France, England, Norway, China, India and Persia.

Now with the death resulting from the Crusades and the Bubonic Plague in mind, look again at the above Scripture describing the Fourth Seal. The death was to be caused by (1), the "sword" (the Crusades) and (2), with hunger and the beasts — the Plague and poverty. The "*beasts*" probably refers to disease-carrying animals.

Isn't it interesting that history reveals specifically that "one-fourth" of the population of Europe was destroyed. Now look at verse seven of the fourth Seal and observe that power would be given over the 'fourth' part of the earth! I believe this is a prophecy fulfillment right before our eyes.

This completes my comments on The Four Horsemen. To summarize briefly:

1. The White Horse------------The 'Conquering' Constantine
2. The Red Horse---------------The 'Swordsman' Mohammad
3. The Black Horse-------------Scarcity (The Dark Ages)
4. The Pale Horse--------------Widespread Death (Black Plague)

Now, recall my analogy of the drive from San Francisco to Atlanta to that of long-range prophecy. I said my instructions would include highlight references such as certain cities you would pass through. Reaching these points would assure you that you were still "on the right path". That's what I think the prophetic highlights of the Historical Four Horsemen are. They were main highlights. Chief attractions. Unmistakeable, historical points easy to identity. Once seen, you can't miss knowing and saying, "Hey, I'm on the right path. This is exactly what the Travel Guide said would occur. Let's stay on this road." Now, let us do that in our prophecy journey by moving on to the next main event.

THE FIFTH SEAL: The Cry of the Martyrs

9 "And when He opened the fifth seal, I saw under the altar the souls of those who had been slain for the word of God and for the testimony which they held.
10 And they cried with a loud voice, saying, "How long, O Lord, holy and true, until You judge and avenge our blood on those who dwell on the earth?"
11 And white robes were given to each of them; and it was said to them that they should rest a little while longer, until both the number of their fellow servants and their brethren, who would be killed as they were, was completed."

This passage represents an obvious breakaway from the type of "highlights" revealed by the first four Seals. Here we get a glimpse of the saints of God of all ages who have given their lives for the cause of defending the God of Holy Scriptures. This would include Old and New Testament times, both patriarchal followers of God and Christians from Jesus' day until now. It is a specific reference to those who, come what may, were willing to give their lives to insure the testimony of Jesus and adherence to Godly principles would continue to go forth.

Looking again at the Scripture, these saints seem to be crying out to receive their immortal bodies. They are told to be patient for there are yet others to join them for the same reason as theirs: martyrdom. In our prophetic and historic 'voyage' through time we have passed the Dark Ages, therefore we can assume the next prophecy coming up after the final

36

horseman would be at some point later than about 1,400 or 1,500 A.D. So, the Fifth Seal here must be predicting there will be many other saints to come who would be martyred in defense of the Gospel. That would include those from 1,500 A.D. up to this present hour, as well as those who will be martyred in the final spiritual conflicts yet to come, especially those in the last half of the "Tribulation".

So, the Fifth Seal here represents a different kind of drama than we saw in the four horsemen. This is sort of an interlude. It is very important prophecy but there is little reference here to indicate <u>exactly where we are</u> on our journey. It's a broad statement from God though, to let us know He is accumulating a people for Himself in heaven. It reveals that we can be confident the souls of saved men and women go <u>immediately</u> to be with the Lord after physical death. There's no getting around this straight-forward interpretation as we study the above three verses. (There are heresies taught in "Christian" cults which say a person merely goes to the grave when he/she dies, there remaining totally dead--meaning the spirit of the person does not leave the body to go be with the Lord in heaven. This cannot be so according to Revelation 6:9-11.)

THE SIXTH SEAL: Disturbances on Earth coming from Above

12 "And I looked when He opened the sixth seal, and behold, there was a great earthquake; and the sun became black as sackcloth of hair, and the moon became like blood.
13 And the stars of heaven fell to the earth, as a fig tree drops its late (some mss. say untimely or unripe) *figs when it is shaken by a mighty wind.*
14 And the sky receded as a scroll when it is rolled together, and every mountain and island was moved out of its place.
15 And the kings of the earth, the great men, the rich men, the commanders, the mighty men, every slave and every free man, hid themselves in the caves and in the rocks of the mountains,

16 and said to the mountains and rocks, "Fall on us and hide us from the face of Him who sits on the throne and from the wrath of the Lamb!
17 For the great day of His wrath has come, and who is able to stand?"

I believe the above six verses describe conditions which bring us, prophetically, to the modern era. The reader may at first think this is too long a jump from the Dark Ages but actually we'll see it provides just the right pieces of the puzzle to fill up yet another section of the overall portrait we're trying to assemble. Remember, Biblical prophecy comes in clumps. It always has. God provided just enough information to "keep us on the main road". The same was true in the Old Testament times.

In the first four Seals we saw key political, religious, and social situations, which were symbolized by Constantine, (representing the Roman Empire and perverted Christianity), Mohammad (representing Europe's chief opponent-force, Islam), followed by the massive death wave caused by unbelievable poverty conditions — the Black Plague and the Dark Ages. And then we saw the Fifth Seal, an interlude, which gave us a preview of more death, specifically referring to martyred saints of God. Obviously God foreknew (and foretold us) that these were the most outstanding features signifying a sin-laden world not submitted to the Lord. (No wonder Jesus instructed the disciples to pray, "Thy will be done on earth as it is in heaven.")

Before going on, please re-read verses 12 - 17 very carefully because we now enter into a new phase in our long-range prophetic journey. As I said earlier, seeing the Sixth Seal as descriptive of 'our day' was the understanding which broke open the book of Revelation for me. I saw this Seal as descriptive of World War One. Let me show you why.

In the Sixth Seal, I suppose John had seen in a vision things very much like what you and I see on film today. Now imagine yourself in John's place, never having seen anything modern as you and I know it — i.e., airplanes, cars, explosives of enormous magnitude, etc. Then all of a sudden, in a vision, you see things exactly as we do today. Next you are instructed to write about what you saw. The catch was that John had to do it using his first-century understanding. What a task! Of course, the Holy Spirit foresaw our day with John's limitations in mind. Thus, the Spirit used John's faculties to form a permanent, symbolic, prophetic-word picture.

Now, let's disect the vision. In verse 12, John refers to the "sun" and the "moon"; in verse 13 he talks about the "stars"; and in verse 14 he mentions the "sky". In interpreting this, it is important to observe that whatever he saw in the sky it caused the earth below to shake like an earthquake (see verse 12). If you knew only this much, in light of 20th century technology, what would you conclude John is trying to tell you? I can think of nothing other than awesome explosives.

John said the sun "became as black as sackcloth of hair, and the moon became like blood". I suspect John had at some time held sackcloth up and looked at the sun through it. This would, of course, cause the sun to become darkened, or "blackened". Black smoke rising from a blast causes a similar filtration of the sun's rays. Also, the moon is reddened when the sky is full of debris and smoke from large-scale explosives. Does this not logically explain what John describes?

Note in verse 13, "*the stars of heaven fell to the earth, as a fig tree drops its late* (or untimely) *figs when it is shaken by a mighty wind*". What were those stars? Were they <u>real</u> stars? Or did John call them stars simply because they fell from the sky? It doesn't make sense to assume real stars were meant because a single actual star striking the earth would totally annihilate this entire planet!

John had obviously seen "shooting stars" and meteors just as you and I have, so that was his only frame of reference when contemplating something falling from the sky. The latter part of the verse adds further insight: He said the "stars" were as "*a fig tree drops its late figs when it is shaken by a mighty wind*". Now have you ever seen figs (or any fruit) fall from a tree when a "mighty wind" blows? I have. They don't fall straight down. When a wind blows strong enough to dislodge figs, they are carried horizontally a certain distance before they hit the ground. Also consider that a fig has kind of a little "tail" on it, not greatly unlike the "tail" of the type of bombs which were dropped from aircraft during WW1. When bombs are dropped from an aircraft they also don't fall straight down. They are carried horizontally a certain distance due to the momentum given them by the flight-speed of the airplane.

Now look at verse 14. It says, "*the sky receded as a scroll when it is rolled together,...*" Have you ever seen the type of scroll John is talking about? In those days, writing wasn't put on sheets of paper as you and I use. It was done on a continuous roll which occupied less space in it's rolled-up state. To read it, you merely pull it out and then it rolls back together (as John described) when you are finished with it. When a bomb goes off, the rising smoke from the blast doesn't simply go straight up! It rolls as it rises. I believe John's first-century knowledge of how a rolled-up scroll works was the best analogy he had at that time. Good job, John! I like it.

Now, if the above analysis is correct, we should expect John would eventually mention the effect the "figs" would produce when they fell. Notice the words in the last part of verse 14: "*and every mountain and island was moved out of its place*". The bombs of WW1 would indeed move the "mountains" and the "islands" out of their places. The violent shaking which occurs during massive attacks would cause anyone to believe all the earth (i.e., the "*mountains and islands*") must surely be coming apart at the seams. (I work at a Veteran's Clinic, consequently am exposed to hundreds of WW1 veterans. They have indeed confirmed to me their experiences of the mighty shaking caused by heavy artillary during World War I.)

40

Verses 15, 16 and 17 explain the response of certain types of people to the devastation of WW1. The *"kings of the earth, the great men, the rich men, the commanders, the mighty men, every slave and every free man, ..."*; in short, <u>everyone</u> felt surely the world was coming to an end. Note their mind-set as John describes it in verse 16. They were saying to the *"mountains and rocks, 'Fall on us and hide us from the face of Him who sits on the throne and from the wrath of the Lamb!"*

We must remember, although there have always been wars resulting in terrific loss of life, never had there been anything unleashed such as began with the first world war. No wonder the leaders of the nations and the wealthy businessmen THOUGHT the "Wrath of the Lamb" had come. But in spite of the devastation caused by WW1, the "wrath of the Lamb" had not, in fact, come. It was the people living under the conditions at the time who were saying, *"...the great day of His wrath has come, and who is able to stand?"*

There is a very important point here. We must look very carefully at WHO was saying the wrath of the Lamb had come. It <u>was not</u> announced by any heavenly representative but merely by those living under the terrible, prevailing conditions of that era. This is a very important distinction! But those people did not have the knowledge, nor right, to make such a declaration.

Only God's representatives make the proclamation of when God's Wrath comes. In our study, we shall see that the real wrath doesn't come until a later time. What the "great men" and the "rich men" witnessed were the results of man's sinfulness and incompatibilities in a world out of Godly order. In fact, this will always be the case until Jesus comes to establish His Kingdom on the earth. God's wrath is a distinct set of out-pourings of His judgment towards wicked mankind and doesn't come until we get to chapter 15. Today's conditions, as awful as they may seem at times, are not God's Wrath. Now, back to the discussion of the Sixth Seal.

Just to summarize, in case you are unaware of the severity of WW1, there were at least 8,500,000 deaths in WW1 and probably many more never accounted for. There were 37,000,000 casualties and the total destruction was incomparable up to that time in history. History records that the Home Front in Europe came under intense bombing and shelling in areas of military operations. The war destroyed the industrial and community lives of many cities, towns, and villages in these areas. It closed or destroyed schools, factories, roads, and railroads. In many countries, people had to depend on food supplied by their governments. Invading troops tried to change the lives of the people in the areas occupied.

I believe it was in these devastated areas where the "great men" and the "rich men" and all the others John named, were crying out that the "wrath of the Lamb" had come. But it had not!

Reader, are you beginning to see just how ludicrous it is to assume that God provided virtually no revelation concerning the history of the past 2,000 years as the Futurists say? Prophecy was given to God's people to alarm us of what's coming. I believe it's happening all around us all the time. It's somewhat like the Gospel message itself — you must first believe it before getting the fuller image created by it inside you. *"God help us to believe, prophecy-wise, so that we can see what you have already said in Your word."*

CHAPTER SEVEN

THE SEALED OF ISRAEL

People usually accept history with little trepidation. I mean, once something is past, we know it, can think about it, make conjectures about it, discuss how it all may have come to be, ponder the consequences and in some instances, even allow it to help guide our future. In fact, history is about the only thing some people find easy to believe. This is because it's over and done with. It has been seen and much of it recorded. We take it in stride. Even atheists agree to the reality of history and in general, accept what historians say about it.

Now ponder this: with God, the future is as plain as the past! I realize that's no great revelation to most of you. But I want you to really think about it. Get hold of it. Let it sink in. Sometimes we *know* things without really letting the truth of it fully absorb. I want you to latch-on-strongly to the fact that God sees the future as easily as the past.

I am sharing this thought with you as an exercise. Thinking in terms of past events gives us an inkling of how it is with God concerning the future too. We may not fully understand God's "omniscience" (all-knowing nature) but if we really believe God's Word, if we really trust Him wholeheartedly, if we place every situation of our lives in His hands, then this should give us a great sense of security regardless of the severity of the present circumstances. Why so? Because knowing God has worked all things out in the past provides the assurance we need that He will do likewise with the future.

Even in this brief study thus far, we have learned that God gave us HIS STORY (*history*) in advance of the occurrences? This is a wonderful truth, folks. Allowing it to penetrate will add immeasurably to our confidence and faith in Almighty God. Christians need to have these facts indelibly sealed in their minds during these days which are filled with sin and temptation. Obviously this is not a new concept for most of you

43

but many of us either act as if it were not true or as if we didn't know it.

Now with that thought in mind (i.e., convinced of God's faithfulness), let me go on with our study of Revelation. Chapter seven is very quiet as compared with surrounding chapters (sometimes called parenthetical). But then, what's wrong with that? Isn't this good "staging"? We all know any good play has peaks and valleys, right? The low points allow us to relax a bit, catch our breath and anticipate the next exciting episode. So, although chapter seven is low key, it is not without its own dynamic.

There are at least three main concepts to note:

1. The sealed 144,000 persons from the twelve tribes of Israel.
2. The great multitude resulting from their testimony.
3. This great multitude comes out of "great tribulation".

Now let's look at John's description of it:

1 "And after these things I saw four angels standing at the four corners of the earth, holding the four winds of the earth, that the wind should not blow on the earth, on the sea, or on any tree.

2 And I saw another angel ascending from the east, having the seal of the living God. And he cried with a loud voice to the four angels to whom it was given to harm the earth and the sea,

3 saying, "do not harm the earth, the sea, or the trees till we have sealed the servants of our God on their foreheads."

4 And I heard the number of those who were sealed. One hundred and forty-four thousand of all the tribes of the children of Israel were sealed:

5 *Of the tribe of Judah twelve thousand were sealed;*
   Of the tribe of Reuben twelve thousand were sealed;
   Of the tribe of Gad twelve thousand were sealed;
6 *Of the tribe of Asher twelve thousand were sealed;*
   Of the tribe of Naphtali twelve thousand were sealed;
   Of the tribe of Manasseh twelve thousand were sealed;
7 *Of the tribe of Simeon twelve thousand were sealed;*
   Of the tribe of Levi twelve thousand were sealed;
   Of the tribe of Issachar twelve thousand were sealed;
8 *Of the tribe of Zebulun twelve thousand were sealed;*
   Of the tribe of Joseph twelve thousand were sealed;
   Of the tribe of Benjamin twelve thousand were sealed.

A MULTITUDE FROM THE GREAT TRIBULATION

9 *After these things I looked, and behold, a great multitude which no one could number, of all nations, tribes, peoples, and tongues, standing before the throne and before the Lamb, clothed with white robes, with palm branches in their hands,*
10 *and crying out with a loud voice, saying, "salvation to our God who sits on the throne, and to the Lamb!"*

11 *And all the angels stood around the throne, and around the elders and the four living creatures, and fell on their faces before the throne and worshiped God,*
12 *saying:*
"Amen! Blessing and glory and wisdom, And thanksgiving and honor and power and might, Be to our God forever and ever. Amen."
13 *And one of the elders answered, saying to me, "Who are these arrayed in white robes, and where did they come from?"*

45

*14 And I said to him, "Sir, you know." And he said to me,
"These are the ones who come out of the great tribulation,
and have washed their robes and made them white in the
blood of the Lamb.*
*15 Therefore they are before the throne of God, and serve
Him day and night in His temple. And He who sits on the
throne will dwell among them.*
*16 They will neither hunger anymore, nor thirst anymore; the
sun shall not strike them, nor any heat;*
*17 for the Lamb who is in the midst of the throne will
shepherd them and lead them to living fountains of waters.
And God will wipe away every tear from their eyes."*

Some people hold that the sealed 144,000 are merely
symbolic; that these twelve tribes of Israel don't really mean the
twelve tribes of Israel! They say this in spite of the fact John
clearly spells it out with specific, Israelite, tribe names! As we
see the believing "multitudes" which follow after the 144,000, it
becomes obvious that the Holy Spirit plans to use this "remnant"
group (the 144,000) for world evangelization at some point in
time. I believe the precise period will be after the Church will
have been raptured, during what is known as **THE GREAT
TRIBULATION** (last half of the final seven years, just prior to
the end of this age).

This chapter is like the quietness between two storms. In
fact, I believe the reason God "sandwiched" chapter seven
between Seal Six and Seal Seven was purposed to give us a clue
as to when the 144,000 are being set aside for their unique,
up-coming ministry. Therefore, since the Sixth Seal described
WW1, this fixes the sealing dates sometime after 1918 (when
that war ended), but before whatever happens in the Seventh
Seal. Once again we see how magnificently God has interwoven
the prophetic highlights of His pre-arranged plan of the ages.
Surely He designed it this way to give us a general idea
(time-wise) of where we are along our journey of His story.

46

During His first advent, Jesus confirmed a covenant (See Is. 61 and Dan. 9) with certain Jews who became His followers. His three and a half years earth mission with them represented the first half of the final, or 70th Week of Daniel.

The 144,000 Israelites will be those with whom Jesus re-establishes that same covenant to finish the last half of the 70th week. The 70th Week was cut short (ending precisely in the middle of it on the day of Jesus' crucifixion). The counting stopped there, leaving 3 1/2 years remaining to be fulfilled between Jesus and last-days, Christian Jews.

The specific time of ministry of the 144,000 Israelites will be during the last half of the Tribulation, usually referred to as The Great Tribulation. (A distinction is usually made between the first half and the second half of The Tribulation. The anti-Christ will be in "full swing" during the second part.)

Assuming you followed all this, you can see that the first half of Daniel's "70th Week", in a sense, is already over! This understanding will come as a total shock to those who have read other prophecy books. However, at the end of the age, there will still be a preliminary, 3 1/2 year "tribulation" for The Church to go through, before the Rapture occurs. This is a separate thing though from the ancient Covenant God made with Israel as spoken of in Daniel chapter nine. We Christians must be very careful to keep our thinking straight when it comes to national Israel (i.e., blood-line Jews) and 'spiritual Israel' (The Church). God made plans and agreements with national Israel and those bonds will be carried out to completion. These plans are separate from what He is doing with and through the Church today. We must understand though that God will stand by all His Covenants and a big factor at the end of this age will be the ministry of the 144,000 set-aside, real Israelites spoken of here in Revelation 7.

Romans 11 makes very plain that God will eventually open the spiritual eyes of national Israel, <u>after</u> the "fulness of the Gentiles" is completed. The new sight given to the 144,000 Jews for their work to do during The Tribulation represents a big part of their restoration.

I will cover "Daniel's Seventieth Week" more thoroughly in chapter 13. However, this present chapter is a key building-block of the book, so if you had any trouble understanding the concepts, please go through it again before moving on.

CHAPTER EIGHT

SEAL SEVEN - PRELUDE TO THE 7 TRUMPETS

Again I want to call your attention to the fact that the Holy Spirit kept separate the Seventh Seal from the other Seals by everything we covered in the last chapter. He obviously did this for a purpose. I have referred to "keys" several times in this study and emphasized their necessity in understanding Biblical prophecy. This passage is one of those. Now let's look at the wording of Seal # 7:

1 "And when he opened the seventh seal, there was silence in heaven for about half an hour."

Don't you find this language very strange, considering what was covered in the first six Seals? It's totally dissimilar from the other presentations. However, it was the very unusual-ness of the language which drew me so strongly to the seventh Seal. Before the understanding came, every time I would read the passage, it was as if something screamed in my spirit — *"There's a secret here. Seek it out. It's understandable."* At times like that during my studies, I became virtually consumed to the point of obsession until I could find the 'hidden element' in the mysterious passage. What I shall say now is not necessarily the exact order in which my understanding came but the presentation is for the purpose of making it more sensible.

"WHAT A DIFFERENCE A 'DAY' MAKES!"

Prophetically speaking, a *"day"* can sometimes mean (1) a single twenty-four hour period, or (2) a full year, and (3) believe it or not, occasionally it can even mean a thousand years! For example, Ezekiel 4:6 says, *"...I have appointed thee each day for a year."* The passage goes on to explain each day the prophet was to lay on his side was to symbolize a year of time. In context we find the number of literal days the prophet was to lay on each side would represent, prophetically, the number of years of a specific coming judgment upon the nation Israel.

But another passage uses a *"day"* this way: 2 Peter 3:8 says, *"...But beloved, be not ignorant of this one thing, that one day is with the Lord as a thousand years, and a thousand years as one day."* Now some will say this latter case is only metaphoric language, never to be taken literally. Well, I believe God uses these concepts for a very specific reason: **Counting prophetic time.**

God is the cleverest writer of all time. He can put simple truths right under our nose and some of us will many times pass them right by. Some forever! Now I agree we must use great caution as we search for these discoveries. But, we don't want to be so fearful as to miss the main reason (the LODR) He included them in His Holy Word! I am absolutely convinced God was giving us time-tools through Ezekiel and Peter. Interestingly, Jesus said in Matthew 16:19 that he would give Peter the *"keys"* to the kingdom of heaven. I believe this is one of them.

Please note exactly how Peter was inspired to write the statement. He began the verse with *"be not ignorant of"*, a Biblical phrase that might better be rendered "PAY ATTENTION NOW"! It's like a verbal alarm-clock, the rather obvious meaning being, "I'm about to give you a secret now so hear me loud and clear". For double emphasis Peter even repeated the "time-tool" backwards!

Now I'm not saying that Peter 3:8 means literally that it takes 1,000 years of earth-time to equal one day of heaven-time. It simply means that certain time references stated in the Bible will make sense only when this 'conversion factor' is used to unlock the meaning. This is one of those incredibly simple ways which was used to keep the passage locked until the "fulness of time" came for it to be understood. (I want to mention again that applications of this kind never changes a straight forward exegesis of the plain, ordinary meaning of a verse in its immediate context. This is how the Law of Double Reference works and I again remind you that this is God's Law, not mine.)

There is a bit of a problem which arises here, though. Since there are two "time-tools" (i.e., one day = one year and one day = one thousand years), how do we know which to use? I'll explain with a parallel situation-story. Suppose I own a mountain cabin (I don't) and I give you permission to use it some weekend. I give you a key ring holding several keys forgetting to tell you which one would unlock the door. What would you do when you got there? Obviously you would merely insert the keys until you found the one which worked.

The same is true of Biblical keys. We try them to see what happens! Once you've tried the correct key, the passage will suddenly come alive with answers which fit all aspects of that particular Scripture. If it's the wrong key, nonsense and frustration will result just as surely as attempting to get into a cabin with the wrong key.

There is another way to determine how to use God's time keys. If the passage is related to a scene in heaven, use one day = to a thousand years; if the passage concerns an earth scene, use one day = one year. This may seem too simple but it works out. Actually, it agrees with God's ways, for the Bible says "...*God has chosen the foolish things of the world to put to shame the wise, and God has chosen the weak things of the world to put to shame the things which are mighty;...*" (1 Cor. 1:27).

Now let's get back to Seal Seven. Why was John inspired to mention the thirty minute "quiet time" in heaven? This question really perplexed me when I was first studying the passage. My reasoning was that a literal-only interpretation just didn't seem right. Then one day this question suddenly came to mind: *"Why not use the 'time-tool' of one thousand years = to a day and see what happens?"* The task was simply to determine how long half an hour of 'heaven-time' would be on the 'earth-time' scale. This can be done with a simple ratio formula:

$$\frac{1/2 \text{ hour}}{\text{X years}} = \frac{24 \text{ hours (a } day)}{\text{one thousand years}}$$

Therefore, $X = \dfrac{1000 \text{ years } \times 1/2 \text{ hour}}{24 \text{ hours}}$

Thus, $X = \dfrac{500 \text{ years}}{24} = $ **20.8 years.**

I have been quite lengthy in developing all this "time business" and you must be asking, "Is it really worth it"? I felt the same way when working this out. Now, with hindsight, I can shout a resounding, "YES!" When I first saw the answer to the above equation, I stared at the answer of **20.8 years** for some time. So what does it mean? I had a number but still didn't understand the Seventh Seal any better than before I started. So, I went back to the way you assemble any puzzle — look again at all the pieces in front of you.

What did I have? I was at the Seventh Seal. I had already come to understand the Sixth Seal as WW1, so whatever Seal Seven means, it must occur some time after the end of WW1. At that time I had also appraised the Fifth Trumpet as WW2. Suddenly it dawned on me! The main idea of the Seventh Seal is **quietness**. "That could mean lack of severe war conflict in the world", I thought. Then, I checked the date WW1 ended — November 11, 1918. Next, I checked the date WW2 started — September 1, 1939. Subtracting these dates indicates that the duration between the two world wars was 20 years, 9 months and 20 days. If this is put in the decimal system, the time-span equals 20.8 years! WOW!

(Wouldn't you know it? I just realized that I wrote this part here on Veteran's Day, 11/11/91.)

I think it is noteworthy for you to realize I saw Seal Six as WW1 and Trumpet Five as WW2 <u>before</u> I tried the steps outlined above. Had it been the other way around, it might be concluded that I had engineered the outcome.

Of course one could still say this is all mere 'chance coincidence'. One well-known-nation-wide radio preacher laughed when he learned about my explanation of the "half-hour" quietness in heaven. That's O.K. I admit it may seem a little far-fetched. But it is my contention that God is as much the God of numbers and arithmetic as He is of words and ideas. The whole universe operates on very precise mathematical laws which mankind continually learns about. And God is responsible for all the "equations" and "formulas" behind what man thinks he has discovered. But the fact remains---it is God's design. Today it seems many Christian leaders fail to recognize this very simple, yet basic truth.

Unfortunately, a high percentage of those in the sciences today are leaving God out of their lives. There was a time when the scientists were in the forefront of the Christian faith, men like Sir Isaac Newton, for example. He and others understood through their discoveries, the necessity of supernatural intelligence behind the great mysteries they were learning about. Yes, God is very much involved in the mathematics of His universe. The "mystery" surrounding the Seventh Seal adds sufficient proof of that to me.

In conclusion on this point, God promised the prophet Daniel (chapter 12) that in the "last days" He (God) would cause some people to comprehend the chronological prophecies which Daniel himself wrote about, but didn't understand. As audacious as it may sound, it just may be that God has elected to show me some of those things He was referring to when He spoke to Daniel. If it is so, I accept the gift in the spirit of Jesus' own words: "*I thank you, O Father, Lord of Heaven and earth, because thou hast hidden these things from the wise and prudent, and hast revealed them unto babes.*"

This is a wonderful thing, folks! God's promise to Daniel was that this understanding wouldn't come until the time of the end. If I'm right, does it not stand to reason that the countdown is here? I believe the Holy Spirit is providing "last-days manna" for those He has chosen. We only need to take and "eat it". This is part of God's 'prep-work' in the lives of believers, designed to strengthen our faith during the world's up-coming, final conflicts. Jesus is coming again to reign over His Own. His Kingdom will be established just as the prophets-of-old said. And right now, the Holy Spirit is stirring the minds of those sensitive to the prophetic word. Dear reader, I hope you are listening to what He is saying to you.

Next we come to the Seven Trumpets. Note carefully that the trumpets are sounded by heavenly angels. They make the announcements as to when and what is happening. This is quite a contrast to the error of the "*rich*" and "*great*" men who thought WW1 was the "wrath of the Lamb". In Revelation, when God is truly about to do something dramatic, He sends angels to make the pronouncements, not the great, rich or sin-laden men.

THE TRUMPETS INTRODUCED

2 "*And I saw the seven angels who stand before God, and to them were given seven trumpets.*
3 *And another angel, having a golden censer, came and stood at the altar. And he was given much incense, that he should offer it with the prayers of all the saints on the golden altar which was before the throne.*
4 *And the smoke of the incense, with the prayers of the saints, ascended before God out of the angel's hand.*
5 *And the angel took the censer, filled it with fire from the altar, and threw it to the earth. And there were noises, thunderings, lightnings, and an earthquake.*
6 *And the seven angels who had the seven trumpets prepared themselves to sound.*"

54

We humans love fireworks. But the apostle John surely saw things in the heavenly scene which would make our 4th of July look puny by comparison! John somehow saw the prayers from the saints here on earth, mixed with a heavenly "incense" (prayers of heavenly beings, I assume). This prayerful blend ascended to God's Throne. Perhaps this incense was the cumulative "THY-KINGDOM-COME" prayers of saints of all time, combined with the prayers of the "heavenly stewards". In response to those prayers, God finally gave the order for the final countdown to begin.

Whatever the actual meaning, we can definitely draw this conclusion: in response to the "incense", God sent "fire from the altar" which was cast to the earth resulting in "voices" (increased communication?) "thunderings, and lightnings, and an earthquake". These words are symbolic of what is specifically spelled out in the Seven Trumpets when they sound. Now, let's look at them one-by-one.

TRUMPET ONE: VEGETATION STRUCK

7 "The first angel sounded: And hail and fire followed, mingled with blood, and they were thrown to the earth; and a third of the trees were burned up, and all green grass was burned up."

Now the Futurists-only school would say this means that we can someday expect a catastrophe to cause 1/3 of all trees and all the world's green grass to suddenly disappear! This is possible, of course. With God, anything is possible. But, my inclination is to first view the 'burning' historically.

As I pondered this Trumpet a few years ago, realizing the time frame following the Seals was somewhere around the 1930s or 1940s, I wondered if there was anything which happened in the world at that time which would relate to John's description of the First Trumpet. So I again looked at the historical facts.

As I recall, the first thing that came to my mind were conversations I used to hear when I was growing up. My Dad owned a small country store in northwest Georgia. On rainy days, the farmers in the region would gather around a pot-belly stove in my Dad's store and talk about *hard times*. I'll attempt to put in Georgia-vernacular a topic often heard:

"Whooooooie, boys! I like this rain we're getting today.", one would say. *"Yeah, I do too. It's been pretty dry lately but of course nuthin' like what we saw a few years ago, huh Claudy"*, replied another. *"You mighty right, son. Those were the driest times I ever saw; couldn't hardly raise a thing. You boys haven't seen anything"*, Claudy would say.

Thus, I grew up believing there was a period in the 30s and early 40s which was tougher than I could imagine and that idea was put there by the common folklore of honest, hard-working — mostly Christian — men. Those of you with farming background in that era, particularly if you didn't depend on irrigation, will identify with the conditions just described.

Recalling those days around the pot-bellied stove while writing this one day made me wonder if perhaps the events were broader in scale than I had been aware, so, back to the library again.

The encyclopedias reveal that the Southwestern states of the U. S. suffered one of the worst droughts in their history from 1931 to 1938. The drought affected the entire country and few crops could even be grown. Food became scarce and prices went up throughout the nation. In 1944, drought also brought great damage to almost all South America. The drought moved on to Australia and then to Europe, where it continued throughout the summer of 1945.

Let me illustrate this history with an imaginary scene: Recent space photography has provided us with magnificent pictures that show tremendous spans of the earth. You've seen them. Now visualize that scene. Also, imagine the time is the 30s and you are up in the edge of space looking down at the Southwestern states. From that high-up position, you observe the drought begins. Now, visualize the earth beneath you suddenly becoming brown instead of lush and green. Next, watch it sweeping throughout the land, killing the "trees and grass" as it goes. Then you see it skip the ocean to continue the same drying effect on the next continent, and the next, and the next, etc. Can you see it?

Now while it's fresh in your mind, reread Rev. 8:7, then read again the above historical facts and I think you'll see that my scenario probably isn't very far from what John actually saw.

Those of you who didn't live in the 30s and 40s probably can't appreciate the severity of long drought conditions and that "all the green grass" and "1/3 of all the trees" **have already** "burnt up" one time. However, Californians should be able to identify with these conditions, because in the mid-70s we had a 4 year drought. Even though that was merely a low rainfall period, the country-side was nearly devastated! Remember? The water reservoirs were almost emptied! Now just think how bad it would be if it had continued for several more years, then you've got the conditions of the thirties and forties.

Except on rare occasions, like where specific war dates can be checked in the history books, it's difficult to establish a precise day when a Seal or a Trumpet begins. But so what? God doesn't expect us to be able to determine His calendar with absolute certainty. That's His business. However, He has given us plenty of information, plus a few 'time-pieces', to get the general picture of where we are on the prophetic journey through time and space. (I might point out here that probably some of the Seals and Trumpets actually overlap in time, particularly those here in the first few Trumpets.)

57

SECOND TRUMPET: THE SEAS STRUCK

8 "And the second angel sounded: And something like a
great mountain burning with fire was thrown into the sea,
and a third of the sea became blood;
9 and a third of the living creatures in the sea died, and a
third of the ships were destroyed."

I believe this Trumpet speaks of the devastation which began
to affect the seas and the life within them, as well as man's
ships which would travel on the seas. Let's talk first about loss
of the sea life. I think this came about in two ways:

1. The WW2 depth charges and torpedos blasting in the seas
   had a lot to do with the loss of life beginning in the forties.
   The following actual story serves to illustrate the effect of an
   underwater blast: When I was a small boy, I went fishing on
   a creek one night with a group of older boys — with "22"
   rifles. (This is illegal by the way and not recommended at
   all!) Here's how we got the fish. We walked upstream,
   shining the beam of our flashlights into the water, looking for
   'sleeping' fish. When located, the fish would be temporarily
   blinded by the light. Then, we simply held the gunbarrel
   under the water and fired, not aiming to hit the fish. Above
   the water a "22" makes a very soft thump this way, but
   underneath, a violent shockwave knocks the fish out,
   sometimes killing it!
   Now let's apply this principle to sea life during WW2. Ships
   were armed with anti-sub "depth charges" (huge barrel-like
   explosives) which were fired overboard. They would then
   sink and were timed to detonate at certain depths. It wasn't
   always necessary for depth charges to even hit a submarine
   to put it totally out of commission. That being the case,
   imagine what this did to the sea life throughout the region
   where this kind of warfare was used!

Sound transmission is extremely strong under water. Have you ever put your head under water and had a friend strike two small stones together at the opposite end of a swimming pool? The apparent closeness of the sound is amazing. And do you recall those old war movies which showed the allied submarine lying motionless on the bottom of the sea while the enemy destroyer moved over them with their sonar devices operating? The men in the sub couldn't make the slightest sound or it would be detected. Hollywood accurately portrayed this one. That's the way it is.

With these ideas in mind, just imagine also how much sea life has been lost resulting from the testing of atomic devices since WW2! Surely it has been great.

2. The other man-caused devastation to the seas, beginning about the same time as WW2, has been water pollution. We have plenty of evidence today to indicate pollution is destroying sea life and river life. "Coincidentally", the time I was studying this Trumpet, I received a letter from Jacque Cousteau[3] describing what mankind has done to the waterways since the 40's.

Mr. Cousteau is widely recognized as one of the world's leading authorities on water life. I know little about the man's faith or spiritual beliefs but I do respect his views and opinions on water life. Incidentally, till this day I still don't know why I received the letter. I'd never responded to any 'plea' from him or had any contact whatsoever with his organization, nor have I since! But the timing was uncanny and the information enormous. I believe in God's sovereign control in matters such as this but always find it amazing.

---

[3]In the midst of writing this section, I received an extensive newsletter from Jacque Cousteau, a world-renowned, expert scientist on water eco-systems. Although the author's approach was non-Christian related, I found the information very pertinent to prophecy.

Mr. Cousteau's insights so graphically describe sea and river pollution, I felt it would be worthwhile for you to hear his own words. The following comments are from his letter I received July 1979.

"Each month we now pour millions of tons of poisonous waste into the living sea. Many of our lakes, rivers and coastal waters have received their mortal wound. The water is undrinkable. The fish and shell fish, if they exist at all, are inedible. I do not say this lightly. During the past thirty years (now 40+ years) *my team and I have spent thousands of hours diving in Aqua-lungs and other underwater devices. During that time I have observed and studied, and with my own eyes I have seen our waters sicken. Certain reefs that teemed with fish only ten years ago are now almost lifeless. The ocean bottom has been raped by trawlers. Priceless wetlands have been destroyed by land fill. And everywhere poisoness effluents. Often, when I describe the symptoms of our environmental illness I hear remarks like "they're only fish" or "they're only birds." I assure you that our destinies are linked with theirs in the most profound and fundamental manner. All life is interconnected and the great life-giving bank is the sea."* (I do not agree with Mr. Cousteau's obvious evolutionary bias. However, I believe his observations of the devastations are correct. He goes on:) *"If the oceans should die---by which I mean all life in the sea would cease---then this would signal the end not only for all marine life, but for all other animals and plants of this earth, including man."* (Here, Mr. Cousteau comes remarkably close to describing one of the Vials, to be discussed later. But, as Christians, we know that all life will not be destroyed because God will intervene before that happens.)

Mr. Cousteau continues:

"I implore you to understand that more than one billion children - and another billion adults - do not have water safe enough to drink. That's half of the people in the entire world. Each year ten million people die from such horrors as cholera, typhoid, dysentery, hepatitis, and schistomiasis - and from disease because of untreated municipal and human wastes dumped directly into streams, rivers, and lakes. I can't understand - what are we doing to ourselves and to our children? why do we let it go on?"

(Though brilliant and clear in his sensitivity to natural phenomena, Mr. Cousteau seems unaware that we are in a sinful world which is coming to it's climax. He epitomizes the apostle Paul's statement in 2 Timothy 3:7, *"always learning and never able to come to the knowledge of the truth"*. But while he may not understand that the underlying cause is sin and its consequences, Mr. Cousteau has probably given us the most profound picture of what is happening to our water eco-systems. It is so important for you and I to see that water pollution is what John is talking about in the Second Trumpet, I want to include more of Mr. Cousteau's analysis:)

"A researcher asked a marine biologist if he could supply a map showing which rivers pollute the ocean. The biologist had a simpler way. He said, "Nowadays, any river that flows through a farm, a city, or an industrial area is loaded with pollutants."
"Almost forty years ago, seven thousand tons of arsenic were put into concrete containers and dumped into the Baltic Sea. If properly administered, this is reportedly enough to kill the population of the world three times over. Perhaps it has begun. The Baltic now has very high levels of this toxic substance."

"Four years ago I knew that the amount of life in the ocean was dwindling at a terrifying rate. Yet I predicted that the fishing tonnage would continue to rise for a few years because of better equipment methods - and I was wrong. The tonnage of fish started down in 1971 and has kept going down ever since, in spite of more fishing vessels and better equipment. I could add thousands more to these examples, and fill ten volumes, but I hope these few will convey my distress and concern at what is happening to our oceans, our planet, and ourselves."

Now, with Mr. Cousteau's words fresh in your mind, re-read John's description of the Second Trumpet. Do the Scriptures not parallel the observations of this world-renowned scientist?

THE THIRD TRUMPET: THE WATERS STRUCK

10 "And the third angel sounded: And a great star fell from heaven, burning like a torch, and it fell on a third of the rivers and on the springs of water;
11 and the name of the star is Wormwood; and a third of the waters became wormwood; and many men died from the waters, because the waters were made bitter."

Nearly everything I said with regard to the Second Trumpet applies equally well here. The main difference is that Trumpet Two related mainly to the seas whereas Trumpet Three concerns the fresh waters — the water we drink. Notice that one-third of all fresh water became "wormwood" which caused many men to die, therefore we can conclude the water would become poisonous. (Recall that Mr. Cousteau pointed out that half the fresh water on this planet is already undrinkable.)

It may be significant to note the recent radiation "accident" which occurred in Chernobyl, Russia. I have read that the meaning of the word - Chernobyl - is WORMWOOD! Isn't that interesting? Certainly the whole earth was alarmed by the severity of that great polluting incident, and unfortunately these occurrences will probably increase. Of course, the final effect the Chernobyl accident will produce remains to be seen.

"WORMWOOD" SPIRITUALIZED

Understanding multiple applications of Scripture doesn't come easy for most of us. However, through careful Bible study, I have become convinced of the truth and reality of it. I believe God designed it and intends for us to seek out and discover His "hidden manna". Once seen, a whole new arena opens up. I do not claim to be the only one who approaches Scripture in this way but some Christian leaders fear over-spiritualizing. They say that in so doing you can make the Bible say anything you want it to. Unfortunately, there is some truth in this position. But we should never become so fearful that we miss the mysteries God *has* planned for us to find.

I would like to add another possible dimension to the Third Trumpet. Remember my approach to prophecy: First, look at a passage with only the immediate context in mind, concentrating on what it might mean specifically during a local situation at the time the writer wrote it. Next, look at the longitudinal aspect. (Chiefly, that's what you are reading in this book). Thirdly, think of the end-of-the-age application, which will again be a local, brief period. All three applications are equally true, each one affecting this planet and the people living at the time the prophecies are coming to pass.

But there is even a fourth dimension which needs to be considered. And sometimes this is perhaps even more important. I will call it the *spiritual.*

I think the word *wormwood* could also mean 'errant Gospel'. Notice that men died because they partook of imbittered waters. To understand what I mean, first imagine physical waters (H_2O) being polluted with poisons of various kinds. When men drink such water, they die. That's the obvious meaning. Now think of real water in its pure state, before being polluted, to the Gospel message as it was when Jesus first proclaimed it. Since then, heresy has crept in at many sites and as a result, the pure Gospel is found today in fewer and fewer congregations. It has been weakened due to Satanic activity operating in all the areas of man's depravity and sin-prone condition. This has resulted in an endless variety of cults, each with its own brand of the 'gospel', many of them so distorted they bear little resemblance to the plain teachings of the first-century New Testament Church.

I wish I was speaking only of cults. Many, once-strong-in-THE-FAITH, mainline denominations are today so backslidden that they can hardly be distinguished from outstanding cults. The gospel-water of these organizations have become polluted with false doctrines ("wormwood"); hence, men are spiritually starving. What does this mean? It means, at best, people who drink this 'water' are spiritually malnourished; and, at worst, have not been saved through it. When normal drinking-water becomes severely polluted, people die if they drink it. Likewise, people die who drink a polluted gospel.

THE FOURTH TRUMPET: THE HEAVENS STRUCK

12 "And the fourth angel sounded: And a third of the sun was struck, a third of the moon, and a third of the stars, so that a third of them were darkened; and a third of the day did not shine, and the night likewise.
13 And I looked, and I heard an angel flying through the midst of heaven, saying with a loud voice, "Woe, woe, woe to the inhabitants of the earth, because of the remaining blasts of the trumpet of the three angels who are about to sound!"

64

I believe Trumpet Four signals the beginning of the problems associated with air pollution. Certainly the timing would be right. In the first three Trumpets, we have seen (1) the drought years, (2) sea pollution and (3) fresh water pollution. All began about the same time. Actually, one would expect simultaneous commencement of these due to the industrial revolution: a sudden appearance of factories, ships, cars, farmers, etc., all contributing to the pollutants being spued into the air and water systems of the world.

Now, let's look specifically at what the Scripture says. One third of the sun, one third of the moon and one third of the stars were dramatically affected. The Literal-only philosophy would here demand that 1/3 of the sun is going to be destroyed, that 1/3 of the moon will be missing and that 1/3 of the stars will disappear. I don't think this is the meaning. Verse 12 says the sun, moon and stars were *"struck"*, *"darkened"*, and *"did not shine"*.

Doesn't it make more sense to assume that this simply means that, as a result of the debris and smog in the air, one would some day be able to *see* only about one third of the stars and that the illumination of the sun and moon would be reduced by one third?

If you doubt that the number of visible stars seen at night have already been reduced by one third, let me share this very simple, but very practical, illustrative story. I grew up in the country about 60 miles from Atlanta, Ga. It was always an amazing sight to just sit outside at night and gaze up at the stars. It was vast. I vividly recall the ease with which I could see them. The stars were bright and their numbers enormous beyond imagination. Viewing them from that same region on an ordinary night in this day and age is far, far less dramatic. Quite dull, in fact. The visible stars are dramatically fewer in number and much dimmer. (That dimmness is not due to failing eyesight, by the way. I still have 20/20 vision, thank God.)

If you are over 40, it will be much easier for you to grasp, and believe, what I'm saying here. But you younger ones can verify my idea by doing a simple test. If you live in, or can visit, a highly populous region, go to a dark region (where you aren't surrounded by street and city illumination which blot out the stars by glare), look up and get a relative count of the number of visible stars, noting also their brightness. Remember what you saw and as soon as possible, do the same thing again, only this time above 5,000 feet altitude. Observe the remarkable difference: it is totally due to air pollution! It may be hard to believe but all this happened in the last forty years!

Surely air pollution and its consequences provide a more acceptable answer to what John saw than taking a Futuristic-only stand. Re-read the text and think through these thoughts again.

There are three remaining Trumpets to sound which John introduces with the words, *"Woe, Woe, Woe..."*. Obviously this indicates conditions which will be even more devastating than those beforehand. The next chapter deals with two of them.

CHAPTER NINE

To introduce this chapter, let's first briefly summarize the historical aspect of Revelation as covered thus far:

1. We have seen the Roman Empire under Constantine's rule;

2. followed by the Empire's chief threat, Mohammadanism;

3. next came the widespread scarcity on earth;

4. and then death on a broad scale brought about chiefly by the "holy" wars and the Dark Ages,

5. during which occurred much Christian martyrdom.

6. We then saw the emergence of the modern era in the Sixth Seal, World War One.

7. Following that was the *"half-hour"* (20.8 year) quiet time between WW1 and WW2, which introduced the first four Trumpets covered in chapter 8, where we saw...

8. vegetation struck, followed then by

9. sea pollution,

10. fresh-water pollution and

11. air pollution.

So, we note the above 11 identifications include seven Seals and four Trumpets which now brings us to the 12th major piece of the prophetic puzzle, **Trumpet Five**.

FIFTH TRUMPET: The Locusts from the Bottomless Pit

1 "And the fifth angel sounded: And I saw a star fall from heaven to the earth. And to him was given the key to the bottomless pit.
2 And he opened the bottomless pit, and smoke arose out of the pit like the smoke of a great furnace. And the sun and the air were darkened because of the smoke of the pit.
3 And locusts came out of the smoke onto the earth. And to them was given power, as the scorpions of the earth have power.
4 And they were commanded that they should not harm the grass of the earth, any green thing, nor any tree, but only those men who do not have the seal of God on their foreheads.
5 And it was granted to them that they should not kill them, but that they should be tormented five months. And their torment was like the torment of a scorpion when it strikes a man.
6 And in those days men will seek death and shall not find it; they will desire to die, and death will flee from them.
7 And the shapes of the locusts were like horses prepared for battle; and on their heads, as it were, crowns like gold, and their faces were like the faces of men.
8 And they had hair like women's hair, and their teeth were like lions' teeth.
9 And they had breastplates like breastplates of iron, and the sound of their wings was like the sound of chariots with many horses running into battle.
10 And they had tails like scorpions, and there were stings in their tails. And their power was to hurt men five months.
11 And they had a king over them who is the angel of the bottomless pit, whose name in Hebrew is Abaddon, but in Greek he has the name Apollyon.

12 One woe is past. Behold, still two more woes are coming after these things."

Now let's see how John's account of this first *woe* fits into the overall picture. We've already learned that the water and air pollution was associated with the growing industrial revolution, becoming particularly evident in the late 30s and early 40s, which was the prelude to this Fifth Trumpet. Therefore, because of the perfect agreement, time-wise, and because of John's beautiful, symbolic word-picture as described in the above verses, I am convinced Trumpet # 5 stands for **World War Two.** Take a look at these seven points:

1. THE "STAR" (Vs. 1)

The *"star"* can only be Satan for he is the one who fell from heaven as described in Isaiah 14 and Revelation 12. Note in verse 1 that he *fell* from heaven, not *sent*. Recall also, he drew 1/3 of the other angels of heaven with him. Satan is behind all evil, including being in charge of the "bottomless pit" (although Jesus holds the key to it).

(I do not believe the *bottomless pit* need be taken as a single place somewhere but more likely represents a conglomerate of all those in rebellion towards God, including both man and angelic demons. Fallen man has little appreciation of the depth of his own depravity, hence the name *bottomless pit.* But the prophet Jeremiah aptly described it for us when he said, *"The heart is deceitful above all things, and desperately wicked, who can know it?")* [Jer. 17:9]

Satan (the *"star"* of the *"pit")* identifies with all rebellion. Although restricted by God's sovereignty, it seems he has certain rights and authority over these in the *"bottomless pit".* Satan wants us all but he seeks out especially vile, intelligent men — those whose character is most like his own. He inspires them to reach high positions of power and influence in the world's ungodly systems. No human agency or office is off limits. It may include ruling positions of all types: kings, presidents, senators, judges...,! You name it.

Note what happened when the "*bottomless pit*" was opened. The sun and air were "*darkened*". This simply says to me that the sky would once again be filled with smoke. Explosive smoke! Our first hint of WW2.

2. "*LOCUSTS*" (Vs.3)

Locusts fly. But these *locusts* (the "*scorpions of the earth*") could also kill men! What kind of natural locust are you aware of that can <u>fly</u> + has the capacity to <u>kill</u>? (John is not talking about grasshopper plagues.) This means something altogether different. <u>Airplanes</u> maybe!? More on this in a moment.

3. THE "SEAL OF GOD" (Vs. 4)

Verse four refers to those who have the "*seal of God*" in their foreheads. Those without the seal were not to be killed, only "*tormented*". Casual reading would cause one to think those with the seal would refer to Christians. But the longer I looked at the passage the less I felt this was correct. Remember, the "*star*" of the "*bottomless pit*" is Satan. It was <u>he</u> who loosed the "*locusts*" which are to hurt those who do not have the "*seal of God*" in their foreheads. I have trouble seeing the true God or Christians implicated here. The fallen "*star*" was the one who would issue the command. I don't want to be dogmatic here but I have other ideas on just what this passage may mean. So stay with me and see if the logic makes sense to you too.

I believe these verses allude to the "supermen" of Germany, the Nazis. They bought *the lie* of the devil that there were certain people who hindered the path of their "march of supremacy" and therefore ought to be destroyed. Namely, the Jews. According to Adolph Hitler's reckoning, Jews were an inferior race, a race without the *'seal of God'* upon them.

Hitler was religious. (He was a baptized Catholic.) But his 'religion' was a distorted caricature of true Christianity. He believed the Jews should be removed from the human race so as not to further 'contaminate' the superior race he visualized. People that did not measure up to Hitler's perspective of a perfect race did not have the "seal of God", by his reckoning, upon them, chief among whom were the Jews!

Of course, Hitler served the 'god' who wanted the Jews annihilated and this is what Satan put in the hearts of the cruel Nazis. They sought to create a 'superhuman' race — a 'purer' race with the *"seal of God"* in their foreheads, whatever that meant in Hitler's mind. Those who did not have the seal were to be hurt. It mainly started with the Jews but actually turned out later to include anyone who got in the way of his intent to destroy natural Israel.

And thus began Hitler's plot against the Jews. Satan had convinced Hitler the Jews were evil. The Jews, through whom God gave the Holy Scriptures and His Messiah, were always the object of Satan's hatred. Satan figured if he could get rid of them, he would have no trouble setting up his earthly kingdom. (Of course, this later got out of hand as Hitler and his regime realized others too would have to be destroyed, namely all those who resisted his endeavor. In fact, this would eventually involve the whole world! But we must remember it was his intense hatred of the Jews which ignited, and fed, his evil mind.)

But, you may have noticed my explanation of the *seal of God* presents kind of a paradox. Verse five says that those without this seal (the Jews according to Hitler's view) were not to be killed, only *"tormented"*. How do we reconcile this in light of the fact that 6,000,000 Jews were later slaughtered? Could it not simply mean Hitler's <u>initial</u> order was that the Jews were not to be killed (which of course turned out to be a lie)?

But why should this surprise us? Satan is a liar and the *"father of lies"*. His regimes always center around lies. As

71

Satan's puppet, Hitler simply fell right in line with the whole delusion. Although at first he told his cronies that the Jews would only be *"tortured"*, he obviously had murder in his heart from the beginning.

4. MEN WOULD SEEK DEATH (Vs. 6)

Verse six says men would seek but not find death. I believe this refers to the awful conditions which developed in the thirties, especially in Germany. I've seen documentary films of the long food lines which existed there in the years just preceding the war. The poverty conditions were severe and I imagine that's what helped mold the thinking of the German people who finally got behind Hitler and supported him. To them he was a 'messiah', promising them deliverance from hard times; times dreadful enough that men wished they could die. But death would *"flee from them"*.

(Recently, I heard the leader of a nation-wide, Christian Seminar say that Hitler used the aged people to build his base. That was a clever move. He obviously reasoned if he could get the elderly behind him, others would fall in line. It worked. This present humanistic age with its sick euthansia programs is forgetting the elderly. We Christians should consider the principle Hitler discovered, only in our case motivated by a sincere desire to love our more mature citizens, meet their needs, and, include them in ministry activities. I'm convinced God would bless the effort.)

5. THE "LOCUSTS" (Vs. 7)

John said these *"locusts"* (flying machines) were like *"horses prepared for battle"*. I believe he was thinking of the way soldiers poised their horses in a straight-line manner before a

72

battle in those days. Similarly, in WW2, squadrons of aircraft fighters and bombers often lined up like this in order to be ready for immediate take-off as soon as the order came to "hit the skies". Not a bad parallel, John!

These "*locusts*" had "*heads*" like "*crowns of gold*". This is a description of the bright metal surrounding the cockpit. In it John saw faces which were <u>like</u> the "*faces of men*". Why do you suppose those faces looked like faces of men? Because they <u>were</u> the faces of men! Of course John had never seen a man inside such a monstrous creature as an airplane so he called it like he saw it.

Then John noted the "*locust*" had a breastplate like "*iron*". Iron is one of the few metals John had seen. What he saw in the vision resembled it. The metallic fuselage of the airplane John saw was more like "iron" than anything else he had ever seen.

Now it's really getting exciting. Next, John heard the noise which the wings produced. (Verse 9.) In John's day, nothing flew which had wings that produced loud noises. But in our day we've got all kinds of them! To make it even clearer, John also said the "*locusts*" sounded like many horses "*running to battle*". Have you ever heard many horses running together? They make a thundering, <u>pounding</u> noise. WW2 aircraft had piston engines. Piston engines <u>pound</u>. On the other hand, jet engines <u>whir</u> and these weren't around until the 50s. This difference (i.e., the pounding engine) directs our attention towards the technological age of the 30s and 40s which makes WW2 the more likely period John is describing, not some war yet to come which will surely involve jet planes.

The description goes on: The rear of these "*locusts*" had "*stings in their tails*". I believe these "*stings*" represent bombs which came out of the "*tails*". Several of the WW2 planes also had what were called tail gunners. In the rear was a little plastic, bubble cabin just large enough to house one man and his machine gun. He was in this strategic position mainly to ward off approaching aircraft from the back and occasionally to fire at the enemy below.

[Recently, I was having dinner with my wife Cindy at **The Nut Tree,** a well-known restaurant in Vacaville, California. There is a small airport there and inside the building complex is a bookstore with the largest selection of WW2 books I'd ever seen — literally a whole wall of them. I fingered one off the shelf and glanced through it. It contained beautiful, illustrative pictures of WW2 aircraft used by all sides. I 'just happened' to go to a page which pictured the most strategic plane Germany used in its bombing missions---the HE-111. It was a fighter-bomber which had the bubble, machine-gun nest (the *sting* in its tail) I mentioned above. I am convinced this is the very object the apostle John saw. The aircraft fits the picture of John's vision, <u>in terms of appearance and function</u>. The article said the Germans had thousands of these bomber-fighters.]

6. "HAIR" LIKE WOMEN AND "TEETH" LIKE LIONS (Vs. 8)

Sometimes the strangest things have gotten my attention which I have later become convinced were timed and related to my on-going prophecy study. Even Halley's Comet streaking by a few years ago brought with it new insights. A secular article I read at the time said that the word "comet" derives from the Greek word meaning <u>*"hair"*</u>. Ancient astronomers likened comets to a running, screaming woman with her hair trailing behind her. (Also keep in mind, John is still talking about the noisy-winged, brightly-headed object, in which he saw faces like men.)

But what new evidence does the *"hair"* tell us? I'll answer with another question: What produces a con-trail in the sky besides a comet? It becomes increasingly clear that John is talking about an airplane. The only thing John had ever witnessed which resembled what he saw in his vision was a comet (or falling star) streaking across the sky. So what else could he use to describe the con-trail (or smoke) of an airplane other than what he had probably heard astronomers of his day call the *hair* streaks eminating from the rear of a comet? Hmm! Only God knows how something so simple can remain so obscure for so long.

Now remember we are still talking about *"locusts"* and John had even more to say. The *"locusts"* had *"teeth like lions"!* (Verse 8.) What could this mean? I believe John is referring to the airplane propellers. As with the other clues, he certainly wouldn't know exactly what to call them. All he knew was that they were long, sharp (like teeth), could move and appeared destructive. In his environment, lions' teeth were the best he could come up with. Good enough, John! I like it.

Now let's summarize the characteristics of what John called *"locusts"* and compare them to the German, WW2 aircraft — the HE-111:

1. They were like *"horses prepared for battle"*, (lined up at the airports);
2. had *"crowns like gold"* (the shiney cockpit);
3. had *"faces like men"* (because they WERE men---in the cockpit);
4. could *"torment"* (with the bombs);
5. had *"stings in their tails"* (the machine-gun nests);
6. had *"hair like women"* (the con-trails produced by engine smoke or by condensation when flying high);
7. had *"breastplates of iron"* (the overall metallic appearance of the aircraft);
8. and their wings produced *"sounds like the sound of chariots with many horses running to battle"* (the pounding piston engines). Clear enough? There's more.

7. THE "ANGEL OF THE BOTTOMLESS PIT" (Vs. 11)

Now some skeptics will say, "Lance, our side had airplanes which also fit the above description. How do you know these refer to Hitler's regime?" The difference is this: the U.S. and allied forces represented <u>retaliation</u> against evil; Hitler's was <u>initiation</u> of an evil plot from the beginning.

In this seventh point, John reveals the identity of that nation's leader. He says he is the *"angel of bottomless pit"*, which, of course, is none other than Satan. But Satan doesn't reveal himself in his own person. He usually does it in the disguise of a man.

"ABADDON" & "APOLLYON"

John called this *angel* by the names of *Abaddon* (Hebrew) and *Apollyon* (Greek). Abaddon means 'destroyer' and Apollyon means 'exterminator'. What a perfect description for Adolph Hitler! I know of no man in history who equals him in vileness, hatred, viciousness, cruelty, pride, selfishness and utter disregard for the sanctity of life. These are the very traits of Satan!

Adolph Hitler is a shining example of what it means to be satanically possessed. Satan was literally living out his character in and through the life of this man. (Surely Hitler was a forerunner-type of the anti-Christ who will rise in the final tribulation period.)

Now let's look a little closer at the words John used to describe this angel from the bottomless pit: Abaddon = Destroyer and *Apollyon* = Exterminator. The word 'destroyer' reveals what Hitler would do — kill; while Exterminator tells *how*. To fulfill this, Hitler and his 'super-race' came up with the idea of the exterminator furnaces, which were used to destory 6,000,000 Jews. Now, look at verse 2 again, *"...and there arose a smoke out of the pit, as the smoke of a great furnace"*. Plain enough?

Next, let's look at some historical facts about Hitler. Once again I found Michael Hart's book, *THE 100,* a very sufficient 'person' manual:

"Hitler's greatest year was 1940. In April, his armies gobbled up Denmark and Norway. In May, they overran Holland, Belgium, and Luxembourg. In June, France capitulated. But later that year, the British withstood a long series of attacks by the German Air Force and Hitler was never able to launch an invasion of England. "In the middle of 1940, Germany ruled a larger portion of Europe than had ever been controlled by any nation in history." (This statement bears witness to my previous comment that Hitler was a type of the final anti-Christ. Satan was probably prematurely prompting Hitler to be the "man of sin" who would restore and solidify the ancient Roman Empire. The timing wasn't yet right for that eventuality but Hitler clearly foreshadowed it.)

Mr. Hart goes on:

"During his regime, the Nazis constructed large EXTERMINATION camps (note Mr. Hart's choice of words keeping in mind too that he is not writing from a theologian's position), *equipped with massive gas chambers for this purpose. In every territory that came under his control, innocent men, women, and children were rounded up and shipped off in cattle cars to be killed in these chambers. In the space of just a few years almost 6,000,000 Jews died in this way. The Jews were not Hitler's only victims. During his regime, staggering numbers of Russians and Gypsies were also massacred, as well as many others who were deemed to be racially inferior or enemies of the state."* (All these would be those without the "seal of God", according to Hitler's philosophy.) *"It should never be imagined that*

77

these murders were spontaneous acts, performed in the heat of passion of battle; Hitler's death camps were organized as carefully as a great business enterprise." (My emphasis.)

Note carefully what Mr. Hart just said. This was a purposeful, widespread attempt to rid this planet of all the 'wrong kinds' as Hitler defined them. I want to emphasize again that Hitler *thought* he was acting as God's agent to eliminate all who did not bear the seal of his god — the master race. This understanding is vital. The reason I'm harping on this so much is that most prophetic writers will say this Fifth Trumpet is a plague against all unbelievers in the world except those who bear the true "seal of God", i.e., the future "Tribulation" saints. I do not believe that's what this Scripture is saying. It's a very 'tricky' passage, so please pardon my repetitious-ness. Mr Hart continues:

"Hitler is widely considered to be the most evil man in all of history and judging by his ability to move people to significant action, it is likely that Hitler was the most effective orator in all of history. It is probable that no figure in history has had more influence upon his own generation than Adolph Hitler. In addition to the tens of millions of people who died in the war that he instigated, or in the Nazi concentration camps, there were millions more who were made homeless or whose lives were entirely disrupted as a result of the fighting."

It is significant to note that even a secular historian arrived at basically the same conclusions I have, mine gleaned from seeing it in God's Word, his from the facts of history. Mr. Hart makes clear reference to Hitler as an exterminator-destroyer. Recall these are the precise meanings of the words the apostle John used to describe the 'angel' — *Abaddon-Apollyon.*

I want to again remind the reader that the purpose of this book is to identify meaningful, real-life, historical situations which seem to fit what Biblical prophecies portray. Remember, while I'm also a believer of a final end-of-the-age, seven-year, prophetic 'countdown' time, I have here elected to concentrate on that which has been overlooked, or totally disregarded, by other writers: the Historical.

Trumpet Five was, for me, one of the more recognizable prophecies. It still continues to amaze me, as I search for (and find) 'hidden' revelations. One day a prophetic passage will appear dark and blurred, the next day (as God allows) a word or a phrase will suddenly come to life giving new meaning to the Scripture, then it all begins to come together. As one classical music composer once gave his explanation of how he wrote music, "...*first a few notes, next a little melody, then comes the harmony, and finally...the whole grows together.*" Now, let's move on in to the 'harmony' — the second "woe", Trumpet Six.

SIXTH TRUMPET: The Angels from the Euphrates

13 "And the sixth angel sounded: And I heard a voice from the four horns of the golden altar which is before God,
14 saying to the sixth angel who had the trumpet, "Release the four angels who are bound at the great river Euphrates.:"
15 And the four angels, who had been prepared for the hour and day and month and year, were released to kill a third of mankind.
16 And the number of the army of the horsemen was two hundred million, and I heard the number of them.
17 And thus I saw the horses in the vision: those who sat on them had breastplates of fiery red, hyacinth blue, and sulfur yellow; and the heads of the horses were like the heads of lions; and out of their mouths came fire, smoke, and brimstone.

79

*18 By these three plagues a third of mankind was killed - by
the fire, by the smoke, and by the brimstone which came out
of their mouths.*
*19 For their power is in their mouth and in their tails; for
their tails, having heads, are like serpents; and with them they
do harm.*
*20 And the rest of mankind, who were not killed by these
plagues, still did not repent of the works of their hands, that
they should not worship demons, and idols of gold, silver,
brass, stone, and wood, which can neither see nor hear nor
walk;*
*21 and they did not repent of their murders nor their
sorceries nor their sexual immorality nor their thefts."*

ASSUMING THE HISTORICAL PICTURE IS TRUE, WHERE ARE WE TODAY?

Obviously at some point along the way through the Historical
Seals and Trumpets we will reach the prophetic-place of our
own day. In my opionion, we are now there!

I think we are presently living in the days of the second
"woe", Trumpet Six, part of which I view as the next major war
conflict. WORLD WAR THREE is a fitting title. If this is so,
all of a sudden Biblical prophecy gets a little more real and
exciting, doesn't it? Let's look at some details of the Sixth
Trumpet and see if there's any more pieces of the puzzle here
which would fit with what has been assembled so far.

The first significant point to note is the *"loosing"* of the angels
who have been bound at the River Euphrates. The Euphrates
serves as the northeast border of the land of ancient Israel. It
separated the people of God from the rest of the world. It also
was the eastern divide of the ancient Roman Empire. It is
believed to be the line between the east and the west. There
have been "world wars" but never have the far eastern nations

80

of the Orient came across the Euphrates divide to invade the west. But the above Scripture says this will not always be the case.

The apostle John reports there have been four *"angels"* bound up at that crossing but that some day they will be "loosed". I believe that day is almost upon us. And when those angels are freed, an army of 200,000,000 men will come across the Euphrates into the heretofore protected West. Their job? — to slay one-third of mankind! (See verse 15.)

Ironically, the now-deceased leader of Communist China, Mao Tse Tung, actually once boasted he could activate an army of the exact number called for in this Scripture. But, there will be more Oriental countries than China coming from the East. In the Sixth Bowl (or Vial) to be discussed in chapter 16 we will see the Euphrates mentioned again. There it says once the Euphrates is "dried up", it paves the way for the "KING<u>S</u>" of the East to come. So, we can expect there will eventually be a <u>confederation</u> of nations which will unite together for this great, coming invasion of the East against the West.

So, at this point in time, it would be good to know if there is anything going on in and about the river Euphrates <u>now,</u> which might give us any clues as to whether the *"angels"* who have been bound at that river may already be in the process of being loosened. I think there are at least four things which may relate. Only one of them applies specifically to the Euphrates but all may be considered a part of the same 'package', when we see the links.

1. The river Euphrates can now be shunted by a dam which has been built in the northern region which <u>could</u> literally cause the river to be dried up. (This may relate to the Sixth Vial which we will discuss in Rev. 16; it says that the Euphrates will be dried up in order to prepare for the "kings of the east". No matter how this Sixth Trumpet is viewed, literal or figurative, it's hard to get away from seeing that this reference is to the Orient nations.)

2. Next, a highway was completed in July 1978, extending from China through Pakistan into the Middle East. It has taken many years to build this road and one wonders what the motivation was behind the builders! Hmm! Only with Biblical prophecy in mind does it make any sense — to prepare the way for "*the kings of the east*".

3. Diplomatic relations were re-established between the United States and China in January 1979. The essence? China is "crossing the Euphrates" — the divide between east and west. She considers herself ready to be "westernized", which will result, of course, in an increased need for natural and other resources, many of which are found in the Middle East region.

4. The "Dead Sea" in Israel is a super-rich mineral resource. I don't know if the information is accurate but I've read that it contains three times the entire wealth of the United States if only it could be acquired! Apparently ways are being learned how to get it out. As this resource becomes easier to produce, it will become an increasingly valuable and sought-after asset by those who need it. Make no mistake, some will purpose to take it by force. These are the kinds of thing which motivate men to go to war. Will it perhaps be the "kings of the east"?

This completes the discussion of the Sixth Trumpet and concludes chapter nine. One final word: It may be that this war, which is initiated by the invasion from the east, doesn't actually come until we get to the Sixth Vial. The reason I say that is because we'll see that the language of Vial Six is very similar to what is said here in Trumpet Six, thus indicative of some kind of connection between the two events.

It seems that the main point we are to see in chapter nine is not the actual war yet but the "*loosing*" of the four angels which prepares the way for the eventual war that is later to come. Perhaps the reason for God giving the advance notice here is so that we can determine a little more accurately where we are now on His time clock. We have done this by discussing those events which have been happening in and about the Euphrates and with regards to China, all of which seem to give adequate and relevant information in fulfilling the prophecy, the "*loosing of the angels*" at the River Euphrates.

CHAPTER TEN

THE MIGHTY ANGEL WITH THE SCROLL

1   "And I saw another mighty angel coming down from heaven, clothed with a cloud. And a rainbow was on his head, his face was like the sun, and his feet like pillars of fire.

2   And he had a little book open in his hand. And he set his right foot on the sea and his left foot on the land,

3   and cried with a loud voice, as when a lion roars. And when he cried out, seven thunders uttered their voices.

4   And when the seven thunders uttered their voices, I was about to write; and I heard a voice from heaven saying to me, "Seal up those things which the seven thunders uttered, and do not write them."

5   And the angel whom I saw standing on the sea and on the land lifted up his hand to heaven

6 and swore by Him who lives forever and ever, who created heaven and the things that are in it, the earth and the things that are in it, and the sea and the things that are in it, that there should be delay no longer,

7 but in the days of the sounding of the seventh angel, when he is about to sound, the mystery of God would be finished, as He has declared to His servants the prophets.

JOHN CONSUMES THE SCROLL

8 "And the voice which I heard from heaven spoke to me again and said, "Go, take the little book which is open in the hand of the angel who stands on the sea and on the earth."

9 And I went to the angel and said to him, "Give me the little book." And he said to me, "Take and eat it; and it will make your stomach bitter, but it will be as sweet as honey in your mouth."

10 And I took the little book out of the angel's hand and ate it, and it was as sweet as honey in my mouth. And when I had eaten it, my stomach became bitter.
11 And he said to me, "You must prophesy again about many peoples, nations, tongues, and kings."

This is the pattern we see in Revelation — first, general information, followed by specific, prophetic details, then pauses, then more apocalyptic things, then again general pictures, etc. Chapter 10 leans to the general-information side but also presents some very interesting, key concepts, though not all that easy to understand.

Recall in our study we are at some point after the Sixth Trumpet. But before showing him the Seventh Trumpet, another mighty angel called John aside to relate some more instructions. However, as with all Scripture (according to Luke 12:2), its truth is designed to be understood at some point in time. Actually, the context itself tells us when: verse 7 says it will be revealed during the "*days of the sounding of the seventh angel*".

As these eleven verses are read carefully, several obvious questions come to mind:

1. What did the seven thunders reveal to John and why was he instructed not to write about them?

2. What did the angel mean by saying the "mystery of God" would be finished in the days (plural) of the voice of the seventh angel?

3. Who are God's "servants the prophets" John referred to here?

4. Why was John instructed to eat the little book?

5. What is the meaning of the book being sweet in John's mouth but bitter in his stomach?

6. What is meant by the statement that John would prophesy again before many people, and nations, and tongues, and kings?

7. When and how would John prophesy again?

Let's try to make some plain sense out of this thought-provoking chapter. The Seven Thunders John was not to write about must have contained information of such a revealing nature that God didn't want John to document it at the time. Instead, he was told to "*eat*" the little book (which likely had the same information that was in the "Thunders"). God said John would "*prophesy again before many peoples, nations, tongues, and kings*". Now, how was he going to do that? After all, John was a prisoner on the island of Patmos at that time and probably never released to preach publicly again. Well, part of the answer lies in the fact that we have John's testimony today in the book of Revelation, and through it, his 'prophesying' is being spread abroad. But, does this satisfy the puzzlying questions about the Thunders or the book he ate?

Surely there is an explanation. I think John's promised, future ministry had to refer to a much later time than his day. In fact, I'm convinced it referred specifically to our day! Of course, this doesn't mean John would later be reincarnated. I believe it alludes to what could be called the *spirit and power* of the apostle John, much like John the Baptist came in the *spirit and power* of Elijah. Actually, the text itself provides most of the answer if we'll only grasp what it says. Verse 7 forecasts, "...in the days of the sounding of the seventh angel, when he is <u>about</u> to sound (i.e., just beforehand), *the mystery of God would be finished, as he has declared to His servants the prophets.*"

Now think about what this sentence really says. Remember, by my reckoning, we are at the very edge of Trumpet Six now, kind of in a 'holding pattern' just prior to Trumpet Seven. If I'm even close to being correct in the Historical picture presented thus far, this means we are very near, if not already, living in the days John spoke about in Revelation 10:7. In other words, I believe we have come to the literal time and place when John was told the "mystery of God" would be unravelled. We had to get there someday, didn't we?

But exactly what is this "mystery of God"? In general, I think it refers to all Biblical prophecy, but more specifically, points to the things the apostle himself wrote about — i.e., the Seals, the Trumpets, the Vials, etc. But further, even to prophecy as being elucidated by the prophetically-sensitive writers of our day, including, as audacious as it may seem, the concepts found right here in the book you are reading.

Today, the Holy Spirit is clarifying prophecy to certain individuals of His choosing. Let's call them what God did — His "servants the prophets". Most of the 'accepted' servants are seminarians. These represent the formally-educated "prophets". It was their books which first got me interested in this subject. But the Bible indicates God also (in fact, usually) calls laymen to be prophetic "servants". The bottom line is that accurate, prophetic understanding is God's work. And regardless of who we are talking about, no amount of ordinary study will equal *one hour* alone with God while He 'feeds' His Own Word to the sealed spirit of the one He has chosen to do so, be he seminarian or layman.

What I'm saying is that John 'heard' and 'ate' certain information which he was not allowed to speak at that time. I think it was just too revealing for those living then to know because it was too long before the fact. The early Church just didn't need to have that information because it wouldn't involve them. It was designed for those living in the last days only. In His infinite wisdom, God reserves certain prophetic clarifications until that point in time is reached which will involve those living then. God has His Own ways of bringing His will to the surface at the right time and the right place. Let's 'allow' Him the right to do that, O.K.?   That, I'm convinced, is what the "Seven Thunders" and the "little book" are all about.

"SWEET," YET "BITTER"

Why was the little book *"sweet in the mouth"* but *"bitter in the stomach"*, to John? To get the answer, let's first look at this from the aspect of normal food and the digestive process. If food tastes sweet, at the outset we know a little about the overall quality of the kind of food we just took in. (Digestion actually begins in the mouth). But as we all know, sweet-tasting food doesn't necessarily reveal how it will affect us later. The stomach and intestines will later 'decide' more conclusively about the exact nature of the food, whether it is good or bad for us.

Now John used this physical concept to help us understand a deeper Biblical truth. When John put the paper containing God's secrets in His mouth, it tasted sweet. This means the <u>initial</u> understanding of those words would be pleasant to think about. The same would be true for anyone who would later read and learn about those thoughts. But when the 'food' (the words) got to John's stomach, it caused bitterness. This means that upon deeper reflection of the words and understanding their fuller implications, much sorrow would come as the fulfillment of those prophecies became a reality. This sorrow is the "bitter" aspect John experienced in the "stomach".

For example, as you have already learned (hopefully) in this book, it's exciting just to take in the basics of Biblical prophecy. I felt that way when I first began to understand the Historical aspect of Revelation. In John's terminology, it was "sweet in my mouth". This was the result of first impressions. It's what happens to everyone when learning about things formerly vague to them. But nothing is ever altogether good (*sweet*) all the way through! The reality of this struck home as I got deeper into Biblical prophecy. Once it soaked in, I then became affected by some of the devastating aspects of it, e.g., the slaughter of 6,000,000 Jews by Apollyon (Hitler). This represents the bitter side of the book which the apostle ate. As I began to see the bigger picture of prophecy, I too can honestly say that what first seemed 'sweet in my mouth', later changed into a 'bitter-sweet' flavor, advancing toward the more bitter side as I learned more about the shaking and upheavals which await mankind as we enter the end of the age.

Let me make this a little clearer by aiming this directly at you. If you are beginning to believe my book has some credibility, you are probably getting a little excited as you see the identifications. If so, that represents the 'sweetness' John referred to. But, before you are finished with this book, you'll probably grow quite weary of seeing the continual flow of labels which will be given to the prophetic symbology. That, plus the associated devastations, represents the "bitter" side of the coin. As of right now, (1994), according to John's vision, there are two more "woes" to go. And after that, things get even more "bitter"! So get ready folks, for the worst is yet to come. (Just how much of the last stages the Church must experience before being removed from the earth is yet to be discussed.)

SUMMARY OF REVELATION 10

(Before going on, read again the 11 verses at the beginning of this chapter.)

Now let's put this chapter in a nutshell: First, John heard something (the Seven Thunders) which most likely would have given plainer explanation of what Revelation is all about. That is, the symbolic descriptions used throughout the book would probably have been more vividly clarified by these Seven Thunders. Next, the same information was probably contained in the "little book" John was instructed to "eat". My view is that the content of the little book would later be 'fed' to others at some future, appropriate time, so that what John was told not to write about in his day could later be known by those whose lives the prophecy would involve: the people of our day.

Secondly, I believe the "mystery of God" (verse 7) is all Biblical prophecy brought to the surface, designed particularly for those who would experience end-time events. Jesus said it in Luke 12:2 like this: *"For there is nothing covered that will not be revealed, nor hidden that will not be known."* And in Amos 3:7 God says, *"...Surely the Lord God does nothing unless He reveals His secret counsel to His servants the prophets."* And even more direct right here in the immediate context (Vs. 7) we find, *"...but in the days of the sounding of the seventh angel, when he is about to sound, the mystery of God would be finished, as He has declared to His servants the prophets."* So, God has promised that His "mysteries" would eventually be made plainer. He is seeing to that. Hallelujah!

Thirdly, the "sweet" and "bitter" simply means this: "Sweet" is knowing what the basics of prophecy mean. "Bitter" is realizing the consequences of those prophecies — the widespread destruction and loss of much human life.

Fourthly, the prediction that John would "prophesy again" refers to the "little book" he ate, which would later be revealed to God's "servants the prophets" who would speak in John's behalf. This does not mean new Biblical words would be given. It simply refers to the spiritual understanding which would later come. The understanding comes through reading the words of prophecy we already have, seeing their real and allegorical content, and relating them to actual end-time events. The requirement for comprehension is based on two factors: (1) the Holy Spirit's call and anointing plus (2) seeing and understanding which historical facts fit the symbolic-word terminology.

Fifthly, I believe the time "John" would *"prophesy"* again is in our day! And if I am correct in my understanding here, these *"thunders"* (the concepts) will eventually go before *"many peoples, nations, tongues, and kings"*, for that's what verse 11 clearly says!

THOSE RECURRING, INCREDIBLE "ELEVENS"

I'd like to share an interesting observation I made as I first studied these Scriptures. A church once invited me to give a talk on Bible prophecy. As I prepared notes and Scripture references I would use in the presentation, I noticed that practically all the references (15 or more) were associated with the number "eleven". The chapters were either "11" or the verses were "11". And if more than one verse was to be used, adding together the numbered verses would total "11" (i.e., two verses, like 5 & 6, would be needed to complete the thought in the passage.)

As an optometrist, numbers are very much a part of my life. Now I realize one can play all kinds of games with numbers but that's never been my 'bag'. However, for all the Scriptures I planned to speak about that night to just happen to revolve around the number 11 was just too much for me to believe or accept as mere-chance-coincidence. I have since concluded God authored the number arrangements in His Word just as surely as He did the word order.

Let me illustrate: The last time Elijah is seen in the Old Testament is found in 2 Kings 2:11. *"And it came to pass, as they still went on, and talked, that, behold, there appeared a chariot of fire, and horses of fire, and parted them both asunder, and Elijah went up by a whirlwind into heaven."* Then the next verse I looked up was Matt. 17:11. *"And Jesus answered and said unto them, Elias* (i.e., Elijah) *truly shall first come, and restore all things."* Next I found Mark 9:11. *"And they asked him, saying, Why say the scribes that Elias must first come?"* (Recall that Jesus was saying in both these verses that John the

91

Baptist was Elijah, meaning he came, unrecognized, in the spirit and power of Elijah.) Then I looked up the Old Testament prediction of the coming of John the Baptist: *"Behold, I will send you Elijah the prophet before the coming of the great and dreadful day of the Lord: And he shall turn the heart of the fathers to the children, and the heart of the children to their fathers, lest I come and smite the earth with a curse."* This is from Mal. 4: 5 & 6.

You will note that all four of the above references are found in an 11th verse, or in two verses which, when added, equal 11. The laws of probability allow only so many coincidences like this before it can be assumed there is intelligence behind it. I find it most remarkable that God would first allow these special insights into certain Scriptures of His Word, then would follow that understanding with little confirmations, such as the *eleven phenomenon.*

As my study progressed, 'coincidences' increased so much in regularity that I would later become expectant that God would add His confirmations in some special way. He was always faithful. And don't get me wrong. I was not looking for signs. I simply became aware of them. This, you might say, was the 'frosting on the cake'. A few others who have already had a chance to study this work in some depth, have also begun to see that these numerical relationships do indeed seem to correlate, and have later given me feedback somewhat substantiating that this is not merely a numbers game I've put together. Now isn't it interesting we would at this point just happen to arrive at the key chapter of my book, chapter **ELEVEN**?

CHAPTER ELEVEN

THE "TWO WITNESSES"

To me, this is the pivotal chapter of the book of Revelation. Once I saw the meaning of the symbolism here, the rest of the book also began to fall into place. In fact, I would go so far as to say that comprehension of Rev. 11 opens the door to understanding Biblical prophecy — period. The information herein links together many of the mysterious passages relating to God's predictions of the Church Age. Don't be surprised if at some point you wonder, "Why didn't I see that?" or, "Why haven't others seen this?" However, what's really important is to realize **NOW** is the time God has elected to unveil some of these mysteries.

(By the way, you need to know I'm not saying that the mysteries of prophecy are so profound that few can comprehend them. Surely you have already noted that there is nothing complicated about the identifications presented thus far. If there's anything tough here, it's only accepting whether the identifications are correct or not. Again I use the analogy of a puzzle: the scattered pieces of a puzzle before assembly may be compared to the facts of history in disarray. The task is merely finding the parts which fit together. Once in place, one wonders how he could have missed it.)

For ease of continuity and because this is such a prime chapter, I'll go verse-by-verse throughout this chapter.

Verse 1.

"And there was given to me a reed like a measuring rod. And the angel stood, saying, 'Rise and measure the temple of God, the altar, and those who worship there."

93

When God begins to measure with a plumbline, action is imminent. (See Is. 28:17; Jer. 31: 38 & 39; and Zech. 2: 1 & 2). The Seventh Trumpet sounds at the end of this chapter and we know (as you'll see later on) that this is the last trumpet. So, the language here — *"measure the temple of God, the altar, and those that worship there"* — quite properly indicates that once human history reaches this point in time, everything is about finished.

Verse 2.

> 2 *"But leave out the court which is outside the temple, and do not measure it, for it has been given to the Gentiles. And they will tread the holy city under foot forty-two months."*

The *"holy city"* here would obviously refer to Jerusalem. I believe there is another side of this too but for now, I'll limit my explanation to the literal city.

Note that the city was to be *"tread under foot"* for *"forty-two months"*. Now forty-two months means 42, 30-day months. (All months were 30-days in duration by ancient Hebrew reckoning.) Therefore, 42 months, times a 30-day month, equals 1260 days. That's a very interesting number which we'll see pop up two more times in Revelation, chapters 12 and 13. In one place, the same time period is referred to as *"a time, times and half a time"*. All these — 1260 days, forty-two months, and a time, times and half a time — are three different ways of saying the same thing. (Learning all the small facts may be boring right now, but later the knowledge will lend tremendous aid to understanding Bible prophecy, so keep them in mind. I confess that it was quite a while before I too gave more than only casual observance to these seemingly-insignificant details. But I discovered that these "nugget" finds are like dynamite — packaged small, but, oh so powerful when used under properly controlled conditions.)

As we continue the study it will become progressively clear as to what is meant by prophetic *days*. But I'm convinced, based on Biblical precedents as well as how it all works out in actuality, that the *"forty-two"* months referred to above, really means 1260 prophetic-year "days".

But even if you accept how I spiritualized these numbers, the question remains: what's the significance? Just this: note that the *"holy city"* (Jerusalem) was to be *"tread under foot"* for the time span of 1260 years. Therefore, we need to know exactly *what* particular 1260 year period this refers to. I believe it's the years between 688 A.D. and 1948 A.D. Now let me show you why those particular years.

After many centuries of dispersion, Israel was re-established as a nation in 1948. Now, the next question is, what act, or incident, best describes the point at which this dispersion commenced? Some would say it was when Titus and his Roman army invaded Jerusalem, tore down the Temple, etc. It is true that Jewish rituals and sacrifices normally held in the Temple could no longer be performed there after that point, but Titus' invasion didn't disperse all the Jews from the land of Israel.

There is a series of events which better-describes what we are looking for. Now remember, we're searching for something which physically, symbolically and historically, would irrefutably represent something which would satisfy what the Scripture demands: namely, that the *"holy city"* (Jerusalem) was indeed *"tread under foot"* for 1260 years.

Now obviously 1948 is one very pertinent point in time which is easily established. No one can deny that that year spelled the beginning of a renewal of Jewish control of portions of the land of ancient Israel. The main documented event which laid the groundwork for the return of the Jews to their homeland was the **Balfour Declaration** of 1917 (put into effect by the British, by the way), and in 1948, the Jews declared their nationality. Today, most other countries recognize Israel as a sovereign nation and all agree that their re-birth date was 1948.

Therefore, by simply counting backwards 1260 years from 1948, automatically establishes 688 A.D. as a year we ought to look at to see if anything happened in the *"holy city"* that year which could be thought to represent when the *"treading under foot"* began. Rambling through history books at the U. C. Davis library one day I made a very interesting discovery. That year (688 A.D.) was the very year the Muslims began placing the "crown" on the Dome of the Rock. Now what's the prophetic implication here? To Muslims, the Dome of the Rock is one of Islam's most treasured holy places, only third in importance to the mosque of Mecca. Now let me explain the importance of all these facts.

Most modern-day Jews, Muslims and Christians presume that the Dome of the Rock was placed at the exact site of the former Jewish Temple. (Surely you have noticed that almost any photograph of Jerusalem presents the Dome as the most outstanding architectural building in the region.) Isn't it interesting that the Muslims would place their 'holy place' precisely where the holy Jewish temple had formerly been? But then, why not? If a group becomes convinced that they are now God's chosen people, then doesn't it make good sense (from their vantage point) to place their own religious edifice at the same temple site of those (historically their primary enemy) they just conquered?

To the Muslims, the Dome (the site from which Mohammad supposedly ascended) would stand forever, proudly-proclaiming to all future generations that Allah (their god) was proving His preference was for the Islamic religion. This would also send a message to Roman Catholicism (another enemy) who had set up their holy shrines in Israel — the Holy Sepulchre and the Church of the Nativity.

THE "ABOMINATION OF DESOLATION"

Jesus once spoke specifically of something *abominable* that would someday *"stand in the holy place"*. Could the Dome of the Rock have been His inference? Here are His exact words:

"Therefore when you see the 'abomination of desolation,' spoken of by Daniel the prophet, standing in the holy place" (whoever reads, let him understand), "then let those who are in Judea flee to the mountains." (Matthew 24: 15 & 16)

Now the Futuristic School say this reference is to the final anti-Christ when he places himself in a re-built Jewish temple claiming to be god. I'm very familiar with this concept and I realize the view is held by practically all modern-day, evangelical, prophetic writers. But again, they have totally missed the historical picture. We must deal with first things, first.

I will cover the historical *"abomination of desolation"* more thoroughly later but the verse we are currently looking at (Rev. 11:2) demands our scrutiny right now. Recall that the Second Seal (the "red horse and its rider") was Mohammad.

Quoting again from Hart's commentary on Mohammad: *"In 642"* (note the date) *"the inspired Arabs, though small then, embarked upon one of the most astonishing series of conquests in human history. They soon conquered all of Mesopotamia, Syria and Palestine."*

Now carefully observe that Palestine (Israel) was conquered by Mohammad in 642 A.D. This is not the date we are looking for but this invasion set the stage. The building which would later be constructed (the Dome of the Rock) would become the symbolic representation of Mohammad's Islamic accomplishments in Israel. And as noted above, the most prominent part, the gold dome, continually reminds the world of the man with the sword (Mohammad) who put the 'finishing touches' on Israel's dispersion. He was responsible for

97

beginning one of the world's largest false religions, most certainly opposed to Judaism and Christianity. (Make no mistake, Islam is determined to spread it's 'gospel' throughout the world. They took their ground in the beginning by force. I believe they will make another attempt in our day.)

In a recent (1988) issue of "Eternity" magazine was this quote: *"Islam, with its one billion adherents worldwide, is the 'greatest threat to Western civilization that exists today,...".* This "greatest threat" religion is based upon a total rejection of God's promise — that His Messiah would come through Abraham's son, Isaac. Mohammad, a descendant of Ishmael, claimed Abraham was the father of their religion because Ishmael was Abraham's son through Hagar. Nothing could be further from the truth. This is one of Satan's great delusions, perhaps even believed by more people than there are true, born-again Christians!

Now with all these thoughts in mind, once again I want you to focus on the fact that there just happens to be 1,260 years (42 "months") between 688 (the year they began construction on the Dome of the Rock) and 1948, (when Israel was established as a nation.) Again recall what the Scripture calls for; "...*and they will tread the holy city under foot forty-two months.*"

The Dome of the Rock clearly satisfies the Biblical criteria as being the Historical *"abomination of desolation"*. One might properly ask what it is about the Moslem mosque that's "abominable" to God. After all, Jesus said that Herod's temple would be destroyed, clearly indicating that God's use of the old temple was now a thing of the past. (From then on, God would indwell human temples — born-again Christians.) Nevertheless, the location of the Islamic Dome of the Rock is a mockery of God's covenanted-commitment to ancient Israel. Mocking God is an abomination regardless of His change of program.

Next, the meaning of the word *"desolation"* simply refers to the fact that the Jews were driven from their homeland. The land became "desolate" of Jews, and remained so until 1948. It obviously was God's plan to allow His former people to be dispersed, but woe unto those who did it for their own selfish reasons.

ANOTHER "ABOMINATION OF DESOLATION"

I mentioned earlier that most prophetic writers identify the *"abomination of desolation"* as the final anti-Christ who will set up his kingdom in a Jewish temple which will supposedly be built near the end of the age. Futuristically speaking, this could be so but, historically speaking, the Dome of the Rock is clearly the intended meaning.

[Not to confuse you, but there is another way to consider this. We know that at the end of the age, Satan will have established his "throne" in the hearts and minds of many people, even several nations. Those people could be thought of as Satan's "temple"; his occupancy in them representing a spiritualized fulfillment of 2 Thes. 2:4, which says Satan *"...sitteth in the temple of God, shewing himself that he is God."* More on this later.]

99

THE TWO WITNESSES

<u>Verse 3.</u>

"And I will give power to my two witnesses, and they will prophesy one thousand two hundred and sixty days, clothed in sackcloth."

Before giving my commentary on the Historical identity of the *"two witnesses"*, let's first note what the Futurists say about them. They are usually believed to be Elijah and Moses — some say Elijah and Enoch. This conclusion is reached because the characteristics of the "two witnesses" (see verses 4 - 6) are comparable to these ancient prophets.

Other explanations go something like this: Enoch and Elijah never saw physical death, God having taken them alive. Since that time they have apparently been kept 'in store' somewhere and will later return to earth during the tribulation period for their 1260-day witnessing ministry.

But those who believe Moses will be one of the "witnesses" say his characteristics also fit the Revelation description. They refer to the fact that Moses was not allowed to enter the promised land when he delivered the people of Israel to the edge of the river of Jordan. Thus, the contention is that Moses' ministry was never completed and therefore, he will get the opportunity to finish his work in the tribulation period. Other proponents of this view would give broader coverage than this brief scenario but these are the essentials for you to know.

A LITERAL MOSES, OR ELIJAH, OR ENOCH?

Let's take Moses' case first: According to Revelation 11:7, the *"two witnesses"* will be killed. But the Bible says, *"So Moses the servant of the Lord died in the land of Moab, according to the word of the Lord."* (Deut. 34:5) Then, in Hebrews 9:27, we are

100

told, "*And as it is appointed unto men once to die, but after this the judgment;...*" So, if Moses is to be a "*witness*" in the tribulation, he will have to die twice! Now some will say, "What's wrong with that? Jesus raised Lazarus from the dead and he died again. Why can't Moses do the same thing?" Well, he could, using the idea that anything is possible with God. But, in Moses' case, it's not reasonable. Moses has already received and experienced a glorified-body resurrection. I say this because of two Scriptures:

> "*Yet Michael the archangel, in contending with the devil, when he disputed about the body of Moses, dared not bring against him a reviling accusation, but said, "The Lord rebuke you!*" (Jude 9)

Now this fact seems to have slipped past the Futurists' thinking. God obviously had a purpose and need for the body of Moses. Michael, the archangel, demanded the body of Moses from Satan. Why did this happen? The answer is found in Mark 9:1:

> "*And he said to them, 'Assuredly, I say to you that there are some standing here who shall not taste death till they see the kingdom of God come with power.'*" (This is speaking of Peter, James and John.)

Then in verse 4 we see, "*And Elijah appeared to them with Moses, and they were talking with Jesus.*" (Mark 9:4) These verses refer to what is known as the Transfiguration. Three men — Peter, James and John — had the privilege of seeing Jesus transfigured along with Moses and Elijah. It isn't necessary here to go into all the ramifications of what this means. I wanted to draw your attention to the fact that Moses and Elijah were there many centuries after their former prophetic ministries. In Moses' case, wouldn't it be some kind of double jeapordy for him to die again in the tribulation? I have trouble with the Futuristic reasoning here.

But what about Enoch? We know very little about Enoch, but one thing is clear: he pleased God. *"And Enoch walked with God; and he was not, for God took him."* (Gen. 5:24) Many Christians see Enoch's being taken by God as a pre-figurement of the rapture of the Church at the end of this present age. I accept that. But what I don't accept is Enoch being kept alive these past five thousand years or so, still living in a corruptible body!

Thirdly, what about Elijah? Well, he too was translated (i.e., taken away, or "raptured"), apparently without passing through normal death. *"Then it happened, as they continued on and talked, that suddenly a chariot of fire appeared with horses of fire, and separated the two of them; and Elijah went up by a whirlwind into heaven."* (2 Kings 2:11)

Therefore, because Enoch and Elijah were translated, Futurists conclude that Enoch and Elijah never died. Actually, close examination shows the passages don't exactly say this. Of Enoch, it says he *"was not"*, and was *"taken"* — whatever that means. In Hebrews 5 we are told Enoch didn't *"see death"*. This doesn't necessarily mean he didn't experience it, just that he didn't *"see"* it. (I'll explain why in a minute.) Of Elijah, it says he was *"separated"* from Elisha and that he *"went up"*. None of these statements come right out and say they didn't die! Why?

I believe that Enoch and Elijah died instantaneously and before they could even fall to the ground, were immediately transformed into a new creation before being *"taken"*. This is why neither of them *"saw"* death. I have specific Scriptures on which to base this reasoning:

"Now this I say, brethren, that flesh and blood cannot inherit the kingdom of God; nor does corruption inherit incorruption. Behold, I tell you a mystery; We shall not all

sleep, but we shall all be changed - in a moment, in the twinkling of an eye, at the last trumpet. For the trumpet will sound, and the dead will be raised incorruptible, and we shall be changed." (1 Cor. 15: 50 - 52)

Now these verses serve several purposes here. First, it explains what really happened to Enoch and Elijah. They simply did not *"sleep"* — i.e., did not die in the usual way. But, they were *"changed, in a moment, in the twinkling of an eye"*, meaning, their old bodies instantly became new, *incorruptible* ones! Also, these verses are believed by most Christians to represent what happens to believers who will be alive when Jesus comes for His Church. There will be some people who won't have to go through usual dying processes, at the *"last trumpet"*. But this doesn't mean instantaneous-death won't come to the old body! For the verse also says the *"corruptible"* body cannot inherit the kingdom of God. There must be a new body for those who enter the kingdom of God. This is what I believe happened to Enoch and Elijah.

I believe this concept truly makes Enoch and Elijah forerunners of what is described in the above passage. Their early "translations" were pictures of what believers, perhaps in our day, can expect to happen to them. But, make no mistake, if you are saved when the Lord comes, you'll have to die to your old body. It will be quicker than you can blink your eye, but <u>you will die</u>! Our present bodies cannot inherit the kingdom of God. But believers won't *see* the death. I think it is only because of the suddenness of Enoch and Elijah's translation that the Scriptures don't come right out and say they died. Instead, God preferred to use the language *"was not"* for Enoch, and *"was taken"* in Elijah's case. Actually it makes good sense to de-emphasize the act of dying if one is taken through it with the suddenness of an eye-blink. I like God's choice of words. However, I don't like the understanding given these particular passages by most Futuristic writers. I think they have missed the point.

JOHN THE BAPTIST = ELIJAH?

There are other questions about Elijah which some readers will have, so I feel the need to address the issue before presenting my views on the identities of the "*two witnesses*". Malichi, the last prophet of the Old Testament, predicted the coming of Elijah:

"Behold, I will send you Elijah the prophet before the coming of the great and dreadful day of the LORD. And he will turn the hearts of the fathers to the children, And the hearts of the children to their fathers. Lest I come and strike the earth with a curse." (Mal. 4: 5 & 6)

The Futurists place a lot of emphasis on this verse because it seems to lend support to Elijah being one of the two witnesses of Revelation 11. But it's also a prediction of John the Baptist. Note:

"He" (John the Baptist) *"will also go before Him"* (Jesus) *"in the spirit and power of Elijah, 'to turn the hearts of the fathers to the children,' and the disobedient to the wisdom of the just, to make ready a people prepared for the Lord."* (Luke 1: 17)

That was a word from an angel of the Lord to Zacharias, about his son, John the Baptist. The angel said John would turn the *"hearts of the fathers to the children"*; this is exactly what Malachi prophesied about Elijah! And if this isn't sufficient evidence, listen to what Jesus said of John the Baptist:

"For all the prophets and the law prophesied until John. And if you are willing to receive it, he is Elijah who is to come." (Matt. 11: 13 & 14)

104

This is all kind of confusing, isn't it? Well, Jesus' disciples were confused too. They expressed their lack of understanding with this question to Jesus:

"...'Why do the scribes say that Elijah must come first?' And He answered and told them, 'Elijah does come first, and restores all things. ...'But I say to you that Elijah also has come, and they have done to him whatever they wished, as it is written of him." (Mark 9: 11 - 13)

What did Jesus mean here? (1), that Elijah had already come and they had done to him *"whatever they wished"* (namely, killed John by cutting off his head), and (2), that Elijah would yet come to *"restore all things"*. Is this double-talk? No indeed. Jesus showed His expectation that this would be hard to hear when He said:

"He who has ears to hear, let him hear!" (Matt. 11:15)

Now let me summarize: Elijah was "raptured" (or *taken*), not dying in the usual manner. If Elijah was going to be returned to earth in his former body, wouldn't he have been allowed to do so at the time of John the Baptist? Now, I'm not emphatically saying it is impossible that the "real" Elijah can't, or won't, return just exactly as he was when he left in the *"chariot of fire"* several thousand years ago. But, I am saying there is another (I think better) way of interpreting the meaning of Jesus' prophesy that Elijah would return to *"restore all things"*.

Since John the Baptist was a 'representative' of Elijah (i.e., he came in the *spirit and power of Elijah,* meaning he had Elijah-like characteristics and anointing), why not assume that's the same pattern which will be followed when "Elijah" appears again? In other words, when it's time for Elijah to return before the second coming of the Lord, doesn't it make more sense that another will come in the *"spirit and power"* of Elijah, just as did John the Baptist?

But let's get back to the Historical side of prophecy. As I've said several times already, Revelation can't be understood with a Futuristic-only bias. I'm thoroughly convinced the *"two witnesses"* has an altogether *other* meaning in addition to the two-person, *"tribulation"* witnesses. Let's look now at an entirely different, and I believe more plausible, explanation of the following passage.

THE HISTORICAL "TWO WITNESSES"

3   "AND I WILL GIVE POWER TO MY TWO WITNESSES, AND THEY WILL PROPHESY ONE THOUSAND TWO HUNDRED AND SIXTY DAYS, CLOTHED IN SACKCLOTH."

4   "THESE ARE THE TWO OLIVE TREES AND THE TWO LAMPSTANDS STANDING BEFORE THE GOD OF THE EARTH."

When I first attempted serious study of this passage (at the time basically believing the Futuristic-only concept), certain words would occasionally trouble my spirit as I would come across them. Today I'm convinced that 'troubling' was the Holy Spirit prompting me. Seeing deeper spiritual truth which over-rides plain and straight-forward truth (i.e., the Law of Double Reference) had already taken root in me because of a few other passages. I now believe that's how God prepared me for Revelation 11. There were three words in particular in the above two verses which got my attention — sackcloth, olive tree and candlesticks. Let's take a closer look, one at a time.

SACKCLOTH

In the Old Testament sense, sackcloth was a garment prophets wore to identify them as a *prophet of God.* More importantly, it came to be known as a sign of repentance because of the stinging messages the prophets would deliver. So, to understand the spiritual significance (i.e., realizing what God wants us to know) of the word *"sackcloth"*, we are to concentrate on repentance, not the actual material the garment was made of. The type of cloth was obviously just the symbol the apostle John used to convey a deeper truth. Sackcloth in itself is no more the intended meaning here than assuming the "10 horned beast" of Revelation 13 signifies some kind of literal, weird animal! Therefore, to see what John was really driving at, forget about the witnesses' wardrobe. Think REPENTANCE!

Thus, as we seek to identify the *"two witnesses"*, an outstanding characteristic we should note about them is that they, like John the Baptist and Elijah, would preach repentance from "dead works". So, before concentrating on who they actually *are,* we must first agree that the *"two witnesses"* would be strong proclaimers of the fundamental Gospel message. By that I mean they would place major emphasis on the fact that man is sinful and must turn from his wicked ways and seek God's salvation through Christ Jesus, not relying on his own self goodness to save him. Thus, in summary, the teaching is simply this: **sackcloth** = preaching the true Gospel.

THE "OLIVE TREE"

Why did John refer to the *"two witnesses"* as *"olive trees"?* What a strange thing to say! As with *"sackcloth"*, to see the light of this we must determine the symbolic meaning of the *"olive tree"*. (Are you catching on to this idea of the LODR? It's fun of the best kind when the light dawns!)

The olive tree was the most valuable tree to ancient peoples. Here are a few reasons why:

1. The oriental nations viewed the olive tree for its beauty, strength, divine blessings, prosperity, signs of friendship and peace. Therefore, even if we regard ancient knowledge

outside the Holy Scriptures, we see that the old world understood the special values surrounding the olive tree. Obviously there was wisdom, secular and spiritual, behind John's usage of the term "olive tree" for the *two witnesses*.

2. The olive tree was valued for its oil resources. When we think of oil in the Biblical sense, we think of the Holy Spirit. Thus, the obvious point here is that the Holy Spirit would be working supernaturally upon and within these *two witnesses*. To the Jew, the olive tree was a symbol of fruitfulness, again typifying the Holy Spirit, thus indicating God would provide his *two witnesses* with great ABUNDANCE.

3. The olive tree was a sign of grace and peace given by God. The first and most notable symbol was when the dove returned with an olive branch to Noah's Arc letting him know that the land was being uncovered after the flood.

4. Zechariah's vision: The Old Testament prophet Zechariah sheds some light concerning the *two witnesses*. (Zech. 4:12-14)

"And I answered again, and said unto him, What be these two olive branches which through the two golden pipes empty the golden oil out of themselves? And he answered me and said, Knowest thou not what these be? And I said, No, my lord. Then said he, These are the two anointed ones, that stand by the Lord of the whole earth."

Now most prophetic writers agree that the apostle John alluded to these two "anointed ones" which the prophet Zechariah saw. However, most interpret these two special 'oil conduits' as Elijah and Moses (or Elijah and Enoch), completely missing the important Historical aspect I'm convinced the symbolism portrays.

To summarize the underlying meaning of the "*olive tree*", look at what John really said: The "*two witnesses*" would be noted for certain attributes which God extended to them — peace, Holy Spirit empowerment, fruitfulness, abundance, channels of blessings towards others, beauty, strength, divine blessings of their own, prosperity, and signs of friendship. Now that puts things into better perspective than merely visualizing an actual "*olive tree*", does it not? (Anchor these traits in your mind and as we move along I think you'll soon get the picture I did.)

THE LAMPSTAND

A lampstand's function is to hold a light source. In ancient times, the stand was placed in a high, prominent place so that the torch could shed its illumination widely into the surrounding darkness. (The torch-lit towns and villages set on hills in Jesus' day typified this.) On the human side, John the Baptist represented such a lampstand, Jesus referring to him as a "*burning and shining light...*", (Jn. 5:35). John (acting like a "*lamp*") openly delivered strong sermons that sinners should repent. (From this, we can see why Jesus referred to John as Elijah, Jesus also foreseeing that the "Elijah task" in the last days would likewise see two more such lampstand-witnesses set on certain 'hills' as God's representatives.)

So, whatever, or whoever, the two "*lampstands*" are, their purpose is clear: that of giving light to the spiritually-dark world. On a strictly physical plane, as I think of the "*two witnesses*", I picture two seacoast lighthouses which are designed to alert those at sea of nearby danger. When you get right down to it, that's what preaching is all about: warning people who are lost in the 'sea-of-humanity' that they are about to go aground if they don't turn around (repent) and flee to safety in the "Ark of Christ."

POWER

I purposely postponed until now what I consider to be the most important of all the *"witness"* characteristics: **power.** (Check your translation of verse three and see if it uses the word *"power"* as one of the gifts from God to the *"two witnesses"*.) A more literal rendering of the Greek word would be **'of me'**, instead of power; meaning God would give <u>of Himself</u> to the *"two witnesses"*. The implication is that the power which would go out from the *"two witnesses"* would be God-power, not their own.

DID JOHN REALLY HAVE ONLY <u>TWO PEOPLE</u> IN MIND?

Now, before going on to verse 5, let's summarize the five characteristics of the *two witnesses* covered so far:

1. They would have God's 'of Me' power;
2. they would prophesy (preach and teach) for 1260 "days";
3. they would be clothed in *sackcloth*---i.e., their main message would be that sinners need to come to repentance;
4. they would be known as *olive trees*, which means that abundant blessings would be theirs; and finally,
5. they would be *lampstands* standing before the God of the earth, meaning they would reflect God's righteousness towards others.

Now as I think of all these terms collectively, a few serious questions come to mind. First, if God meant the *"two witnesses"* were only two people, like Elijah and Moses (or Elijah and Enoch), why didn't He just simply come right out and say it? After all, the prophet Malachi named Elijah, saying he would come and restore all things. (With Jesus' Own personal interpretation we know now that Malachi was referring to John

110

the Baptist.)   If God wanted John to convey that only two persons would come and prepare the way for Him in a brief, 3 1/2 year tribulation period, I can see absolutely no logical reason to mask the *"two witnesses"* in all the symbolic-word format.   Surely, if only two men were meant, He would have either told us their names, or left no reason to interpret the two witnesses other than two people.

Before attempting a commentary on Revelation 11, I had already become convinced the book was a prophetic portrayal of long-range proportions.   As I read and studied the verses outlined above, it caused me to wonder how might the subject of the *"two witnesses"* fit into the Historical framework rather than assuming a mere literal, 1260-day period.   Pondering this one day I wondered, *"Wouldn't it be more reasonable that the two witnesses represented conglomerate entities?"*   That is, God fore-seeing two large masses of Christian people in two separate places, identifying all of them with the designation, *"two witnesses"*.

A few writers who have believed in the Historical perspective have suggested the two witnesses are perhaps the Old and New Testaments, or Judaism and Christianity, and things of this sort. While some of these ideas seem to have a little merit, they won't hold up as one views all the characteristics John listed for us to examine in Revelation Eleven.   When an identification is attempted, one must look for something that won't break down anywhere.

More evidence is forth-coming but it's now time to tell you who I believe the *"two witnesses"* are. I'm convinced they are nations!   There are two national entities which have been endowed with both physical and spiritual abundance, surpassing other nations so much that I'm amazed other writers haven't made the correlation. Many have seen the power and influence in them, but not the Biblical identity.   The historical powers, (both secular and spiritual) which I'm persuaded fit the complete, prophetic picture is —— **The Church within Great Britain and the United States of America.**

GREAT BRITAIN AND THE USA = THE "TWO WITNESSES"

Even if the reader is becoming convinced about the Historical aspect of Revelation, there will probably be many skeptical questions arise at this point. So, let's address a few which I can already anticipate.

1.   Why do I think whole nations are meant by the *"two witnesses"*?

There are many reasons. First, practically all of Revelation deals with national organizations, such as the *"ten horns"* of Revelation 13 which refers to ten nations, or the *"city"* of Revelation 18, which must be taken as an all-inclusive word actually signifying many cities of the world, (to be discussed later), etc. Knowing this understanding is even accepted by many other prophetic writers caused me to ask *why not the 'two witnesses' also?*

Take the *"horn"* for example:

First, Scripturally, sometimes a *"horn"* refers to a single individual but more often indicates entire nations. (It seems to always be true in Revelation.) The context determines which is meant. However, everybody knows that even the 'horns' may not be fully identifiable until the time of fulfillment approaches.

Secondly, the symbolic characteristics which John used to describe the *"two witnesses"* fit the idea of nations far more accurately than simply two persons.

Thirdly, these New Testament "prophets" would have power to affect <u>the whole earth</u> (verse 6). That was not a typical characteristic of the ancient, singular prophets, whose

112

ministry generally affected local situations. (Now this is not to say that God couldn't anoint two individuals to have this kind of influence. I just believe it is not the case and I have many reasons for saying this which will be further explained ahead.)

2. Some will say, *"But Britain and the USA aren't Christian nations today. In fact, they are becoming the world-centers of ungodliness and immorality, a modern type of Babylon. So how can you possibly identify them as God's primary 'two witnesses' on the earth?"*

It may surprise you to learn this is exactly what the Scriptures call for when the *"testimony"* of the *"two witnesses"* draws to a close. (To be discussed shortly).

3. Some people ask, *"Lance, don't you know God is no respecter of persons? Your idea suggests He is."*

Many have missed the point of this Scripture. Essentially it means that anyone who believes the Gospel and are willing to come to Christ can be saved. It certainly can't be construed to mean God doesn't sometimes select and/or specially-gift certain individuals, groups, and yes, even nations. As I've faced this question before, it causes me to wonder if the inquisitor has carefully looked at Scriptural precedence. The whole Bible is filled with examples of God's sovereign selection (or 'election') process that He has used to identify Himself and His ways to others. It was true in ancient history. It is true today.

Now, it is quite accurate to say that God's salvation is adequate for every individual in the whole world (God being no "respecter" of persons) but we cannot extend this understanding to the degree of eliminating God's right to choose for special ministry both individuals, and/or, nations, as a part of His Divine Plan of the ages. That's the real meaning of the Scripture *"...many are called but few are chosen."* Matt. 20:16.

4. Others have said to me, *"Lance, I've heard of what you are saying here. It's called 'British Israelism'"*.

That was the response from a pastor who read the first draft of this book. At the time, I had never heard the term "British Israelism"! But as I understand it, there arose a belief by certain groups in England a number of years ago (perhaps centuries) that they had been given the 'mantle' of what was once Israel's. The story goes that since Israel rejected God's Messiah, God rejected Israel and subsequently transferred His power to another nation — namely England. Hence, British Israelism was born. Great Britain, according to this thesis, became the new "Israel".

Now, I want the reader to hear me loud and clear here. My classification of Great Britain as one of the *"two witnesses"* has nothing to do with British Israelism. I've learned that this belief is deeply rooted in the Old Testament but I find no passage which would either directly or indirectly lend support to these ideas. My view of the *"witnesses"* is New Testament teaching, born out of seeing and rationally-relating several allegorical Scriptures to an abundance of actual historical facts. Regardless of how it may look now, before I'm through, you'll see that what I present is not at all a statement of national pride as is the case of "Britism Israelism"! Those who confuse my understanding with these concepts are making a gross error. As you can see from my comments above, that is not how I arrived at the understanding, nor is my interpretation that of the "British Israelites".

Herbert Armstrong (now deceased), former head of the World Wide Church of God, taught strongly concerning America in Biblical prophecy. As with all cultic concepts, we Christians might agree with them on certain facts, but on the whole, Armstrong's understanding is more like (perhaps exactly like) "British Israelism". His view is not mine at all.

114

There are others (Christians) who teach fragmentary concepts about Britain and America in Biblical prophecy. They get their ideas from terms such as *"ships of Tarshish"*, certain *"islands"*, or *"young lions"*, and things like that, from verses scattered throughout the Old Testament. Some of these views may have merit but this is not where my thinking originated either nor is it the way I base my concepts. What I have discovered is a broad, straight-forward, clear identification of God's primary *"witnesses"* that He would use for a period of 1260 years during the Christian era.

WHAT DO OTHER CHRISTIAN LEADERS SAY ABOUT BRITAIN AND USA IN PROPHECY?

From my readings and listening to large T. V. and radio ministries, I conclude most preachers are very much aware of the Christian roots and Christian heritage of G. B. and America. Today especially, many ministers are even trying to affect our local and national governments by reminding politicians of the facts that many of our founding fathers were Christians who strongly influenced America's beginning. I agree with them but have gone one step farther. I have identified us not merely as nations which 'just happened' to have a lot of foundational Christian input but rather that we were actually chosen and set aside by God from the beginning. We are more than nations which have shown a measure of love <u>for</u> God; rather we are nations which possessed the <u>**"of Me"**</u> power of Almighty God.

Some may feel my identification of the *"two witnesses"* is prideful. Actually, just the opposite is true. The idea that Britain and America have been "christian" nations is far more arrogant than my position. What I'm saying gives God the glory, whose honor it is. What others are saying gives man the glory. Their ideas are based on the understanding that Christian men have done the things which have given us our rich blessings and heritage. On the other hand what I'm saying is that <u>God chose</u> the sites and the people He would anoint.

115

I see it much like the prophet Elijah throwing his mantle across the shoulders of his follower, Elisha. Elisha didn't even know what had been done to him. Similarly, Britain and America's power was a result of God throwing the 'mantles' across our shoulders and we likewise haven't even known it. The same was true of John the Baptist. Jesus said John was Elijah, but we have no record that John ever understood this fact. Thus, to whatever degree we have been, and are, 'Christian' nations, is God's doing, not ours. He is the igniter; we are the matchstick.

I believe my concepts on the *two witnesses* fit the patterns and guidelines of Scripture. In my opinion, and I say this with due respect for the office they hold, with regards to prophecy, many ideas of pastor-teachers on prophecy do not.

I believe there are many, specially anointed men of God today whose ministry has been more thwarted by people within the Church than from without. They think themselves knowledgeable when, in fact, they are the blind in these areas. Let me conclude my 'beef' on this by leaving you with this Scripture; *"Despise not prophesying"*. (1 Thess. 5:20.)

A note to pastors:

(I realize there has been much abuse within the body of Christ on the spiritual gifts and the "offices" of ministry (Ephesians 4:11). In spite of everything I've said, which may seem offensive to some, I agree with much of the apprehension and reluctance in accepting the claims of many so-called and self-described "prophets" of Christ. In most cases it's a healthy, Godly skepticism. But being a Christian myself, believing God has touched me in several peculiar and distinctly-different ways, I must also disagree with the way many in Church leadership positions respond to people like me. The net result has been to throw the proverbial 'baby out with the bath water'. I'm convinced God has shown me these things so I feel I have no alternative but to share them with the body of Christ. Accept what you can.)

Now, let's move on. We must face the question of who is anointed in these two nations. Is it everyone or just the Christians? And what about Great Britain? Historically speaking, they have been spread virtually all over the world. Was it only mainland-England which received the gift or was the whole empire involved?

Let me address the last question first: Of the two, England was the easier to historically identify relative to the beginning date of the *"witness"* missions. In earlier days, as England spread their influence throughout the world, politically and otherwise, the Gospel went along with it. (From God's perspective, the Gospel was actually leading the way and the politico-mercantile movements only incidental to the greater endeavor — evangelization.) And, as the British Empire grew, so grew godliness in the regions affected by England's outreach.

Now someone will say, *"Lance, don't you know that the Gospel message was perverted by many of the English clergy?"* Or, *"do you not know of the atrocities which were committed among the 'such and such' group, or in the 'so and so' country by the British Empire builders?"* Yes, I'm aware of these shortcomings. The Gospel has many times been distorted and abused in the past, and will, unfortunately, probably be so in the future. But that doesn't detract from the good that was done.

No, the British-Christian influence was not perfect. (Read the letters to the seven churches again. Rev. 2 & 3.) Perfection is not guaranteed — even among God's anointed. It never has been. Jesus alone holds the distinction of a perfectly-maintained human life. It wasn't so in the anointed kings of Israel, the ancient prophets, the whole nation of Israel, nor even Jesus' apostles. Even Paul, who taught most of what we know about Christian' maturation, referred to himself as *"chief of sinners"*.

No, we haven't been perfect, Christian nations. But, in my opinion, one has to be nearly blind not to see the unique blessings (reflecting the reality of the anointing) which has been the historical possession of the British and the Americans, regardless of how decadent our societies appear now. The downward trod shows the success Satan is having in our nations today. This makes it rather obvious he knows who we are. In fact, that's why the devil is trying to destroy us.

THE ANOINTING; EXACTLY WHO RECEIVED IT?

The Bible shows that anointing power from God is always manifested in a twofold way — both **physical** and **spiritual**. It's as true of entire nations as of individuals. The blessings upon the British and the Americans has been (and still is) clearly manifested in the form of <u>physical</u> blessings and <u>spiritual</u> blessings.

On the physical blessing side, in terms of natural resources, and the ability to be resourceful outside their countries when needed, no nation has equalled the British and the Americans.

The spiritual blessings have been similarly countless. It is utterly awesome to simply look at the number of Christian churches in Great Britain and America. This remains true even until this day in spite of the soaring apostasy presently manifested in our lands.

An imporant spiritual blessing has been (and still remains so) the saved individuals who have been 'called out' here. Of equal importance is the missionary work which has followed in the wake of evangelization among our own people. The financing as well as the training of most missionaries has occurred in one of these two national structures. I believe this mission work is a fulfillment of the 1260-day *prophesying* by the *two witnesses* as spoken of in Revelation 11:3. Remember, the *prophesying* = the preaching of the Gospel. Individual Christian work is part of this prophesying but it also includes many Christian organizations which were birthed in one of these two nations. In combo, these represent a big part of THE GREAT COMMISSION[4].

Keep in mind, God has done this, not man. We have merely been His instrumental servants. What an awesome responsibility! But have we been completely faithful? Let me ask the Christian reader, are you faithful today to do your part in this "Elijah Task"? If you are truly a born-again Christian living in the land of one of the *two witnesses,* you are a part of the heritage. I'm sure there have been times when you have thanked God for the blessedness of just being born where you were. Some of you have probably had an inner feeling there was more to it than "good luck", too.

Now, does this understanding that you were actually chosen by God to be a part of His "witness" not stir up in you a sense of awe and responsibility? You and I have our parts in the mandate to reach others for Christ. I know you are thinking this is true for Christians everywhere and you are right about that. But I'm talking about something entirely different. What has been true of our nations as a whole is also yours as one individual. Never has there been a more critical time than now that the people of God in America and Great Britain band together to resist the growing evil influences in our lands, and to *be* the righteousness of God for others to see. A personal holy life is the strongest "prophesying" one can do.

THE INVISIBLE WALL

Everybody knows about the 'invisible wall' of protection that has been around GB and the USA (oddly, foreigners seem

---

[4]There are two very worthy statistical books I would recommend to those who wish to see the validity of my conviction that 90% of missionary work goes forth from the *two witnesses:*
OPERATION WORLD by Patrick Johnstone and
LET THE EARTH HEAR by Paul E. Freed.

more aware of this than some of us). I work with veterans as an optometrist and some of them like to tell about their wartime experiences. Now there are certain types of individuals who tend to sort of 'stretch' things (you know what I mean) but many of their stories were so amazingly similar, I'm convinced they are true.

The old heroes recount how God often protected them individually (sometimes even whole groups) during certain battles — these included land, sea and air conflicts. They retell in vivid detail the unexplainable thoughts that would come to mind that things would somehow be all right when the circumstances clearly indicated they were done for. Understand me, I'm not talking about an occasional thing. These seemed to be ordinary occurrences. Now, we might expect this from believers, right? But the point I want to drive home is that these incidences were common among non-Christians as well! This is the sovereignty of God in action, folks.

These stories are only a small example of the invisible wall of protection of the *two witnesses*. It has been true throughout the histories of these two powerhouses. (More on this later.)

WHEN DID THE "PROPHESYING" COMMENCE?

From a Biblical, historical perspective, I shall base my response on the prophetic principle of a 'day' = one year. Let's start with England. In my search regarding this point, I read a book called THE HISTORY OF ENGLAND[5]. In it the author says:

"Five years after the Synod of Whitby, Theodore of Tarsus became the new Archbishop. His organizing and administrative abilities were manifested in the

---

[5]THE HISTORY OF ENGLAND by Harold J. Shultz.

precedents and reforms that shaped the organization of the English church. *He doubled the number of bishopries, set up regular church councils, and laid the groundwork for the modern parish system.* *By providing counsel to rulers and offering the one basis for unity among feuding kingdoms, the power of the clergy increased.* *Under Theodore's successors the church flourished both in missionary enterprise and in the dissemination of culture.* *It sent missionaries to the Continent and established schools in England whose graduates provided moral leadership and scholarly achievement.* *The caliber of scholarship is exemplified by the 'father of English history,' the Venerable Bede (671-731)* (remember this date), *whose writings caught the unity of the English as a people and, also, as part of the greater unity - the Church Universal.* *By the* eighth century *English scholarship was at least the equivalent of that in western Europe, and Christianity had again brought Britain into the mainstream of western civilization."*

Now this last sentence is of particular importance from my perspective. Even from a secular historian's view, we see Christianity was observed as being the most outstanding attribute which resulted in England's becoming a significant part of the *"mainstream of western civilization".*

I have become convinced that it was in this exact era (i.e., the 8th century) that England's anointing commenced. Let me tell you why. The above author, Mr. Schultz, mentioned the "Venerable Bede" as being the "father of English history". There is an amazing fact in Bede's life which Christians should note: Mr. Bede is given credit for performing the first English translation of the Bible. History reveals he died (731 A.D.) right at the very moment he penned the last word of the Gospel of John! Isn't that fantastic? God is the ultimate dramatist when the occasion calls for it.

121

Thus, with Bede began the translating and the eventual supplying of the Word of God to the English people. And later it would be those same peoples who would become God's chief resource for translating and disseminating the Bible into hundreds of other languages. You have all surely heard of the fine organization called "Wycliffe Bible Translators". John Wycliffe (1320 - '84) was a noted Bible translator and a church reformer. He typified in his generation one of the outstanding English persons God used along the way during the past "1260 days".

One could write a book on Christian scholarship just to summarize the vast academic contributions the British have provided to the Church. But that is not the intent of this book. What I'm trying to do is merely relate what I believe is the correct understanding of what Revelation 11 is all about. Once readers get the essence of what I've been saying, I'm convinced some of you may very well provide better substantiating-information to support my 'theory' than I've presented myself. That's the way real truth operates. It builds and grows once a correct principle is established.

BUT WHAT ABOUT AMERICA?

Some readers will probably believe I've trapped myself with the claim that the *two witnesses* are GB and the USA since America wasn't even discovered until 1492. If England's ministry began around 731 A.D., how can this apparent discrepancy be reconciled?

This illogical situation at first troubled me too. But nevertheless, I believed in the identification I had given the *two witnesses* long before I could reconcile the delimma. I sought the Lord about it. The convictions wouldn't go away. There has always been a pervasive, over-riding peace which caused me to move on. I think it was an inner-knowing. I just believed that some day the incongruity relative to the 1260-year time issue as it applies to America would somehow work out. And it did!

One morning I 'just happened' to tune in the "700 Club" and saw a documentary film story. Ironically, I felt prompted to record the program that morning and still have the video. At that time, CBN was doing several special programs involving the Christian heritage of America. They had heard of a recent, very interesting discovery in a cave located in Boone County, West Virginia. Their T.V. crew went there and filmed the researchers' findings.

Archaeologist Robert Pyle had found and studied carvings in the cave and became convinced that the markings were not Indian as was formerly assumed. They sent for an expert witness on ancient languages. Professor Emeritus Dr. Barry Fell, of Harvard University, came and made careful studies of the "petroglyphs" (the carved markings on the walls of the cave). To everyone's amazement, he identified the markings as a form of ancient Irish (English in its rudiment stage). They were even able to approximate the time the markings were inscribed, being somewhere between the 6th and 8th centuries!

When I first saw that program I literally leaped for joy! Even though I was already convinced and expectant that God would one day provide a satisfactory explanation of the position I held concerning America as one of the "witnesses", I could hardly believe my own eyes that morning. God was confirming my viewpoint right in my own family room! And to find out that these special, ancient English-speaking 'visitors' came about the same time England's Venerable Bede had begun the translating work of the Scriptures into English (which would later broaden into the largest base for Bible dissemmination the world had ever known), well, it was just too good to be true. But nevertheless, there it was.

THE MESSAGE

Discovering that ancient English people were here in America around the 8th century would have been sufficient evidence to confirm my convictions about the second of God's *two witnesses*, but there's even more.

As a Christian visiting a foreign land for the first time and you wanted to leave an inscription on a cave wall for future generations to know you were there, what would *you* say? The visitors chose a brief message of the Gospel! It told of Jesus being born of a virgin and that He was the Savior of mankind. Also of interest was the fact that on the winter Solstice (believed by the discoverers to be the day the markings were inscribed), a ray from the sun pierces through a certain notch on a nearby mountain, landing on the markings in the cave. (This fact may cause some to think the early visitors to America were sunworshipers. Not so. They were people who loved Jesus and, by God's providence, also very smart!)

Obviously these were Christians who were thinking of their Savior on the day which had traditionally been set aside for remembering Jesus' birthday. I like their idea. What a fantastic 'calling card' — a giant-sized Christmas greeting left indelibly inscrolled in a cave where a sun beam just happened to fall only on that day. The Scripture in Malachi (Mal. 4:2) about the *"sun of righteousness"* who would come with *"healing in His wings"* must surely have been on their minds. The T.V. program speculated on the route and method the visitors used to get here, which really isn't all that relevant. The important fact is, they came!

But why did the ancient Irish come? What motivated them? I think, although likely hidden from their own minds at the time, they came to put a *"seal"* on America. That little record would indicate God had chosen this land; God's plan being He would some day take this first tiny gospel message and later expand it into the world's most prominent and influential Gospel base.

There may even be an inference of God's sovereign influence here in the name of the area where the *seal* was placed: West Virginia — *virgin* land of the *west.*

But why did God keep this secret so long? Perhaps because of the prideful tendencies in man. If a person, or a nation, thinks of himself as "God's anointed", the natural tendency is often to develop a self-righteous attitude. God's way has always been for humble people to wear His mantle. Therefore, I would offer the suggestion that God designed the circumstances so that the people of America would not know all the facts surrounding their inheritance. God's "witnesses" can accomplish His goals without understanding everything about their own background.

STILL NOT ENOUGH PROOF?

Now I realize there will still be skeptics who have all kinds of reservations and unanswered questions about this matter. Sorry, I don't have all the answers. But for those with honest doubts, I will say a few more things.

The reservation I personally had (after learning who really "discovered" America) was this: Even if there were ancient-English Christians here in the 8th century, the Christian influence wasn't effective until after the 15th century when Christian settlers began to arrive. After 1492, America's Christian "witness" is easy to see. But how does the 8th century discovery of America, by ancient Irish, correlate with the fact it was much later before America began her 'prophesying' to the world?

A satisfactory answer came to mind when I noted how Elijah's 1260 literal-day prophesying seems to parallel America's prophetic days. Biblically, we know of only a few incidental situations of Elijah's 1260-day preaching period — those things God felt were of importance to us. Similarly, it is not important that we understand all God has in mind when He works things out in an entire nation He plans to use in special ways. Not knowing all the specific details of those ancient English peoples who came here and left their "mark", and the long lag time from then until 1492, should not worry us. If God thinks we need to know about this seeming paradox, He'll eventually reveal it. It's that simple. Our God is a faith-God. He always gives just enough information to identify things, to make reasonable judgments based on the sound facts of the situation, and then once we sense, "This is of God!", we, by faith, must move on from there. This may be a simplistic viewpoint but it sufficiently satisfies my curiosity. I hope it does yours.

NATIONAL RIGHTEOUSNESS

The next day after I concluded the above remarks went like this: My customary morning activities is to rise early (between 2:00 and 4:00 A.M.), spend time in prayer, have breakfast and then work at whatever project is going, which right now is this manuscript. During my quiet time I read two or three daily devotionals, one of which is "Days of Praise", published by the Institute of Creation Research in San Diego, Ca. Dr. Henry Morris, the Institute's president, writes most of the one-page commentaries. Because of the precise place I am now writing in this book, the reader can understand my amazement at the topic of that morning's devotional. It was called "National Righteousness"[6]. Although I am truly awed at the timing of this, I shouldn't be shocked, for I've learned God has been faithful throughout the writing of this book to provide confirmations as I go along — and I praise Him for it!

I was so impressed with Dr. Morris' comments I think it is worthwhile to include his remarks here. He said:

---

[6]"Days of Praise", a daily devotional written mainly by Dr. Henry Morris and published by the Institute of Creation Research.

"Righteousness exalteth a nation: but sin is a reproach to any people." (Proverbs 14:34)

"*Modern Christians place great emphasis on personal salvation, but we must remember that God is also the God of the nations. That being so, our own nation, so greatly blessed of God in the past, may well be in great peril, for 'the wicked shall be turned into hell, and all the nations that forget God' (Psalm 9:17).*
"*Our nation was founded by men who had strong faith in God, and its laws were based on the laws of God. The schools all honored the Lord and His Word, taught the truth of special creation, and enforced Biblical morality among the students.   Today, God and anything associated with Him are banned from the classroom, His laws are no longer taken seriously in the courts and legislatures, and evolutionary humanism is, in effect, the state-endorsed religion.   Divorce and immorality are affecting most of the nation's homes; business and finance are ubiquitously plagued with greed and dishonesty; the sins of homosexuality, drunkenness and drug use are rampant, and atheistic communism is an imminent threat at our gates.*"
"*God would even have spared Sodom, though, if there had been ten righteous (Genesis 18:32), and America has evidently been spared thus far because it is still the nerve center of world missions and Christian literature, as well as aid for the sick and needy. The modern revival of true creationism is centered in this nation, and serious Biblical interest is growing in many places, yet worldliness, apostasy, and compromise are eating away at the heart of American Christianity, and there is great need for a revival - not of religious emotionalism, but of genuine commitment to the integrity and authority of God's Word.   "Blessed is the nation whose God is the LORD"* (Psalm 33:12). End.

Now, what would you think if you were writing a commentary of your convictions that there are two Biblically-prophesied, anointed nations of God, and then woke up to read the above concepts of someone else at a point when you were trying to say something to inspire belief among your readers? Well, it was a bright word for me that day, the kind I've learned to expect from God. He's gracious. He's a confirmer. He's totally sufficient and faithful to prompt us onward if and when we are faithful in our ministry in His Kingdom.

Now, I'm not saying Dr. Morris interprets the two witnesses as I do but his comments cogently explain a deep, Biblical principle — one which just happens to fit my interpretation concerning the two witnesses. The main difference between us is that I have gone so far as to state my belief that the principle is set forth in God's Word in the form of a prophetic proclamation, not just seeing a general spiritual law — that *"righteousness exalts a nation"* — which would apply anywhere.

CHRISTIAN ROOTS

There has always been a sister-like union between England and America. And, like sisters, we haven't always been in perfect agreement with each other. But just let someone else interfere with that relationship or try to hurt the other in any way, then, traditionally, the invader has had a fight on his hands! Note these quotations from some quite old history books. (Sorry, title and authors unavailable.)

"The very purpose of the Pilgrims in 1620 was to establish a government based on the Bible. The New England Charter signed by King James 1 confirmed this goal: '...to advance the enlargement of Christian religion, to the glory of God Almighty...'. The goal of a government based on the Bible was further reaffirmed by individual colonies such as the Rhode Island Charter of

1638: "We ... submit our persons, lives and estates unto our Lord Jesus Christ, the King of Kings and Lord of Lords and to all those perfect and most absolute Laws of His given us in His Holy Word."

Those absolute Laws became the basis of our (USA) Declaration of Independence and the writing of our national Constitution. A walk through the halls and monuments in Washington D.C. still portrays the evidence of these truths as excerpts from the Scriptures are displayed in many areas. In a Supreme Court Justice room, the ten commandments were inscribed above the judges' seats, with the American Eagle's wings protectively surrounding them. (I heard this was recently removed. Many ungodly people in authority today are methodically getting rid of the reminders of our nation's Christian heritage. However, that doesn't destroy the reality of our history. They can <u>never</u> do that!)

Further evidence of God's guidance in the establishment of the USA as a particular and 'peculiar' nation for His good pleasure is revealed in history books relating the true motivations of the early English settlers of the Jamestown expedition. It said, "...*first to preach and baptize into Christian religion, and propagation of the gospel, to recover out of the arms of the devil, a number of poor and miserable souls...*". This book (again, I don't have the reference) also related how the first permanent English settlers in the New World had landed at Cape Henry for the occasion, and their chaplain, Rev. Robert Hunt, led them in prayer, dedicating the land to God. About two weeks later they established Jamestown, England's first overseas colony. (Isn't it interesting that English people did this, and very near the site where the ancient English pilgrims had left their "mark" approximately seven centuries earlier!)

129

In their book,[7] Peter Marshall and David Manuel present a beautiful historical picture of the Christian roots of this nation. Even though these authors nowhere imply that Great Britain and the United States represent the two witnesses of Revelation 11, I think their views lend credibility to the idea. Like Dr. Morris, they see the principles behind "national righteousness". Now, back to the Bible's description of the witnesses:

THE "FIRE" AND THE "RAIN"

5. *"And if anyone wants to harm them, fire proceeds out of their mouth and devours their enemies. And if anyone wants to harm them, he must be killed in this manner."*
6. *"These have power to shut heaven, so that no rain falls in the days of their prophecy; and they have power over waters to turn them to blood, and to smite the earth with all plagues, as often as they desire."*

Historically speaking, verses 5 and 6 are somewhat easier to see than some of the other passages we've covered. Once the identities of the two witnesses are known, the ensuing verses help clarify and further substantiate who they are, as well as provide information relative to their historical functions.

For example, verse 5 lets us know that if anyone attempts to hurt one of the two witnesses (GB or the USA), it will result in *"fire"* coming out of their *"mouth"* and the offender himself will, in *"this manner"*, be killed. This simply means that those who would attack or attempt to destroy GB or the USA, would themselves be defeated in the same way they had purposed to kill us. In short, their attempts would backfire! If they would

---

[7]"The Light and The Glory", by Peter Marshall and David Manuel.

send bombers (as Japan did in WW2), they would be destroyed in like manner by our retaliatory defenses; i.e., *"fire"* would come out of our *"mouths"*.

A similar thing could be said of Germany's strategies against England. History records that Hitler could never mount a death-blow offense against England. This was a real frustration for Hitler. In fact, the retaliatory *"fire"* from the combined forces of the two "sisters" back-fired against him and his regime was destroyed — just as the above prophecy predicted! Other war conflicts could also be cited but these are the two best examples to get the idea across.

Verse 6 carries this same concept further. All blessings come from above but God often distributes the control of certain blessings into selected human agencies. Having the *"power to shut heaven"* simply means God has allowed the blessings (physical and spiritual) to flow from our shores into the lands of many other nations. For example, America's history of philanthropy has always amazed me. Giving money, food, clothing, shelter, health resources, and providing military assistance against others who would strip poorer nations of their assets, are, historically, British and American attributes.

In general, no nation could have a better ally than either GB or the USA. If a country had one — or better, both — on their side, they would automatically reap certain benefits just by being their partner. Why? Because God blesses those who support 'God's anointed'. It's a spiritual law. God promised Abraham that He would bless those who blessed Israel. In like fashion, He has blessed those nations who joined the British and the Americans in their endeavors. Thus, having the power to control the *"rain"* (blessings) during the days of their prophecy, means as long as a portion of their *"1260 days"* remains, the two witnesses will still hold much of the control of God's blessings upon this planet. This responsibility obviously escapes the awareness of today's politicians. (O *God, give us some Spirit-filled leaders!*)

The last part of verse six says that the two witnesses can *"smite the earth with ALL PLAGUES, as often as they will"* (i.e., as long as their <u>desire</u> lasts to do it.) The essence of this is that we have had God-given physical and spiritual powers right in our hands (military, mercantile, Bible-publishing capabilities, missions, etc.,) and, for the most part, unaware of it! How much military control? The Scripture tells us: enough to turn the *"waters to blood"* as we have seen the need to do it, against those who would attempt to destroy God's anointed. (*"Waters"*, by John's own definition, means PEOPLE.)

It is quite obvious that both the ungodly and the godly have enjoyed the blessings God gave us. Even in the midst of pervasive apostasy and extreme wickedness within our nations today, God is still blessing us abundantly. Why does God do this? Because of a group known as "the remnant" — the remaining Christian believers who comprise the true Church. They still hold the mandate of the Gospel in their hands! Take the followers of Christ out of these lands and the current decadence would intensify dramatically, as will indeed happen one of these days! God said He would not destroy Sodom if there were even ten righteous people left there. The principle still applies.

But, I believe the main reasons God specially chose these two nations were:

(1) to demonstrate that "righteousness does indeed exalt a nation" and,

(2) that they would be God's main national witnesses (bearing testimony) to the rest of the world. This would be achieved in three ways:

    (a) through regular worship services held openly throughout our lands — including hundreds of radio and television broadcasts;

(b)   the witnesses would be international providers of God's Word, Christian literature, plus radio, television and numerous other worldwide distributions; and

(c)   they would send missionaries forth throughout the world.

THE APOSTASY IN GREAT BRITAIN AND AMERICA

Some people refuse to accept my concepts of the two witnesses because of the ungodly extremes which now pervade our societies. They just can't believe we are "Christian" nations. Well, in a sense they are right! I recently learned that less than 4% of the people in England attend church regularly anymore! While church attendance is much higher in the USA, this does not excuse the fact that Americans have also become very backslidden from God. But in spite of these facts, we must also face the reality that the Gospel is going forth at an unprecedented rate, via radio, television, the printed page, and through missionaries on the foreign field. And the preponderance of this work, Biblically called The Great Commission, originates within the confines of the 'British factor' and/or the USA.

THE BRITISH-FACTOR

When one thinks of the British, there is an ever-persistent question which says, "Where are those who represent the British side of the two witnesses"? That's a good question in light of the fact that, historically, GB set up their regimes all over the world (even attempting that here initially). It was called the British Empire, or the British Commonwealth. Well, early Americans would have no part of it, hence, the Revolutionary War and eventually America's Declaration of Independence.

It was God who determined that America would be separate from Great Britain; an ally to GB, yes, but not under her. I think of our former relationship like an older sister who so-dominates a younger sister that both have trouble learning that the younger is her own person. But just as any loving, yet over-powering, older sister must eventually come to her senses and let her baby-sister grow up, such was the case with Great Britain. Once GB understood her status, she reluctantly became resigned to be what she was — a protective, older 'sister'.

But the question remains, is England the only anointed part of the British aspect of the two witnesses? I think not. I believe it applied to Scotland, Wales, Australia, Canada, and all others which came to be a part of the Commonwealth. To get my perspective, think of it like this: witness number one (Great Britain) is like one house with a large dining room. On the dining table are many plates, each plate representing one of the outlying territories which would come under British rule. Collectively, as the empire grew, each added plate became a part of the Commonwealth. That which was shared was not merely the humanistic ideologies brought in by the British influence to the new land (i.e., the physical blessings) but also, and more importantly, God's spiritual blessings which came along because His anointing power was upon them. Over the years, the torch would be carried in succession by different territories at different times, the timing and power being established by the leadership and control of the Holy Spirit, of course. (It is probably only in retrospect that this understanding can really be seen. Some, I suspect, never will.)

The Christian Canadians presently appear to be having a greater zeal for God than any of the other British regions which have exercised their part of this witness at some other point in time. Whether you agree with my identification of the two witnesses or not, surely it is obvious to all that there is an unmistakeable kindred spirit between the Canadians and the Americans. The union is far more than the casual eye would see, though. It is deeply rooted in our ancestral heritage, but even that explanation is not nearly good enough. It is far more important to realize that we are, as nations, deeply rooted in God. It is, and has been, His idea and plan from the start.

Some of you will have strong reservations about all this "plate" business and the like. For now, I only ask that you keep the ideas in mind, allowing the Holy Spirit to guide your thinking as you continue to read and ponder the historical significance of this new line of reasoning.

CANADA

Canada recently broke from the "motherland" of England, and has become a sovereign nation. At first, that seemed to disturb my overall concepts on the British-witness factor. But the more I've thought about it, it seems quite fitting that the two 'sister-lighthouses' would end up side-by-side to make their last stand for God as His primary witnesses in the world. That, I'm convinced, is where we are right now. God has used all the 'plates' of the British Commonwealth at certain times and we may yet see revivals break out within some of them. How glorious that would be! However, it is my conviction that, today, Canada and America are the prominent "*olive trees*" the prophet Zechariah said would empty themselves of their "*golden oil*" — the very same the apostle John refers to in Rev. 11 as the witnesses. (When England joined the Common Market of Europe, I believe that union spelled the end of her being the main British "torch bearer". More later on this.)

I hesitate writing at this point because eventually, as the saying goes, 'all good things must come to an end'. That will be the case as the assignment of the two witnesses draws to a close, as depicted in the next verse. But, it is necessary to go on. In fact, the next two verses are perhaps the most confirming of the way I've identified the two witnesses.

THE "WITNESSES" ARE KILLED

7 "And when they finish their testimony, the beast that ascends out of the bottomless pit will make war against them, overcome them, and kill them."

Verses 1 - 6 needed word-deciphering to get the picture, but verse 7 is plain and can be taken quite literally. The two witnesses will be killed when their testimony (witnessing) is completed. Exactly who will be killed? As you've seen, witness number one (starting in GB) is complicated, having been spread all over the globe. America, being more localized, is easier to see. So, when the 'testimony' is over, which nation (or nations) of the British witness will be destroyed? (I think England and Northern Ireland will be destroyed later, but for different reasons than that which is predicted here in Revelation concerning the two witnesses. More on that later, too.)

I believe Canada and the USA will be "killed" simultaneously. We sit right next to each other and, in general, agree philosophically, economically, governmentally, and more importantly, spiritually. As such, we are somewhat at odds against the rest of the world, many growing stronger each day in their resentment towards us. And, at some point in time (perhaps not long from now), some country, a representative of the *"beast that ascends out of the bottomless pit"* (Satan), will rise up to MAKE WAR, OVERCOME and KILL the two witnesses. Let's look a little more closely at these three terms I've underscored.

MAKE WAR

Let me urge the reader to be alert here! Don't miss this point! If you'll really concentrate on what I'm about to say, I'm convinced the next few points will convince you of the absurdity of the view that the two witnesses are only two people.

136

"Make war" is a very revealing term. The phrase is altogether inappropriate if the inference were only to two individuals. Think about it. It would be grossly misleading to use the word *"war"* if one wished to convey the idea that only two people were to be destroyed. Let me illustrate: Suppose a criminal plots to kill someone, the terminology used in such a situation, now or in Biblical times, wouldn't be 'make war'. The word *war* is reserved for conflicts between nations (or sometimes of course, between large groups in a single nation such as the Civil War). I'm persuaded that John's use of this word was carefully Spirit-directed, even designed, to give us a clue as to the proper identification of the two witnesses.

This word *war* served as one of the main clues to confirm my convictions about national "witnesses" as opposed to only two people as held by the Futuristic-only school. God doesn't waste words nor does He use words to confuse or mislead us, which would most certainly be the case if we take the position that the *beast* would make war against two God-anointed preachers.

OVERCOME THEM

The above rationale applies equally well here. To *overcome* implies tremendous resistance has been involved. Are we to believe that the two witnesses are two individuals who God has so-gifted with supernatural abilities that the *beast* must use all sorts of offensive forces against them, and finally after great conflict, overcome them? If God had any such supermen in mind, no amount of energy against them would be sufficient. It could only work if and when God's power in them was removed.

But, if the assumption is made that the two witnesses refer to two national entities, then things fall into place. To *make war* and to *overcome* two mighty nations makes much better sense.

Think of what is happening in Canada and the USA today. Apostasy is unquestionably upon us. That's one area of the *beast's* attack. Broad-scaled immorality is at an all time high. That's another area of attack. Greed and materialism is everywhere around us, even in the Church. On another front, hatred is growing against us, particularly in some of the Middle East and some of the Third World nations. Need I say more? Satan (the real force behind the *beast*) is on the attack at every point of vulnerability within the *two witnesses*. And, he knows them all! The *beast* is rising, *"making war"* and beginning to *"overcome"* us.

"KILL THEM"

Although important, weapons are not Canada's and America's greatest defense. The apostasy, idolatry, immorality, greed, materialism, etc., within the two witnesses are the forces responsible for weakening our best defense — **Righteousness**. As already discussed, the Bible clearly teaches that righteousness *"exalts a nation"*. Neither of the two witnesses has achieved perfection in this area but throughout the ages, the characteristic has been our heritage. And the degree to which that righteousness has been manifest, God has abundantly blessed us.

On the other hand, as righteousness diminishes within a nation, the blessings also diminish. This is happening in our two countries today. Slowly but surely we are being *"killed"* by these nebulous, satanically-inspired forces. These alone would ultimately spell our defeat and wipe out our positive influence in other nations if allowed to run their natural, downward course to completion. However, our destruction will reach a far more definite climax than a mere *"withering on the vine"* because of the apostasy and gross negligence on our part. Verse seven says the two witnesses will be **KILLED** and I'm convinced it means exactly that! Now, no Canadian or American wants to hear that, including me. But according to the Scripture here, the two witnesses will be killed.

WHO DOES IT?

Who will the *"beast"* inspire to kill the two witnesses? As of now, we can only speculate. I find no clear Biblical reference to it. (Later in the study we'll discuss one candidate in detail, the "10 horned beast", but I feel the beast of Revelation 11 and the "10 horned beast" of Revelation 13 are not one and the same.) I find it very interesting to note that Russia and America are making an attempt at peaceful co-existence to reduce the possibility of a conflict which might result in annihilation of one, or both, our nations. At a time when the devastation-potential is at an unbelievable heighth, we are discussing peace! But then, wasn't this predicted? Note what the apostle Paul said regarding world conditions just prior to the return of the Lord:

"For when they say, "Peace and safety!" then sudden destruction comes on them, as labor pains on a pregnant woman. And they shall not escape." (1 Thes. 5:3)

Most of the world's leaders are focussing today on **"peace and safety"**. That's a primary topic among all current international leaders. Not long ago we had the largest single-day stock drop in all history. This too was a strong indicator that the *"labor"* has begun. Actually, the 'labor pains' the apostle spoke of started before the *"peace and safety"* talks and the stock market tumble. But these facts are strong indicators.

We know labor pains in a pregnant woman begin with slight discomfort at wide-spread time intervals, then grow in intensity with shorter and shorter time spans between them, until finally the baby is born. Such, I believe, will be the case in the breakdown of the Canadian and American strongholds. The "killing" will come by slow, internal blows to our "mid-section" at first, followed by a military knock-out punch by some other nation in the end. That nation could be one which we do not suspect as having such capability today.

It's not even inconceivable that it could be done from within our shores. Who really knows just how much technical expertise is secretively held by any nation in our day? Several nations may have atomic warfare capabilities, just waiting for the right time to set them off. Or it might be done by common explosive devices strategically planted throughout our nations, timed for precise detonation; an awful thought, but it's possible. Folks, we have let our gates down. Our nation is filled with irresponsible outsiders who have no respect for our God or our country. And, unfortunately, many of our people are listening to them!

(Much of the above was written several years ago, but recently, 1/17/91, we entered a war conflict with Iraq (the modern name for ancient Babylon). In light of this, my overall presentation appears to take on more credibility since what is now unfolding right before our eyes was predicted at a much earlier time. The *birth pains* are here. Oddly, and almost prophetically, and even though he lost the war, the tyrant Saddam Hussein made the comment that the "**mother of battles has begun**". I agree. But, regardless of who, when or how it's done, and in spite of our seemingly-invincible war strength as demonstrated in the Gulf War, the final hour for the two witnesses is coming. Perhaps sooner than most think.)

John the Baptist was beheaded when his mission was over, and even our Lord Jesus Himself was crucified at the end of His ministry. On a national scale it will be similar when the two witnesses complete their ministry. I believe this means a simultaneous, physical destruction will occur in America and Canada — leaving some alive, of course, but both rendered militarily helpless.

However, we can take comfort in this fact: death does not come until *"they finish their testimony."* You may be wondering if all the nations which have been a part of the British witness will be destroyed along with Canada and America. I think not. Today, it is well known that most of the international evangelistic outreach is eminating from Canada and America. Therefore, I believe that's where the attacking nation will concentrate their efforts.

In spite of the prevailing apostasy and ungodliness, Canada and the USA still represent the main threat against Satan's present kingdom-building process. Satan is limited in knowledge but he most definitely knows where God's primary work is being done at any given moment. It's always been this way. In spite of his evil nature, he understands the principle of "binding the strong man" before he can enter to "steal". For this reason he will focus his murderous, anti-Canadian-American scheme into the minds of those who are listening to his 'inspirational' suggestions. The binding is under way. But, for the moment, we are still here! The main question is, is the righteousness of the Church' remnant sufficient to resist the devil's plot?

THE "WALLS" OF ISRAEL

Ezekiel 38 and 39 are prophetic previews of an invasion of Israel. This is widely agreed upon among most prophetic writers. The leader, *"Gog"*, is believed (by most) to be Russia; the nations aligned with her will be Ethiopia, Persia (modern Iran), Libya, Gomer (some suggest this means Germany) and

141

Togarmah (apparently modern Turkey). Exactness of this coalition is debatable. However, I want to emphasize here one very interesting verse from that passage: (Ezek. 38:11)

> *"And thou* (i.e., Gog) *shalt say, I will go up to the land of* <u>*unwalled*</u> *villages: I will go to them that are at rest, that dwell safely, all of them dwelling* <u>*without walls*</u> *and having neither bars nor gates."* (My emphasis.)

The main essence of this passage is that in the "last days" there will be a group of nations who are intent upon annihilating the regathered nation of modern Israel. However, there is a very key concept here which others have apparently overlooked. It's found in the phrases *"without walls"* and the *"unwalled villages"*. That the passage refers to modern Israel is certain but we need to examine other implications here.

In ancient Israel, as well as other nations, walls were built around cities for their protection against invaders. Obviously such walls would not be effective in Israel's behalf against modern warfare, so the prophet Ezekiel surely had some other kind of *"wall"* in mind. What could this mean by today's standards? That's the issue.

We must see the spiritual side of this verse in order to get its intended meaning. It seems rather clear to me that these 'walls' allude to the fact that Israel has allies who help protect her. There are two main nations today which continue to stand by Israel — Canada and America. In fact, if it were not for these, modern Israel would probably be gone already. But here's the main point I want you to see: looking at the above verse again, note that *"Gog"* doesn't come until the *"walls"* are gone! If this is what a *"wall"* really means, we can only conclude America and Canada (the British remnant) will have to be removed <u>before</u> *Gog* invades Israel. From Russia's perspective, this makes good sense. Russia has already indicated she wants to avoid an all-out, direct confrontation with us which, they fear, could result in world-wide devastation. But once we are out of the way, then "*Gog*" — whoever that is — will move against Israel.

Because of Russia's fear of their own demise should they have a direct battle with Canada and America, it seems quite logical to me that our final defeat will come from some other source than her. Russia may very well supply the weaponry to the nation which responds to the inspiration of this "beast", but avoiding direct involvement.

The main revelation here is that the two witnesses (the "*walls*" of Israel) will be destroyed <u>before</u> Gog invades Israel. This may be the most important point of enlightenment in my entire book, insofar as the chronology of "last-days" events are concerned. I say this because almost all modern, Christian seers say the <u>next</u> main event on the prophetic agenda is Gog's attack on Israel. But if I'm right about Ezekiel 38:11, you can see the fallacy of that argument. Canada and America's destruction comes <u>before</u> Russia's invasion of Israel — and I think this is prophetically important!

I'm constantly amazed at the responses of famous prophecy experts to questions from their radio audiences such as, "What about America in Bible prophecy?" Or, "Where is America while Russia invades Israel?" Their answers are invariably weak, vague and, even evasive! Equally shocking is their assumption that God was Biblically-quiet about nations whose God is the Lord, at the same time speaking prolifically about nations which [they say] the Bible alludes to — in passages far more obscure than those I'm saying portray the two witnesses! I have to suppose their rationale goes something like this: since God didn't mention "Great Britain", "Canada", or "America" by name or identify them geographically, He didn't say anything about them. I'm convinced I have already shown you far more logic to confirm the correctness of the British and the Americans as the two witnesses than they can present to prove Gog is Russia.

Typically, modern day 'prophets' criticize and deny allegorical analyses of the Bible. This makes one wonder how in the world they ever arrived at "*Gog*" being Russia, or that the "*ten horns*" of Daniel, chapter 7, is the revived Roman Empire, etc. The fact is, their spiritualized conclusions are based on far less information than I have found to support my convictions. Oh well, enough bickering. Let's look at some more evidence.

SODOM AND EGYPT

8 "And their dead bodies will lie in the street of the great city which spiritually is called Sodom and Egypt, where also our Lord was crucified."

This verse may lend the greatest support of all concerning my position on the two witnesses. Notice where the bodies lie after they are killed. John emphasized we are to think *spiritual Sodom* and *spiritual Egypt* (not the literal city of Sodom or the literal country of Egypt). The wording is obviously designed to direct our attention to the underlying <u>characteristics</u> of those places — not to their geographic locations. Now the literal-only Futurists say the two witnesses will be killed in Jerusalem. They get that from the phrase, "*where also our Lord was crucified*". Well, certainly there is no argument as to where Jesus was crucified. But note that the apostle John had just instructed us to look for the <u>spiritual</u> meaning here, even giving us two very identifiable terms to focus our thinking — "*Sodom*" and "*Egypt*".

Jesus was not crucified in either Sodom or Egypt and if John only wanted to relate that Jerusalem was the place where the dead bodies of the two witnesses would lie, why didn't he just come right out and say it? What value could there possibly be to beat-around-the-bush? What conceivable reason could the Holy Spirit have had to not name the city of "Jerusalem" if that's all He meant? It just doesn't make good sense.

The logical approach to Revelation 11:8 is to take John's pictures (i.e., Sodom and Egypt) and concentrate on the implications. Just to make sure we get the point, John even qualified Sodom and Egypt with a modifier word — *spiritual*. There's just no way that John was talking about a single town so let's 'spiritualize' his words just like we are told to do.

Jerusalem was the center of religious life. But, in Jesus' day, it had become a *"den of thieves and robbers"* and all kinds of perverse activities — even causing Jesus to weep over the city. But *Jerusalem,* thought of as the center of religious life, was John's intentional inference to us. In our day, the center of religious life must be seen on a much broader scale. It now includes entire nations, the leading ones today, evangelistically, clearly being that of Canada and America.

So, the questions are very simple: What were the characteristics of ancient Sodom and Egypt? And, how do those characteristics apply to the two locations where the dead bodies of the two witnesses shall lie after they are killed? Many things could be said in answering the first question but I believe we need to look only at the outstanding traits in order to understand what John meant for us to grasp. Let me summarize it like this:

1. Sodom is remembered for its sexual immorality, and in particular — homosexuality.

2. Egypt was always a spiritual enemy of God's order, best known for its idolatrous practices and paganism.

So, discovering what is meant by a *"street"* in a *"great city"* filled with signs and symptoms of gross IMMORALITY and IDOLATRY will lead to the correct identification of the location of the dead witnesses.

Reader, is it not plain to see that Christian Canadians and Americans live today in the home office of those very characteristics? We are the *"street"* of this *"great city"*. Look about you. Start anywhere you like — the local newspapers, television, radio, magazines (secular or Christian), your home town, the very street you live on — all will testify today to the facts that our nations have reached the pit of sexual immorality and idolatry. Immoral sin, cultic groups of all kinds, the New Age movement, even outright Satan worship, have all permeated every aspect of Canadian and American societies today. Now let's focus our microscope even finer.

SODOM

When writing the first draft of this manuscript 15 years ago, I predicted if my interpretation of the word "Sodom" in Rev. 11:8 was correct, that something would soon happen to substantiate the conviction. At that time I had no way of knowing AIDS was about to break out and become a national scandal and frightful health problem. And yet I'm not at all surprised at the occurrence. It validates that God saw all this two thousand years ago and, amazingly, it was necessary for the Holy Spirit to inspire John to write only two words in his book — *spiritual Sodom* — which would give us sufficient insight to know what was being conveyed.

I do not believe God has only recently sent AIDS as a present judgment against modern sodomites. This disease is the inherent result of the sin of sodomy. God made the judgment thousands of years ago! It has been there all the time waiting to erupt as the perverted lifestyle reached its full, widespread potential. It is as the apostle Paul said in Romans 1:27:

"And likewise also the men, leaving the natural use of the woman, burned in their lust toward one another, men with men committing what is shameful, and RECEIVING IN THEMSELVES THE PENALTY OF THEIR ERROR WHICH WAS DUE."

146

Yes, God saw AIDS a long time ago. It is an awful disease, although completely commensurate with the sinful practice which causes it. It is true that the disease is now also affecting some who are not guilty of sodomy, people who have received blood transfusions from the blood of other people with AIDS, drug users who share dirty needles with other AIDS' victims, babies born of mothers with AIDS, the spread through bi-sexuals, etc. But it is well documented where the disease started. AIDS is the direct result of the practice of sexual immorality, particularly amongst male homosexuals.

EGYPT

Canada and America are also becoming "spiritial Egypt". MOODY MONTHLY did a series of articles focusing on the rise of the cults and false religions in Northern America today. The numbers of adherents devoting their lives to these leaders and philosophies are staggering. The demons are making their last bid for the souls of human beings. Traditionally, I think no people on earth are more worship-prone than those here in America, but unfortunately it also seems many will go for anything wild and different. There is one commonality among all these cults: they don't consider the sinful nature of mankind. Demons and false teachers know that if you avoid that one fact, you can bring in 'believers' by the millions. Taken collectively, these groups spell *spiritual Egypt.*

One could perhaps write a book on just this one verse of Scripture (Rev. 11:8). However, I believe any open-eyed Christian can relate to the reality of my brief statement here. **Canadians and Americans are living in spiritual *Sodom* and in spiritual *Egypt.*** Just as Jesus died in the ancient world's center of worship (His beloved city of Jerusalem), which had in that day become a *Sodom* and *Egypt,* so also His *two witnesses,* Christian-Canada and Christian-America, will die in the "*street*" of our beloved "*city*".

Now, this thinking should put to rest forever any conclusions that I am saying Canada and America are altogether Christian nations. Obviously, we are not. However, the *"witnesses"* of Revelation chapter 11 are here within the confines of these nations. It is they who God has used, and will do so until the end, to reach the ends of the earth with the Gospel of Christ. You and I, brothers and sisters in Christ, are the *"witnesses"*. How does the label feel? What does the understanding do to your sense of responsibility? What shall you do with the time and energy you have that remains?

Of course God's Hand of protection and blessing is upon every person and nation in the world, and especially so upon Christians, regardless of where they are. But nowhere has His blessed-touch been so evident as here in Canada and America. It has not been because of who we are but because of Whose we are. God did the choosing. It is He Who has done the work here, in and through the people He anointed. And, for the most part, without our even knowing it!

THE ROAD TO EMMAUS

After His resurrection, Jesus once chose to walk with two particular disciples on the road to Emmaus. I liken that incident to God's choice of the two witnesses. They had nothing to do with the encounter. Theirs was only to hear what He had to say to them. Here's the Scriptural account:

"And behold, two of them went that same day to a village called Emmaus, which was about seven miles from Jerusalem. And they talked together of all these things which had happened. And so it was, while they conversed together and reasoned, that Jesus Himself drew near and went with them. But their eyes were restrained, so that they did not know Him." (Luke 24: 13 - 16) But then look at verse 27 and 31.

148

*27. And beginning at Moses and all the Prophets, He
expounded to them in all the Scriptures the things concerning
Himself."*

*31. "And their eyes were opened and they knew Him; and
He vanished from their sight."*

It could be these two witnesses commenced what eventually
grew to be the two national witnesses, them handing the "baton"
on to others, until eventually it reached the final stage of two
nations. The parallelism is strikingly similar. Who can deny the
reality that Jesus has chosen to be with Canada (the British
remnant) and America in a special way? And like those two
disciples, we have not recognized His unique walk with us,
although as we went "down the road" we have enjoyed the fact
He has clearly and especially opened the Scriptures to us.
Yes, we have known His wonderful grace and love as it was
shed abroad in our hearts on a national scale, but somehow we
have not been fully cognizant of the fact that Jesus has singled
us out from among the other nations for a unique ministry (like
the two individual disciples Jesus singled out from among the
others). I really believe the two disciples were a spiritual
forecast of America and the British.

God has not favored Britain and America due to inherent
goodness. We are no more pure than anyone else, individually
or collectively. True goodness is revealed only by the Presence
of Christ in the lives of His people. Near the end of Jesus'
ministry, the apostle John realized Jesus had "loved" him
specially. It has been the same with us as nations.

"HOORAY! THE WITNESSES ARE DEAD! LET'S HAVE A PARTY!"

*9 "And those from the peoples, tribes, tongues, and nations
will see their dead bodies three and a half days, and not
allow their dead bodies to be put into graves.*

10 And those who dwell on the earth will rejoice over them, make merry, and send gifts to one another, because these two prophets tormented those who dwell on the earth."

Many times individuals who receive a special blessing, such as a firstborn son for example, are scorned by other family members. This is also true on a national scale. The blessedness of the British and the USA has been like a thorn in the side to many other nations, especially hostile enemies. From the beginning of the national witnesses (my guess being some 1250+ years ago), starting with England, our greatness and endowments have been incomparable. Ironically, other nations seem to know it perhaps even better than we! Political power, economic power and the power of the Gospel eminating from our lands, have reached nearly every region of the world. Some have received it gratefully, some not so gratefully.

Satan is building a throne to sit on and true Christianity is his only threat to that end. The devil also knows where the "witnesses" are today, and where they have been over the centuries. At various times throughout the Christian age, he has put it in the hearts of ungodly leaders to destroy us, but until our "testimony is finished", he can't do it. However, when our course is completed, the destruction will come and those who hate us will rejoice. That is what the above verses predict. In fact, they will be so happy they will *"send gifts to one another"*.

But why do they rejoice? Not understanding 'the blessing' aspect of course, from our opponents' perspective, the British and the Americans have simply hoarded and greedily consumed the best of what the world has to offer. (This has sometimes been true, by the way.) So, with us out of the way, now the rest of the world will have their chance to be on top for a while. You see, so much of the world's abundance being at our disposal has been, and still is, a "torment" to the others that dwell on the earth. For that reason, a world-wide celebration will break out at our destruction.

Also, the Godly-joy and Gospel-proclamation which still goes forth from here acts as a hindrance to those (both here and abroad) who violently oppose the true and living God we proclaim. Knowingly or not, those in false religions of the world are Satan's puppets. Thus, when the two witnesses are killed, they will surely be delighted, believing their "god" is the true god, made evident by the fact of our death! Such, we have seen, is the thinking of Muslims who regard their mosque in Jerusalem as an obvious and tangible stamp of God's (Allah) approval of Islam as the true religion. (Today, one-fifth of the world's population are Muslim, and growing! Certainly many in this group will be thrilled when we are gone — maybe even the cause of it!?)

WHY NO GRAVES?

Verse nine says that the dead bodies of the two witnesses will not be put into graves. Now why do you suppose John would tell us that? What value is there in knowing the bodies aren't buried? There is another clue here which will lead us further into the correct understanding of this whole chapter.

The Futurists say that after "Enoch and Elijah", (or "Moses and Elijah"), are killed, those who kill them will want to use the incident to demonstrate to the whole world just who really is in control. So, the murderers will allow everyone to see the dead men by focusing television cameras on their bodies for 3 1/2 days, broadcasting the images into television sets all over the world. This would be quite a grandstand play, if true. As usual though, I have trouble with this line of thinking.

I believe there will be millions of dead bodies because of nuclear blasts! Oh, I know the news media and certain politicians say there will never be a limited nuclear war, believing that once it starts the whole world would be destroyed. That's humanistic reasoning and bears no Scriptural evidence. I suspect there may be a continental atomic attack on Canada and America and that's what would eliminate God's two witnesses. I don't know who will do it but I believe it may happen this way. And when it does, what nation would want to "come take a spoil" from a land devastated by nuclear blasts where radiation lingers long after the attack? That would explain why no one puts the bodies into graves. The only ones around will be those who remain in the land and they won't be too thrilled about burying bodies either. It'll be hard enough for them just trying to survive as they seek to reach safer areas as far as possible from the sites of the atomic explosions.

So, we have several conditions prevalent today which indicate we are fast-approaching the end of the two-witnesses' testimonial. The nations are crying "*peace and safety*" (peace talks, disarmament agreements etc.), there is an undeniable apostasy in our lands (falling away from Biblical faith), our beloved countries are filled with symptoms of sodomy and idolatry, and we have animosity growing in the world against the remaining Christian witness in Canada and America. These are the very characteristics which must be present to be in line with prophetic, Scriptural revelation.

It grieves me to say it but I honestly believe the final destiny of Canada and America may soon come. That is not to say that we must not resist it in every possible way. Christians need to pray unceasingly. We need to repent of our sinfulness and we must recognize our negligence in having allowed the humanists to become so influential in all systems of our societies today. We need to become involved at every level of government, seeking to restore that which has been lost, and above all, we need to be proclaiming the Gospel to a lost and dying world more fervently than every before. But even if we do all these things, there is a day coming when God will allow the "beast" which ascends out of the bottomless pit to "*make war*", "*overcome*" and "*kill*" the two witnesses. But do not let this word lessen your day, Christian friends! A brighter day is coming for us!

RESURRECTION BEGINS

11 "And after three and a half days the breath of life from God entered them, and they stood on their feet, and great fear fell on those who saw them."

Earlier, I pointed out how often the number 11 is associated with my understanding of prophecy. Isn't it interesting that the happiest note in my book "just happens" to be Rev. 11:11?

To remind you now of the Futuristic viewpoint — that God will raise up two individual witnesses to do a particular testimonial for Him at the time of the end, then lasting a literal 1260 days. If this is so too, I believe their ministry will begin at the death of the two national witnesses.

In the above verse we see that the dead bodies of the national witnesses will come to life after three and one-half "days", (with long-range application still in force, this would indicate 3 1/2 years). Immediately upon the death of the national witnesses, the two individual witnesses would commence their 3 1/2 literal-year testimony which would last the duration of the same 3 1/2 years the national witnesses lie dead; then they too would be killed and remain dead three and one-half literal days. Their death might possibly occur in literal Jerusalem. And if so, you now see how, and when, the Futuristic aspect of Revelation really begins to fit in.

(Do you follow the reasoning of this explanation of the Law of Double Reference? This isn't double-talk, folks. It's double-application. It's the Law of Double Reference in operation. It's not some bizarre story I cooked up either. It's very Biblical and anyone who seriously studies the prophetic word of God should recognize this is nothing more, nor less, than a repetition of the pattern laid down in the Old Testament. Careful thinking will insure your grasping it.)

153

THE TRUMPET BEGINS TO SOUND!

Looking back at verse 11, we see that the dead stand upon their feet as the *"breath of life from God"* entered them. This must be the beginning of the rapture! Now if we read carefully, we will see that the rapture will be a <u>progression</u> of events, rather than a single happening. In fact, it covers everything described in the group of verses, 11 - 15. Want some proof of this? Look again at Rev. 10:7.

> *"...but in the <u>**DAYS**</u> of the sounding of the seventh angel, (i.e., the LAST TRUMPET) when he is <u>**ABOUT TO SOUND**</u> the mystery of God would be finished, as He has declared to His servants the prophets."*

Note the apostle says during the *day<u>s</u>* (plural) of the *sounding...* Therefore, even though we know that when God "energizes" Christian bodies at the end of the age causing an immediate transformation to take place, nevertheless, the above passages strongly suggest there is a <u>sequence</u> of events, not merely one, momentary occurrence. Thus, it appears the "changing of the guard" will last at least a few days. (More on that later).

[This idea may very well come as a surprise to most readers. It was for me. I certainly had no preconceived notion about this progression concept. I was reading this passage one day and suddenly, there it was. I decided a long time ago not to argue with the Word of God. If it says something which goes against what I supposedly already understood, it doesn't particularly bother me to re-check my thinking. When I did that here, I had no problem agreeing with what John said and simply took it at face value, *"...in the <u>DAYS</u> of the sounding, ...the mystery will be finished."*]

154

Now let's look at the two passages most often considered when thinking in terms of the rapture. (1 Thes. 4: 15 - 17 and 1 Corinthians 15: 51 & 52)

15 "For this we say to you by the word of the Lord, that we who are alive and remain until the coming of the Lord will by no means precede those who are asleep. For the Lord Himself will descend from heaven with a shout, with the voice of an archangel, and with the trumpet of God. And the dead in Christ will rise first. Then we who are alive and remain shall be caught up together with them in the clouds to meet the Lord in the air. And thus we shall always be with the Lord." Then, Paul tells us in 1 Corinthians:
51 "Behold, I tell you a mystery: We shall not all sleep, but we shall all be changed-
52 "in a moment, in the twinkling of an eye, at the last trumpet. For the trumpet will sound, and the dead will be raised incorruptible, and we shall be changed."

These two passages help clear up the matter of the mysteries of the rapture. Actually it really isn't complicated, but in my opinion, many writers and expositors have made it so. We are told the time of the event will be *"at the last trumpet"*. I take that just as it is, the LAST TRUMPET. And what is the last trumpet? It's the seventh trumpet, of course, which will be discussed in Rev. 11:15.

Now, I've heard some otherwise terrific preachers try to make Paul's statement here mean all kinds of things other than what it simply says. They say the *"last trumpet"* doesn't really mean the seventh trumpet, even though the seventh trumpet is the last trumpet! It supposedly means some other last trumpet. That's confusing and totally wipes out common sense. The fact is, there can be only one *last trumpet* and it would logically be the last of the numbered trumpets described by the apostle John in Revelation 11:15 — the seventh. And, its sounding signals the rapture. It's that simple.

155

Recall now that the two national witnesses will be dead for 3 1/2 years, (the same 1260 days the two individual witnesses will be ministering) at the end of which their dead bodies will begin to raise up as the Spirit of God gives them life. This being the case, and in line with the above passage from First Thessalonians, which indicates that the "*dead*" rise before the witnesses who weren't killed, one can come to only one logical conclusion: **THE RAPTURE BEGINS AT THE MID-WAY POINT OF THE FINAL SEVEN YEAR COUNTDOWN!**

Therefore, by simple deduction, leaving all mental pre-conditioning aside, I can only conclude that the Bible teaches a Mid-Tribulation[8] rapture concept, not Pre-Trib, not Post-Trib. Both the latter views set certain Scriptures at odds against themselves which is absolutely not allowable. Once you've got the right answer, all the Scriptures will fit, not just those one might use to establish his already-decided viewpoint.

Regardless of all you've heard about how God allows our varying interpretations, etc., etc., the truth is, there's not but one valid answer concerning when the rapture will come. I certainly don't expect my analysis to be taken without reservation, but I am convinced the views presented above does less violence to God's Word when all the Scriptures are considered than do the typical, Futuristic beliefs.

---

[8]Ed Moore, author, pastor and prophecy teacher, in his recent book "APOCALYPSE WHEN", has also taken a "mid-Trib" rapture position. His overall stand on prophecy is not like my own but it's interesting that other writers are re-thinking their eschatology these days.

ASCENT OF THE TWO WITNESSES

12 "And they heard a loud voice from heaven saying to them, "Come up here." And they ascended to heaven in a cloud, and their enemies saw them."

Recall that Futurists believe Revelation 4:1 pictures the rapture. The apostle John was caught up to heaven "in the spirit" at that point and then saw, and/or heard, the rest of what we read about in Revelation — a 'preview' of coming attractions. At least part of the basis for this viewpoint is that the Church is no longer mentioned by name from this verse onward, therefore the assumption is made that Christians have been removed from the earth.

I, of all people, can't criticize the Futurists for over-spiritualizing. It's true that the word Church does not appear after Rev. 4:1 so their conclusion is reasonable. However, the Church is described in so many other ways after this, I have no difficulty believing it is still here during part of the final seven year period. Of course, the real reason Futurists take this position is because the whole "pre-trib" concept says the Church cannot be here during the dispensation of the Seals, Trumpets and the Vials, which begin at Revelation 6. Thus, they need a Scripture to fit how they see Revelation as a whole. Rev. 4:1 is the best they have found.

But notice how Revelation 11:11 & 12 above more appropriately agree with 1 Thessalonians, chapter four's prediction, which says the *"dead shall rise first"*. The ones who *"heard a loud voice from heaven saying to them, 'Come up here"',* were none other than those who had been dead for 3 1/2 *days* (meaning years). And, by the Historical stand I take, those were very specifically the bodies of dead Christians in the countries of Canada and America. Since we know the dead rise before the alive, we must therefore conclude those Christians which remain alive all over the world can't be raptured prior to the point in time as described here in Revelation 11:12.

157

A "SPIRITUAL" POSSIBILITY

I hope what I'm about to say doesn't confuse you but I have another idea relative to this verse which probably came to mind due to the fact the enemies of the two witnesses don't allow their dead bodies to be put in graves. This verse could be seen as an inference to a time of great apostasy. Imagine the Church in Canada and America becoming so backslidden that they become "dead", spiritually speaking — i.e., people going through religious motions but possessing little, true spiritual life. If this were the case, their "dead" bodies would not be put into graves because they wern't actually dead at all, physically speaking. This idea may not be the correct Biblical meaning, but it is happening nevertheless.

If this is a correct interpretation of the passage, carrying this thinking on to its logical conclusion, after 3 1/2 years the *Spirit of life* enters the *"spiritually dead"* giving them new life. This would be predicting genuine repentance in those who were formerly *"dead"*.

Even if this is an LODR' meaning of the passage, it wouldn't really change my overall understanding of the identity of the two witnesses. It simply forecasts a revival for Northern America and what Christian wouldn't want to see this happen? If this explanation is true, verse 11 says those who were formerly *"dead"* (spiritually speaking) shall rise to their feet and their enemies will see them do it. This would mean the spiritual, downward spiral in Canada and America will come to an end and, furthermore, that our *"enemies"* would see the coming revival. ('Enemies' here refers to anti-Christian humanists here among us including also all those like them in the rest of the world).

Canadian and American Christians should be working towards making this become a reality, regardless of whether this discussion correctly interprets the Scripture or not. I'm convinced the only reason our countries haven't already been destroyed is because of the presence of the true and faithful, Christian-remnant here. Therefore, it behooves us to be diligent about making restorative moves at every front of opportunity. It begins as each individual Christian pursues a greater degree of commitment.

(Now reader, don't forget that the last few paragraphs are just suggestions. I admit it deviates a bit from my overall thesis concerning Biblical prophecy in the historical sense. It could be that both meanings are correct---i.e., that "dead" here means literal dead bodies as well as indicating a time of spiritual "deadness". In any event, let's now get back to the main road.)

EARTHQUAKE

13 "And in the same hour there was a great earthquake, and a tenth of the city fell; and in the earthquake seven thousand men were killed. And the rest were afraid and gave glory to the God of heaven."

Several key phrases are found in this verse:

1. *"same hour"*
2. *"great earthquake"*
3. *"a tenth of the city fell"*
4. *"7,000 men were killed"*
5. *"the "rest" were afraid and gave glory to God"*

As time progresses we see the prophetic "signs" and "seasons" of the last days clearer but I think we can all agree the exact timing of things remains blurred. For example, we see that this earthquake occurs during the *"same hour"*, which implies it happens near the same time but not necessarily the precise moment the dead bodies rise.

To add to the puzzle, when the witnesses are killed, then comes this shattering earthquake which brings its own awesome devastation, killing "*7,000 men*". Some will say, "Lance, this must occur in a single city for only 7,000 people will be killed, thus negating the national-witness idea." I must admit being troubled, at first, with this passage.

But then one day I checked the literal meaning of this verse in a Greek New Testament. A word-for-word translation says "*7,000 names of men*" will be killed. I thought it rather odd John said "*names of men*" rather than just "*men*". As I was pondering it, this thought suddenly sprang into my mind: many men have the same last name! There could be 5,000 "Smiths" killed. That would be one "*name of men*". There could be 4,000 "Jones" killed,...and so on. Therefore, the passage could be saying that there will actually be hundreds of thousands killed, perhaps millions, and that the total number of the peoples' last name will be exactly 7,000!

Or, there is yet another way of seeing the prophetic meaning of this: 7,000 is a special Biblical number. By itself, seven means perfection, or completeness. 7,000 is 7 multiplied by 1,000. Could it be that this 7,000 is simply God's way of revealing an amplified form of completeness, like the 'nth degree' of a situation, rather than a literal number of persons?

In any event, from the Historical viewpoint, this idea made the passage come alive for me. There just had to be a specific inference for the Holy Spirit to instruct John to include the phrase "*names of men*", rather than simply saying "7,000 men", which, I reasoned, is what would have been stated if the only intent was to convey the understanding of 7,000 literal people.

I was also somewhat perplexed by the phrase, "*the rest were afraid and gave glory to the God of heaven*". Are we to believe that many former-unbelievers will suddenly be saved! I think that's unlikely. No, we must assume these who glorify God are already Christians. A possible explanation is that these people are those "alive in Christ" who remain a little while after the *"dead in Christ"* rise to meet the Lord in the air. Remember, in 1 Thessalonians 4:15 we are told the *"alive will by no means precede those who are asleep."* And in verse 16, further emphasis is made that the *"alive"* will leave at a later time as it says, *"And the dead in Christ will rise first."* Finally, in verse 17 we are told, *"THEN, we who are alive and remain shall be caught up..."*

The word *remain* is very revealing: the dictionary's definition of the word is 'to stay behind or in the same place'; another says, 'to be left after the removal'. These simple definitions suggest that there will be a definite lag-time between rapturing the *"dead"* and those *"alive"* at the mid-way point of the final, seven-year countdown period.

If you follow my logic, note just how carefully we must read the Scriptures before accepting someone's interpretation of what a passage means. I have always assumed, because of what others told me, that the *"alive"* in Christ immediately follow the resurrected *"dead"* in Christ at the rapture. But Rev. 11:13, combined with the 1 Thessalonians passage, adds strength to the idea that God, for reasons He has chosen not to fully reveal to us, will keep the two events separated by a definite period of time. The next few verses may help us understand this further.

WOE # THREE

"The second woe is past. Behold, the third woe is coming quickly." Verse 14.

You'll recall John told us of three *"woes"*. The first I've identified as WW2. The second, just discussed, is the death of the "two witnesses", which included the devastating earthquake. (This earthquake, by the way, could be the nuclear attack on the two witnesses). Lastly, verse 14 here tells of the third woe. I believe this is a prediction of Satan's final reign as the anti-Christ, which will include basically everything during the last three and one-half years of the final countdown.

161

(I continue to treat the common concept of the tribulation with respect, and yet, as you well know by now, with specific reservations about whether it fully satisfies the overall Biblical prophetic message. The fact is, we have been in the historical tribulation for almost 1260 years now! What the Futurists call the tribulation is, to me, simply the last of the "last days", a more intense recapitulation lasting for 1260 literal days (3 1/2 years), spiritually paralleling what has already transpired in the previous 1260-year, historical sense. So, basically, that which will be discussed over the next several chapters will embrace everything John captions as "THE THIRD WOE". This will be the last half of the final, seven year Tribulation period, which will include the 200,000,000 soldiers who invade the Middle East for the Battle of Armageddon, finalizing then with *God's Wrath* put upon all earth's remaining, wicked, unrepentant mankind; i.e., the Vials).

"15 And the seventh angel sounded: And there were loud voices in heaven, saying, 'The kingdoms of this world have become the kingdoms of our Lord and of His Christ, and He shall reign forever and ever!'"

This verse kind of wraps up the Rapture issue. Pictured is the Seventh (and last) trumpet. Scripture presents no more trumpets after this one. Don't forget this Biblical fact! Remember, there are many who refuse to accept the 7th as being the last Trumpet. Don't ask me how they arrive at a conclusion which says the last Trumpet doesn't really mean the last Trumpet, but I'm not kidding you, that's the pre-tribulation-rapture position.

Well, I prefer to accept it just as the Scripture says it. The seventh Trumpet of Revelation 11 is the last of the sequence of seven Trumpets which started back in Revelation chapter 8 and I see no reason not to call the *last* Trumpet, the **Last Trumpet!**

Now, let me show you why the Futurists probably don't like to interpret the seventh as the last Trumpet. Looking back over our study thus far, we see that we are now past the seven Seals and six of the Trumpets. We noted that the Seals and

Trumpets followed, sequentially and logically, the main historical events of the past several centuries. Now, let's look at a plainly stated verse of Scripture which upsets the Futuristic apple-cart. I believe, and even the Futurists agree to this, that 1 Corinthians 15: 51 & 52 describes the last Trumpet and that it signals the final rapture of the Church.

51 "Behold, I tell you a mystery: We shall not all sleep, but we shall all be changed-
52 in a moment, in the twinkling of an eye, AT THE LAST TRUMPET. For the trumpet will sound, and the dead will be raised incorruptible, and we shall be changed."

I see no reason not to take this passage at face value. We should never allow our allegorizations to cancel the obvious intent of a plain passage. The literal passages set the standards and define for us the intended meaning of the more obscure, prophetic statements. Such, I think, is the case here in 1 Corinthians. Surely the "LAST TRUMPET" here refers to the final, seventh Trumpet of Revelation 11, which, we have already learned, sounds at the mid-way point of the final seven year count-down period.

Recalling verses 11 - 15 again, we saw that the Rapture is not a one-moment-in-time event. It seems to occur over a short span of time but exactly how long, we just don't know. The important thing is to see the overall picture God has given us and leave the finer details to Him. He always keeps enough to Himself to let us know that **He** is the God Who is putting all this together!

HEAVEN'S "HALLELUJAH CHORUS"

16 "And the twenty-four elders who sat before God on their thrones fell on their faces and worshiped God,

163

17 saying: 'We give you thanks O Lord God Almighty, The One who is and who was and who is to come, Because You have taken Your great power and have reigned."

When important transitional things happen in God's heaven, (or when they are about to occur here on earth), the elders and other heavenly beings are always on the scene in a big way. It seems as if they are God's 'Amen Corner'! These obviously know that a long-awaited day of reckoning has come and they sing and shout about it. They realize God is about to finish His plan of the ages, bringing together His Heavenly Kingdom, including then — saved humanity. That's the greatest event Christian believers ever anticipated! However, as usual, there is another side to this coin.

GOD'S WRATH IS ANNOUNCED

18 "And the nations were angry, and Your wrath has come, And the time of the dead, that they should be judged, And that you should reward Your servants the prophets and the saints, and those who fear Your name, small and great, And should destroy those who destroy the earth."

A terrific stirring occurs in my spirit as I look forward to the conditions described in verses 16 and 17, and then read the contrast of verse 18. On the one hand, we see a picture of the most glorious event possible will have been reached. However, concurrently, it is the worst time in history — for the unsaved! (See verse 18.) Just when the saints will be honored by going into the presence of the Lord, back on planet earth will begin the most grievous time in mankind's history. The reign of the anti-Christ will reach its greatest height of power and influence at this time. Then in the wake of the anti-Christ comes the WRATH OF GOD upon wicked mankind! Oh Christian friends, we must reach the unsaved — TODAY!

There is a very important technical point to see here. Do you recall back in the sixth Seal (WW1), John explains there that those under attack in Europe were crying out that the *"wrath of the Lamb"* had come. We have noted that Futurists use that verse to establish their position that the Seals and Trumpets describe the beginning of God's Wrath. But, we must remember <u>who</u> said that. It was those experiencing war devastation, the worst in history up to that time. But, the Bible establishes *God's Wrath* with the above verse, Revelation 11:18, which will some day be proclaimed by the 24 elders in heaven who say that God's Wrath has come. (Read the above verse again).

The fact is, God tells no one but the elders in heaven when it's time for His *Wrath* to come. The <u>men</u> described in the sixth Seal were mistaken. Things were tough during the tribulations of man during those days but that was nothing compared to what will occur when the seven Vials will be brought upon the earth. The Vials spell out God's Wrath, not the Seals and Trumpets. (We will discuss this later.)

GOD'S FAITHFULNESS (Verse 19)

"And the temple of God was opened in heaven, and the ark of His covenant was seen in His temple. And there came lightnings, noises, thunderings, an earthquake and great hail."

I like the description given this verse by Jamieson, Fausset and Brown's "Commentary on the Whole Bible": They said,

"As in the first verse, the earthly sanctuary was measured, so here it's heavenly antitype is laid open, and the anti-type above to the ark of the covenant in the Holiest Place below is seen, the pledge of God's faithfulness to His covenant in saving His people and punishing their and His enemies."

CHAPTER TWELVE

THE WOMAN AND HER CHILD

As previously noted, most of the book of Revelation is written in such a way as to present a continually-unfolding description of events which began during the first century, and continues up to the end of time as we now know it. For this reason, unfortunately, many prophetic writers follow the rule that *everything you read in Revelation must be a description of a later time period than all previous passages.* However, there are some very important exceptions to this format. In fact, if one insists on absolute non-deviation from this general rule of progression, then chapter twelve is one which can't be understood — period.

There are also other chapters which prevent this ironclad approach. For example, we saw that by the time the Sixth Seal was opened we were up to WW1. Then we found chapter 11 presents a description of the two witnesses who began their 'testimony' in the early 700s. Thus, chapter 11 discusses events of the 8th century and yet an earlier chapter covered things clear up to the 1900s — a terrible dilemma if no re-tracing of history is allowable in a later chapter!

Next, we shall see that Revelation Twelve gives a generalized recapitulation of God's plan of the ages relative to the nation Israel. It reveals some of her troubles in a very broad sense, plus provides an explanation of what her main, God-designed purpose would be.

It is amazing how much wisdom God can pack into seventeen short statements. Let's look now at the very interesting way John describes it, noting just how far God allowed him to see into the past, and future. It is a view which clearly and thoroughly refutes the above-described 'rule of exegesis'.

*1 "And a great sign appeared in heaven: a woman clothed
with the sun, with the moon under her feet, and on her head
a crown of twelve stars."
2 "And being with child, she cried out in labor and in pain
to give birth."*

In Genesis 37:9, there is a description of a man named
Joseph, the next youngest of the twelve sons of Jacob. Now
Jacob's name was later changed to Israel, the indication being
that all the nation of Israel would come from him. That is,
Jacob's twelve sons would become the foundation of the twelve
tribes of Israel.

Joseph once had a dream, seeing the *sun* as his father, the
moon as his mother, and 11 *stars* which signified his 11 brothers.
Joseph foresaw them all eventually giving obeisance to him.
And as we study the Scriptures about this family, we learn that
the dream was truly prophetic. Joseph did indeed rise to a
great position in Egypt under King Pharaoh. Later, Jacob and
the other eleven sons would come to seek food and counsel
from Joseph, and did, in fact, bow down to him. (It is
important to note in this Old Testament pre-figurement, that
they did not at first recognize Joseph.)

John's vision was very similar to Joseph's dream. Once the
ancient, foreshadowing model is seen, it becomes clear that the
"woman" John saw could only be the nation Israel. The twelve
stars John saw would be the same "sons of Jacob" in Joseph's
dream; except, in John's case, the twelve stars comprise the
whole nation which, collectively, he identified as the *"woman"*.
Another point which needs to be observed here is this: Just as
Joseph's father and brothers didn't recognize him at first in
Egypt, so likewise national Israel didn't recognize their
"brother", Jesus, as the one to whom they must eventually give
obeisance if they wish to receive His "food".

The apostle Paul describes vividly the spiritual state of
national Israel in Romans 11: 25 - 27: (This remains in force
even till this day.)

25 "For I do not desire, brethren, that you should be ignorant of this mystery, lest you should be wise in your own opinion, that hardening in part has happened to Israel until the fulness of the Gentiles has come in."
26 "And so all Israel will be saved, as it is written:
'The Deliverer will come out of Zion, And He will turn away ungodliness from Jacob.
27 "For this is My covenant with them, When I shall take away their sins."

Here Paul is predicting national Israel will eventually see and understand who their Messiah is. If not for the fact that God's Word declares it, it seems incomprehensible that the vast majority of national Israel can't see that Jesus was their Old Testament-predicted Messiah. But, that's the nature of God's sovereignty in action. It is for the benefit of the rest of the world, the Gentiles, that God has seen fit to allow Israel to be in the state of spiritual blindness these past 2,000 years. (Suggested reading: Romans, chapters 9, 10 & 11.) After reading this, I think you will probably have a greater appreciation of Israel and, more importantly, praise God for this fantastic piece of Great-Commission strategy.

Israel was the nation which God chose, beginning with Jacob's grandfather, Abraham, to deliver God's total revelation to all humanity. For 2,000 years God called and anointed kings, prophets, and priests of Israel and through them, painstakingly gave His Wisdom we have recorded in 39 books we today call the Old Testament. Thus, God chose one nation to deliver His plan of salvation, not only for Israel, but eventually all people.

The irony is that the nation responsible for all this, except for a remnant, virtually missed the point! They remained hardened-of-heart and refused to believe their own prophets, even promoting the crucifixion of their promised Deliverer, Jesus Christ! No nation (other than perhaps the British Commonwealth or the USA) has been more blessed than Israel.

God "clothed" them with every good thing. Being "*clothed with the sun*" implies Israel was surrounded and protected by God Himself. Being "*clothed with the moon*" (the moon being closer to earth than the sun) alludes to having God-given, physical, earthly benefits.

In short, Israel had it all. God's chosen people. The problem with them was that they thought all these benefits were either of their own making, or resulted from inherent goodness. They were lifted up in pride and subsequently (again, except for a remnant) God elected to leave them in a state of spiritual blindness during the whole Christian era.

THE 'TRAVAIL' AND THE 'CHILD'

Israel went through tremendous struggles and pain from 2,000 B.C. up until the birth of Christ. The *wilderness* years, continuous battles with surrounding nations, the captivities, etc., all attest to the reality of this conclusion. The combination of these facts relate to John's comment that the woman "*cried out in labor and in pain to give birth*" (see verse two above). The Lord God told the serpent (Satan) that some day a child would be born of a woman who would ultimately spell his destruction. We read in Genesis 3:14 & 15.

> 14 "*And the Lord God said unto the serpent, Because thou hast done this, thou art cursed above all cattle, and above every beast of the field; upon thy belly shalt thou go, and dust shalt thou eat all the days of thy life:*"
> 15 "*And I will put enmity between thee and the woman and between thy seed and her seed; it shall bruise thy head, and thou shalt bruise his heel,...*"

Satan is smart. He knew from that time on, if he could stop the "*seed*" from developing, he could prevent the final crushing of his own "*head*". Volumns could be written just discussing his attempts to stop this prophecy from occurring as described

169

throughout the Old Testament. For now though, it is only important that we focus in and see that the intended meaning and relationship between the *"woman"* and her *"travail"* described here in Revelation 12, is the very same *"woman"* God alluded to in the Garden of Eden. (This *"woman"* shifts her identity from the first woman in the Garden, Eve, who later gave birth to righteous Seth, then broadening in meaning to include the whole nation of Israel, and finally narrows to one *"woman"* again (Mary) who gave birth to "THE SEED" — Jesus.

So, in summary of Revelation Twelve, verses 1 & 2, we can be definite on these conclusions: (1) A certain *"child"* would be born through a particular nation. (2) Israel would be the nation who, through great pre-birthing difficulties, is seen here as the *"woman"* that was responsible for delivering this *"child"*. (3) Furthermore, the *"child"* can be none other than the Lord Jesus Christ Himself, as will be made even plainer as we proceed.

(The wide assortment other writers give the identities of this woman and her child is amazing. I won't confuse you here with all those views. However, concerning the understanding as given above, I only ask that you search the Scriptures and see if the thoughts and ideas presented align with God's Word.)

THE DEVIL AND HIS ARMY OF DEMONS

3 "And another sign appeared in heaven: behold, a great, fiery red dragon having seven heads and ten horns, and seven crowns on his heads."
4 "And his tail drew a third of the stars of heaven and threw them to the earth. And the dragon stood before the woman who was ready to give birth, to devour her Child as soon as it was born."

Most evangelical Christians agree that this passage is speaking of Satan (the "*red dragon*") and his demons (the "*stars from heaven*"). Since even the Futurists agree here, I feel impressed to point out that these two verses greatly weaken their own stand of the literal-only interpretation of the book of Revelation. If their view is followed completely, i.e., with the assumption that everything from Revelation 4:1 onward describes only the last seven-year tribulation period, then this chapter completely destroys their position. If the "*red dragon*" is the devil and if the "*stars*" here are fallen angels (demons), which most agree to be so, this passage can't possibly be referring to some future time from now because the devil and his angels have been here since Eden!

The apostle John was getting a post-view of what happened a long time ago when he saw the "*dragon*" and the "*stars*" thrown to the earth. However, some hold to the notion that Satan and the fallen angels, although already found guilty of treason and sent to live in the space among the stars we see (including earth), somehow, still have access to come and go as they please into God's heavenly throne until we get to the time forecast by John here in Rev. 12. I don't buy it.

(It is believed by most students of Biblical prophecy that this passage reveals that Lucifer (Satan), before his fall, enticed one third of all God's angels to agree with and follow him in his act of rebellion against God. I accept this concept but an interesting thought has just occurred to me. If the predicted time here is yet future, as the Futurists claim, why are demons called "*fallen* {past tense} *angels*"? Think about it.)

THE "MULTIFACETED" DRAGON

John mentions that the "*red dragon*" (Satan) had seven heads, ten horns and seven crowns on his heads. In the next chapter we will see a *beast* which has seven heads, ten horns and ten crowns. Although they are not identical, these "beasts" must be inter-related in some way. I'll reserve part of my explanation until chapter thirteen. But the multi-headed, multi-horned, multi-crowned "*dragon*" here in Revelation 12 seems to be a picture of the spiritual heirarchy of Satan's regime. Therefore, since these two verses refer mainly to the devil and his army, one reaches the inevitable conclusion that John got a glimpse of Satan's entire strategic forces in the spiritual realm.

I think for every spiritual reality in the heavenlies, there is a physical, earthly counterpart. Watch this carefully now: Satan has his demonic armies set up in a certain power structure (similar to nations and governments), over which are leaders, commanders, etc. We must remember that Lucifer didn't keep his first estate, whatever that was. He rebelled and subsequently has tried to usurp god-like authority over mankind. Ever since his fall, Satan has desired and plotted to superimpose his spiritual heirarchy upon the world and its human systems, in order to have tangible evidence of his power to control and influence people here on earth. He wants to be worshipped as god. If this presumption is correct, it should be possible to analyze worldly powers and determine which nations and powers (historical and current) would best fit Satan's ways, ways clearly described in the Bible. If such a system exists and can be identified, much credibility would be added to my overall position on prophecy.

SATAN TRIES TO KILL THE "WOMAN'S" CHILD

Verse four says the *dragon* attempted to devour the *woman's Child* (Jesus), as soon as it was born. How did the devil try to destroy the baby Jesus? To fulfill his desires among humans, Satan usually lures certain people whose fallen nature is in agreement with his own nature. In this case it was King Herod. Note: (Matt. 2: 7 & 8).

172

7 "Then Herod, when he had secretly called the wise men, determined from them what time the star appeared."
8 "And he sent them to Bethlehem and said, "Go and search diligently for the young Child, and when you have found Him, bring back word to me, that I may come and worship Him also."

But, Herod was lying, as proven in Matt. 2: 13 & 16.

13 "And when they had departed, behold, an angel of the Lord appeared to Joseph in a dream, saying, "Arise, take the young Child and His mother, flee to Egypt, and stay there until I bring you word; <u>for Herod will seek the young Child to destroy Him."</u>...
16 "Then Herod, when he saw that he was deceived by the wise men, was exceedingly angry; and he sent forth and put to death all the male children who were in Bethlehem and in all that region, from two years old and under, according to the time which he had determined from the wise men."

But Satan and Herod were unsuccessful. God protected the *"Child"*. God's Garden-of-Eden promise of the *"seed"* had come to crush the head of the serpent and He was overseeing every eventuality to see to it that this would ultimately occur. Satan would be able to *"hurt the heel"* of the *"Child"* (implying Jesus' human death at the crucifixion) but in the end, this *"Child"* would destroy the adversary (the dragon) and his works, through His perfect obedience to the heavenly Father.

A "CHILD" RULER?

5 "And she brought forth a male Child who was to rule all nations with a rod of iron. And her Child was caught up to God and to His throne."

Some view this *"Child"* as the Church. By now you know that it's fine with me to look below the surface to see if anything can be seen other than that which appears obvious. But defining this "*Child*" as the Church won't hold up in its own context nor will it stand in light of all the other Scriptures. It's okay to explore seemingly far-fetched ideas but in the final analysis, conclusions must be based on sound balance of the Scriptures *and* the facts of history. God authored both!

Using the balancing system of interpretation, I see no way to accept that the "*Child*" of this passage alludes to the Church. Note this important point in verse 5: the "*Child*" is precisely identified as <u>male</u>! Now why in the world would John make such a specific fact known unless he wished to convey (1) individual personhood and (2) even the Child's gender? Therefore, if this male-Child is the Church, one would have to conclude no women would go to heaven!

But there are other excellent Scriptural confirmations that the "*Child*" can only be Jesus. Most expositors agree that psalm 2 is a picture of the Messiah. Whoever the "*Child*" is here in Revelation 12:5, we see that he eventually rules the nations with a "*rod of iron*". Look at this prophecy from psalm 2: 7 - 9:

7 ..."Thou art My Son, Today I have begotten Thee..."
8 ..."and I will surely give the nations as Thine inheritance,..."
9 ..."Thou shalt break them with <u>a rod of iron</u>,..."

Note the perfect language agreement. But, that isn't all. In Revelation 19:15 we again find that same phrase:

15 "And from His mouth comes a sharp sword, so that with it He may smite the nations; and He will rule them with a <u>rod of iron</u>; and He treads the wine press of the fierce wrath of God, the Almighty."

Further, in verse 19:13, the one who uses the "*rod of iron*" is identified this way: "*...and His Name is called The Word of*

God". Remember now who is recording Revelation: the apostle John. The very same man who wrote here that the *"word of God"* would rule with a *"rod of iron"*, said in his Gospel that the "Word of God" was the Lord Jesus Christ (John 1:14). Folks, things equal to the same thing are equal to each other. There is no getting around it: the *"Child"* of Revelation 12 is Jesus!

THE "CHILD" ASCENDS UP TO GOD

We see also in verse 5 that this *"Child"* is *"caught up to God and His throne"*. I guess those who hold the 'Child-Church' idea assume this describes the rapture. However, not only do they ignore all the above better references indicating John is speaking of Jesus but they also forget that Jesus too was, in a sense, raptured. (See Acts 1:9.) The Bible says that Jesus is at the right hand of God the Father today making intercession for Christian believers. He is at the throne of God. That's clearly what Revelation 12:5 is talking about.

THE "WOMAN'S" WILDERNESS YEARS

Now John brings the *"woman"* back into the picture again. We read in Revelation 12:6:

6 "And the woman fled into the wilderness where she has a place prepared by God, that they should feed her there one thousand two hundred and sixty days."

The literal-only Futurists, who see practically the whole book of Revelation (chapters 4 - 18) as all yet future, have this verse worked out this way: they correctly identify the *woman* as Israel but say that it only applies to a small remnant who will be living in Israel near the end of the tribulation. The persecution against them by the anti-Christ will become so intense that they must flee from the cities out into *"the wilderness"* and there find a place to hide. They even speculate on the exact site. It's called "Petra", which means rock. (The Petra people ought to run to and hide in is Jesus Christ — the Rock of our salvation.)

However, as you might suspect, I have a different viewpoint of this passage. It is much clearer if interpreted historically. Actually, I have already partially discussed this in Revelation 11:2, which spoke of the *"holy city"* being *"tread under foot"* for *"forty-two"* months, which we learned is the same time period as the 1,260 prophetic-days as indicated here in 12:6. I'm convinced both passages, (as well as verse 14 coming up), refer to the same time and the same situation. Now, let's look briefly at it again.

We've agreed (I hope) that the "woman" is national Israel, God's national, prophetic-time-piece. Her fleeing *"into the wilderness"* where God would *"feed her there one thousand two hundred and sixty days"* means Israel would leave her homeland for 1,260 years, although remaining in God's sovereign care. As pointed out previously, that would have commenced around the time Mohammad and his followers devastated Palestine; I gave it a beginning date in accord with the crowning of the Dome of the Rock, 688 A.D. Why then? Well, the thinking correlates so well with Jesus' words in Mark 13:14:

4 "But when you see the 'abomination of desolation,' spoken of by Daniel the prophet, standing where it ought not" (let the reader understand), 'then let those who are in Judea flee to the mountains."

Note Jesus' words carefully. He referred to:

1. An *"abomination"*. The Dome of the Rock sits where the old temple used to be.
2. *"Desolation"*. The land of Israel became *"desolate"* of Jews from 688 A.D. until 1948. This *abomination* would be...

3. *"Standing"*. Implication of a structure. A building.
4. *"Those in Judea"* = Jews in the Land.
5. *"Flee to the mountains"*. The Jews would flee to certain other nations (= "mountains") where God had prepared a place for the Jews during most of the Christian era.

Can you see how closely Jesus' comments parallel John's description of the "woman" here in Revelation? Re-read verse 12:6 and note the striking similarities, then skip over to Rev. 12:14 and read that verse. Note how all these Scriptural passages fit the historical facts surrounding Israel: her plights throughout the world these past several centuries, the reality of the Dome of the Rock as it still sits in the very place God originally planned for Jewish temples, etc. Surely these are not mere-chance-coincidences. Perhaps in time the Futuristic analysis of these verses and events will also have credibility, but let's not leave out that which we know is already so!

SATAN THROWN OUT OF HEAVEN

7 "And there was war in heaven: Michael and his angels fought against the dragon; and the dragon and his angels fought,
8 and they did not prevail, nor was a place found for them in heaven any longer.
9 And the great dragon was cast out, that serpent of old, called the Devil and Satan, who deceives the whole world; he was cast to the earth and his angels were cast out with him.
10 And I heard a loud voice saying in heaven, "Now salvation, and strength, and the kingdom of our God, and the power of His Christ have come, for the accuser of our brethren, who accused them before our God day and night, has been cast down.
11 And they overcame him by the blood of the Lamb and by the word of their testimony, and they did not love their lives to the death.

177

12   Therefore rejoice, O heavens, and you who dwell in them! Woe to the inhabitants of the earth and the sea! For the devil has come down to you, having great wrath, because he knows that he has only a short time!"

Again, we have a passage which doesn't fit in with the Futuristic concept. This is not a "will be" situation. Satan and his angels were cast out of heaven centuries ago!

The war between Satan and Michael is difficult to understand. Apparently there was some kind of great conflict between these two, including other angels which followed each of them. It's hard to believe this war occurred in heaven where the Father and the Lord Jesus reside. So, it makes me think the war took place in another heaven. Biblically, *heaven* is described in at least three ways:

(1)   heaven, where God is;
(2)   heaven, meaning the outer galaxies, and
(3)   heaven, where the planes and birds fly.

Perhaps John is referring to the second of these. Satan and his angels were kicked out of heaven, where God is, prior to Adam and Eve in the Garden. After that, he was allowed freedom to explore everything you and I can see in the upper heavenlies and maybe it was there where the war occurred between Satan and Michael. But, the main thing to realize is that it was Jesus Christ who really defeated Satan when He took the sin-penalty for all mankind at Calvary. That's when salvation, strength, the kingdom of God and the power of His Christ came to man. (see verse 10 above).

Satan has been persecuting the Church ever since the ascension of Christ but Christians overcome him by the "*blood of the Lamb and by the word of their testimony*" (verse 11). This is all history, plus current events, not merely some yet-to-come tribulation period as the Futurists ascribe to it.

178

Satan's warfare has been intensifying throughout the past 1,950 years and his time is ever-diminishing. As he realizes this fact, he becomes more wrathful in his vengeance against God's plans and against mankind. Satan's chief pre-occupation is influencing humanity. He has a plan similar to God's (although perverted) to reign over and be among mankind. The Church represents the only threat against this plan so it should come as no surprise that Christians will always face spiritual evil forces in our days on this earth. But we can have joy in the midst of these conflicts, knowing we can overcome Satan and his angels by the "*blood of the Lamb*". The writer of Hebrews admonished the Church as to what Christians must do as we approach the end of the age:

"Not forsaking the assembling of ourselves together, as the manner of some is; but exhorting one another; and so much the more, as ye see the day approaching." Hebrews 10:25.

This is not talking about ecuminism (all denominations together under one ecclesiastical roof), but about Christian unity. Satan understands arithmetic. He likes to single Christians out because he knows that strength multiplies rather than adds when Christians come together to fellowship in true, Godly love. Jesus was illustrating this principle when He told the story about the shepherd leaving the large group of sheep to go after the lost one.

THE "WOMAN" IS PERSECUTED

13 "And when the dragon saw that he had been cast to the earth, he persecuted the woman who gave birth to the male Child.
14 And the woman was given two wings of a great eagle, that she might fly into the wilderness to her place, where she is nourished for a time and times and half a time, from the face of the serpent.

15 And the serpent spewed water out of his mouth like a flood after the woman, that he might cause her to be carried away by the flood.
16 And the earth helped the woman, and the earth opened its mouth and swallowed up the flood which the dragon spewed out of his mouth."

Recapping the identities in chapter 12, the *dragon* (or serpent) is Satan; the *woman* is Israel; the *male Child* is Jesus. Verse 13 reveals Satan would persecute the *woman* because she gave birth to the *Child,* Jesus. Many historical events testify to the reality of this persecution. Here are the 3 main ones:

1. The destruction of the Jewish temple in Jerusalem in 70 A.D., by Titus and his Roman army.
2. The final dispersion of the Jews from their homeland by Mohammad and his followers in the seventh century.
3. Hitler's annihilation of 6,000,000 Jews during WW2.

(Let's skip verse 14 for now.)

THE FLOOD

We need to learn what is meant by Satan spewing water out of his mouth like a *"flood"* in his attempt to destroy Israel. The devil had a twofold purpose in all this:

(1) to eliminate Israel — the *"woman"* who delivered the *"Child"* into the world, and
(2) to eliminate the *"Child's"* followers — the Church. Since Satan was kicked out of heaven, Israel and the Church have been his only two spiritual enemies.

In the early Church era, Satan's enemies involved primarily Jews. However, as the Gospel spread, Satan realized the conflict was now broadening to include God-believing Gentiles (who he probably presumed were already his). He could no longer limit his attacks to one target, so he had to broaden his scope hoping to wipe out everybody connected to the God of the Bible. There are many examples of his strategy but two are of particular importance we should note:

(1)   Satan 'joined the church' — that is, he began working within certain ecclesiastical structures, perverting the doctrines etc., and
(2)   He also inspired wars, aiming especially at those nations which housed most of the Jews and the Christians.

Then things got further and further out of Satan's ability to control so he stepped up his activities. The *"waters"* (see verse 15) would have to reach *"flood"* level — the world wars. But God came to the rescue and the *"earth swallowed up the flood"*, His instruments being the 'of God' nations (i.e. the *two witnesses*). The British and the Americans (plus some Godly, behind-the-scenes, German Christians), were the main allies of Israel and they were chiefly God's agents who were responsible for *"swallowing up the flood"* which Satan *"spewed out of his mouth"* in his attempt to destroy Israel.

THE ABOMINATION OF DESOLATION

Now, let's back-track a little and look more critically at verses 6 and 14:

6 "And the woman fled into the wilderness where she has a place prepared by God, that they should feed her there one thousand two hundred and sixty days."
14 And the woman was given two wings of a great eagle, that she might fly into the wilderness to her place, where she is nourished for a time and times and half a time, from the face of the serpent."

Now, read these two verses again and note the incredible similarity when they are placed side by side. They are so nearly alike one wonders why both were included. But there is a key difference. First of all, the *"woman"* (Israel), was dispersed into different nations to be protected by the sovereign influences of God in those places. Surely America is one of the main locations as one-third of all Jews remain here until this day. England and Canada were also very much involved in Israel's hiding place. This is the central meaning of these two verses.

Clearly, the *"woman"* and her *"fleeing"* is identical in both verses. But the time factors are stated differently. In verse 6 the *"woman"* would be in the wilderness for *1,260 days;* but in verse 14 it would be for a *time, times and half a time.* Now what conclusion can we draw from this?

A mathematical law is again applicable: things equal to the same thing are equal to each other. In other words, if the two women here are one and the same (which they obviously are for there is no change in their identities suggested anywhere throughout chapter 12), and if they are describing the same movement — into *"the wilderness"* — (of which there can be do doubt), then the two time statements are one and the same also. This was God's way of telling us that a *time, times and half a time* is equal to *1,260 days.* (We will later see just how needful this discovery is in order to unscramble a few other appropriate Scriptures.)

I entitled this section the "Abomination of Desolation" and you may be wondering why I didn't put this part in the earlier discussion of verse 6. At times, our understanding is enhanced if we group certain verses from different passages once we discover they are obvious references to the same thing. There's nothing wrong with this approach as long as we don't abuse the context. After all, Jesus Himself often referred to seemingly-obscure passages which He said alluded to Him. The Pharisees hated and accused Him for doing this, in spite of His clear explanation which would follow that He was fulfilling Old

Testament prophecy. With this thought in mind, I would like to put 4 verses before you, all of which indirectly relate to our current topic — Israel in 'the wilderness' for 1,260 years.

I mentioned the Abomination of Desolation earlier in chapter 11, suggesting that it refers to the Muslim Dome of the Rock which sits in Jerusalem at the site where King Solomon's Temple once stood. Jesus declared Daniel as a Prophet of God, and He told the Jews in His day, (1), to be aware of what Daniel said about the *"abomination of desolation"*, and (2), that those Jews who saw it should *"flee to the mountains"*.

Now, let's look at the pertinent Scriptures:

1.

"Therefore when you <u>see</u> the <u>abomination of desolation</u>, spoken of by Daniel the prophet, <u>standing</u> in the holy place' (whoever reads, let him understand), then let those who are in Judea flee to the mountains." Matt. 24:15&16.

2.

"But when you see the 'abomination of desolation', spoken of by Daniel the prophet, standing where <u>it</u> ought not' (let the reader understand), 'then let those who are in Judea flee to the mountains." Mark 13:14.

3.

"And forces shall be mustered by him, and they shall defile the sanctuary fortress; then they shall take away the daily sacrifices, and <u>place</u> there the <u>abomination of desolation</u>." Daniel 11:31.

4.

"And from the time that the daily sacrifice is taken away, and the <u>abomination of desolation</u> is <u>set up</u>, there shall be one thousand two hundred and ninety days." Dan. 12:11.

There are many points which could be made here but I want to draw your attention mainly to four key words in these four references to the "abomination of desolation".

Matthew says the *abomination* <u>STANDS</u>.
Mark calls the *abomination* an <u>IT</u>.
Daniel says the *abomination* was <u>PLACED</u>.
And lastly, Daniel tells us that the *abomination* was <u>SET UP</u>.

Something which is called an IT, is PLACED, SET UP, and STANDS is a clear description of a <u>building</u>! The only thing ever <u>set up</u> in Jerusalem (the Holy City) which was <u>placed</u> where <u>it</u> "ought not" be (since 688 A.D.), is the Islamic Dome of the Rock. And, this building <u>stands</u> till this day as a constant reminder that it was the Muslims who made the land "*desolate*" of Jews for 1,260 years — or a *time, times and half a time* — the exact number of years between 688 and 1948 when the Jews were re-established as a nation.

One final point in this regard: you need to read all of Matthew 24 to see the obvious tie-in concerning the old Temple and its site. For example, in Matt. 24:1, Jesus spoke of the Jewish Temple He and the disciples were then looking at:

2 "...*Do you not see all these things? Assuredly, I say to you, not one stone shall be left here upon another, that shall not be thrown down.*" Matthew 24:2.

Titus and his Roman army invaded Jerusalem, fulfilling this prophecy in 70 A.D. But, history clearly records that it was the Muslims who much later made sure no Jews remained in the land of Israel and later <u>placed</u> their "holy shrine" on the same site as the Temple Jesus and His disciples were discussing. I believe it is reasonable to assume that the Lord Jesus was seeing into the future when another building would sit in the same site as the Temple they were then observing, referring to it a few moments later as the *Abomination of Desolation,* today's Dome of the Rock. Surely we must come to this conclusion as we study everything the Bible teaches on this subject and relate it to plain, observable, historical facts. To me, all these truths just can't be meaningless, unrelated chance-coincidences. Also, we have seen even simple arithmetic and a little common sense confirms it.

Friends, let's be rational. We shouldn't be so quick to dismiss a 'painting' set so blatantly-plain right before our eyes. The Futurists would say giving this inference a historical label just isn't important. They believe Jesus was alluding to the final anti-Christ who will someday sit in the holy place (a supposed new Jewish Temple). Well, again, these Futuristic concepts may have LODR validity too, but those views do not change nor supplant the historical fulfillment of God's Word.

IF YOU CAN'T KILL "MOM", THEN KILL HER KIDS!

17 "And the dragon was enraged with the woman, and he went to make war with <u>the rest of her offspring</u>, who keep the commandments of God and have the testimony of Jesus Christ."

It may sound sadistic but I love this verse. It shows that God is sovereignly watching out for His Own. Here John introduces us to a new personality. We already know two he mentions but look at the third:

1. We know the *"dragon"* is Satan.
2. We also know the *"woman"* is national Israel.
3. But who is this *"rest of her offspring"*? It can be none other than those who believe in the *"Child"* and the Gospel delivered to them through the *"woman"*; namely, the Church.

185

How did I arrive at that? The answer is right in the verse itself: the *"offspring"* are the ones who *"keep the commandments of God and have the testimony of Jesus Christ"*. Folks, Christians alone meet the requirements of this definition! (Futurists will tell you that this verse is a reference to other saved Jews and/or those who become believers during the tribulation, leaving history out altogether.)

As I said earlier, Futurists make a lot out of the fact that the word "Church" is not mentioned after Revelation chapter 4. Thus, they conclude the Church isn't here. They obviously haven't discovered that Israel's *"offspring"* = the Church. (The whole book of Esther never mentions the word God! Does that mean that God isn't in it?)

THE DRAGON "MAKES WAR" with the OFFSPRING

Now where else did we see the expression *"makes war"*? Wasn't it back in Revelation chapter 11? My, My! Are we at last establishing a point here? Is this not a Biblical confirmation of the interpretation concerning God's *"two witnesses"*? Surely it is so. We, the saved, are the *"offspring"* of the *"woman"*.

As already suggested, the national two witnesses may have been started by two individual disciples who were first-century Christian *offspring* of the *woman.* Perhaps they found their way into England and Scotland, or England and Ireland, and began their testimony of Jesus to people there. Later, what those two disciples commenced, may have broadened into groups which led eventually to the English-speaking British nations and English-speaking America. It was against these that the *"dragon"* exerted his greatest attention. From their beginnings, he has "made war" against them. He has been unsuccessful only because of God's protection reigning over them.

Now, those Christians in lands other than GB, Canada or America, may tend to be resentful of my views here. I understand that but truth must prevail over the ridicule. I'm really not prejudiced against other peoples or other nations. I'm simply declaring what I believe the Scriptures teach. If two other nations were just as strongly implied in prophecy as Great Britain and America I would be just as quick to make the identification regarding them.

SUMMARY OF REVELATION 12

Brothers and sisters in Christ, God deals in the affairs of men! It is He that ties historical events together. Never forget that. Israel, the British and the Americans have been, and are, inexorably-linked together by God Almighty. We shall also see this in chapters yet to come. Again, please understand that I'm not saying ALL people within the confines of these national entities are believers. However, I am saying the anointing of God is, and has been, upon these nations like no others. Therefore, there are God-given benefits everyone receive by just being here — although obviously not extending to eternal life being given to anyone other than Christian believers.

The next chapter will give us further insights regarding how the "*dragon*" has operated in the past, and what his plans are for the future.

CHAPTER THIRTEEN

THE BEAST FROM THE SEA

1 "And I stood on the sand of the sea. And I saw a beast rising up out of the sea, having seven heads and ten crowns, and on his horns ten crowns, and on his heads the name of blasphemy."

There are so many "*beasts*" in Revelation it makes it kind of hard to keep them all straight. Some of the confusion can be erased by observing that the *beast* of Revelation chapter 12 and the two *beasts* described here in chapter 13 arise from different places. We noted the *beast* of the last chapter came out of heaven, indicating it was of a spiritual nature and was none other that Satan and his demonic forces. John also helps us distinguish these two *beasts* here in 13 by saying one comes from the "*sea*" while the other rises out of the "*earth*".
So, to summarize the three "*beasts*", there is:

1. From "*heaven*", a beast with seven heads wearing seven crowns and also has ten horns. This was Satan's army.
2. From the "*sea*", a beast with seven heads and ten horns with ten crowns on the horns. Prophetically, the word "*sea*" symbolizes all humanity. We will see that the seven heads, the seven horns and the ten crowns represent specific, governing-power structures within this "*sea*". A little later in this chapter we will also see:
3. From the "*earth*", a beast with two horns "*like a lamb*". While "*sea*" alludes to the totality of humanity, "*earth*" narrows to include only the religious community.

In this chapter we will discover just how the beasts from the "*sea*" and the "*earth*" work together under the influence of the heavenly beast, as discussed in chapter 12. Therefore, all 3 represent ungodly forces, eminating from either the "*air*", "*sea*" or "*earth*". We should be able to relate each *beast* to historical facts and not based solely on yet-future conjecture. The first *beast*, the devil and his angelic power structure, attempts to superimpose his spiritual organization (from the *air*) on the human agencies of the other two *beasts* of the *sea* and the *earth*.

The beast from the *sea* represents a string of certain earthly kingdoms. These began a long time ago and will extend to the end of all the earthly empires of unregenerate man. Many powerful empires have come and gone over the ages which are not included in this particular group but there are key ones which have had world-wide influence that are historically and Biblically discernible. Each of the heads of the *beast* from the *sea* is believed to signify one particular world power. There is not consistent agreement among the commentators as to exactly which nation represents each of these "*heads*" but I'll present two possibilities. I think both lists have some merit and it probably won't be terribly destructive to our overall prophetic understanding regardless of which is correct.

This first group of empires are well known and are identifiable — Biblically and secularly.

1. Egyptian
2. Assyrian
3. Babylonian
4. Persian
5. Grecian
6. Roman
7. Germanic-Slavonic

The outstanding commonality among these kingdoms was their passion against Israel. The aggression was so wrathful it seems unquestionable that Satan was the spiritual powerhouse behind them all. These could easily represent the seven heads John saw as described in Rev. 13:1. The last empire, the Germanic-Slavonic, is not listed in the Bible but the character of many European 'kings' during the Christian era (such as

189

Hitler's for example) with their intense hatred of the Jews certainly puts them in league with the other six empires.

Another solution can be determined by relating John's vision to Daniel's, as described in Daniel chapter 7. Daniel had a vision in which he saw four beasts. The first beast had one head, the second had one head, the third had four heads and the fourth had one head, making a total of seven heads. Now if this group-of-seven is the same John saw in his vision, the list would likely be as follows:

1. Babylonian
2. Persian
3, 4, 5 & 6.　The third beast had 4 heads which is explained this way: Alexander's empire was dispersed among four smaller ones headed by Seleucus, Cassander, Ptolemy and Lysimachus.

7. Daniel's "*fourth beast*" (the seventh kingdom) had one head, like John's, but on its head were ten horns. Most prophetic writers agree that Daniel and John are referring to the last of man's earthly empires — the final anti-Christ system. Chapter 13 here concentrates almost exclusively on this last empire.

Both these groupings are interesting and all are pertinent to our study. A strong case can be made for either list but I am more comfortable with the first group as being what John saw. Here's why: It appears that John was getting a glimpse further back into history than was contained in Daniel's dream. Daniel's first "*beast*" was the Babylonian empire, which was well after the Syrian and the Egyptian and these latter two are just too relevant in overall history to omit. Actually, one sees list #2 contained within list #1. Therefore, list #1 is broader in scope and more in keeping with the wider perspective John's vision seems to encapsulate. For these reasons, I will assume and write as if list # 1 is correct.

THE COMMON THREAD IS THE "TEN HORNS"

Read verse 1 again and note that John's beast had ten crowned-horns. We may disagree on some of the earlier kingdoms but as we get towards the last one, we had better put on our best 'thinking caps' lest we be completely deluded and side-tracked by Satan in these last days. Remember, he is the one who is really heading these earthly entities. The human leaders are merely his earthly puppets, (not to excuse mankind's responsibilities for his own wicked ways, of course.) So, let's look carefully at one extremely important relationship between Daniel's and John's visions.

Daniel and John both saw a beast with ten horns. What I want to do now is get to the kingdom which will be in power at the time Jesus Christ returns to call Christians out of the world. Daniel gives several insights about this political system. Quoting now from Daniel 7:7.

7 *"After this I saw in the night visions, and behold, a fourth beast, dreadful and terrible, exceedingly strong. It had huge iron teeth; it was devouring, breaking in pieces, and trampling the residue with its feet. It was different from all the beasts that were before it, and it had ten horns."*

(This passage goes on with much more information about this final world power and I will get back to that aspect later.)

We can be very positive that the above-described kingdom will be the last empire on earth just before Jesus establishes His throne. Let's look now at the explanation that was given to Daniel concerning his vision of the *"ten horned beast"*: Daniel 7:23-27.

23 *"Thus he said:*
'The fourth beast shall be a fourth kingdom on earth, Which shall be different from all other kingdoms, and shall devour the whole earth, trample it and break it in pieces.

24 The ten horns are ten kings who shall arise from this kingdom. And ANOTHER shall rise after them; he shall be different from the first ones, and shall subdue three kings. (Practically all writers agree this "another" is the anti-Christ.)
25 'He shall speak pompous words against the Most High, shall persecute the saints of the Most High, and shall intend to change times and law. Then the saints shall be given into his hand for a time and times and half a time.
26 'But the court shall be seated, and they shall take away his dominion, to consume and destroy it forever.
27 'Then the kingdom and dominion, and the greatness of the kingdoms under the whole heaven, shall be given to the people, the saints of the Most High. His kingdom is an everlasting kingdom, And all dominions shall serve and obey Him.'"

As believers, our hope is spelled out in the last verse in the above passage because ultimately we win. Or I should say — Christ wins the kingdom for us.

Let's look at the nature of earth's final kingdom. We see that it consists of *ten horns* (meaning ten nations and their rulers) and that they will do quite a bit of destruction before their kingdom is taken away from them. We see also that an eleventh horn (the "ANOTHER" nation and its leader), will rise up after the ten. It is this particular ruler we as Christians must learn about, for he is none other than a satanically-possessed man who will become the leader over all the other ten. Ironically, this last leader will ultimately destroy three of his own nations! The eleventh *"little horn"* is the man all prophetic writers refer to as the anti-Christ. Daniel's expression *"a little horn"* seems to imply he will seem to be an insignificant man at first. If so, we must be watchful for someone with subtle power in his beginning days of authority, remembering he will eventually rise to an unparalleled, grandiose state of authority and influence.

The reader will note I write <u>anti-Christ</u> rather than the more common way, <u>Antichrist</u>. To me, the capitalized "A" puts the emphasis on the beast himself which doesn't sit well with me (or Scripture). Whereas, "anti-" (with a hyphen) emphasizes not so much <u>against</u> but *instead of.* This is an important distinction. This final leader is really Satan in disguise. It is in this manner the devil plans to rule humanity. Remember, Satan's dream is to be God! And in his heyday, as the anti-Christ, he actually gets that privilege to a certain extent. He will establish a throne from which to rule mankind in a real temporal sense. He will be the *instead of* Messiah who reigns over lost, depraved humanity who reject the true and living God — Christ Jesus. I hope this explanation helps clear up any confusion caused the reader by the unusual way I write "anti-Christ".

Let's see now how this *"little horn"* gets all that power as we read on in the chapter currently being studied, Revelation 13:2:

2 *"Now the beast which I saw was like a leopard, his feet were like the feet of a bear, and his mouth like the mouth of a lion. And the <u>dragon</u> gave him <u>his power</u>, <u>his throne</u>, and <u>great authority</u>."*

Interestingly, John describes this beast in the same way as were the first three beasts of Daniel's vision, only in reverse order. In Daniel, the first kingdom was like a lion; the second, a bear; and the third, a leopard. One commentator says these meant (1) Babylonian voracity, (2) Persian tenacity and (3) Alexandrian swiftness. This seems right. However, the final anti-God system will not only have the above characteristics but will also have a fuller measure of the devil's power as we see in the phrase "...*and the dragon gave him his power and his seat, and great authority.*" In other words, the anti-Christ will be possessed by Satan who will give him ALL his power with which to do his conquering. (All the empires — *"heads", "horns",* and *"crowns"* — of the past have been under Satan's influence too but God has never allowed any to rise to the full measure of strength which the last kingdom will possess. Paul refers to the resistance God has always placed upon Satan to keep him 'in check' as he says in 2 Thessalonians 2:6, *"And now you know what is restraining* — i.e., the Holy Spirit — *that he* (i.e., the final anti-Christ — *may be revealed in his own time."*)

Some people get nervous when they hear a preacher trying to specifically-identify those nations who represent the "horns" and/or other powers spoken of in Scripture. However, that philosophy is not in agreement with our Lord's command concerning these things. Speaking to his disciples about the final days of this age, Jesus stated that His followers should observe the trends so that they might <u>KNOW</u> approximately when He would return:

> *"And He spoke to them a parable:* *'Look at the fig tree and all the trees.* *When they are already budding, <u>you see and know for yourselves</u> that summer is now near.'"*
> (Luke 21:29&30)

The *"fig tree"* is a well-known allegorical, Biblical-name God gave Israel. That being the case, the rest of the above phrase *"and all the other trees"* would refer to the other nations of prominence in the end times. And God is saying **"Look at them!"** during the last days in order to ascertain the nearness of Christ's return. Jesus was pointing out that just as summer can be predicted by the activities observed on the branches of a fig tree, so also the general time of His coming again can be predicted by observing the activities surrounding national Israel in the last days.

But what about these *"other trees"*? If the *"fig tree"* refers to national Israel then logically it would follow that the other trees would signify all other nations which have pertinent, discernible roles in prophecy. I'm convinced these refer to the countries being highlighted in this book, such as America, England, Canada, Russia, the Orient, Arabic and European nations.

Actually, I believe Jesus' instructions to the disciples was really directed more to us in our day than to them then. Surely the heavenly Father, Whose instructions Jesus was always following, knew the end of the age was not going to come in the lifetimes of the people of the first century. So, the answer Jesus gave to the apostles' question concerning the timing of the end was worded in such a way that it would make more complete sense to those of us whose lives would actually be affected by the conditions He was describing.

The next verse will help us zero in a little closer as we try to discern "the signs of the times".

THE DEADLY WOUND IS HEALED

3. *"And I saw one of his heads as if it had been wounded to death, and his deadly wound was healed. And all the world marveled and followed the beast."* Rev. 13:3.

Now let me again briefly set the stage of our current topic. We are discussing the seven-headed beast and you recall I mentioned two possible lists, indicating my preference for this one: Egyptian, Assyrian, Babylonian, Persian, Grecian, Roman and Germanic-Slavonic. Now, none of these empires are presently ruling. But in their day, I'm sure it would have appeared to all who observed them that no new power could ever unseat any one of them. And yet, they have all come and gone! In essence, they are all *"dead"*. That's what verse 3 above is talking about. However, note that one of them will come back to life and rule again. Which will it be? Answer that and you've got the final anti-Christ system identified.

Because of the vast amount of literature already written on the subject I must again mention the Futuristic understanding of this verse. Most say it refers to a certain *man,* who will die and return to life. By this reckoning, Satan will be given the power to restore a dead man back to life, enter his body and become what Paul called the *"man of sin",* the final anti-Christ. Now we know anything is possible with God but I believe it's far more reasonable to assume the seven *"heads"* of this beast are

<u>national</u> powers, not merely seven kings over them. If this is true, we are faced with only one possible conclusion: that which comes back to life is something of national proportions, not merely an individual person! (But again, even if it turns out that the Futuristic view actually occurs too, this still would not preclude the Historical view.)

As you now know, I too believe in a literal, one-man anti-Christ. But, I am most certainly not looking for one who comes back from the dead before being convinced of who he is. He will have far more important characteristics to see than that. (Of course, the Futurists don't think they'll be here anyway, believing they will have been raptured, so I'm a little confused as to why they even bother with this particular prophecy!)

As we have seen, both Daniel and John saw this final kingdom as having *"ten horns"*. This means ten nations will group together in some way; i.e., a confederate coalition of ten national powers will eventually agree to formulate some kind of connective bond because of their mutual interests. That will be quite a feat since most nations, we know historically, can't even get along very well among themselves, let alone maintaining cordiality in a group of ten. Consequently, they will need a leader with a lot of influential 'cement'. I believe the prophet Daniel gives us some tremendous help here: Read all of Daniel 7, especially verses 7 & 8, then 19 - 24. Here, I'll quote only partially:

"...and it had ten horns. I was considering the horns, and there was another horn, a little one, coming up among them, before whom three of the first horns were plucked out by the roots...." Dan. 7: 7 & 8.

Many students of prophecy agree on this group of "horns", believing its rudiments are found in the EEC (European Economic Community), or more commonly known as the Common Market. I agree on this assessment. However, I'm amazed that most of the commentators say that one of these ten becomes the anti-Christ nation. Now this isn't at all what Daniel revealed. He clearly says that *"another"* horn, a *"little horn"*, would arise and that he would *"pluck up"* three of the others *"by the roots"*. Folks, *"another"* after <u>TEN</u> means there must be at least <u>ELEVEN</u> nations involved in the final coalition. The *"ten"* are the ones over which the anti-Christ wishes to rule, but he is not one of ten himself. He is the <u>eleventh</u>.

When I finished the first draft of this book (in 1981), Greece had just become the tenth member of the Common Market. At the time I thought, "WOW, the end is near because the ten horns are in place!" Many other prophecy experts were also watching to see just which of those nations housed the anti-Christ, and wondered how soon he would make his move. I knew that we were entering a new era because Greece's joining the EEC fulfilled a specific prophecy in Daniel (to be explained in greater detail later). But I wasn't looking for one to rise to stardom in the completed *"ten"*. I was already convinced there had to be *"another"* included, making at least eleven, before the *"little horn"* could be seen.

WHY THE EEC?

There are wonderful Christians in all the present nations who make up the EEC. Therefore, many people are understandably troubled with the identification of this organization as Satan's final anti-Christ system. Frankly, the thought grieves me, too. However, I must also be realistic. After all, the anti-Christ system must come from somewhere and God's Word clearly teaches we can identify it. I think this is it.

Why do most prophets believe the EEC is the one? Well, as I said earlier, (1) it must be a power which has already existed and (2) one which comes back to life again. Looking at a map of the ancient Roman Empire as it existed in the first centuries of this age and comparing it to today's Common Market nations reveals a striking similarity of the territorial lines. This alone is enough evidence to cause serious speculation that this is indeed the Roman Empire coming back to life again. But there's more.

ROME

There is an old adage which says, "All roads lead to Rome." Well, that's the way it actually was in the ancient Roman Empire. Roads were built all over Europe (some remaining till this day) and they were, in fact, designed to lay a path for all Europeans to Rome, the 'home office' of the Roman Empire. You will recall this was the great city the apostle Paul longed to go, and did, to defend himself and to win people there to Christ. (People there still need to be won to Christ, by the way. I know a missionary family who has been in Italy for many years. They say it is one of the hardest places in the world to be a witness for our Lord. I suspect it is largely because Satan has such a tremendous grip on that nation.)

On January 1, 1958, the organization of the Common Market was born. It was referred to then as the **Treaty of Rome**! At that time it consisted of six nations but, mysteriously, even the signers seemed to have a sense of their ultimate destiny. In 1971, Great Britain became the seventh national member of the coalition. Note this very interesting news report from an encyclopedia:

"Almost ten years after its first application to join the Common Market, Great Britain's negotiations were completed at 4:30 A.M. in the 23 story Kirchberg European Center. Weary negotiators ended a 48 hour meeting with a toast to 'THE TEN'."

This is a remarkable fact. Why do you suppose they would specifically acknowledge the "magic" number **TEN**? Was this just someone's play on words? Or could it be that they originally planned to limit their organization to ten member-nations, and if so, why? Or, maybe it was God's sovereign way of showing His Word coming to pass, that would likely be overlooked by all except prophecy sleuths.

GREECE

On January 1, 1981, Greece became the tenth national member of the Common Market, thus completing a group of "TEN" member-nations of the EEC. Now, I must tell you about a specific incident that happened to me in May of 1981, which I believe God literally set up to teach me something:

I had been writing this manuscript, ironically working on the topical area you are now reading. The Common Market, Greece, and the whole European scene, were all heavily on my mind. (It was practically all I thought about in those days. I 'ate' it, 'lived' it, and 'slept' it. Ask my dear, patient wife!)

One morning at the breakfast table I was glancing over the front page of a San Francisco newspaper. There staring me in the face was a picture of a shaggy, white goat, with a single horn growing out between his eyes! It was not a drawing of the mythical unicorn but was a photograph of a real, live goat which had a single horn between its eyes! [The article explained that its owners had discovered an ancient technique of how to achieve the single horn. I don't know the technicalities of this, nor is it important for this discussion. I regarded it, then and now, as an act God allowed (perhaps *caused*) for a very specific reason. The shaggy goat was being kept at Africa-Marineworld U.S.A. in Palo Alto, Ca. I saw it again that same night on a T.V. news program.]

There were many occasions in the writing of this manuscript that I had the joy of seeing God confirm His Word through real-life occurrences. When I saw that goat's picture, there was again that unmistakeable stirring in my spirit. *"What is it, Lord?"*, I thought. I knew there was something there but didn't immediately see it. As I said, I had been studying the book of

199

Daniel a lot at that time, then I remembered the white shaggy goat the prophet saw in his vision as described in Daniel chapter 8. I remembered it also had a horn coming out between its eyes, much, I reasoned, like the one I was looking at in the newspaper that morning. What was the importance of this? (I'll cover Daniel's vision more thoroughly later but for now, I want to summarize this one aspect concerning the white, shaggy goat.)

The goat, as explained to Daniel by the angel Gabriel, represented the nation of Greece, and the horn between his eyes symbolized its first great leader — Alexander the Great. The prophet was told how this man would overcome the world's primary kingdom of that time; that he would quickly build a greater empire; and then die in the prime of life — all of which occurred just as Daniel predicted, followed by Alexander's death at age 33 in 323 B.C.

In that same chapter a reference is made that 2300 "*evenings-mornings*" would transpire before there would come a "temple cleansing". (I won't explain here the usual 2300 literal-day interpretation. As you might guess, others have plenty of thoughts along those lines.)

In 1981, I had learned that the expression "*evening-morning*" was a term sometimes used in those days to indicate a yearly cycle. The idea goes like this: An "*evening*" implied the darker portion of the year (i.e., fall-winter, when the days are shorter and darker) and "*morning*" indicated the lighter portion of the year (spring-summer, when the days are longer and brighter). So, when one wished to emphasize the whole cycle, he'd say, "*evening-morning*", thus indicating one year of time. (This is obviously not a well known fact but if true, and I'm persuaded it is, it certainly puts some chronological mysteries in perspective.)

Now, if you look in your particular Bible, it may say 2300 "*days*", or 2300 "*evenings and mornings*", or something similar to that. But if the translators were thorough in their explanation, they have shown somewhere, perhaps a marginal note, that the best English rendering of what is said in the Aramaic is, *"evenings-mornings"*. I want to emphasize the hyphen. The original doesn't say *"and"*, which, if it did, would be more implicit of a literal day. The hyphenated expression is a better transliteration which helps us to understand what Daniel was really trying to convey.

That this is a correct interpretation is strongly suggested by Gabriel's comment to Daniel concerning the 2300 evenings-mornings: *"And the vision of the evening-morning which was told is true: wherefore shut thou up the vision; for it shall be FOR MANY DAYS."* (Daniel 8:26) If Daniel's vision was merely referring to 2300 literal days, surely the angel Gabriel would not have been so emphatic with the words *"many days"*. The whole thrust of the entire 8th chapter of Daniel clearly refers to the extremely-distant future, although set in a very local situation concerning the renowned Alexander-the-Great and his kingdom.

You say, *"O.K., suppose I accept the meaning that 2300 years would pass before the 'sanctuary cleansing' comes, how does all this fit together?"* The whole 8th chapter of Daniel revolves around Greece and its first leader, Alexander. Amazingly, right at the same time I saw the picture of the shaggy goat in the newspaper, I learned that Greece had just become the tenth member of the Common Market, January 1, 1981.

(Somehow, I had missed the news of their joining a few months earlier. I have to suppose God had disallowed my seeing that sooner, waiting until I was writing exactly where I was in May when the "shaggy goat" would come on the scene. I think it's important for you to realize that similar ordered-steps have occurred many times during the years of the preparation of this manuscript.)

Now, let's carry this a step further. In the previous chapter (7), the same prophet (Daniel), who is telling us about Alexander the Great and Greece in chapter 8, wrote about the *"ten horns"* and their ruler which would be upon the world scene in the last days — one _like_ Alexander, but even more empowered. What God was showing me, I believe, was that Greece' recent membership completed a group of "ten" nations as of January 1, 1981. Now, that was a very, very important date, friends! Let me show you why:

Already believing that the 2300 "_evenings-mornings_" referred to years, not literal days, prepared me for doing a little more arithmetic. I reasoned that since the whole prophecy in Daniel 8 revolved around the great Grecian-Empire-builder (Alexander) and since the tenth member of the Common Market was that same nation in our day (Greece), perhaps the 2300 year period somehow related to the time span between Alexander's death and the time when Greece would become the tenth member of the EEC. I checked the records in several reference books and was amazed to find that every single one gave 323 B.C. as the year Alexander died. I assumed it was another example of those incredible acts of God, designed to make-certain history recorded this particular date.

Most scholars agree that Jesus was not born 1994 years ago (as of this writing). It is thought to be somewhere between 2 and 6 B.C. In that very significant year, 1981, when I was first writing this, I had acquired a Bible called "The Reese Chronological Bible". Edward Reese had attempted to put the Scriptures together in chronological order rather than the usual book fashion. His purpose was to provide a reference source which allows the reader to see all the Scriptures grouped in one place which pertain to the same subject matter and same time period, to avoid the necessity of thumbing from book to book when doing cross-reference work.

Reese worked twenty years on this project. Based on his own background and drawing from the knowledge and work of others interested in Biblical chronology, he put together a book to help Bible believers see more clearly not only the facts of history but also the time-setting of that history. Because of my own interests in chronology, and his obvious dedication, I decided to use his views.

Reese's conclusion is that Jesus was born in 5 B.C. Admittedly trusting in his scholarship, I saw no reason not to use his concepts in my computations regarding the Alexandrian issue. Here's what I did: I simply counted forward 2300 years from the time Alexander died, and made correction for the calendar error of Jesus' birth:

$$
\begin{array}{rl}
 & 2300 \text{ years} \\
- & 323 \text{ years} \\
= & 1977 \text{ years} \\
+ & 5 \text{ years} \\
= & 1982 \text{ years} \\
- & 1 \text{ years} \\
\\
= & 1981 \text{ A.D.}
\end{array}
$$

(When making corrections for calendar errors, at the point of the crossover — at Jesus' birth — you must either add or subtract one year, depending on which way you are counting: forward, minus one year; backward, plus one year. The reason for this is that there is no "0" year. You go from 1 B.C. to 1 A.D. the day Jesus was born.)

Now, when I first did this calculation I nearly 'jumped out of my skin'! I quickly re-checked my math to see if I had made any mistakes. None. Using the above-described presumptions, I had actually 'proven' that there were 2300 years separating the time span between Alexander's death and the time when the kingdom he commenced, would join with nine others to complete a confederation of ten European nations in our day.

Was this the completion of the "ten horns" Daniel saw in chapter 7 and "THE TEN" which the EEC heads toasted in 1971? I believe it was. There were just too many coincident facts there for me to assume otherwise. I didn't premeditatively assimilate a bunch of data which, when combined, would confirm a previous conviction. I simply used the information which was there before me; things which God had sovereignly allowed to come my way, in that particular, let's call it *fullness of time*. Nor did I engineer Daniel's vision, or the 2300 *"evenings-mornings"*, or Alexander the Great, or the timing of his death, or Reese's stand as to Jesus' birth date, or the date Greece became the tenth member of the EEC, or the fact that they were the tenth member, nor the year and day I just happened to see a picture of a real, white, shaggy goat with a single horn between his eyes! No, these were all events out of my control. I saw the pieces of this 'puzzle' and God graciously allowed me to put them together. Do the pieces create a fulfilled-prophetic-picture? You be the judge.

THE "TEN TOES"

In Daniel chapter 2, the prophet tells us of a dream Nebuchadnezzar had. The dream was actually a picture of all the future kingdoms which would come upon the earth, beginning with his own, and ending with the final kingdom just before Christ returns to earth. The last kingdom in the string was symbolized by *"ten toes"* on the feet of the man-like image Nebuchadnezzar saw. These toes are generally believed to be the same symbolic entities as the *"ten horns"* of Daniel's personal vision of chapter seven.

A study of the *"toes"* give us a little more insight into the exact nature of the final ten-horned kingdom. It's significant to note they were comprised of *"iron and clay"*, a combination known not to mix well, thus implying disharmony among THE TEN can be anticipated. It is well known that the greatest problem in the EEC lies in their inability to get along and make unified decisions. News accounts of their annual meetings show that often they are unable to come to a single, major decision relative to the agenda they had previously arranged. That's because they are made up of *"iron and clay"*! However, in spite of their differences, there will ultimately come one with just the 'right' abilities to unite them. Amazingly, by their own admission, that's exactly what they are looking and waiting for.

THE "ELEVENTH" HORN. WHO IS IT?

So, today we have "*the ten*" setting 'on ready'. It's now just a matter of time before it all comes together. The big question is, which nation and what person, will join them and unify the present, great-potential forces of the EEC?

As of now, the main commonality of the EEC is based on economic considerations. And, perhaps on the whole, most of those within the Common Market are chiefly motivated to help living conditions for their own constituency. But, that's today. We must think of tomorrow. Mere economy is not what will be in the mind of the one who comes to draw the EEC together. His mind-set will be as it always has been — to rule and destroy. He will do it through intrigue, flattery, deception and, ultimately, all-out war.

"THE TEN"..... + 1?

A few years ago, Spain and Portugal became members of the EEC. When that occurred, I was confused by the fact that there are now twelve Common Market members. I had become convinced there would be only eleven. At first I wondered if I had been totally wrong about the "*ten horns*" + "*one little horn*" concept. Perhaps the "*ten horns*" and the "*ten toes*" had nothing to do with the EEC, I thought. Maybe this whole idea of a revived Roman Empire was incorrect. Then I sat down and prayfully-rehearsed the whole situation, going step-by-step back through the whole prophetic picture as described up to this point in my book. And once again I came to the same, inevitable conclusion: to me, the EEC is the only organization that even remotely meets the criteria demanded by the prophetic Scriptures. So, right now, I'm presently content to wait, watch, think, study and pray. And, while I'm waiting, I might as well think out loud and share my present thoughts with you.

AN INTRODUCTORY NOTE TO THE NEXT SECTION:

(Before I continue, let me say this: I know that within the confines of all the Common Market nations, including of course even the one in which the anti-Christ will rise, there are good and faithful, Christian people. It is not my purpose to cast an "evil eye" against individuals or nations. My intent is to see and report the *trees* as they really are. While I believe strongly in the validity of the spiritual nature and anointing of the *two witnesses*, I must also remind you that I'm fully aware that we have also become the havens of all kinds of ungodly practices within our shores, certainly equal, if not worse, to evils manifest within the European nations! Regarding the Common Market nations, or any other highly, satanically-influenced nation, I want the reader to realize that what I am doing is merely relating certain national conditions to that which best conforms to what the Scriptures teach, as I see it. In spite of having just said that, some people will still probably think I'm being prejudicial at times, but please believe me, it just isn't true.)

SPAIN AND PORTUGAL

Being somewhat surprised with the news that the EEC had passed up the special number "TEN", I began to seek the Lord on this issue. I won't dogmatically say that it was the Holy Spirit prompting me but let me tell you what came into my mind while pondering this. As I was looking at a map one day, it occurred to me that Portugal and Spain have the geographical appearance of <u>one</u> nation, not two. Get a map and see what I mean. I'm sure Spanish and Portuguese people would regard this idea with great indignation but I mean no disrespect.

However, it is a fact "*the ten*" of the EEC voted on Spain and Portugal for admission through a 'two-package deal'. The reason was that they felt if only one of those two particular nations was voted in, she might later disallow (through the veto vote) any possibility of the other ever becoming a member. I presume this was based on the EEC's sensitivity to the long-existing rivalry between Spain and Portugal.

So, these two facts — (1) the territorial boundaries being the way they are, and (2) these two nations coming into the EEC as a unit — have caused me to look at this situation in a different light. I am no longer concerned that there are, mathematically speaking, 12 members of the EEC. Spiritually speaking, I believe Daniel's predicted "ten horns" are in place, and that within the package of "2 = 1" (Spain and Portugal), the eleventh "*little horn*" has now been added. Thus, if the logic is correct, the skeleton of the anti-Christ system is here.

Now I'm not saying that the intents and purposes of the EEC today is one of willful, anti-God strategies. The European union is based on what seems to be sound economic principles. However, that's only today's foundation. It will change. In the future it will move towards **power** and **force**. Wait and see.

Let's face it, man's chief priorities have always been to feed his belly and to surround himself with possessions. Once power gets out of the hands of those who today may very well be honest people, and into the hands of evil leaders, these motivations will change into <u>taking</u> whatever they want from others when the economic-cooperative effort no longer works. When the EEC becomes the USE (United States of Europe), the economic priority base will give way to a desire for world domination. In fact, when in full operation, the rest of the world's opinion will change to one of awe at United Europe's new ability to control and influence people. How will all this happen? It can only occur when the *"man of sin"*, the *"lawless one"*, the man who *"understands dark sentences"* — the "anti-Christ" — comes upon the scene to head up the organization. I think this man is alive today and will likely come from either Spain or Portugal, my belief being Spain.

WHY SPAIN?

I have no personal ax to grind against Spain. Let me tell you why I picked this nation to produce the anti-Christ: Spain is the eleventh member of the EEC. That's clearly what the prophetic Scriptures of Daniel 7 demand. (Remember, Spain and Portugal's entry was as a unit, even though *on paper* they are separate. And don't forget this, Portugal was not even a nation until after 1000 A.D.). But I also have Biblical reasons:

PAUL AND SPAIN

I have always wondered why the Holy Spirit forbade the apostle Paul to follow through with his burden over Spain. (See Romans 15:24 & 28). Some modern writers believe he did eventually go there. Purportedly, Spain cherishes a certain "Black Madonna" (a Mary-and-Child painting) that the apostle supposedly carried to Spain himself. This story alone is sufficient proof to me Paul never entered the country. It is absurd to even think he was involved with the heretical teaching of 'Mary worship'. And the fact that Paul wanted to go to

Spain, with no account of it in God's Word that he did, is strong evidence that he never went there.

When we come across unfulfilled "dreams" and/or "visions" of God's people in the Bible, we must keep in mind the incident probably has prophetic content. God always has a reason for allowing someone to allude to something (such as Paul's strong wish to visit Spain) and then not allowing it to come to fruition in that man's lifetime. In this case, I believe Satan had been given, let's call it *temporary spiritual authority,* over Spain, which impeded the true Gospel message from entering there until some God-ordained, future date. This doesn't mean Paul mis-read the Holy Spirit's mind regarding Spain. I believe Paul indeed had a God-given vision of ministry to Spain, but did not himself realize it. Only his timing was off.

Is there any proof to substantiate the idea that Satan has had a certain hold on Spain? Let's look at the facts. The atrocities committed by the Spanish Inquisitions are well-known historical facts. Perhaps not so well-known is that this was all done under the authority of the Roman Catholic Church with full papal indorsement! From the beginning of the Roman Catholic Church, under Constantine's rule, efforts were often made to stamp out what they called "heresy" within the "christian" faith.

This particular form of "christianity" was not Christianity at all. The Roman-Catholic backing of the Spanish Inquisitions simply represented an on-going continuance of Constantine's "law and order" principles. (Many non-Catholics fear viewing Roman Catholicism as non-Christian because (1) Christ is supposedly the head of their church and (2) because they use the Bible to authenticate themselves. But these suppositions do not automatically confirm their 'gospel' and their 'Jesus' as the true Church of Jesus Christ.)

Stamping out heresy (i.e., getting rid of that which wasn't Roman Catholic) continued throughout much of the Christian era and around 1229 the Inquisition was established. It was chiefly centered in Spain and Portugal plus a portion of Italy, lasting until 1884! People who did not conform to the "faith" as defined by the Inquisitors were considered heretics. They were tried, many of them killed, and remember, <u>all in the name of God and with papal authority</u>! Jews and born-again Christians (Protestants) were the outstanding 'heretics'. (This, I believe, was part of the "*flood*" which Satan spewed out of his mouth in his attempt to devour "*the woman*" {the Jews} as discussed in chapter 12.)

Spain is still predominantly Roman Catholic. Many modern Spaniards may be truly grieved and embarrassed by the evil practices of their forefathers. But for several centuries these were the facts in that nation and *that,* after all, is what we are trying to get across here. (I suspect many readers had no idea what the Spanish Inquisition was all about. I confess that until recently, I've known very little about it myself and was shocked when I learned these things. If you have doubts about what I'm saying relative to the Spanish Inquisitions, look it up in almost any encyclopedia.)

Discussing things of this nature are always regarded with skepticism and disdain. People say, *"Why don't you just leave it alone? America has also done some awful things in the name of 'righteousness'. What about Vietnam? What about North Korea? What about Hiroshima? What about this? What about that?"*...and so go the questions. Some people often try to associate these kinds of American conflicts as being just as bad as the Spanish Inquisitions but actually there is no parrallelism here at all. Those in charge of the Spanish Inquisitions were purposefully annihilating human beings who didn't conform to their, self-proclaimed "holy order". The U.S.A. has done some devastating things, true. However, typically it has been in retaliation towards invaders of our own nation or to protect other nations from attempts of oppression and domination by outside evil forces coming against them.

Recall in Revelation 11:5 a characteristic of the "*witnesses*" was this: "*And if anyone wants to harm them, fire proceeds out of their mouth and devours their enemies. And if anyone wants to harm them, he must be killed in this manner."* THAT is greatly different than what occurred through the Spanish Inquisitions, all under the authority of the papacy — the office which, according to the present Pope, Jean Paul II, acts 'infallibly' as God's agent here on earth.

Christian friend, there are some nations more righteous than others. It is obviously not up to you and I to do the judging in these matters but let's not be so naive as to be unaware of reality. As I have said repeatedly now, there are saved people in *unrighteous* nations and there are saved people in *righteous* nations; just as surely, there are many unrigheous individuals in both! But some of the nations have in the past (and will in the future) been Satan's more primary seats of opportunity. We must see that there are nations which have followed a Judas-like pattern — operating outwardly as a member of Jesus' group but inwardly filled with the devil himself. (Brothers and Sisters, join me now in this prayer: *"God bless and protect the innocent ones who are trapped within the confines of any and all nations held by Satanic bondage".*)

I'm thankful not to be Judas' or Spain's judge. However, it is foolish to stick our heads in the proverbial sand and act as though their sinful acts didn't, or don't, exist. They have a Judge Who has graciously allowed us to see and understand them both to a certain degree. We Christians are not to regard these things with hate or vindictiveness, but with Godly, righteous indignation, in the manner Jesus instructed His own — being *"wise as serpents but harmless as doves".*

But even though Spain has historically been one of Satan's primary tools of carrying out his endeavors in the past, this alone certainly doesn't absolutely confirm this nation as being the one from which will come the final anti-Christ. But if "the ten" which was completed in 1981 when Greece joined the EEC is, in fact, the *"ten horns"* of Daniel 7:24, how does one get around identifying the "*another* shall rise after them" (same verse) as the next member of that same group? The "*another*" was none other than Spain!

"But what happens if more nations join the present group? Wouldn't this upset the numbers altogether?", someone asks. Good questions. At this present time (1994), one certainly thinks about the upheavals and the walls which are coming down in Eastern Europe. Perhaps some of those nations may eventually join up with the present EEC. What happens to our "ten" scenario if that occurs? Or suppose the EEC ends up with 15 or 20 members? It's kind of confusing, isn't it?

> Some writers have pointed out that *"ten toes"* are comprised of five *"toes"* on each foot of *"two legs"*. In this scenario, the two legs represent the Eastern and the Western sides of the old Roman Empire. Thus, they conclude, the final *"ten"* must have five nations from the east and five from the west. (I'm not trying to confuse you. I just want to keep you abreast of the variations within the overall prophetic, Christian community regarding how the old Roman Empire will reunite.)

There is a relatively new organization (called Opus Dei) being established right now throughout the world that has all kinds of "anti-Christ" implications which, not unexpectedly, was established in Spain. (To be discussed further later in this chapter.) But regardless of who the anti-Christ is or where he comes from, we can increase our ability of discernment by studying his Biblically-described characteristics.

PERSONAL TRAITS OF THE ANTI-CHRIST

Here is a list of Scriptural phrases believed to allude to the anti-Christ. Most commentators agree on this group of verses as indicative of the anti-Christ who will be the reigning ruler in the last-days of the restored Roman Empire. The purpose of knowing the nature of the anti-Christ is to help sharpen our sensitivity to him as he comes on the scene. I believe that we will actually be able to make the identification simply by observing current events via T.V., radio, newspapers, etc.

THE ANTI-CHRIST'S CHARACTER LIST

1. A *foolish king.* Zech. 11:15. Does not have Christ's character. Doesn't visit the sick; doesn't heal, etc. Zech. 11:16.
2. A *willful king.* Jn. 5:43; Dan. 11: 36-45; 2 Thes. 2:3-12.
3. A *deceiver.* 2 Thes. 2: 9-11; Matt. 24: 5, 23, 24 & 26; Mark 13:6; Luke 21:8; 1 Jn. 2:18 & 22; 1 Jn. 4:34.
4. *Speaks* great words. Dan. 7:25.
5. *Wears out* the saints. Dan. 7:25.
6. Tries to change the *times and laws.* Dan 7:25. The 'spirit of anti-Christ' is already at work on this point. For example, the Biblical, foundational principles right here in the USA are being replaced by immoral, humanistic philosophies. Expect an increase of it.
7. Will have a *fierce countenance.* This man's face will literally be awesome to look at. Dan. 8:23.
8. Understands *dark sentences.* Dan. 8:23. Mr. Intelligent. He will have a remarkable ability with words. In short, he will be Super-Smart. This is what the EEC — indeed, the world — wants today.)
9. *Destroys wonderfully.* Dan. 8:24
10. *Prospers* for a while. Dan. 8:24
11. Destroys the *mighty and the holy people.* Dan. 8:24.
12. *Deceit prospers* under him. Dan. 8:25.
13. Destroys many by *peace.* Dan. 8:25.
14. Eventually *stands against Christ.* Dan. 8:25.
15. *Exalts himself.* 2 Thes. 2: 1 - 12.
16. *Speaks* against God. Dan. 11:36 & Dan. 8:36.
17. *Prospers* till *indignation is accomplished.* Dan. 11:36.
18. Doesn't regard the *god of his father.* (Could mean he is Jewish but refuses to worship the God of the Jews. Dan. 11:36.)
19. Honors the *god of forces.* (A mighty, military strategist.) Dan. 11:38.

20. *Divides the Land* for gain. Watch for drastic changes in Real Estate philosophy. Dan. 11:39.
21. Almost deceives the *very elect* (true Christians). Matt. 24:24.
22. Heads up a *10-horned* confederacy. Dan. 7:24; Rev. 13:1-10; Rev. 17:7-14.
23. Tries to *confirm the Covenant.* (This covenant was already confirmed by Jesus. The anti-Christ will do his perverted form of it.) Jn. 5:43; Dan. 9:26&27.

There are other Scriptures which add further insights regarding knowledge of the anti-Christ and his system but these are the key personal characteristics. Let's face it, he will be a human dynamo! Although I'm presently convinced he will be of Spanish descent, if a man rises in another nation who shows the signs as depicted above, I will not hesitate to re-focus my attention on *him* and the nation in which *he* rises.

(Of course, the Futuristic approach avoids all these uncertainties with the assumption the Church will be gone and therefore, Christians need not worry about it. Strange! This understanding causes me to wonder who prophecy was written for in the first place? The heathen? The unsaved? Those who remain after the Church is gone? Who would be left to explain to them what it means? Rapture before tribulation makes no sense. Rapture before *God's Wrath* is what the Bible teaches.)

Let's move on and see how the world responds to 'superman'.

LOST MEN WORSHIP THE NEW 'MIGHTY KING'

4 "And they worshiped the dragon who gave authority to the beast; and they worshiped the beast, saying, "Who is like the beast? Who is able to make war with him?"

214

The eleven nations (actually twelve) of the EEC today represent a vast array of cultural differences. For this reason, it seems as if there is no possibility of agreement on important issues. I have read accounts of some of their meetings during which they had prepared a large-scale agenda to follow, only to report at the conclusion — no newly-established purposes.

We have division in America; so does Canada; it's the nature of men of different backgrounds. But the diversity in Europe is a 'horse-of-a-different-color'. Ironically, cultural pride is at its fullest among nations which seem bent upon becoming united. And, because of this reality, they are looking for, and need, a masterful unifier-organizer.

With this understanding, we can see the stage is now set in the EEC for the one *"who understands dark sentences"* to make his showing. I shall not speculate now on exactly how or when this might be. But the major Biblical characteristics listed above should help make us sensitive to the man described in the above verse, (Rev.13:4). The new European leader will be one who *"honors a god of forces"*, and the apostle John reveals just how 'right on' the prophet Daniel was with that prediction. The people will *"worship the dragon"* (unwittingly perhaps, not realizing the *"beast"* is actually being controlled by Satan). His power and influence will be so extremely effective and coercive, it will cause those who regard him to say: "Who is able to make war with him?" In short, today's EEC (tomorrow's USE) will eventually become a powerhouse of unparalleled proportions.

THE BLASPHEMER

5 "And he was given a mouth speaking great things and blasphemies, and authority was given to him to continue forty-two months."
6 "And he opened his mouth in blasphemy against God, to blaspheme His name, His tabernacle, and those who dwell in heaven."

These two verses are about a man but they actually reveal the nature of Satan himself. Remember, he was kicked out of heaven because of his desire to be God's equal. Since that time, Satan has been attempting to prove his equality with God. He still believes he can pull it off. Satan hates God furiously. We got a glimpse of the intensity of this hatred in Adolph Hitler. But in the final *"man of sin"*, this will be demonstrated to the fullest degree possible, when Satan will then have complete control of the will, mind and emotions of one human being. Satan has waited for this a long time.

The above two verses are clear statements of what will come out of the mouth of this ruler. He won't be able to control himself. Eventually, he will literally and openly blaspheme the name of Jesus Christ, the One who crushed Satan's head. I doubt this will be true in the beginning stages. At first, he may even claim belief in Jesus. But when his time comes, i.e., when he is convinced he's 'got-the-world-on-a-string', the real anti-Christ nature will come forth from his lips. He won't be able to control his ego nor his contempt for God. His 23 characteristics will become reality.

There is an excellent passage of Scripture which the apostle Paul left us regarding the anti-Christ, and this is the place we need to study it: 2 Thessalonians 2: 1 - 12:

1 "Now we ask you, brethren, by the coming of our Lord Jesus Christ and our gathering together to Him,
2 that you not be soon shaken in mind or be troubled, neither by spirit, nor by word, nor by letter, as if from us, as though the day of Christ had come.
3 Let no one deceive you by any means; for that Day will not come unless the falling away comes first, and the man of sin is revealed, the son of perdition,
4 who opposes and exalts himself above all that is called God or that is worshipped, so that he sits as God in the temple of God, showing himself that he is God.

5 Do you not remember that when I was still with you I told you these things?
6 And now you know what is restraining, that he may be revealed in his own time.
7 For the mystery of lawlessness is already at work; only He who now restrains will do so until He is taken out of the way.
8 And then the lawless one will be revealed, whom the Lord will consume with the breath of His mouth and destroy with the brightness of His coming.
9 The coming of the lawless one is according to the working of Satan with all power, signs, and lying wonders,
10 and with all deception of unrighteousness in those who perish, because they did not receive the love of the truth, that they might be saved.
11 And for this reason God will send them strong delusion, that they should believe the lie,
12 that they all might be condemned who did not believe the truth but had pleasure in unrighteousness."

If I was limited to only one portion of Scripture to study Satan, the anti-Christ and last-days events, this would be my choice. If this Scripture is new to you, or if you haven't studied it in depth, would you right now read these twelve verses several times — nonstop. I shall list segments which are most meaningful and it will help your understanding tremendously if you can immediately recall the verse as soon as you see the phrases I'll be commenting on.

"...the coming of the Lord Jesus...and our gathering.."

At the outset of this chapter we see that it concerns the return of Jesus Christ to the earth to receive His Own. Paul goes on:

"...Be not soon shaken..."

Here, Paul is making it clear that <u>Christians will see</u> the things he is about to discuss concerning the coming anti-Christ system. This passage has strong suggestions which reduce the pre-trib-rapture concept. I'm amazed that the Futurists so easily glide right over this very clear passage of Scripture on this issue.

"...that day will not come unless..."

Then Paul goes on to explain that there will be a *"falling away"* first. This refers to an apostasy, indicating that believers begin to drift away from deep, Biblical faith. We see this in process right now, do we not? Ungodliness and unrighteousness is on the rise everywhere, especially here in our own beloved Canada and America. This clear statement by Paul is one of the great Biblical signs confirming that we are nearing the end of the age.

"...and that man of sin is revealed, the son of perdition."

God has many identifying names in the Bible; so does Jesus Christ; so does Satan. Two of Satan's, in the form of the final anti-Christ, are revealed in this verse, the *"man of sin"*, and the *"son of perdition"*. The *"man of sin"* is indicative of man's sinful nature at its highest ebb; while the *"son of perdition"* tells us from where the underlying power comes — the devil himself.

"...in the temple of God, showing himself that he is God."

The Futurists are waiting for a new Jewish temple to be built in Jerusalem before the anti-Christ can come on the scene. I believe this thinking may be one of Satan's cleverest schemes, (perhaps another example of Daniel's suggestion that the anti-Christ would think to *'change the times and the laws'*). If this theory is correct, there would be no need to even study prophecy! We could just wait for the new temple to be built and then we'd know the anti-Christ would soon come!

I don't agree with the reasoning. The only real foundation it has is that a great number of influential people have bought it and are broadly proclaiming it to others. There is a large, relatively-new synagogue in Jerusalem today which could suffice to meet this interpretation, if indeed the idea has any credence at all. Personally, I am skeptical concerning the new temple-in-Jerusalem idea.

It's more important to see that this is referring to a spiritual temple — someone's body! I don't think it's necessary to quote verses because I'm sure that the reader knows the New Testament is filled with the concept that our bodies are the *"temple of God"* in this age. And it is in the anti-Christ's body that Satan will be *"showing himself that he is God"*. This will be Satan's 'incarnation' — his best attempt at perverting what Jesus Christ was — god in the flesh.

Jesus, when presenting Himself to the Jews as God's Messiah, alluded to the anti-Christ in John 5:43: *"I have come in My Father's name, and you do not receive Me; if another comes in his own name, him you will receive."* Jesus was teaching two profound truths here:

1. He was claiming to be the fulfillment of all the Old Testament prophecies of God's Messiah to Israel.

2. He was also predicting Israel would some day receive a false messiah — the one none other than the anti-Christ!

You heard me right folks. Israel will one of these days actually accept Satan's counterfeit as their messiah. They rejected Jesus many years ago and, as a nation, still do. This one who comes respecting the *"god of forces"*, who will demonstrate his abilities as a great military strategist, even calling himself *"god"* in his latter days, is the same kind of king the Jews wanted in Jesus' day. They will finally be impressed to receive the one who will not be coming in Someone else's behalf, as our Lord did representing the true and living God, but coming in his own name, presenting himself as god.

> *"...you know what is restraining....until He is taken out of the way..."*

Notice that the *"what"* of verse 6 becomes a *"HE"* in verse 7. It is refreshing to find that most prophetic students agree on the identity of this Person — *He* is the Holy Spirit. However, I do not wholeheartedly agree with some of the other conclusions. Many say that the Holy Spirit will be removed from the earth, along with the Church, thus allowing Satan to indwell the *"man of sin"* who will then proceed to build his kingdom. My position is that the Holy Spirit remains very much here, but assuming a "hands-off" policy thus allowing Satan to complete his assignment. The verse says nothing about this *"He"* leaving; it is His *"restraining"* power that is removed.

The Holy Spirit, and to some extent in this age the Church too, has been the *"restraining"* force against Satan since the beginning of time. Satan would like to have built his throne long ago but has been thwarted by God's Sovereign plan to draw out of this world a people for Himself. However, this *"restraining"* power will discontinue at a certain point on God's time-table, then Satan's operation will be allowed to go to completion. We'll see later a better picture of what the Holy Spirit is doing during the final seven year "Tribulation".

> *"...then the lawless one will be revealed, whom the Lord will consume..."*

When great difficulties are predicted in the Scriptures for God's people, in the same context we always find God's offer of hope and ultimate deliverance to His Own from the forces of evil in this present world. We see an example of this in the above verse. Paul is in the process of explaining the most ungodly time, under the most ungodly ruler of all time, and then simply says, *"whom the Lord will consume..."*. Isn't that great? God will always bring His people through any situation. We have His Word on it.

"The coming of the lawless one is according to the working of Satan with all power, signs, and lying wonders,..."

This is probably the best summary statement of the anti-Christ in the Bible. In it, we see that Satan is the real power source behind the *"lawless one"*, who will put on a demonstration of strength greater than the world has yet seen by an ordinary man. It appears as though we can expect supernatural phenomena to come through him, i.e., the *"power and signs"*. But note the qualifying phrase *"lying wonders"*. This latter trait makes me believe a lot of what will seem supernatural will actually be tremendous displays of false deception. Recall the magicians under Pharaoh who through trickery seemed to duplicate some of Moses' miraculous signs.

"...they did not receive the love of the truth...God will send strong delusion..."

This is an incredible illustration of God's justice in action. Note that it is God Who sends the strong delusion! Why would God do this? The answer is right in the verse: *"...because they did not receive the love of the truth."* In other words, this reference is to those who continually refuse to hear and believe the Gospel, preferring instead the deceptive nature of Satan himself. In essence, God is saying to unbelievers, *"I've offered you life. If you refuse it, I'll send the opposite"*. In the end, God will remove the Restrainer, (the Holy Spirit), allowing Satan, that *old dragon* and *deceiver,* to come and put his greatest efforts before men who willingly receive his anti-Christ system.

221

The apostle Paul then concludes this passage with this:

"...that they should believe the lie, that they all might be condemned who did not believe the truth but had pleasure in unrighteousness."

There is a *"lie"* which weaves its way throughout mankind's history. Paul even goes so far here as to call it *"the"* lie. This lie was introduced to man in the garden of Eden — that man himself can become god. Never has *the lie* been more evident than in our day.

The above excerpts and their explanation are key to understanding certain aspects of the person of the anti-Christ and other end-time events. I would encourage you to once again read the whole passage of 2 Thessalonians 2:1-12, then also glance through these notes again.

Next, we need to look at another super-important subject, usually referred to as the *"seventy weeks* of Daniel".

DANIEL'S "70 WEEKS"

In case you've forgotten, we are still focusing on Rev. 13:5 & 6. In verse 6 we see that the anti-Christ will be allowed to *"continue 42 months"*, which we have already learned is the same as *"1260 days"* or *"a time, times and half a time"*, which I view as having both a literal application at the end of the age and also a certain 1260 year, long-range application. I admit not yet knowing exactly *what* 1260-year time span in the Christian age God is referring to here but I'm convinced about the concept. Perhaps God will someday reveal it to us.

However, as we move toward the end of the Historical aspect of Biblical prophecy, we must look for the literal 2,520-day age to begin. I prefer to call this the Tribulation-Wrath period rather than just "Tribulation" as most writers refer to it. (Note that I said a 2,520-day age. That's two, 1,260-day periods. As I see it, the final seven years will be broken down into two segments. In the first half the anti-Christ builds his forces; the second half will be his ruling heyday. More on this later.)

Now let's focus our 'microscope' a little finer. We need to learn more about this final seven year period. You may wonder why prophetic writers always refer so specifically and dogmatically to a final seven year period of devastating times, which supposedly occurs just before Jesus sets up His Kingdom on earth. Well, it comes from several places in the Bible, although chiefly found in Daniel and Revelation. The description is most clearly set forth in Daniel 9: 24 - 27. Let's start with only the first two of these verses:

24 "Seventy weeks are determined upon thy people and upon thy holy city, to finish the transgression, and to make an end of sins, and to make reconciliation for iniquity, and to bring in everlasting righteousness, and to seal up the vision and prophecy, and to anoint the most Holy."
25 "Know therefore and understand, that from the going forth of the commandment to restore and to build Jerusalem

unto the Messiah the Prince shall be seven weeks, and threescore and two weeks: the street shall be built again, and the wall, even in troublous times."

I hope you are fresh and alert as you read this section because every phrase in these four verses is extremely important. Misunderstanding any aspect of it will distort your whole thinking relative to Biblical chronology, especially as it relates to our day. I am separated from practically all other prophetic writers mainly because of the different way we interpret these few, but oh-so-profound, verses. You will see right here the very foundation of my overall understanding and presentation as rendered in this entire book, so stay with me.

At the outset, we must understand that this prophecy was given to <u>Israelites</u>, therefore demanding that we must also keep national Israel in mind as we interpret the time framework. The language of this passage in the original text says something more akin to "seventy sevens", rather than *"seventy weeks"* as our English versions render it. From what I've read, no serious Bible scholar doubts that the reference means *seventy...sevens,* or more simply, 70 x 7. With this in mind then, it is quite easy to see we are talking about 490 YEARS.

Thus, Daniel is saying that within the time span of 490 years in the life of national Israel, certain things can be expected to happen. Let's look at the specifics:

(1)   the *"transgression"* would be finished, (this is not complete yet for people are still transgressing against God);

(2)   that the *"end of sins"* would come (obviously not completed yet);

(3)   that *"reconciliation for iniquity"* would prevail (this is fulfulled in that Jesus Himself took the human sin penalty);

(4)   that *"everlasting righteousness"* would be brought in (true in a spiritual sense — the righteousness of Jesus);

(5)   that *"vision and prophecy"* would be sealed (true, assuming the intended reference is to Jesus' completed work during His first advent; this could also be talking about the total Word of God, the Bible; and finally,

(6)   that the *"most Holy"* would be anointed. This was fulfilled the day the Holy Spirit descended upon Jesus right after John baptized Him.

Going on to verse 25, Daniel then tells us how much time will lapse before ALL these things would come to pass. He said that from the going forth of the commandment to re-build Jerusalem, 7 weeks plus 62 weeks (49 + 434 years), would pass leading up to the coming of the Messiah. So, beginning at the commandment, there would transpire 69 weeks of years — 69 x 7 = 483 years — concluding with the coming of Christ. Now right here is where I diverge from the mainstream of most who have written on this subject.   Before giving you my interpretation, let me summarize theirs.

Writers vary somewhat but, in general, it goes something like this: They say the counting commenced in 445 B.C. when the Persian King Artaxerxes issued a command to the Jews, instructing them that they could re-build their city and temple, and ends the day Jesus Christ rode into Jerusalem on a donkey just before His crucifixion. Some have even gone so far as to calculate the exact number of days (using the 360-day Hebrew year) in order to arrive at Jesus' Calvary appointment. I've read very-detailed accounts about this in several books but will not present it here, primarily because of my conviction that their overall, prophetic-theological-premise suffers so severely. The worst error is their assumption that Jesus presented Himself as Messiah for the first time on the day of His crucifixion. It isn't even rational, let alone Scriptural.

First, let's look at this using mere logic. If God is going to send His Son (Israel's Messiah), doesn't it make more sense to assume it would occur at the moment the *"most Holy"* one (mentioned in verse 24) was anointed? And don't you think God would do this publicly in order to establish an undeniable time of fulfillment? And if these two presumptions are true would God not in some way confirm it? The Scriptures clearly provide the answers to these questions.

By now you know very well that I also work things out mathematically whenever possible. But the counting procedure mentioned above is just a little too perfect, even for me! Jesus said we would not be able to make exact, *"day and hour"*, prophetic determinations. He said even He was not always aware of exact dates ahead of schedule. These things were in the Hands of the Father only.

The verses here in Daniel, confirmed by others I'll share momentarily, demand Jesus' Messianic commencement as being early in His ministry, not at the end. I agree with the others that the commandment came from Artaxerxes, as given to Ezra (see Ezra 7). But by Reese's reckoning (whose chronology I have followed throughout my book), the commandment was issued in 458 B.C. Simply counting forward 483 years brings us to 25 A.D.; and adding the necessary 4 years (due to the present calendar error) we come to 29 A.D. Let's look at some pertinent Scriptures: Luke 3:21-23.

"Now when all the people were baptized, it came to pass, that Jesus also being baptized, and praying, the heaven was opened, and the Holy Ghost descended in a bodily shape like a dove upon Him, and a voice came from heaven, which said, thou art My Beloved Son; in Thee I am well pleased. And Jesus Himself began to be about thirty years of age,..."

So, right here in one 'package' of Scripture, we have several interesting facts:

(1)   This occurred right at the beginning of Jesus' ministry.
(2)   He was *"about thirty years of age"* (the *"began to be"* indicative that Jesus was still 29).
(3)   The Holy Ghost was there descending on Jesus, (this was the *"anointing"*), and

226

(4)   the Father spoke His declaration from heaven that this was His "*Beloved Son*" in Whom He was "*well pleased*".

It is extremely important to note here the emphasis that all three Persons of the Godhead were present for that very critical appointment in history. Surely this is the occasion which spelled the commencement of the Messiah being presented to Israel. Also, Scripture strongly indicates that it was at the beginning of Jesus' ministry when his forerunner, John the Baptist, introduced Jesus to the Jews as the "*Lamb of God*" Who would take away the sins of the world which, of course, is the whole essence of Messiahship.

As I see it, Jesus' Messianic-ministry commenced on the day of His anointing by the Holy Spirit, then was <u>confirmed</u> by His 3-1/2 year teaching and miracle-performing power.   Also, remember that the Father was "*pleased*" with the Son on that <u>first day</u> of Jesus' ministry; He didn't wait until the crucifixion before making that very important statement.

Timewise, one's whole end-of-the-age prophetic analysis hinges on how this particular issue is viewed. So, could I urge you to re-read the last five pages if you had any difficulty following what was said. It is essential to have this foundation in order to comprehend what is yet to be discussed regarding the "seventy weeks".

26 "*And after threescore and two weeks* (62 weeks) *shall Messiah be cut off, but not for himself; and the people of the prince that shall come shall destroy the city and the sanctuary; and the end thereof shall be with a flood, and unto the end of the war desolations determined.*
27 "*And He* (keep track of this HE) *shall confirm the covenant with many for one week; and in the midst of the week He shall cause the sacrifice and the oblation to cease, and for the overspreading of abominations He shall make it desolate, even until the consumation, and that determined shall be poured upon the desolate.*"

Before going on, recall where we left off prior to quoting these verses. Sixty-nine "weeks" (483 years) of this covenant had transpired, ending when Jesus was baptized. The prophet Daniel repeats the 62-weeks phrase, saying that *after* that amount of time the Messiah would be "*cut off*". Now this is very important. Note: He didn't say how much time after the 62 weeks before the "*cutting off*" would occur, only that it would be "after"; he will tell us exactly *how much after* a little further on.

I apologize for continually interjecting Futuristic thinking in this commentary, but if I don't, assuming you have heard these views, you'll be wondering how my thinking is going to fit with theirs. Only certain parts will. Also, you must understand that their whole approach is different than mine and therefore, they arrive at different, overall conclusions.

For example, their explanation of the above two verses is something like this: They see the Messiah being "*cut off*" (Jesus' crucifixion) at the end of the 7 and 62 "*weeks*" (483 years), leaving one week of years not completed. Now, this is where the one week of years comes in, which will not be completed until the final seven years. In other words, according to them, the prophetic time-clock went "on hold" at Jesus' crucifixion, not to start again until the beginning of the "Tribulation". The destruction of the "*city and the sanctuary*" would be fulfilled by Titus' invasion of Jerusalem in 70 A.D. Next, the "He" of verse 27, according to the Futurists, is a prediction of the anti-Christ who will make an agreement with national Israel for seven years. Then, at the half-way point of that seven years (the "*midst of the week*"), he will break the agreement, enter the Jewish temple, stop the Jews from sacrificing (which they presume the anti-Christ will have allowed the Jews to resume) and once again, cast out the Jews (i.e., "*make it desolate*").

It may surprise you to hear me say it but I can accept some of these positions, and in the Futuristic sense, this may be close to what will happen. But, let's go back and review verses 26 & 27 very carefully. There are some very critically-stated phrases in this passage which some seem to have missed.

First of all, we must not forget *who* is center-stage here. The **Messiah** is the main "He" of the passage, **not** the anti-Christ!

In his heyday, the anti-Christ may pervert this prophecy when he will present himself as the Jewish messiah. But we don't want to forget that the main inference here is to Jesus. Now, verse 26 says, after "62 weeks" the Messiah would be "*cut off*". This was indeed fulfilled at Jesus' crucifixion; we all agree on that point. Being "*cut off*", but "*not for himself*", refers to the sacrificial nature of His death; i.e., He was "*cut off*" for the sins of others, not His own.

The latter part of verse 26, "*unto the end of the war desolations determined*", means this: The "*war*" is the ongoing battle between Godly and satanic forces, referring particularly in this passage to Israel's "*desolations*". You will recall that we saw this in Revelation 12 — Israel described there as the "*woman*" in the "*wilderness*". The inference here is that the land would become desolate (void) of Jews for many centuries.

WHO HAS THE AUTHORITY TO CONFIRM GOD'S COVENANT WITH ISRAEL?

This is the key question to this whole passage here in Daniel chapter 9. If the identity of the "covenant-Confirmer" is missed, one's whole analysis of the passage will obviously be in jeapordy. We must never forget who the primary parties are in this passage. The "deal" is between God and Israel! The commencement, we learned, started when a certain king was given the authorization to tell Israel when they could rebuild their city. (This was at the end of the Babylonian captivity.) The primary intent of verse 27 above is to tell us that one will come at some future date to "*confirm the covenant*". This means someone who has the God-given right would someday come and validate the 490-year agreement between God and Israel.

Now, the Futurists put all their emphasis on the anti-Christ's perversion of this confirmation, to be done at the beginning of the final seven year period. But this understanding misses altogether the far more important aspect: the **Messianic** message. I'm really amazed that God-fearing "scholars", in their zeal to find all the allusions they can to the anti-Christ, somehow lose sight of the far more important issue of this passage — the "He" who has the real authority to confirm God's dealings with Israel. Question: Would God not first send His true covenant-Confirmer so that the Jews could hear, and thus have a chance to accept His God-Given proclamation? If God allowed only Satan's perversion of the real thing, God's nature and ways would be inconsistent. I'm sure the reader agrees this could never be so.

Before we think on how Satan may twist this passage to his own advantage, let's look at the primary intent of it. Not until the first and most important part is understood does the second part have any meaning. Let's look now at some very pertinent Scriptures which plainly reveal the who, when, where, what and how, of the covenant-confirmation.

THE ACCEPTABLE YEAR OF THE LORD

Right after Jesus was baptized, he went to His home town of Nazareth and entered the synagogue He grew up in. Luke tells about the incident in Luke 4: 16 - 21.

16 *"And He came to Nazareth, where He had been brought up. And as His custom was, He went into the synagogue on the Sabbath day, and stood up to read.*
17 *And He was handed the book of the prophet Isaiah. And when He had opened the book, He found the place where it was written:*
18 *"The Spirit of the Lord is upon Me, Because He has anointed Me to preach the gospel to the poor. He has sent Me to heal the brokenhearted, To preach deliverance to the captives And to recovery of sight to the blind, To set at liberty those who are oppressed,*
19 *"To preach the ACCEPTABLE YEAR OF THE LORD."*

20 "And He closed the book, and He gave it back to the attendant and sat down. And the eyes of all who were in the synagogue were fixed on Him.
21. "And He began to say to them, "Today this Scripture is fulfilled in your ears."

WHEN?

Many answers to our present puzzle are right here. First of all, we must note when this occurred. Clearly, it was right at the beginning of Jesus' ministry — not the end. Jesus said, *"Today is this Scripture fulfilled in your ears."* Note also that the *"anointing"* occurred at the BEGINNING of Jesus' ministry, not the end.

WHO?

Jesus of Nazareth is the One Who made this great statement. That makes Him the main *"He"* of the Daniel 9 passage.

WHERE?

Jesus carefully chose exactly where this proclamation should be made. It was in His own hometown synagogue. Although elsewhere Jesus said a prophet is not without honor except in his own country, Nazareth was the most fitting place in all Israel for Him to begin His ministry. (Other men of God discover this principle continues to hold true as they have experienced rejection in their own community.)

WHAT?

In my opinion, nothing surpasses "WHAT?" happened in Nazareth on that very special day when Jesus stood and read from Isaiah. Visualize the setting exactly as it was: As has been shown, Jesus (the "Who?") is standing in His hometown synagogue (the "where?") right after He had been anointed (the "when"?) to commence His ministry. [Without clearly seeing the importance of each of these points, the fourth "what?" will fly right by without recognizing God's 'staging'. And, if you miss it, you too, like many others, will never be able to see the correct view of Daniel's "70 weeks". This is no boast. It is the plain, simple truth. Stick with me and you'll see what I mean.]

Now, imagine yourself sitting in a "pew" on that eventful Sabbath Day in Nazareth's synagogue. Jesus, Who you know has already been proclaimed by John the Baptist as Israel's Deliverer, rises and is handed the Old Testament. Every eye is glued on Him. Everyone in town is already intrigued by this young carpenter, Who — the most fervent preacher in the region had been screaming — was the *Lamb of God*. And now they all sit in wonderment as Jesus turned to Isaiah chapter 61 and began to read.

Note especially these words: "...*TODAY is this Scripture fulfilled in your ears.*" The prophecy was fulfilled THAT day, which is to say, the day He read it. This means right at the beginning of His ministry. We can be sure this incident probably occurred within a few hours of His anointing because Jesus' first words were, "*The Spirit of the Lord is upon Me...*".) Thus, since Jesus Christ, the Savior of the world, the One by Whom the world was made, placed such a major emphasis on the fact that a prophecy was being fulfilled that day, we had better pay heed to every aspect of the prophecy He was pointing out to them.

We know Jesus was reading from Isaiah but I wonder how many have actually taken the time to read the whole chapter from which Jesus was quoting. I admit I never had, until one day while studying these passages, I felt prompted to read Isaiah 61. Now Jesus merely quoted the first two verses of the chapter, obviously reading just enough to indicate to everyone what prophecy was being fulfilled "*in their ears*" that day. But as I read on I saw the passage contained much more information of what was surely in Jesus' mind that day than just

232

the part He read out loud to those in the synagogue. When I got to verse 8 I was stunned as I read these words:

"For I the Lord love judgment, I hate robbery for burnt offering: and I will direct their work in truth, and I will make an EVERLASTING COVENANT with them." (My emphasis.)

The four *"I"*'s in this verse are the same *"I"* on whom resides the *"Spirit of the Lord"* as given in verse 1, and Jesus was saying that was Him! Now, please note carefully what this "I" said in verse 8, *"...I will make an EVERLASTING COVENANT with them."* I am convinced this is the same covenant spoken of by the prophet Daniel. It has to be. There are just too many facts here to believe otherwise. Remember, we have already shown that 483 years of that 490 year time-span Daniel wrote about, transpired between the issuance of the proclamation (458 B.C.) that Israel could re-build their city, up until the year (25 A. D.) Jesus would have been 29 years old. Now, as indicated in Luke and Isaiah, we find Jesus, 483 years later, claiming the right to make an *"everlasting covenant"* with the Jews present in the synagogue that day. It is also important to note that there was no doubt among the Jews in the synagogue of what Jesus was claiming, for a little later in the same chapter we read of their reaction to Jesus' statements:

"And all they in the synagogue, when they heard these things, were filled with wrath, and rose up and thrust Him out of the city, and led Him unto the brow of the hill whereon their city was built, that they might cast Him down headlong."
Luke 4:28&29.

In other words, the Jews tried to kill Jesus for His audacious words. We must also recognize that another main *what* is indicated here. Jesus said He was preaching *"...the ACCEPTABLE YEAR of the LORD."* What was the year in

233

which Jesus was speaking? It was the <u>first year</u> of His 3 1/2-year ministry! And, what did Jesus mean by the "*acceptable year*"? Obviously it means exactly what it says! On the very day He spoke those most-treasured words from Isaiah 61, was *the* day — the "*acceptable year*".

Thus, beginning with that small group of Jews gathered in Jesus' hometown synagogue, in God's typical low-key fashion, was given the honor and privilege of receiving the *everlasting Covenant* mentioned in Isaiah 61:8 and Daniel 9:27. Jesus was claiming to be God's Covenant-Bondman and He was, that very day, stating *that* was the "*acceptable year*". Jesus was "confirming" the predictions of Isaiah and Daniel.

(When John the Baptist was in prison awaiting execution, in a moment of bewilderment, he once sent word to Jesus asking if He was the Messiah of Israel or whether they should look for another. Interestingly, rather than simply saying "yes", Jesus mentioned the ministry-functions we find in these very passages of Luke and Isaiah. Jesus knew John would be familiar with those Scriptures and that he would understand what they meant. I believe Jesus also knew John would understand Isaiah and Daniel's predictions, for anointed prophets were lovers of God's Word. Deeper understanding of the prophetic word is a gift to prophets, thus, Jesus knew the kind of answer He gave would be more persuasive to John than mere assent to the fact that He was the Messiah.)

HOW?

Jesus did all the above under the anointing of the Holy Spirit, <u>Who</u> knew all about the right timing and circumstances in which to bring all the prophecies to pass. Remember, Jesus later said that He did nothing unless He saw the Father do it. This was possible because of His perfect obedience to the Holy Spirit's promptings. This is *how* He did it. [Here's a Scriptural summary of how this all fits together. You might want to lay my book aside now and, in the order given, do several readings of the following Scriptures: Is.61:1-8; Dan.9:24-27; & Luke 4:1-30.]

THE COVENANT WAS CONFIRMED FOR "ONE WEEK"

Now it may seem as if I've taken us way off-course but actually this is not the case. Everything I've said is directly related to the "70 weeks" of Daniel. (Our current baseline is still Daniel 9:27, you remember.)

We have now identified that the "*HE*" Who confirmed the covenant mentioned in this verse could be none other than Jesus Christ. Next, we must make careful note of the duration of that Covenant:

"...He shall confirm the covenant for ONE WEEK."

Again, to remind you, the Futuristic analysis of this 'confirmation' is when the anti-Christ makes some sort of agreement with today's national Israel (perhaps a promise of national protection, and maybe even allowing resumption of their Old Testament rites and rituals — such as animal sacrifices, temple worship, etc). In the Futuristic sense of the LODR, this is a distinct possibility. But, we must first deal with the more primary meaning of the prophecy — the Historical.

Jesus was obviously confirming the *covenant* predicted by Isaiah and Daniel when He spoke that day in His own hometown synagogue. I have emphasized the need for recognizing the fact that Jesus quoted Isaiah 61 at the beginning of His ministry. And I have shown you the Biblical evidence that some Jews *then* recognized and understood what Jesus was doing. Now listen to what Andrew, one of the first disciples, said soon after Jesus' remarkable, confirming proclamation:

"He first found his own brother Simon, and said to him, 'We have found the Messiah'..." (John 1:41)

We have here a clear declaration that Andrew had received the prophetic message of God as recorded in Isaiah 61 and Daniel 9. This occurred right at the outset of Jesus' 3 & 1/2 year ministry. Shortly after Andrew, John and James came Peter and the rest of the disciples, all receiving Jesus as the promised Messiah. Then from their testimonies other believers were added to the fold. The combination of these groups represent the ones to Whom Jesus confirmed the Covenant.

Jesus' confirmation of God's Covenant started at the end of 69 *weeks* (483 years). It is imperative to understand that the counting of the 70 *weeks* DID NOT STOP when Jesus selected His disciples. After the initial declaration in the synagogue, for the next 3 1/2 years Jesus continued the confirmation through teaching, performing miracles, etc. Now isn't it interesting that this just happens to be precisely one-half of 7 years? What does this mean in terms of Daniel's expression of "weeks"? It's very simple: 3 1/2 is one-half of 7 (a week). This conclusion may not seem all that profound but folks, so many seem to have missed the essence of it. Let me show you why:

THE "MIDST" OF THE WEEK

Daniel was very careful to point out in verse 26 that the Messiah would be "*cut off*" after the end of the 69 "*weeks*". But then in verse 27 he explains exactly *How much?* after. It's stated this way: "*...in the midst of the week*", the Covenant-Confirmer would be "*cut off*". If a *week* is seven years, then the "*midst*" of the *week* would be half of it---namely, 3 1/2 years. The *midst* of the week (3 1/2 years) coincides precisely with the 3 1/2 years Jesus ministered with His disciples!

So, what does this indicate? You can see that by careful analysis of the plainly-stated Scriptures (and a little simple arithmetic) we have arrived at the unmistakeable conclusion that 486 1/2 years of God's 490-year covenant with Israel had transpired at the completion of Jesus' first-advent ministry.

But the Futurists insist only 483 years of the "70 weeks" have been fulfilled. Now at first, this discrepancy may not seem like any big deal to you. But actually, one's whole end-of-the-age,

236

theological-base hinges on which of these views is believed to be correct! To me, the 486 1/2 years far-better fits Daniel and Revelation, as well as all the other prophecies we've studied. Let me explain:

We've seen in Revelation a certain period described in one place as — *1,260 days,* and in another — *42 months,* and also as — *a time, times and half a time.* We learned that these are all the same amount of time: three and one half years (on the 360-day, Jewish-year scale). I believe that the 3 1/2 years remaining of the 490 year covenant (i.e., the difference between 486 1/2 and 490), is that very 3 1/2 years the apostle John constantly refers to in Revelation. It'll require a little time and determination but if you'll go back and re-read this whole section, I believe you'll see how perfectly it all works out. It's taken me years to see it. You can do it in a matter of minutes. (More on this later.)

THE SACRIFICE AND OBLATION CEASED (Dan.9:27)

Before I tell you what I think this means, it is worthwhile to first explain how this is ordinarily interpreted. After the anti-Christ will make his 7-year pact with national Israel, in the middle of it (3 1/2 years later) he will break the covenant and stop what he had formerly allowed the Jews to do — performing their religious rites and rituals, etc. This could be so. But what could it mean with regards to the far more relevant "*everlasting covenant*" Jesus had confirmed with the Jews 2,000 years ago?

When Jesus was crucified, *that* was what actually put an end to the temple rites and rituals of that time. No longer would God allow the old order to continue which He Himself had instituted centuries earlier. When God tore the "*veil*" in the temple at the moment of Jesus' death (Luke 23:45), He was causing "*the sacrifice and the oblation to cease,...*". Note that this occurred at the end of Jesus' 3 1/2 year ministry — one-half of a "*week*".

237

MAKING IT DESOLATE

Some modern versions of the Scriptures have so-modified this portion of the Daniel passage that if you have one of those Bibles, you will find it very difficult to interpret and/or follow my explanation. So, I would advise you to use an Authorized Version of the King James Bible and stick with it for this part.

> Although some of the words are archaic by today's standards, thus slowing the reader down at times, the KJV-translators did a better job where prophecy is concerned than many of the modern translators. In their zeal to make the obvious side of Scripture even plainer, some modern versions have masked much of the deeper, double-referenced material which is so vital to prophetic understanding.

The Futuristic appraisal of the Daniel 9:27 phrase *"make it desolate"*, means the anti-Christ will drive the Jews out of their key cities in the last part of the Tribulation. But if one reads the verse carefully, another altogether-different and far more important conclusion can be seen. Note this especially: The verse itself provides the reason the land is made *"desolate"*. It is *"...for the overspreading of abominations"*. Now, is it reasonable that the anti-Christ would want to harm anyone, or run them off, because of their *"abominations"* — i.e., evil practices? This notion is preposterous. The anti-Christ will not be at all interested in Jewish sinfulness.

We must look at this in light of both history and the Scriptures. HISTORY SAYS that the land of Israel became desolate of Jews after Christ's first advent. The BIBLE SAYS this would happen. Daniel predicted it. GOD permitted it. God allowed Satan (through Titus, Mohammad, and others) to do the handiwork, but it was God's Will that the *"desolation"* was to occur.

God allowed the destruction of Israel's Temple and the city of Jerusalem followed by the dispersion of the Jews because they rejected Jesus' proclamation that He was THE

238

EVERLASTING COVENANT-MAKER! From the Cross onward, any practices of the old order under the old covenant would be an "*abomination*" to God. Not receiving God's Messiah — Jesus, Israel's Deliverer — was, and is, abominable to God. It was for this reason He made the land "*desolate*" of Jews for centuries after Jesus' crucifixion. Israel's rejection of Jesus and their subsequent dispersion defines the *abomination of desolation*. *This* is what Daniel 9:27 is talking about!

THE "MANY"

"*The many*" of Daniel 9:27 is a term of Biblical accounting. It refers to the ones with whom the "Covenant Confirmer" would agree. It is talking about those Jews who *would* hear, understand and receive Jesus as being their Messiah — the very Messiah predicted here in Daniel. Near the end of his life, the apostle John reflects on this and writes in his gospel:

"He came unto His own, and His own received Him not. But as "MANY" as received Him, to them gave He power to become the sons of God, even to them that believe on His Name." Jn. 1: 11 & 12.

Some of you are probably wondering why the prophetic clock didn't keep ticking off the remaining 3 & 1/2 years of the 490 year *covenant* at the end of Jesus' ministry. After all, He was no longer dead and the calendar didn't really stop! This is one of those great mysteries we find in the Bible. But God's reckoning, especially when the subject *TIME* is being considered, is not always the obvious. However, the understanding is not beyond our ability to discern once we get hold of God's idea on the matter.

The old covenant was between GOD and NATIONAL JEWS. God still has a plan for His ancient people. Many folks think God's total plan has already been completed with the Jews and that the Church is now His final, and only, means of communication with lost people. This is not so. God will yet have, even in this age, a short time during which He will once again work with national, believing Israel. It will last for 3 1/2 years at the end of this age.

This is the 3 1/2 years yet remaining of the 490-year covenant Jesus confirmed almost 2,000 years ago with that certain group John referred to as "*the many*". Remember, Jesus has already fulfilled 3 1/2 years of the final "*week*", then He was "*cut off*". He will fulfill the last portion of that "*week*" with another certain group we can appropriately call the "*many*", <u>after</u> the Church has been raptured. We'll cover this particular "*many*" later.

It may seen to the reader that I have steered us way off course. However, all this discussion of Daniel's "seventy weeks" and on Jesus as being the Covenant-Confirmer of the "70 weeks" agreement, and the exposition of the anti-Christ description as given in 2 Thessalonians, were all very pertinent and necessary pieces of the prophetic puzzle. Without clear understanding of these particular passages, it is absolutely impossible to comprehend the upcoming, end-of-the-age events. But now, we can come back to Revelation 13 where, you recall, we left off studying the "*ten horned*" beast.

ANTI-CHRIST SUBDUES THREE KINGS

Remember that the 11th "*little horn*" will subdue three of the "*ten horns*". This is usually interpreted to mean that the anti-Christ will destroy three nations in his own empire. I agree with this and even go so far as to suggest their identities: I believe two will be England and Northern Ireland. I picked these two because of their powerful, historical influence and leadership in the Church, believing that perhaps they will eventually come out of their present spiritual lethargy.

(I can hardly believe these two are in the Common Market in the first place. But then, that's the way of apostasy, isn't it? Once an individual — or entire nation — starts sinning and rebelling, stopping becomes a real problem. At some point, usually requiring a major crisis, a nation may repent. If so, God will once again restore the nation. I hope this happens to England and Northern Ireland. Pray for this eventuality, fellow Christians!)

It may surprise you but I believe Germany may be one of the three the anti-Christ will "subdue" — surprising because she is given credit for starting the last two world wars. But then why should we be shocked at this paradox? After all, it is Satan who tries to destroy the work of God. I do not believe it was any accident that Germany housed so many of the Jews during WW2. Surely their being there was to some degree beneficial for them, even part of God's overall plan of the ages, certainly not merely so that 6,000,000 of them could be slaughtered. Also, we must remember the Godly Germans who hid many of the Jews and gave them protection during Hitler's nightmare-ish regime. It may surprise you to learn that West Germany is one of the world's largest supporters of America's Christian radio-mission work. (Ref: Footnote 4.)

We must ask what exactly is meant by the "*little horn*" (anti-Christ) "*subduing*" three other "*horns*". Now that could mean destruction through warfare, but it could also mean other things. I say this because of the odd phrase in Daniel 7:8 which tells us the three "*horns*" will be "*plucked up by the roots*". Could "roots" suggest <u>foundational principles</u>? A root is the base of something. This could mean that deep beliefs and former commitments (the roots) would be destroyed. England, Northern Ireland and Germany have backgrounds similar to America. They were deeply grounded in the Christian faith but today are in gross spiritual slumber, nationally speaking.

It may mean both both. That is, the anti-Christ may keep banging away at (subduing) the "roots" of the "*three horns*" until they repent and return to Godly principles, at which time he would feel the need to destroy them entirely, militarily. I'm uncertain about this, of course. In any event, Christian friends, join me in regular prayer for God's people everywhere to repent and return to the "God of our fathers".

WAR WITH THE SAINTS

7 *"And it was granted to him to make war with the saints and to overcome them. And authority was given him over every tribe, tongue, and nation."*

Many Christians have been martyred defending *the faith,* refusing to turn away from proclaiming the Name of Jesus and His Gospel. That takes a special kind of boldness. God-given kind. I'm all for it. I hope we have many of these types around right up till the end.

Some preachers talk today about us Christians "winning the world for Jesus". Sounds bold but I'm not sure these have clearly understood end-time prophecy. There's nothing wrong with Christians having a positive attitude and commitment to send the Gospel into every region of the world. In fact, this must have been in Jesus' mind when explaining what it would be like at the time of the end:

"Blessed is that servant whom his master, when he comes, will find so doing." Matt. 24:46.

The "so-doing" refers to being faithful doing the master's work at the time Jesus returns. The Church must do everything in its power to reach out and touch a spirtually-dying world. Nevertheless, we must also face the facts stated in the above Scripture, Rev. 13:7. It clearly says the anti-Christ <u>will</u> "*make war*" with the "*saints*" and that he will "*overcome them*". Just how certain groups fit this verse into their prophetic scheme — that Christianity is going to overcome the world — I don't know.

The Futurists handle it like this. First, recall they believe nothing concerns the Church between Revelation 4:1 and 19:1, their concept being that the Christians will have been raptured. Now obviously John is referring to saved people in the above verse for he calls them "*saints*". A Biblical saint is simply a

242

Christian. (It most assuredly has no reference to "sainthood" as defined by the Roman Catholic Church, which is someone reaching a certain 'divine statehood', as determined by heirarchy-approved accomplishments. It's a "works" milestone.)

So, according to the Futurists, the Church can't be on earth when the anti-Christ is "*overcoming*" these particular "*saints*". But then, who are they? They say these are the people who become saved during the Tribulation. I disagree. My answer to this really is this entire book. But right here in context is provided a worthy answer to the 'mystery'. Actually, Rev. 13:7 substantiates in large measure the position I take — that the Church is very much here on earth when we get to that point in time. Compare the language of Rev. 13:7 to Rev. 11:7:

"And when they finish their testimony, the beast that ascends out of the bottomless pit will "MAKE WAR" against them, OVERCOME them and kill them."

I believe these two passages address the very same event. The only difference is that Revelation 11 is specifically talking about the "*two witnesses*", while Revelation 13:7 is more inclusive, embracing the "two witnesses" as well as all "*saints*" in the remainder of the world — i.e., the total Church. (Note the last part of Rev. 13:7, "...*And authority was given him over EVERY tribe, tongue, and nation.*")

The fact is, the Church is in a condition of apostasy, <u>not</u> moving toward some grandiose state of perfection as some claim. Our perfection is in heaven. His Name is Jesus Christ. If you are "*in Him*", that's your perfection. Certainly we want to do everything possible while here, in our attempt to "*perfect*" our walk with Christ. Our character needs to be in a constant state of transformation into the likeness of Christ and we have something to do with that. Neither do I wish to imply that the Church should allow the anti-Christ to rise unabated. My caution here is that we not be deluded by the current efforts being made by some to bring the splintered, physical church organizations together under one ecclesiastical roof in order to achieve some form of unity calling it *The Church.*

WHERE HE LEADS, WHO WILL FOLLOW?

8 "And all who dwell on the earth will worship him, whose names have not been written in the Book of Life of the Lamb who was slain from the foundation of the world.
9 If anyone has an ear, let him hear.
10 He who leads into captivity shall go into captivity; he who kills with the sword must be killed with the sword. Here is patience and the faith of the saints." Revelation 13:8-10.

There's a wonderful old Christian hymn entitled "Where He leads Me, I will Follow", which speaks of our Shepherd, the Lord Jesus Christ, leading His "lambs" (Christians). All Christians should have that mindset. However, We saw in 2 Thessalonians that another "shepherd", an unlovely one, is going to come some day and many will follow him. We also saw God will send strong delusion that *"they should believe THE lie"*, to those that refuse to receive the love of the truth. Satan initiated this lie in the garden of Eden. I think it really takes on many forms but chiefly it means that man, not God, is the center of everything. Those who teach this believe man is 'one' with the universe and that once he learns to understand and wholeheartedly follow this philosophy, nothing can stop him from achieving his highest goals, including even godhood.

The "New Age" Movement ascribes to this philosophy; most of the world's political forces are motivated by it; much of the job force is getting into it, (and I mean right here in the good-ole USA); all false religions have embraced it (whether they realize it or not); and even many of today's churches (so-called) are buying "THE LIE".

Looking again at the above verses, we see that most of the world will succumb to the anti-Christ's power, deceptions and promises; all those except those "written in the Book of Life".

244

(If your name isn't in <u>that Book</u> yet, my friend, see to it that it is before it's too late. How do you do this? Believe the Gospel. This basically means seeing yourself as God does — a sinner who is lost, spiritually dying and on his way to hell. Once you can believe that, you can "repent" — turn around and go in the opposite direction! To do this means to turn <u>from</u> your own selfish way, <u>towards</u> Jesus, the Messiah. Realize that His death on the cross of Calvary was God's requirement for the penalty of sin, and that it was done in *your* behalf to release you from the bondage of sin, both now and forever! When you really believe this, the Holy Spirit will seal you as God's possession and your name goes in the Book of Life — permanently. This is the central truth of all prophecy.)

Those who are a part of "THE LIE" are the ones John says here lead "*into captivity*" and consequently they themselves "*shall go into captivity*". As each day passes it's becoming easier and easier to discern who *they* are. The end is coming. We are getting close. I sense it strongly and see it with increasing clarity each day as I watch the world buying "THE LIE". But Christians can avoid the deception by seeking God with their whole heart. That's the requirement to become an overcomer.

"ANOTHER BEAST". This one is from THE EARTH

11 "And I saw another beast coming up out of the earth, and he had two horns like a lamb and spoke like a dragon."

Of all the topics discussed in this book, nothing troubles me more than to comment on this *beast.* I think I understand how Jesus must have felt when He prayed over His beloved earthly Jerusalem. (Luke 13:34.) But, I believe there are pertinent insights of this passage which are essential for those of us living in our day, so, here goes. (Before you read, please do this: stop right now and pray that God will give you an open mind and that He will truly bear witness whether my discernment of this passage is accurate.)

The coming of the anti-Christ will follow a perverted pattern of Jesus' first coming. Jesus had a forerunner in John the

Baptist. The second *"beast"* in the above passage is the anti-Christ's forerunner, his 'way-paver'. He will be a world-renowned man himself who becomes committed to the ever-growing, popular and influential secular leader and the regime he heads and the endeavors he espouses. He will be a noted 'spiritual' leader.

We have learned that the anti-Christ will likely be the leader over today's Common Market nations of Europe, which will ultimately unite in a tighter relationship than it has today, representing at that time a revival of the ancient Roman Empire. Now let's identify his cohort.

Verse 11 says beast #2 comes out of the *"earth"*. Recalling that the first beast came from the *"sea"* (the general populace of mankind), it follows that one who comes out of the *"earth"* would represent a more specific region of humanity. Since he will be involved with establishing worship of the *"beast from the sea"*, we can logically presume the *"earth"* beast is from the religious community.

Remember, the anti-Christ is Satan-personified — a perverted "incarnate-god", if you will. As such, he must have a religious organizer, someone who can bring the world's people together in one accord, making them ready to receive the man described throughout this chapter. Just as John the Baptist came on the scene before Jesus — making ready a people to receive the true Lamb of God, Israel's Messiah — in like manner the *beast from the earth* will come in advance of the first *beast,* anti-Christ. Note that the "earth beast" had *"two horns like a lamb"*. What could this mean?

For one thing, the dual horns imply double-mindedness. It convinces me that the "earth beast" speaks of God and Christ but underneath is serving quite a different master. He comes usurping the name and authority of the Lord Jesus Christ but following rules and guidelines totally contrary to clear Scriptural teaching. Jesus was THE LAMB of God. The double-horned "earth beast" comes "like a lamb". He will be outwardly meek. Lamb-like, but inwardly serving a "spirit" other than the God of

246

the Bible. So, we must look for a person and an earthly system which meets these criteria:

(1)   The organization will have a semblance of respectability. Otherwise, no one could be deceived.
(2)   It must also have been around for a long time. Otherwise, how could it possibly fool people? Historically-sound roots are a necessity.
(3)   It must be very widespread. Otherwise, how is it possible to prepare "*all who dwell on the earth*" to receive the anti-Christ?

The question is, is there such an organization present <u>today</u> which fits the requirements? Surely there is and I'm persuaded it is none other than the Holy Roman Catholic Church, which has been headed for centuries by a string of institutionally-proclaimed 'vicars* of Christ' — the popes. (Interestingly, today's EEC was formulated under what was originally called, "*The Treaty of Rome*". As far as I know, there is not yet any formal link between the EEC and the Vatican. But, if my presumption is right, the union will eventually occur.)

WHY THE ROMAN CATHOLIC CHURCH?

I'm convinced there are many, true Christians in the Catholic Church. It is for that reason I regretfully and reluctantly state my convictions about their parent-organization. But we cannot overlook the atrocities which occurred under Constantine and others in the Catholic Church. For example, how does one look at endorsed murdering, as occurred in the Spanish Inquisitions, and remain convinced that the leaders who stood behind it speak for God?

* (Vicar — a papal title — refers to one who supposedly speaks in Jesus Christ's stead with absolute perfection.)

But even more important than the historical abuses this 'church' is guilty of, is the perverted 'gospel' it embraces and teaches. I certainly don't know all about Catholic beliefs and doctrines but born-again Christians ought to be aware of at least a few of the primary ones:

1. The Worship of Mary.

Catholics are taught to believe that Mary is a mediator between Christ and them. They pray to her for her divine protection and plead to *her* because of her supposed intercessory-accessibility to Jesus. This they do in spite of the fact that the Scriptures plainly teach that there is but ONE Mediator between God and Man, the Man Christ Jesus. (See I Tim. 2:5.) I'm sure you have heard of the many supernatural "appearances" Mary has made to Catholics throughout the ages — and are supposedly occurring right up to the present hour. I've recently heard Catholic priests discuss these things quite openly on television. No doubt about it, they believe in her divinity and visitations.

Even the "Beatles" sang about these phenomena in a song which said, *"Mother Mary comes to me, whispering words of wisdom, let it be..."*. Don't be deluded. Mary's appearances are nothing more than <u>demonic</u> apparitions. They are 'angels of light', designed to insidiously steer believers off course and into Satan's trap.

2. The Infallibility of the Pope.

Catholics believe in this. I have heard the present pope, John Paul II, positively affirm his position about it. He has said he doesn't deserve spiritual perfection but that it is a gift to him because of the the office he holds. This "Holy Father" has also made it very clear he plans to see to it that this belief is reinstituted, along with other traditions, throughout the world's entire Parish system.

3. Purgatory.

Apparently, the Roman Church has determined the relative 'weights' of sins, and categorized them on some kind of graduated scale that only they know the answers to! Catholics believe in a place called purgatory. It is a place 'saints' go after physical death to sort of work out the 'debit' sheet. That is, if you still have sins remaining on your 'account' when you die, you must go to purgatory and, somehow, make restitution. The bottom line here is they do not believe the shed blood of Christ cleanses a believer of all his sins. In short, they do not really believe the Gospel!

4. Prayers for the dead.

Catholic tradition teaches Catholic believers to pray for unbelievers who have died, (particularly while the dead are in purgatory.)

5. The Holy Eucharist.

Communion, according to Catholic teaching and practice, means the priest-blessed wafer and wine actually (not figuratively) become the real body and blood of Jesus. So, when ingested, the partaker is quite literally eating and drinking the body and blood of Christ. That is how one gets Christ in himself! This practice and phenomenon is called transubstantiation. What a gross perversion of what Jesus said in John 6:53-58.

6. Baptism.

When a Catholic priest baptizes someone, he is transferring his divinely-given grace to them. The priest is actually "saving" the person! This would explain why babies are baptized in the Catholic Church.

Some of you may have trouble believing that these six points are Vatican doctrines and beliefs. The descriptions and conclusions were determined from their own literature and television discussions (I personally saw) among Catholic "Fathers" who defend these practices. These perverted beliefs and practices are convincing-proofs that Roman Catholicism is a works-religion, not faith-Christianity. In fact, when you get right down to it, the beliefs are not greatly unlike other religions outside Christianity. They have defined *"another Jesus"* than the One Holy Scripture reveals.

Now as I said before, I believe there are individual Catholics (and priests) who really love God and have trusted Christ as their personal Lord and Savior. In spite of their blindness to the maze of gross errors within this institution, by God's grace some have seen and experienced enough of the true Gospel that God has wonderfully and miraculously saved them.

I am certainly in no position to judge these people for Jesus loves all who come to Him in true repentance. I believe I shall go into eternity with many Catholics. However, and that's a big, capital-letter — HOWEVER — I'm thoroughly persuaded the organization itself, along with many of its leaders and adherents, has been, and is, the very seat of the *"beast from the earth"* as described here in Revelation 13:11. I also believe this is the earthly 'house' upon which Satan has for centuries attempted to superimpose his spiritual kingdom.

Please don't get the idea that I think Protestantism is completely devoid of being part of the ecclesiastical 'beast'. The watered-down 'gospel' taught in many Protestant churches today is little better, if any, than the above-described Catholic doctrines. I have singled out and discussed the perversions of the Roman Catholic Church because I believe Scripture presents her portrait. The history, beliefs and practices of the Roman Catholic Church are the convincing-proofs that this is the only organization on earth which matches the Biblical picture of the second beast.

THE FALSE PROPHET

In Revelation 19:20, the *"beast from the earth"* is named the False Prophet. Therefore, when we see this term we must realize that the inference is to the '2nd beast' here in the latter part of Revelation 13.

False Prophet is an appropriate title for anyone, or any organization, who is preparing the way for the anti-Christ. Obviously Satan will be the spiritual force who lies in the background empowering the False Prophet. That being the case, *deception* will be the key sign to look for as we contemplate who the False Prophet is.

Satan has always used the Scriptures in his scheming. He did in the garden of Eden. He even had the audacity to quote Scripture to Jesus! But we know that in doing so, Satan always has an evil, ulterior motive. We must be sensitive to these patterned-truths if we are to be discerners of who is and who isn't a true follower of Christ.

Carrying a Bible around doesn't automatically prove one's godliness or insure that he is Christ's representative. Using the Scriptures and claiming to be 'christian' can be a mere cloak of decency — just as Satan attempted against Jesus. I'm convinced this tendency has prevailed in the upper echelons of Roman Catholicism from its beginning. (If the truth were fully known, I suspect reams could be written about what is currently going on in the Vatican to prepare and pave the way for the coming restored Roman Empire. It's mostly hidden but I am aware of a few things which should help the reader understand why I'm rather firm in my convictions about this issue.)

THE VISITS --- THE INVITATIONS --- THE PREP WORK

Today in Roman Catholicism, three things stand out rather distinctly which, to me, loudly proclaim "FALSE PROPHET". Let's look at them one at a time.

THE VISITS

Pope John Paul II has probably done more visiting throughout the world than all previous popes combined. What's his motivation? Is it because he is such a wonderful man of God? Is it because of his compassion for a world in chaos, filled with sick and sin-laden people? Does he take the true Gospel message to them? I can't accept these premises, because I can't ignore that this pope BELIEVES all those previously-stated church doctrines. Believing *what* he believes makes the Pope wide open to deception. After all, that's how more deception comes — having a false base to begin with. False beliefs lay the groundwork for being a false teacher — a 'false prophet'. Deception builds on deception.

The Vatican's present Pope is warmly received by nearly everyone, including, you must have noticed, much of the Protestant world. But then, isn't this exactly what verse 11 predicted? It says he would come *"like a lamb"*. This implies he will be gentle, warm and kind. A 'grandfather' type.

But also note that the apostle John indicated this 'lamb' would have *"two horns"*. I think this (partly) means he has two sides for us to look at. There is what he wants the world to see and there is also that other person inside. Pope John Paul II is trying to draw the masses to himself, not Christ. Don't ever forget that <u>he believes</u> that he is literally the mouthpiece of God on this earth right now.

Did you know that Pope John Paul is also sitting down at the bargaining table with the leaders of other religions, too? Oh yes, Muslims, Hindus, Buddhists, you name it. He obviously feels all mankind must come together in order to have "peace on earth and good will toward all men". (However, Christians know that this will only happen when Jesus physically reigns as Lord and King of planet earth. But this particular pope believes it is *his* duty to accomplish this feat.)

The visitations are not aimed merely at seeing the masses though. John Paul is meeting with the cardinals, bishops and

252

other great political leaders as he makes his rounds. I believe the purpose is to draw attention to the Vatican and Rome, seeing himself as the ultimate spiritual head over all the lands he visits. In fact, even Gorbachev said to the Pope that he recognized him as the earth's greatest religious leader.

It is reported that when the Pope kneels and kisses the earth, as he has in some places, it is not so much an act of papal condescension but rather that he is claiming that land for the kingdom he envisions himself building. Thus, it appears the VISITS are working.

THE INVITATIONS

The Church of England, The Episcopal Church in America and Canada, The Lutheran Church in West Germany, and others, are receiving 'honored' invitations from the Vatican to consider compromising their differences and to rejoin their "mother" — the Roman Catholic Church. This ecumenical movement is widespread and many leaders in these institutions are definitely trying to get the people in their churches ready for reattachment to Rome.

Friends, I don't know of a shred of Biblical evidence to substantiate that Jesus wanted all Christians under one, earthly, ecclesiastical roof; certainly not one which embraces the unscriptural tenets of Roman Catholicism. It's right and good to be in a local congregation with people who are trying to develop Christ-like character and who embrace the clearly-spoken doctrines as recorded in the Bible. But this ever-increasing, international *"beast"* eminating from Rome has nothing to do with the real body of Christ — that body which comprises the priesthood of all born-again believers.

But, in spite of what seems very plain to ordinary Christian believers, many of the mainline-denominations are giving strong consideration to the ecumenical movement towards Roman Catholic rule. Thus, I conclude, the INVITATIONS are working.

THE PREP WORK

In order to comment on the PREPARATION WORK going on in the Roman Church, we need to look at the remainder of chapter thirteen.

12 "And he exercises all the authority of the first beast in his presence, and causes the earth and those who dwell in it to worship the first beast, whose deadly wound was healed.
13 And he performs great signs, so that he makes fire come down from heaven on the earth in the sight of men.
14 And he deceives those who dwell on the earth by those signs which he had power to do in the sight of the beast, saying to those who dwell on the earth that they should make an image to the beast who was wounded by the sword and lived.
15 And he had power to give breath to the image of the beast, that the image of the beast should both speak and cause as many as would not worship the image of the beast to be killed.
16 And he causes all, both small and great, rich and poor, free and slave, to receive a mark on their right hand or on their foreheads,
17 and that no one may buy or sell except the one who has the mark or the name of the beast, or the number of his name.
18 Here is wisdom. Let him who has understanding calculate the number of the beast, for it is the number of man: And his number is six hundred and sixty-six.

This is another one of those large segments which is rather difficult to digest all at once. For most of us, symbolic language isn't easy to keep in mind with only one reading. So, in order to follow what I'm saying, it will be helpful to read this passage several times.

I won't be taking the time to go through each phrase here. But, I draw your attention to one key word in each of several of these verses: In verse 12 we see the False Prophet *"exercises"*; verse 13, he *"performs"*; verse 14, he *"deceives"*; verse 15, he has *"power"*, and finally in verse 16, he *"causes"*. In other words, the second *"beast"* is the one who effectualizes things. He's the 'up-front man', a person of action, one who makes things happen. The False Prophet is obviously going to be very visible in order to do all the things which are outlined here.

It is also plain to see that he holds a position of high authority because he directs the worship of his people towards the first *"beast"* whose *"wound was healed"*. Therefore, it's significant to note he does everything in favor of the first *"beast"*, the anti-Christ. He does the great *"signs"*. He causes the *"mark"* to be placed on everyone, which will eventually become necessary in order to *"sell"* or *"buy"*. In short, the False Prophet ultimately becomes the practical head of all that entails the final, 666 system. This may not sound like the kind of activities you'd expect to find in a Church, does it? But...,

THE "OPUS DEI"

Just as the true prophet, John the Baptist, was quite visible and outspoken before the coming of the real Messiah, Jesus Christ, so also is the False Prophet who comes before the anti-Christ. Actually, the PREP work has been going on since the days of Constantine (the white horse rider of Seal # 1, you recall). Constantine wanted to 'christianize' the Roman Empire and that philosophy hasn't stopped till this day. The restored Roman Empire will likewise show a form of 'christianity', having been prepared long in advance of the coming of the final anti-Christ. This is its cloak of decency.

Therefore, the world-wide network of Roman Catholic parishes, with their leaders, is already in place. We don't have to speculate on how the office of the False Prophet shall come; the ground work has already been laid and presently stands right before our eyes. But there is one fairly new organization within the old system that needs to be discussed. It's called the Opus Dei, which means, "Work of God."

I first became aware of Opus Dei on June 11, 1984 through an article in TIME magazine[9] entitled, "Building God's Global Castle". More recently, INSIGHT magazine[10] also published an article on the same organization called, "An Elect Few Assume God's Work".

The articles agreed there are approximately 74,000 of these new "priests" who have been spread across 40 nations. TIME says, *"Since its founding in 1928, Opus Dei has become one of the most influential, controversial and mysterious movements in Roman Catholicism. John Paul's presence at Opus ordinations is only one of many signs of his approval..."* Opus is *"a corps of well-educated, disciplined, profoundly committed Catholics who, <u>as laity in ordinary jobs, can penetrate society in ways that priests cannot.</u> In the Opus concept, each lay Catholic is to <u>SANCTIFY the secular world and his own career...</u>"* They reportedly work *"at 487 universities and schools, 694 newspapers or periodicals, 52 TV or radio stations, 38 publicity agencies and twelve film companies."* Some who have dropped out of the Opus refer to the secretive organization as *"the Holy Mafia,"* or *"Octopus Dei".* One *"drop-out"* said, *"leaving becomes difficult for members, because 'their spirits are broken, and they have lost all touch with everyday life'".*

Some Catholic leaders are not in favor of Opus Dei but two events have enhanced the Opus stature. *"In 1981, the Vatican took the first steps toward the canonization of Opus' founder, <u>Spanish Monsignor Josemaria Escriva de Balaguer,</u> who died in 1975. Sainthood would vindicate the movement's creation*

---

[9]TIME Magazine. June 11, 1984.

[10]INSIGHT Magazine. November 16, 1987.

under 'divine inspiration,' as the pope described it." The other *"momentous mark of papal favor occurred in 1982, when John Paul granted Opus a new status known as personal prelature."* This gave the organization *"autonomy as a worldwide, nonterritorial jurisdiction with its priests and laity subject to Opus' prelate."* The TIME's article also said, *"A senior Vatican official says that the Pope has asked for private commitments from Opus that it will seek out all levels of society and will cooperate with local bishops and other lay movements."*

The author also had this to say: *"...The members of Opus Dei now seem to represent, for John Paul, an ideal for today's lay church member. There is speculation that the organization will gradually fill the traditional role of the Jesuits as an elite vanguard ready to DO THE BIDDING of Pope and church, and that John Paul has important evangelizing duties in mind for the organization..."*.

That the leaders in Opus Dei are strongly committed to the pope is suggested by this quote by an Opus' member of the men's General Council: *"We are among the most committed defenders of the notion that undebatable truth exists. Doctrine is not debatable, and when doubts arise over what is binding truth, the final word is the Pope's and not some theologian's."*

(Reader, does this not tell us where the authority really lies within the Roman Church? To Opus members, the Scriptures are not the final word of authority. The Pope is. This is not a Christian concept.)

The article in INSIGHT magazine confirms nearly every detail mentioned above which also reported that there are, in addition to the 74,000 bonafide Opus members, 700,000 "cooperators" around the world who may not necessarily be "christians". According to the INSIGHT article, *"..'.Opus Dei focuses on where political, economic and social power lies,' says an English prelate at the Vatican, 'this carries with it a danger that the movement could lose its freedom to challenge the existing order by becoming part of it."*

This last comment by the Englishman expresses tremendous sensitivity and insight. What he is saying is that one of the main objectives of Opus Dei is to challenge things the way they presently are in the world, on every level of existence. I understand where the prelate is coming from when he says Opus will *"become part of it"* (i.e., the politico-economic-socio scene). He's close to the truth but not quite 'on the beam'. It isn't as though Opus is unwittingly endangering themselves through ignorance as they move into the whole world's marketplace; indeed, this is their very objective! I believe their aim is to eventually supplant what is in existence today. It appears that not only the leaders but also that all Opus' members are fervent in their belief and commitment that they are *the* element which will ultimately solve all the political, economic and social woes in today's world.

OPUS DEI'S FOUNDER: Jose Maria Escriva de Balaguer y Albas

Escriva, a priest of Spain, created the Opus Dei society in 1928. The story goes that when he was on a retreat in Madrid in 1928 at age 26, he was pondering what God wanted of him. Suddenly nearby church bells began to ring and Escriva "saw" the answer. It was to set up an institution that would *"tell men and women of every country and of every condition, race, language, milieu and state of life that they can love and serve God without giving up their ordinary work, their family life and their normal social relations."* This is a remarkable conviction Escriva had. But how does this fit in with *"numeraries who perform periodic, brief sessions of mortification of the flesh, using braided thong 'disciplines' for self-flagellation. Some wear a wire with prongs, which members call a cilice, tied around the leg above the knee."* Such mortification is

258

supposed to remind the Opus member of the suffering of Jesus. One of their leaders, Monsignor Cormac Burke, said this *"is something which cannot be omitted from a fully religious life,..."*

INSIGHT also reported *"the group is said to exert great political influence in Spain and to be vastly wealthy."..."In part, the criticism Opus Dei inspires stems from its being the product of traditional, Catholic Spain and its Spanish leadership, which infused it with values that have become alien in countries of liberal civilization."* The article goes on to say, *"...an Irish priest working in America who has observed Opus Dei in Spain, Mexico and the United States, says the society's practices are much milder here (USA) than in the two Hispanic countries."* (*"The organization came to the United States in 1949 when three Spaniards arrived in Chicago from Rome. One was a nuclear physicist taking up a university position. From among their new friends and acquaintances, they won adherents to Escriva's teachings. But the movement's growth in the U.S. has not been as great as elsewhere in the world."*)

Escriva died in 1975. His replacement today, another Spaniard by the name of Monsignor Alvaro del Portillo, worked directly with Escriva for forty years. Pope John Paul II is obviously very close to Opus Dei as he established the society as the first *"personal prelature"* set up in the Roman Catholic Church. *"A prelature is similar to a diocese, but instead of having a territorial jurisdiction, a personal jurisdiction is exercised by the prelate over the spiritual formation and work of members WHEREEVER THEY ARE."* According to a historian named Johnson, John Paul II has said, *"Escriva had the right combination; a robust adherence to the traditional dogmas and moral standards of Catholicism together with the missionary zeal to apply them in the modern world."*

Now, compare the above facts about Opus Dei to the "AIMS" of the EEC as stated in an encyclopedia in the library of the

University of California at Davis, California. It said:

"To promote throughout the Community a harmonious development of economic activities, a continuous and balanced expansion, an increase in stability, an acceleration in the rise of the standard of living and closer relations between Member States, by establishing a common market and by progressive rapprochement of the economic policies of Member states."

Interesting parrallels, aren't they? They are, I'm convinced, the <u>same</u> concepts because they come from the <u>same</u> "author".

SUMMARY AND CONCLUSIONS

Revelation, chapter 13, describes two *"beasts"*, one from the *"sea"* (representing all humanity) and one from the *"earth"* (the religious community within). The first *"beast"* we have seen is a politico-economic-social system, which has been identified as the Common Market of Europe. The second *"beast"* is identified as the Roman Catholic Church as headed by the Vatican under the leadership of its Pope.

The prophet Daniel said the <u>eleventh</u> member of an already-existing ten nation confederacy would produce a leader, the likes of which the world has never known, which we have called the anti-Christ. As of January 1, 1981, The EEC had ten members and on January 1, 1986 the eleventh joined — SPAIN. (You recall the explanation of how Portugal was included along with Spain. Now let me share a new insight with you.)

MORE ON THE TWO HORNS

Remember the picture of the white shaggy goat which I saw in the San Francisco newspaper the year Greece became the tenth member of the EEC, and that it had one long single horn? It was reported the way this is achieved is by some kind of manipulative fusion of two normal horns into one! It may be a wild thought but one day it occurred to me this parallels Spain and Portugal's entry into the EEC: two nations voted in together — 'fused', if you will, by the others. Is it possible that this is God's way of resolving for us the mystery that there are now 12 EEC members instead of the expected 11?

Carrying this thought further, recently I learned that in the 15th century the Pope authorized two nations to "claim" the remainder of the undiscovered world for the Vatican. Those two nations were Spain and Portugal!

It just may be that Daniel's single horn ("fused-from-two"), which arose after the "ten horns", was the very same as the two horns the apostle John saw on the head of the False Prophet. In Daniel's case it appeared as <u>one</u> to indicate the single source of power from which the fusion came; in John's case the horns appeared as <u>two</u> to indicate that there were in fact two separate nations set up to accomplish the False Prophet's desires. Can you accept this possibility, my friends?

NOW BACK TO THE TWO BEASTS

This whole chapter of Revelation makes clear that these two "*beasts*" (not to be confused with the "*two horns*" of the False Prophet) will join forces in the end. We learned the second "*beast*" is preparing the way for the first. This second one is called the False Prophet and it is his duty to link the religious community to the world's work force into one structure. We also learned that a Spanish man named Escriva produced the idea of how to accomplish this very feat and that Rome's present Pope, John Paul II, is not only in agreement with Escriva, but is trying to promote his "sainthood" in order to "sanctify" his ideas. The Pope is also "anointing" his secret emissaries and sending them all over the world to "DO HIS BIDDING". He is living out the very words of the text as the apostle John described him — he *"exercises"*, *"performs"*, *"deceives"*, has the *"power"* and *"causes"* it all to happen. Admittedly, there are some things described in this chapter which haven't yet happened. However, much of what John said is unquestionably already in place.

The identifications I've made in this chapter will make many uncomfortable. I will probably be accused of discriminations and prejudices. That is neither my nature nor my intent. I would merely admonish the Roman Church to repent of their sins and turn from their wicked ways — unbelief of the simple Gospel truths and usurpation of the authority that only Jesus Christ Himself holds.

It is not my intention to stir up Christians to the point of anger. God Forbid! This kind of information must always be handled with extreme delicacy. Unsaved people, who may have good morals, and demonstrate high patriotism, etc., can do great harm with knowledge such as this. 'Good' people (though unsaved) who have virtually no understanding of the things of God, often think it's alright to take up an offense and attempt to destroy those they believe to be 'tools of the devil'. That, of course, is not our responsibility. Look at Jesus! He did not try to get rid of Herod nor did He try to stop Judas. Christians must keep in mind that all the prophecies will be fulllfilled.

In the process of what lies ahead, Christians are to be *salt* and *light* in the world. For this reason, I have even hesitated to share these convictions. Many times I ask, "Why God?" That is, "Even if these things are true, why have You shown them to me?" And as I try to hear His answer, all I can tell you is that I seem to be driven on in my search to understand prophetic truth as contained in the Holy Scriptures. Obviously I take this to mean someone needs to know. However, if you believe and accept the thoughts, ideas and identifications I've suggested here concerning the Roman Catholic Church and its heirarchy, please use great discretion as you share the insights with others. There are innocent, honest, Godly Christians caught up in this web. We'll see more about this in Revelation 18.

CHAPTER 14

JESUS AND THE 144,000 ISRAELITES

We have already covered the main points I felt were lacking in other prophecy books on the following subjects:

1. The longitudinal aspect of Biblical prophecy as understood in the light of the Law of Double Reference.
2. New thoughts and concepts on the "two witnesses".
3. Clarification of the confusion about Daniel's "seventy weeks".
4. Giving a few clues on how to recognize some of Satan's delusions and handiwork within certain worldly empires and 'religions'; and how these relate to the 'kingdom' he is building.

Therefore, to keep this book reasonably-sized, from here on I shall present even larger blocks of Scripture, followed by less commentary on the main highlights of those passages. This in no way means the Scriptures yet to be discussed are of any lesser importance.

1 "And I looked, and behold, a Lamb standing on Mount Zion, and with Him one hundred and forty-four thousand, having His Father's name written on their foreheads.
2 And I heard a voice from heaven, like the voice of many waters, and like the voice of loud thunder. And I heard the sound of harpists playing their harps.
3 And they sang a new song before the throne, before the living creatures, and the elders; and no one could learn that song except the hundred and forty-four thousand who were redeemed from the earth.
4 These are the ones who were not defiled with women, for they are virgins. These are the ones who follow the Lamb whereever He goes. These were redeemed from among men, being firstfruits to God and to the Lamb.

*5 And in their mouth was found no guile, for they are
without fault before the throne of God."*

From Genesis to Revelation there are many stories which
seem to traverse the following pattern: God makes a promise
to fulfull a certain act, then Satan <u>precedes</u> and perverts the
real thing God had originally purposed and prophetically
revealed. Example: Abraham and Sarah had an idea on how
to "help" God fulfill His promise of a son to them. Since Sarah
was too old to conceive (they reckoned), Abraham could have
sexual relations with their servant, Hagar. He did and Ishmael
was born. (The reader will recall that Mohammad is a
descendant of Ishmael. Isn't it amazing how one's sin will
invariably find him out? Today, Israel continues to be
threatened by the Arabic, descendant-nations of Ishmael.)

Initially, Abraham and Sarah looked to reason instead of
believing God. But in spite of their first actions, God remained
faithful. Sarah did have a son (Isaac) who became the line
through which eventually would come God's Lamb, and Israel's
Messiah, Jesus Christ.

In our present study of prophecy, we see man continues this
particular sinful pattern. In chapter 13, John gave us a
description of Satan's best effort to pervert what God will one
day accomplish. That is, the anti-Christ and his lamb-like
forerunner, the False Prophet, will make their attempt at being
the messiah the world wants. Like the distorted, evil idea Satan
planted in Abraham and Sarah's minds, it won't work. It will
come. It will go. Afterwards, God's Kingdom will be set up.

Following the pattern, immediately after chapter 13 where we
see Satan's best perversion of God's plan, next comes the
appearance of God's true Lamb. Also with Him are the
144,000 — a unique group chosen for a special mission. There
is much speculation among Bible students as to the exact
identity and purpose of these people. I don't see any reason to
guess about it. In chapter 7 we saw that 12,000 individuals from

each tribe of Israel (which totals 144,000) were set aside for some eventual function. We have now reached the chapter which describes their destiny.

THE 144,000 BORN-AGAIN JEWS

Since chapter 7 so explicitly pointed out that there would be 12,000 people from each of twelve tribes of Israel, there's no reason not to accept this at face value; i.e., they will be 144,000 Israelites. It is very important to realize that the population in national Israel today does not necessarily represent all the tribes of Israel. I think the majority of modern Israel came from the tribe of Judah. I also believe the twelve tribes of ancient Israel are scattered all over the world and I doubt whether most of them have any idea that they are ancestorally-rooted in one of the twelve tribes of Israel! However, God knows who and where they are and I think these 'Israelites' are being set aside this very day. Also, the number is probably almost complete. Presently, each one becoming a member of this particular group is most likely coming into God's Kingdom just like any other Christian — hearing the Gospel with a believing heart. But one of these days, I believe an anointing will come upon these Christian-Israelites (born-again, blood-line Jews) larger in scope than anything yet seen in all Christian history.

THE LAST HALF OF THE "70TH WEEK"

Earlier I left you with the idea that 486 1/2 years of the 490-year Covenant Jesus confirmed, had transpired at Jesus' ascension. The counting stopped at that point, leaving 3 1/2 years to be completed at some future time. I believe God put this particular prophetic time-clock 'on hold' for the duration of the Christian Dispensation. Although brief, the 3 1/2 years remaining to be completed is a very important time period. I believe this particular 3 1/2 years is the last half of the final seven year countdown of this age. Now, it will be during this last half of what is commonly called the "Tribulation" that these 144,000 set-aside Israelites will become Jesus' co-workers for the final harvesting of souls. The Church will have just been raptured when this group 'takes over'.

[Now let me again summarize how I see the final seven year period. The first half can accurately be called Tribulation. (*Tribulation* being defined as "trouble in the world resulting from man's gross sinfulness and rebellion toward God"). The last half (i.e., the final 3 1/2 years) is more correctly called **THE GREAT TRIBULATION**, Scripturally referred to as the "*time of Jacob's trouble*". This latter half will be far more intense than the first half in terms of living conditions and manifested-hatred towards God and Godly people. Up until now the Holy Spirit has always restrained wickedness but will then have removed His restraints on satanic activities, thus allowing evil to rise to its full capacity. It is during this latter half that the 144,000 will be performing the work they were called to do.

So, the Tribulation should actually be broken into two distinctly different time segments. In the first half of the anti-Christ's build-up, the Holy Spirit will still be "restraining" evil; while in the second half (after the Church has been removed), the Holy Spirit adopts sort of a "hands off" policy concerning evil and the anti-Christ system. However, He will obviously still be here in order to seal the Great Tribulation believers.] (See 2 Thes. 2:1-12).

"ELIJAH'S" TASK OVER --- "ELISHA'S" TASK BEGINS

As I pointed out in Revelation 11, I'm not at all convinced Elijah will be one of the "*two witnesses*"; one like him perhaps, similar to John the Baptist, but not Elijah personally. But, there is one aspect to this reasoning which interests me. According to those who believe Elijah is one of the two witnesses, when Elijah was caught up (see 2 Kings, chapter 2), the incident was a glance into the distant future, believed to be prophetic of the rapture of the Church. (Insofar as the timing of the Church's rapture, you can see that the Futurists and I actually disagree only by a factor of 3 1/2 years. But oh, what an important 3 1/2 years!)

O.K., let's assume Elijah's rapture <u>was</u> a picture of the time when Christ calls His Church to be with Him. One day while pondering this issue (at the same time studying this chapter, Rev. 14), a question suddenly came to my mind: "If Elijah represented the Church, why stop spiritualizing there? Could Elijah's replacement, *Elisha*, likewise have been an Old Testament foreshadowing of yet another distant-future event?"

I'll leave it to you to read 2 Kings chapter 2 in depth but the story goes something like this: Elijah knew that he would soon be *"taken away"* and he had already placed his *"prophet's mantle"* on Elisha's back (see 1 Kings 19:19&20). That act sealed Elisha as the one who would take up the former prophet's role, somewhat like the transfer of the baton in a relay race.

But prior to departure, Elijah asked Elisha if there was anything he might do for him before he left. Elisha said, *"let a double portion of thy spirit be upon me"*. Elijah told him if he saw him leave, then the request would be granted. Elisha did see the event as Elijah was swept away in a *"chariot"*. Soon thereafter, it seems Elisha wanted to check whether his *"double portion"* had been given. He walked over to the river Jordan and struck the waters with his mantle (as he'd seen Elijah do) and cried out, *"...where is the Lord God of Elijah?"* And the waters parted in response to God's new prophet in the Land of Israel. (Later, Elisha saw his new power demonstrated again when he *"cursed"* — in the name of the Lord — 42 mocking children. Two *"she-bears"* came out of the woods and killed the youth. Lesson: don't mess around with God's anointed.)

From then on, the Scriptures reveal that Elisha did indeed receive the *"double portion"* of the *"spirit"* that was upon Elijah. Here's what I want you to get: if Elijah pictured the alive *"saints"* who would be raptured at the end of the Church age, what future role might Elisha forecast?

I believe Elisha foreshadowed the 144,000 as described in Revelation 7 and here in Revelation 14. Carrying this logic to its natural conclusion, just as Elisha received a *"double portion"* of the *"spirit"* that was upon Elijah, so also shall be the case with the 144,000 called-out Israelites after the Church is removed. (The "*spirit*" which was referred to by Elijah and Elisha is, of course, Holy Spirit empowerment.)

Why must the anointing upon the 144,000 need to be double-portioned? We must remember that the 144,000 will be working during the GREAT TRIBULATION, the last half of the final seven year countdown period. This will be concurrent with the reign of the anti-Christ — a period we know that will be extremely tough for believers. Therefore, it doesn't stretch the imagination to realize it will require "*double portions*" in order to provide endurance for the 144,000 prophets of Israel to minister during the "*time of Jacob's trouble*".

Thus, when the anti-Christ is functioning under his full 'anointing' from the devil, the 144,000 will also need a fuller measure of power to continue and not faint. It is noteworthy to observe that Elisha was not all that fearless prior to his "*double portion*". In fact, when first called through Elijah to be the next prophet, his natural flesh resisted tremendously. He wanted to remain on the farm and work. But, *after* the anointing, he became a different person altogether. The same will be true when the 144,000 receive their anointing as soon as the Church is raptured. They will "*strike the river Jordan*", so to speak, with their "*mantles*", it will part and multitudes of people will come to believe in the Messiah they will proclaim, Jesus Christ.

INTERESTING IMPLICATIONS

Earlier I suggested that everyone does not necessarily know whether they are in the lineage of one of the twelve tribes of Israel. Marriages within national Israel haven't remained purely within the framework of their own; some have married 'Gentiles'. Consequently, I'm sure many have lost track of their own racial background. There are likely thousands (perhaps millions) of people of Israel background without the slightest awareness of it.

Remember also, Assyria took the ten northern tribes of Israel about one hundred years <u>before</u> the Babylonian captivity of the Southern Kingdom. (The Southern Kingdom consisted mainly of the tribes of Judah, Benjamin and a few Levites). The far greater number of tribes (10) were in the Northern Kingdom. There is no Biblical account as to what happened to those ten northern tribes. My conviction is that those people were <u>then</u> dispersed throughout Europe and <u>now</u> are scattered all over the world, most unaware of their link to national Israel.

But God knows who and where the Israelites are. And when the *last trumpet* sounds, calling the Church to meet Christ in the air, certain Christ-believing Israelites will suddenly be anointed with a "*double portion*" of God's Holy Spirit and a new work will begin. The 'mantle' will have passed from "*Elijah*" to "*Elisha*".

I'm persuaded that those 144,000 are being saved <u>today</u>. They are coming into the kingdom just like everyone else: hearing the Gospel with a believing heart. If you have read between-the-lines here, you can see that some Christians will not leave when the Church does! That'll shock some readers. But, someone has got to stay behind and finish the work God has purposed during the final wrap-up — the 144,000.

Some can't accept the implications as I see them here. But I ask you to consider the logic of this presentation. If, as most Futurists would say, all Christians were to be raptured at the end of this age, there wouldn't be even one remaining believer in the world! Now, even the Futurists believe there will be multitudes saved during the tribulation. QUESTION: Who is going to be leading this multitude to salvation?

There will be a multitude of Christians right up to the end of the Christian age (mid-point of the Tribulation). There will also be a sizeable number (144,000 to be exact) to take over the mantle at that point. I'm convinced the "Elijah-task" is about over now and that the "Elisha-task" is about to begin. All signs point to it. If you, dear reader, happen to be here at that time and come to realize that you are in fact one of the *144,000,* take courage my 'Israelite' friend and, good harvesting!

PREACHING ANGELS?

6 "And I saw another angel flying in the midst of heaven, having the everlasting gospel to preach to those who dwell on the earth---to every nation, tribe, tongue, and people---
7 saying with a loud voice, "Fear God and give glory to Him, for the hour of His judgment has come; and worship Him who made heaven and earth, the sea and the springs of water."

If this is to be interpreted literally-only, this is an amazing prediction; an angel gets to preach the Gospel! How does he do it? Perhaps the same way the Holy Spirit prompts our minds today. But maybe it has a symbolic meaning. The angel was seen in the *"midst of heaven"* proclaiming the Gospel to those on earth. Perhaps the inference is to the gospel coming down to earth via satellite transmission.

"BABYLON" FALLS

8 "And another angel followed, saying, "Babylon is fallen, is fallen, that great city, because she made all nations drink of the wine of the wrath of her fornication."

Ancient Babylon epitomized man-centeredness: materialism, ungodliness and paganism. Paradoxically, the greatest apocalyptic Scriptures of the Old Testament were revealed to the prophet Daniel during that time. The apostle John also speaks of a *"Babylon"*. However, the *"Babylon"* referred to in verse 8 above is a "spiritual Babylon" rather than a particular place. I think the instruction here to us Christians is that the spiritual nature of the sins practiced in the original Babylon are now dispersed throughout the world. We will see this *"Babylon"* discussed later in much greater detail.

SOWING AND REAPING

9 "And a third angel followed them, saying with a loud voice, "If anyone worships the beast and his image, and receives his mark on his forehead or on his hand,
10 "he himself shall also drink of the wine of the wrath of God, which is poured out full strength into the cup of His indignation. And he shall be tormented with fire and brimstone in the presence of the holy angels and in the presence of the Lamb.
11 "And the smoke of their torment ascends forever and ever; and they have no rest day or night, who worship the beast and his image, and whoever receives the mark of his name."

This passage describes what happens to those people who submit to the anti-Christ's rule and authority. I call your attention to a very important point here: Note that his followers *will* (future tense) receive the Wrath of God. I emphasize this because, as you recall, the Futuristic viewpoint is that the Seals and Trumpets are a part of God's Wrath. But we saw the first mention of God's Wrath in Revelation 11:18 and John now speaks of it again here, doubly assuring us that God's Wrath still hasn't come, and we are now well past all the Seals and Trumpets! The Wrath of God will be spelled out in chapters 15, 16 and 17.

Notice that GOD'S WRATH will be dispensed *"without mixture"*. I take this to mean God will not temper or soften His final judgment. By then, God's righteous indignation will have reached the point of climax. Man will have rejected God as far as He will allow. You see, God is a loving God. He is longsuffering and merciful. He has always held back His wrath against man, knowing that he is such a weak vessel. And God wants to win mankind to Himself, giving him all kinds of chances to wake up and repent of his evil deeds and rebellion towards God. But even God has His limitations. When we get

271

to the time described above, God will have gone as far as He will go and those who have "*sown*" badly will "*reap*" badly. As the apostle says in verse 11, "*And the smoke of their torment ascends forever and ever; and they have no rest day or night, who worship the beast and his image, and whoever receives the mark of his name.*"

ATTENTION UNREPENTANT SINNERS!!!

This is a good place to talk to non-Christians. If you are unsaved, I invite you to receive the gift of eternal life right now. There is a day coming, and I think not too distant future, when God will pour out His Wrath on those who have refused His offer of eternal life to be spent with Him in His Kingdom. It's not something which <u>might</u> occur (as though an accident), dependent upon how good you may have been in this life. God does not judge on the merit system. We don't win 'brownie-points'. Nor does He gauge you relative to me and then pick the better of the two.

Self-righteous thoughts won't get us to heaven. God sent His Son Jesus Christ to die on the cross for our sins. He is the "bridge" between us and Almighty God. There are no other substitutes. All the religions and philosophies in the world will not provide you the gift. The gift is A GIFT. It's there for the receiving. You and I receive it by faith.....faith in the already-accomplished work of One Person — **Jesus**. Faith must be exercised in order for salvation to commence. This involves believing with your mind and your heart that what Jesus did was for *you*.

The Bible teaches that we need to confess our sins before God with the mouth. Tell God you are sorry for your sins and that you want to be forgiven and cleansed. Tell Him you've heard that the shed blood of Jesus paid the price for all your sins and that you understand this is the only acceptable sacrifice to Him to remove your sins. And tell Him you believe this to the best of your ability. Then, ask Jesus to come into your heart, mind and soul to become your Lord and Savior. When you do this, the Holy Spirit will seal you as God's purchased possession and give you guidance and help you to turn away from your old sinful ways and habits.

God bless you, fellow sinner, as you purpose to do what I just shared with you. And if you did it sincerely, welcome into the Kingdom of God. You've received The Gift. You and I are now fellow Christians. We're going into eternity together. Don't let anyone, or anything, cause you to stumble or turn away from your new conviction. I say this because you still have a mental storehouse of knowledge of your former ways. Your "old-man", who gets kicked out when you receive Jesus (authority-wise, he dies), may try to tell you, "Nothing happened. You're not saved. You're going to hell," blah, blah, blah... These thoughts are stirred up by Satan, the one hell was designed for. Once saved, Satan knows he's lost in the battle for your spirit; now he's trying to destroy your witness for Christ. He knows you won't tell others about The Gift if he can get you to doubting whether you received it.

One final word to you as a new believer — read your Bible every day. Begin with the New Testament. Read in this order: John, Romans, Acts, then go back to Matthew and read the whole thing, straight through. Pray every day. Get together with other like-believers, in a Bible-believing, joy-filled, local church. You have received what the Bible calls the BREAD of life. Jesus IS that BREAD. He is the gift. So, enjoy Him to the fullest, my friend!

BLESSED ARE THOSE "IN THE LORD"

12 Here is the patience of the saints; here are those who keep the commandments of God and the faith of Jesus.
13 And I heard a voice from heaven saying to me, "Write: 'Blessed are the dead who die in the Lord from now on.'"
"Yes," says the Spirit, "that they may rest from their labors, and their works follow them."

This passage makes clear that right in the middle of the worst times of recorded history, there will be faithful saints of God around. Note that patience is emphasized. Why so? Because it will be very trying and tempting to face the reality of not being able to buy or sell anything unless one has the "mark of the beast" on him which identifies one's eligibility to operate within the anti-Christ system. Thus, extreme patience will obviously be required of believers in those days.

273

But, verse 13 reveals a great promise to those who are willing to resist the 'mark'. *"Blessed are the dead who die in the Lord from now on,"* the Scripture says. Why does he say, *"from now on"*? Again, it must be an implication of just how difficult it will be to become a believer then. (This further substantiates the need for the *"double portion"* being given to the 144,000 Israelites). But, although difficult times are predicted here, never forget that God sustains those who trust Him; and the measure of the power He gives them to maintain will be proportional to the intensity of the trouble they are in. It's always been that way, as typified in the case of Meshach, Shadrach and Abednego in the furnace. (See Daniel 3.)

REAPING THE EARTH'S HARVEST

14 "And I looked, and behold, a white cloud, and on the cloud sat One like the Son of Man, having on His head a golden crown, and in His hand a sharp sickle.
15 And another angel came out of the temple, crying with a loud voice to Him who sat on the cloud, "Thrust in Your sickle and reap, for the time has come for You to reap, for the harvest of the earth is ripe."
16 And He who sat on the cloud thrust in His sickle on the earth, and the earth was reaped."

These verses summarize the actual evangelization which will be going on during the last half of the *Tribulation,* better called the GREAT TRIBULATION. One like the *"Son of Man"* directs this great in-gathering of souls. Jesus often used the title "Son of Man" in reference to Himself. Since John says *like* the Son of Man, he intimates perhaps a special representative sent in Jesus' behalf. Note that John saw Him "on the cloud". So, whoever it is, it appears he won't actually have touched the earth at that time.

Exactly how the transition of the rapture of the Church and the re-establishment of God's Covenant with national Israel occurs is not clear. But this we can be sure of: Jesus will become especially involved with the 144,000, just as He has been with the Church during the Christian era.

Remember, God's 490-year Covenant was specifically with Israel's twelve tribes. That covenant was "confirmed" and lived out for 3 1/2 years between Jesus and the "*many*" who received Him during His first advent. It will, I believe, be finalized between Him and the 144,000 during the remaining 3 1/2 years of the 490 year covenant — the GREAT TRIBULATION.

Admittedly, there is a bit of a mystery here. But then, we don't have to understand God's design of everything in order to know it will work out perfectly.

REAPING THE GRAPES OF WRATH

17 "And another angel came out of the temple which is in heaven, he also having a sharp sickle.
18 And another angel came out from the altar, who had power over fire, and he cried with a loud cry to him who had the sharp sickle, saying, "Thrust in your sharp sickle and gather the clusters of the vine of the earth, for her grapes are fully ripe."
19 And the angel thrust his sickle into the earth and gathered the vine of the earth, and threw it into the great winepress of the wrath of God.
20 And the winepress was trampled outside the city, and blood came out of the winepress, up to the horses' bridles, for one thousand six hundred furlongs."

God is very patient and long-suffering. We see the evidence of this truth historically. We also see it currently. It will be even more manifest during the GREAT TRIBULATION. We saw in verses 14 - 16 above that as wickedness increases, God increases His standards against it. Simultaneously God gives more and more of His blessings, protection and Holy Spirit anointing to the needs of those who love Him. But, there always comes a time when God says, "No more!" to the wicked. That's the above picture.

Earlier I spoke of the pattern of how Satan often comes first, pretending to fulfill God's promises through perversion and deceit. However, in the concluding text of this chapter we see that God has the last word. For those last ones on earth who refuse to receive "The Gift", there awaits for them a measure of *wrath* never-before witnessed by any man.

SUMMARY

In this chapter we have seen Jesus re-confirming the remaining 3 1/2 years of the 490-year Covenant which God made with Israel with the 144,000 born-again Israelites. We saw that many souls will be saved during the GREAT TRIBULATION as a result of the witnessing done by these double-portioned sons of Jacob. And just as the seemingly-untouchable, ancient Babylon fell, so also the 'Babylon' of our day will fall. And finally, we saw that, while Satan will have his heyday, God's justice will be served when God's *wrath* is poured upon all those who resist Him — those who choose instead to follow Satan's counterfeit system.

CHAPTER 15

THE WRATH OF GOD

1 "And I saw another sign in heaven, great and marvelous, seven angels having the seven last plagues; for in them is filled up the wrath of God."

<u>Now</u> we have finally arrived at the point which begins to spell out *GOD'S WRATH* against wickedness. I remain amazed by those who embrace the idea that the Seals and Trumpets contain any portion of God's wrath. I don't wish to sound harsh but in light of the above verse, the concept is ludicrous, yet it seems to be held by practically the whole evangelical Church!

As previously explained, the idea apparently stems from a misinterpretation of Revelation 6:16&17 which speaks of men who were experiencing the awful conditions of that time. I suggested the inference in that passage was to Europeans who were crying out because of the horrifying consequences of WW1. It was ordinary men who said the *"wrath of the Lamb"* had come. It is important to note that neither God, nor an angel, or any heavenly representative, made that announcement.

But whatever they thought was the *wrath of the Lamb,* it was obviously not the same thing as the *Wrath of God* which quite clearly is not introduced until here in Revelation 15:1. The Seals and Trumpets were tribulation troubles; problems man would bring upon himself as the consequence of sin. But the seven last plagues represent Divine judgments of an entirely different magnitude — it is the **WRATH OF GOD.**

Even Christians have never been allowed the privilege of avoiding tribulation. Think of those who were martyred for the cause of Christ during the past 2,000 years. Nor will tribulation pass Christians by in the first 3 1/2 years of the final seven year countdown.

Once again my position is understood in the light of the Law of Double Reference. There will yet be a specific Tribulation

277

as most prophets understand and talk about. There will be a LODR repetition of the Seals and Trumpets. But this time it will last 1260 days, (3 1/2 years), not 1260 years. Christians will still be here for that.

The only reason there is to be a rapture AT ALL is:

1. so that Christians living then may avoid the anti-Christ's time of total control (the last half of Daniel's 70th Week) and
2. not face **God's Wrath**. *"For God hath not appointed us to wrath, but to obtain salvation by our Lord Jesus Christ."* (1 Thes. 5:9).

THE VICTORIOUS SAINTS

2 "And I saw something like a sea of glass mingled with fire, and those who have the victory over the beast, over his image, over his mark, and over the number of his name, standing on the sea of glass, having harps of God.
3 And they sing the song of Moses, the servant of God, and the song of the Lamb, saying:
'Great and marvelous are Your works, Lord God Almighty! Just and true are Your ways, O King of the saints!
4 Who shall not fear You, O Lord, and glorify Your name? For You alone are holy. For all nations will come and worship before You, For Your judgments have been manifested."

These glad-hearted saints are apparently those who will become saved during the GREAT TRIBULATION. Their triumph seems to be especially awesome, probably due to the great intensity under which they became believers. They will have refused the anti-Christ's special-rights system — i.e., the "mark of the beast". During the anti-Christ's rule, God will miraculously preserve those who are willing to trust Him to the fullest. Thus, these beautiful words of praise here.

Notice what they sing: the "*song of Moses*" and the "*song of The Lamb*". What are these two songs? Moses was the deliverer of the people of God in his day, so his song must mean *Song of Deliverance*. The *song of the Lamb* obviously refers to Jesus, the Savior, which must mean, *Song of Salvation*. Both songs will be spectacular realities for these adulating Great-Tribulation saints. Even thinking about it now should cause any Christian to shout, "HALLELUJAH".

Another great promise here is that the Lord will ultimately rule the earth, for it says, "*...all nations will come and worship before You...*". Isn't that fantastic?

> (With clear Biblical statements like this I cannot understand how anyone could say, as some do, there will be no millennium during which Christ literally and personally reigns as King.)

SEVEN ANGELS WITH SEVEN "BOWLS OF WRATH"

5 "And after these things I looked, and behold, the temple of the tabernacle of the testimony in heaven was opened.
6 And out of the temple came the seven angels having the seven plagues, clothed in pure bright linen, and having their chests girded with golden belts.
7 And one of the four living creatures gave to the seven angels seven golden bowls full of the wrath of God who lives forever and ever.
8 And the temple was filled with smoke from the glory of God and from His power, and no one was able to enter the temple till the seven plagues of the seven angels were completed."

The seven angels are here given the Bowls which contain the WRATH OF GOD. The next chapter describes the actual sequential "dispensing" of these Bowls upon the ungodly, unrepentant world. It is not clear how long a period of time is involved during which the Bowls are emptied, but I believe it will occur rather quickly at the end of the anti-Christ reign. Here is my reason: Note that verse 8 says no one can enter the *"temple"* during the time these Bowls are being poured out. This means no one can be saved then. However, we know there will be multitudes who come to Christ during the Great Tribulation (the last half of the final seven years), so this places God's Wrath at a later time; namely, at the conclusion of Daniel's 70th Week, which is the end of this age. This will occur right after the last day of the final seven year countdown.

CONCLUSION

The thrust of this chapter should be a stimulus for Christians to become more fervent in our plea for sinners to repent. It's easy to just sit back and wait for the end to come. But we are not called to do that. Evangelizing requires willful and conscious effort. One must sometimes force his mouth open to say the words that lead people to salvation. The Bible says, *"Faith comes by hearing and hearing by the word of God...".* When we are with any unsaved person, our prayer, hope and attitude should always be to seek an opportunity to introduce them to Christ. The Holy Spirit will help, but you and I are expected to do our part. That's the way the Gospel works!

CHAPTER SIXTEEN

SEVEN BOWLS FILLED WITH GOD'S WRATH

1 "And I heard a loud voice out of the temple saying to the seven angels, 'Go and pour out the bowls of the wrath of God on the earth.'"

God wants to make it virtually impossible for us to be mistaken concerning the difference between tribulation and wrath. So, let's pull our comprehension-belts a little tighter. We need to know <u>when</u> and <u>who</u> receives God's wrath:

1. We already know that the anti-Christ will be in full power when the Bowls will be poured out. Therefore, obviously the first half of the final seven years will be over.
2. This also means the Church will have been raptured.
3. We know the 144,000 Israelites will have already brought multitudes to salvation-knowledge.
4. According to Revelation 15:8, we know no one can be saved during the dispensing of the Bowls.
5. The task of the 144,000 is finished (which we know lasts for exactly 3 1/2 years).

Considering these facts and by simple deduction, plus a little arithmetic, we are left with only one possible answer as to the timing of the Bowls: they will be emptied right AFTER the completion of the last half of the final seven year period.

As we shall see in this chapter, the Wrath of God is against the anti-Christ, the False Prophet and all wicked mankind. Thus, the Bowls of Wrath are against all who refuse God's grace, the "wicked" choosing instead to follow Satan's delusions.

The exact timing may also somehow relate to Daniel 12, where the prophet refers to 1290 and 1335 days. It (could) be that the Bowls commence at the end of the 1260th day of the last half of the Great Tribulation, intensifies at 1290 days, then continues until the 1335th day, making a total time of 75 days for the dispensation of all seven Bowls. This passage in Daniel seems to remain somewhat unclear to all writers. (You know, of course, that throughout this book I defined a 'prophetic day' as one year. Therefore, the 1290 and 1335 days probably also have had a long-range application. But remember, one application doesn't preclude the reality of the other.)

Whatever is actually meant by the 1335 days, it must relate with Jesus' second coming because Daniel said, "*BLESSED is he that waiteth, and cometh to the thousand three hundred and five and thirty days*" (1335 days). Dan 12:12. I believe this is talking about the point at which the earth will be prepared for the second coming of the Lord Jesus Christ to reign as Lord and King. Daniel's comment "*Blessed is he...*" refers to those who are chosen to begin the millennium with Christ.

THE FIRST BOWL: THE "MARK OF THE BEAST" BECOMES INFECTED

> 2 "*And the first went and poured out his bowl on the earth, and a foul and loathsome sore came on the men who had the mark of the beast and on those who worshiped his image.*"

God's Wrath seems to start at the bottom of the anti-Christ system and from there progresses upwards throughout the heirarchy. This first Bowl is against those who have given their allegiance to God's adversary, the satanically-energized anti-Christ. These are the ones who will have believed the "*strong delusion*" the apostle Paul spoke of in 2 Thessalonians 2:11. (This should be a strong stimulus for us to be bold in our testimony to the lost that Jesus is their only hope of deliverance — today, and forever).

THE SECOND BOWL: THE "SEA" TO BLOOD

3 "And the second angel poured out his bowl on the sea, and it became like the blood of a dead man; and every living creature in the sea died."

I find this verse hard to understand, whether viewed figuratively or literally. We have learned that *"sea"*, allegorically speaking, refers to mass humanity. If we take it that way here, then it would appear that every human being would die. This can't be true as the ensuing verses will testify.

But, if we are to take it literally, then we have to ask the question, "Does the second angel kill every living thing in the oceans?" If so, this would mean there would be no living things in the seas during the millennium! I think that is equally false. Since the word John used is singular, *"sea"*, one wonders if it refers only to one specific sea. However, I fail to see the value in that since what we are talking about here is God's Wrath against wickedness all over the world. ???

But let's look at another phrase in the above verse: The *sea* became..."*as the blood of a dead man*". What is the blood of a dead man like? Motionless, right? Blood in motion carries life to all parts of the body via an elaborate network of blood vessels. If the blood stops, so does the sustenance of body-life. With this thought in mind, perhaps the second Bowl is aimed at destroying the elaborate net-work the False Prophet and the anti-Christ will have in effect at that time.

This last postulation seems most acceptable in light of the fact that all the Bowls are specifically targeted, each one aimed at a particular aspect of Satan's earthly kingdom. It appears that God brings down the anti-Christ system in a "domino" fashion. Perhaps the outstretched-network of Opus Dei and similar satanic operations within the *"sea"* of humanity are part of the line-up.

THE THIRD BOWL: RIVERS AND SPRINGS BECOME BLOOD

4 "And the third angel poured out his bowl on the rivers and springs of water, and they became blood.
5 And I heard the angel of the waters saying: 'You are righteous, O Lord, The One who is and who was and who is to come, Because You have judged these things.
6 For they have shed the blood of saints and prophets, And You have given them blood to drink. For they are worthy of it.'
7 And I heard another out of the altar saying, 'Even so, Lord God Almighty, true and righteous are Your judgments."

Using the same line of reasoning presented above (i.e., that Bowl # 2 represents God's Wrath against the peripheral aspect of the anti-Christ's system in the *"sea"*), then next up in the ladder of authority, the *"rivers and springs"*, would logically signify THE LEADERS over Opus Dei and other mainline command-links.

To clarify, consider this: picture a sea — a large body of water which receives it's nourishment from rivers and streams that flow into it. Since we know that *"sea"* symbolically refers to the general populace, where Opus Dei is designed to feed their 'wisdom' to the masses, then it seems reasonable to assume that *"rivers and streams"* would refer to the next step up in the chain-of-command of the anti-Christ's system.

But whatever is the actual meaning of *"rivers and streams"*, we can certainly be sure that the term suggests <u>human beings</u> and not flowing bodies of ordinary water. I say this because verse 6 tells us that these particular *waters* will *"shed the blood of saints and prophets"*. I think we can all agree that <u>people</u> are responsible for killing the saints and prophets, not literal waterways.

284

THE FOURTH BOWL: MEN ARE SCORCHED

8 "And the fourth angel poured out his bowl on the sun, and power was given to him to scorch men with fire."
9 "And men were scorched with great heat, and they blasphemed the name of God who has power over these plagues; and they did not repent to give Him glory."

Talk about hard-headedness! In spite of everything that has already happened, ungodly men still refuse to repent of their sins! Even though much torment will have already been experienced and witnessed by lost mankind, he will, on the whole, still *"blaspheme the name of God"*. I see no way of interpreting how this plague comes other than to assume that the intensity of the sun's rays are going to be greatly increased upon the earth. It appears this particular Bowl of God's Wrath is more general than we've seen in other Bowls, this one affecting all mankind. However, that's what we should expect to happen eventually.

THE FIFTH BOWL: THE "BEAST" GETS IT

10 "And the fifth angel poured out his bowl on the throne of the beast, and his kingdom became full of darkness; and they gnawed their tongues because of the pain."
11 "And they blasphemed the God of heaven because of their pains and their sores, and did not repent of their deeds."

As suggested earlier, it seems that God's Wrath started at the bottom of the anti-Christ system, affecting first those who were deceived into receiving the *"mark of the beast"*, followed then by the next Bowls, going right on up through the ranks. Now, the Fifth Bowl reaches the upper echelons of Satan's earthly kingdom. This probably refers to the political leaders in power within the revived Roman Empire at that time. (Note the continued hard-heartedness. Men still refuse to acknowledge

God's authority, preferring rather, in spite of their misery, to remain self-centered, self-sufficient and unrepentant.)

THE SIXTH BOWL: THE EUPHRATES DRIES UP

12 "And the sixth angel poured out his bowl on the great river Euphrates, and its water was dried up, so that the way of the kings from the east might be prepared."

Most apocalyptic-Scripture writers seem to be agreed that the *"kings of the east"* refer to the oriental countries, chief of which would probably be China. Recall that the Sixth Trumpet mentioned the Euphrates river in conjunction with a 200,000,000-man army. It is doubtful any group of nations other than the Eastern Orient could even conceivably amass such a large number of soldiers as this.

We noted earlier that in 1978 a road was completed, extending from China, through Pakistan, into the Middle East. This could actually pave the way for that 200,000,000-man army. Also, it is said the Euphrates River can now be shunted near its head, therefore making it possible for a literal *"drying up"* of its present course. This would make it quite conceivable that, in our day, the Euphrates could become a dry bed over which a broad band of foot soldiers could approach a battle field in the Middle East.

THE "UNHOLY TRINITY"

13 "And I saw three unclean spirits like frogs coming out of the mouth of the dragon, out of the mouth of the beast, and out of the mouth of the false prophet.
14 For they are the spirits of demons, working signs, which go out to the kings of the earth and of the whole world, to gather them to the battle of that great day of God Almighty.

15 "Behold, I am coming as a thief. Blessed is he who watches, and keeps his garments, lest he walk naked and they see his shame."
16 And they gathered them together to the place called in Hebrew, Armageddon."

There is a real heavenly Father, a real Holy Spirit and a real Son of God — Who together comprise the Godhead. Person-wise, all are distinctly different, yet Biblically presented as One. They are always in perfect agreement. Everything that is done by either is always respected and 'approved', if you will, by the others. I confess that I cannot fully understand this. However, a mere reading of the Scriptures shows that these conclusions are clearly and unquestionably taught. What one does with the teaching is either believed or rejected.

Satan has his own plans for perverting the real Godhead. Some have called the above passage a Biblical portrayal of his 'unholy trinity' — the *"dragon"* being Satan, the *"beast"* is the anti-Christ and the *"False Prophet"* his forerunner. I don't know if this is correct or not. But it does serve the purpose of understanding the delusion God said He would send to those who believed NOT the truth. (See 2 Thes. 2.) In essence, God is saying, *"Either believe Me or I have no other alternative than to allow you to follow the one who perverts my ways".*

Today there are many false religions. But in the final analysis, there will be only two choices: one way leads to eternal life; one way leads to eternal destruction. The *only* way to be saved from the latter is to believe the former, which means to accept God's delivering Messiah — the Lord Jesus Christ.

It seems Jesus deemed this passage so crucial He sent no angel but broke His personal silence by saying, *"Blessed is he who watches, and keeps his garments, lest he walk naked and they see his shame."* What does it mean to keep one's *"garments"*? The only apparel you or I can wear which hides our real nature (our spiritual nakedness) is the *"righteousness of Christ".* God *imputes* the righteousness of Jesus to those who trust Him as

287

Lord and Savior. The very Perfection of Jesus spiritually clothes those who are "*in Him*".

Thus, when God looks upon a believer at Judgment Day, He sees His Own Son's perfection, not the guilty sinner. Jesus is the 'apparel' the heavenly Father sees. The sinful nature of a believer and the sins he commits are covered (actually removed) by Jesus' shed blood. That's what Jesus paid for at the Cross of Calvary. What a price has been paid for us sinners! How can one neglect so great a salvation? (See Hebrews 2:3.)

ARMAGEDDON

Notice verse 14 says demons are the ones behind the scenes inspiring and luring humanity into the battleground of Armageddon. They will do this through "*great signs*" which will effectively deceive the "*kings of the earth*". That battle will involve many kingdoms which Satan will have banded together, the kings of the east, the Arab nations, the revived Roman Empire, and others, presumably designed to attempt annihilation of Israel once and for all.

It is not altogether clear exactly *who will be against who?* in this last war. In any event, we know Christ ultimately intervenes and will begin the process of putting all nations under His feet. (This is another one of those places where identifications are very difficult, perhaps impossible, to make. In certain instances, I've come to rest in the assurance that God has reserved some facts which just won't be fully known until the time comes. If it is necessary for the Church to have the understanding, it'll come right on time.)

THE SEVENTH BOWL: THE EARTH UTTERLY SHAKEN

17 "And the seventh angel poured out his bowl into the air, and a loud voice came out of the temple of heaven, from the throne, saying, "It is done!"

18 And there were noises, thunderings, and lightnings; and there was a great earthquake, so mighty and so great an earthquake, such as had not been since men were on the earth.

19 And the great city was divided into three parts, and the cities of the nations fell. And great Babylon was remembered before God, to give her the cup of the wine of the fierceness of His wrath.

20 And every island fled away, and the mountains were not found.

21 And great hail out of heaven fell on men, every stone about the weight of a talent. And men blasphemed God because of the plague of the hail, since that plague was exceedingly great."

This is the final Bowl of God's Wrath. It will be a literal earth-shaking experience. When the Bible goes to the extent of saying something is so severe that *"such as had not been since men were on the earth"*, you better believe this is going to be some tremendous event. Cities will fall; islands will *flee away;* mountains will not be found. Does it literally mean the islands and mountains in the world will be gone? Or could *"islands"* symbolically refer to small nations and *"mountains"* be indicative of large nations? Again, I just don't see enough information here to be sure. In any case, clearly, God will have intervened to take control in order to show forth His might which He has had in store for a long time.

This morning I just happened across a passage in Job which could be an Old Testament prophecy concerning these Bowls of God's wrath. Note the language: *"...Hast thou seen the treasures of the hail, which I have reserved against the time of trouble, against the day of battle and war?"* (Job 38:22 & 23). Now compare this to Rev.16:21 above.

The next chapter spells out in greater detail that which is predicted here.

CHAPTER SEVENTEEN

THE "BEAUTY" AND THE BEAST

1 "And one of the seven angels who had the seven bowls came and talked with me, saying to me, "Come! I will show you the judgment of the great harlot who sits on many waters,
2 with whom the kings of the earth committed fornication, and the inhabitants of the earth were made drunk with the wine of her fornication."

As with most of the symbolic figures we see in Revelation, such as the *"ten horns"*, the various *"beasts"*, the *"false prophet"*, etc., there is also much controversy and speculation as to the identity of the *"great harlot"* here in this chapter. Actually, I don't see the reason for so much confusion since, beginning in verse seven, the angel who showed John these things explains the mystery to a great extent. I believe the fact is, there are many who <u>do</u> understand this passage but are fearful of saying what they really believe. It's high time we stop hiding our convictions on this matter and speak out.

At the outset, let's simply use a little common sense as we look at some of the terms used in this passage. First, what is a harlot? The dictionary defines her as *"a promiscuous woman"; "an immoral woman"; "one whose body is for hire"*. I would add this: *"one who enters into fornication* (sinful intimacy) *with virtually anyone interested and willing to pay for her services"*. A man who lies with such a woman reduces himself to the same level of her own immorality, thus exposing himself to all the harlot's 'business' acquaintances.

Now with the above definitions of a literal harlot, we can unmask the *harlot* of this chapter with a little better insight. We see in verse 1 that the harlot *"sits on many waters"*. So, whoever 'she' is, we must look for a personality of broad-scale proportions, not some obscure entity or vaguely-familiar organization.

(I work in a district well-known for prostitution. An outstanding feature of the community is the seductively-dressed, overly-made-up, street-call-girl. It is with an attractive, up-front display that the harlot makes herself known and desirable to the passers-by. Just as the prostitute lures her "prey" through her outward-beauty, so also does the *"mystery harlot"* of Revelation chapter 17. Therefore, we must look for something unhidden, well-known and outwardly beautiful; i.e., things which would lure the lustful, not-so-well-informed, unsuspecting world. Men who are seduced by the "call-girl" get caught up in her world and become *"drunk"* with sensual pleasures. In like manner, the harlot of this chapter makes her 'partners' — the *"kings of the earth"* — drunk with the *"wine of her fornication"*. That is, many leaders of certain nations will become infatuated and seduced by the teachings and ideas promulgated by the "mystery harlot".)

THE "BEAUTIFUL" SIDE OF EVIL

3 "So he carried me away in the Spirit into the wilderness. And I saw a woman sitting on a scarlet beast, full of names of blasphemy, having seven heads and ten horns.
4 And the woman was arrayed in purple and scarlet, and adorned with gold, precious stones, and pearls, having in her hand a golden cup full of abominations and the filthiness of her fornication.
5 And on her forehead a name was written:

**MYSTERY
BABYLON THE GREAT,
THE MOTHER OF
HARLOTS AND OF THE
ABOMINATIONS OF THE
EARTH."**

The Bible teaches that God has in mind a perfect dwelling place for all those He has purposed to save to be with Him. This is a wonderful thing to think about; indeed, the hope and belief of every Christian. It will be a time when power and worship will be perfectly unified, totally planned and executed by God Almighty. God has shown certain bits-and-pieces of that coming age and we can be assured, as with all other Biblical prophecies, it will come to pass.

Conversely, fallen mankind, under the perversive inspiration of Satan, has always had in mind to bring about a state of 'perfection' here on this unregenerate earth, representing a spiritual parallel of God's Divine plan as briefly described above. Many kingdoms and empires have come and gone which attempted to do this very thing, obviously none having achieved their goal. Those who have believed they could pull this off have had many ideas in common, the main one being to strike a balance between religious power and temporal power. With these thoughts in mind, the above Scripture passage will be a little more sensible. Let's look at the key points:

THE "WOMAN" AND THE "BEAST"

John pictures fallen-man's perfect-blend as that of a *"woman"* (the religious part) who sat upon a *"beast"* (the temporal part). We have already touched on this in previous discussions but John broadens it here. The seven heads of this beast are the same ones spoken of in Revelation 13. Recall, they represented seven sequential kingdoms: Egyptian, Assyrian, Babylonian, Medo-Persian, Grecian (or Alexandrian), Roman, and the various Christian-age attempts some have grouped and called the Germanic-Slavonic. I believe history shows that few, if any, of the rulers over these kingdoms had any real, sincere respect for their religious counterpart within each of their regimes. They were known for their stubborn arrogance, egotism, high-mindedness, in fact most desiring to be worshipped themselves.

However, these "kings" were forced to admit that they couldn't achieve success without the religious-leaders' help, who the masses looked to for 'spiritual' guidance. This tendency represents the spirit of antichrist at work in them.

But the problem was, the religious leaders liked authority and praise too, thus often resulting in great struggles between these two power-hungry, self-worship-prone offices. (Later we will see the final result of this kind of sick harmony.)

So, while no kingdom ever seemed to achieve the perfect match-up, past ages demonstrate that unregenerate-man would continue searching all his days, obsessed with the conviction he would find it some day.

There is a key thought in verse 4 having to do with the beautiful adornment of the "woman". This refers to outward beauty, typical of all harlotry — whether speaking of real-life prostitutes or the spiritual harlot of erroneous religion. So, what should we look for in the world as we attempt to identify this "woman" of Revelation, chapter 17? The Scripture says one dressed with "gold, precious stones, and pearls". As one regards the wealth and museums of the Roman Catholic Church along with her great cathedrals and all the pomp that goes with it — the dress of the popes, bishops, cardinals, etc. — , I'm convinced we are seeing what John is describing.

To be successful, each kingdom of the past has embraced the religion of the hour — whatever was then popular. Beginning with the Egyptian, all seven kingdoms had its own religious adornment. In the Christian era, it was the 'Holy' Roman Empire. For nearly 2,000 years now, Rome has presented the world perverted-christianity. Oh, this 'church' has a "form of godliness", even using the Bible as its basis, but has really missed the mark of true Christianity.

As already said, I'm sure there are real Christians trapped within this ecclesiastical prostitute. But knowingly or not, they are giving their allegiance to one of Satan's cleverest attempts at cementing earthly-religion and temporal-power. (More later on this.)

THE "MYSTERY"

Why does John call the woman "*mysterious*"? I think it is mainly because the winding course she has traveled has been so incredibly long. The religous aspect of man's kingdoms (under Satan's guidance) have always been chameleon-like. They have taken on the 'color' of whichever leader and his heirarchy that has captured the people's imagination at any given time or age. To understand our 'hour' with the *harlot* we need only address the kingdom (the "*horn*" of the Holy Roman Empire) that affects our age because the book of Daniel and Revelation clearly indicate it will be <u>the last</u> of human empires.

I have lately been reading some interesting historical accounts of the Roman Empire beginning at the time of Jesus' day, going right up through today. Even a sketchy view of this particular Empire's ever-changing nature, noting the power struggles between the Roman emperors and the popes, seeing the abuses, the perversions, the Spanish Inquisitions, the immorality of the emperors and some of the popes, the wars, etc., provides sufficient and irrefutable evidence to conclude the Holy Roman Empire must to be the harlot of Revelation 17.

(Paradoxically, one German king, Frederick II, desiring to rule all Italy, including Rome, was called the "Antichrist" by Pope Gregory. Isn't that amazing? Frederick, not to be outdone, reacted by calling Gregory the Antichrist!)

Although the leaders on both sides (religious and secular) basically wanted the same things (total control in the earth), the back-and-forth bickering and accusations, plus the never-ending battle for supremacy among the European kings and the popes, prevented the Empire from reaching a unified state. But then, we must remember that's exactly what the prophet Daniel said would be the primary characteristic of this "ten-toed" kingdom. He said it would be mixed with "*iron and clay*" (Dan. 2:43), an obvious indication that they wouldn't get along well.

But, although they have never been able to put 'Humpty-Dumpty' (the old Roman Empire) back together, every generation or so a new leader would rise somewhere within the confines of the territorial boundaries of the old empire, who would be convinced he could do it. Many of them were Germans, some French, some Austrian, some Spanish, etc.

(The seventh kingdom is labelled "German-Slavonic" because there was a preponderance of German and Slavic kings, particularly in the middle ages, who saw themselves as head of all Europe. Actually, it is BECAUSE of a lack of unity amongst the European nations of the past 15 or so centuries which makes it near impossible to give a specific title to the Christian-age, seventh-head empire. But as loose as the bonding was, the baton went on. The *iron and clay* kingdoms can definitely be identified and understood even if we don't have an agreed name for it.)

Amazingly though, there was always an obvious driving force behind these European leaders, each convinced he was THE one, some even believing God was behind them! I have no doubts that many of these men had dramatic encounters with spirit beings. Clearly, they were (and are) in touch with the *"prince of the power of the air"*, the *"angel of light"*, the devil.

Satan is the power source behind these kingdoms. He started with the pharaohs of Egypt, then came the Assyrians, continuing on to Nebuchadnezzar in Babylon, the Medes and the Persians, followed by Alexander the Great, the Caesars of Rome, and finally the string of European kings of the Christian era, including Napolean, Hitler, etc. He'll also meet with the 'grandaddy' of them all — the final one — the one who will seem to get all the splintered kingdoms (Europe's EEC) to quit their bickering and follow him. Simultaneously, the final leader's forerunner and cohort, the *False Prophet* (the pope), will be re-gathering the divided 'churches' throughout the world, telling them to follow Europe's new leader.

295

Most of the kings and emperors of Europe's past were egotistical and believed themselves to be destined-rulers of the entire world. Some even presumed they were anointed by the God of heaven to hold that position.

At the same time though, the popes saw themselves as the spiritual leader of the planet and, therefore, the only one with absolute authority to convey power upon anyone else. The popes saw the emperors as mere heads of temporal power, not nearly so important as the more authoritative spiritual office (the papal) they themselves held. And make no mistake, today's pope, John Paul II, believes (as he has been quoted as saying) his spiritual headship is divinely declared. But keep in mind, the final "emperor" will not only assume headship of temporal power and authority, he will ultimately declare himself to be god! (See 2 Thes. 2:1-12).

In the early days of his 'mission', I believe the anti-Christ will honor papal authority, perhaps even demonstrating a form of humility at first. He will do this to get the people behind him. Remember, the papacy and its heirarchy will have molded the world into a useful framework consisting of a balance between religion and the work-place, via the parish system, Opus Dei, etc., likely then including many re-united Protestant churches.

Satan is powerful but he is not omni-present. He must work through structure. He has a limited number of demons at his disposal. Also, he has only a specific number of humans to do his bidding, so he must operate within the functional systems of the day. The only difference between Satan's control and influence in past kingdoms and the final one is that in the end, Satan will be allowed to be more up-front, when the restraining force of the Holy Spirit is removed. Satan will then make his move, no longer content for temporal headship from "*god*", via the pope's administering power, but then stating himself to be *god!* This has been Satan's motivation from the time of his fall. It continues today and the obsession will drive him onward throughout this age, until God puts him in hell.

So, although Satan is a very real, spiritual being, we mainly see him operating within the lives and systems which bear his trademarks. The *"harlot"* and the *"beast"* she rides are two of the most prominent places we find these indicators. Let's move on now and let the apostle John's words help remove some of the mystery of "Mystery Babylon".

6 "And I saw the woman, drunk with the blood of the saints and with the blood of the martyrs of Jesus. And when I saw her, I marveled with great amazement.
7 And the angel said to me, 'Why did you marvel? I will tell you the mystery of the woman and of the beast that carries her, which has the seven heads and the ten horns. "'

We must remember John saw (in his vision) an image of a literal woman who was spectacularly dressed and adorned. He did not see an empire. In verse 6, he sees her becoming intoxicated, not on alcohol but on the *blood* of Christians! What does this mean?

John differentiated between *"saints"* (ordinary Christians) and *"martyrs"* (Christians sacrificed for the cause of Christ). Some of the intoxicating beverage (blood) would be provided by the martyrs. Some would be provided by Christians who are members of the Roman Catholic church, not realizing they are in the middle of Satan's earthly heirarchy.

Therefore, the harlot's method of acquiring this 'drink' would range from physical death to the 'heretics' (true Christians) through the Spanish Inquisitions, etc., to *blood* donated unwittingly by the saints within the Roman church itself. This caused John *"great amazement"*. At that point the angel intervenes, consoles the alarmed apostle, and tells him to 'relax' and listen to an explanation about the *woman* who rides the *beast* with *"seven heads"* and *"ten horns"*. Let's listen in on the angel's explanation — — —

THE SEVEN KINGDOMS - EXPLAINED

8 "The beast that you saw <u>was</u>, and <u>is not</u>, and <u>will ascend</u> out of the bottomless pit and go to perdition. And those who dwell on the earth will marvel, whose names are not written in the Book of Life from the foundation of the world, when they see the beast that <u>was</u>, and <u>is not</u>, and <u>yet is</u>.

9 Here is the mind which has wisdom: The seven heads are seven mountains on which the woman sits.

10 And there are seven kings. Five have fallen, one is, and the other has not yet come. And when he comes, he must continue a short time.

11 And the beast that was, and is not, is himself also the eighth, and is of the seven, and is going to perdition.

12 And the ten horns which you saw are ten kings who have received no kingdom as yet, but they receive authority for one hour as kings with the beast.

13 These have one mind, and they will give their power and authority to the beast."

Verse 8 presents us with a puzzle. How can something (the *beast*) be an entity that <u>WAS</u>, and <u>IS NOT</u> and yet <u>IS</u>? Thank God we have the explanation in the ensuing verses.

1. Verse 9 tells us the seven "*heads*" refer to *mountains* (meaning nations) upon which the "*woman*" (religion) sits. Verse 10 says five had already come and gone. They would be the Egyptian, Assyrian, Babylonian, Medo-Persian and Grecian — five bygone empires. These represent that portion of the beast that "*was*".

2. The sixth *mountain* would have been the "*is*" empire, the Roman, which was in existence as John was being told these things — the very one responsible for his imprisonment at that time.

298

3. The *mountain* which had not yet come would be the splintered remainders after Rome's fall, (the one identified as the Germanic-Slavonic). This seventh kingdom actually represents all the various attempts (from roughly 500 A.D. until the present day) of various European kings and popes to restore the broken Roman Empire. However, none of these kingdoms would last but a short time. And none can be thought of, by itself, as one of the heads of the *"beast"*. All of them put together represent the one, seventh head, each in succession carrying the proverbial "baton" for a little while, the final destiny being to get it in the hands of the last kingdom — the eighth.

Verse 11 tells us about this most-important eighth kingdom. It says this beast *"was"*, *"is not"* and yet will be *"of the seven"*, which means it has already existed. This is the verse where most prophetic analysts get the idea of a restored Roman Empire. It makes too much sense to ignore the concept, for in the next verse (12) the angel tells us there will be *"ten horns"* (and here he specifically says the horns are *"kings"*) who will have *"one hour"* with the *"beast"*. (I believe by saying *"one hour"*, the angel is merely emphasizing the shortness of the last kingdom, not specifying a 60-minute time period.)

We have already learned that the Common Market presently has 12 national members, thus passing up the *"ten"* (where many prophetic experts thought it would stop). You recall I believe Spain and Portugal, although separate nations today, actually represent only one 'fused' horn, making a total of 11 members at this time, which is the requirement as revealed in Daniel 7:24. But there are other views on this.

Some expositors see it this way: They remind us that the final kingdom, as Daniel interpreted it, hung from two "legs". These would be the Eastern and Western sides of the old Roman Empire, the capitols being Constantinople (east) and Rome (west). For the past 40+ years there has been a strong division between eastern and western Europe as a result of the 'iron curtain' influence of

Russian power. Now, some prophetic writers feel the east must fit in the final anti-Christ system in some way. One wonders if the dramatic changes going on recently (1990-1992) in the Slavic countries (eastern Europe) may possibly be the beginning of the restoration of the "eastern leg" of the former Roman Empire.

Let's assume that eastern and western Europe could represent the two "legs" of the figure Nebuchadnezzar saw in his dream. So, to carry this line of reasoning on to its logical conclusion, since each leg has one foot and each foot has five toes, (completing the "ten toes" of the vision as recorded in Daniel chapter 2), the final "ten-horned" kingdom would have five nations out of the eastern bloc and five nations out of the western bloc.

So, even though the Common Market has passed the *"ten horns"*, some current member-nations may drop out of the market to be replaced by certain eastern nations. But, in the end, there will be the required *"ten horns"* as both Daniel and John saw them.

Well, I hope all that didn't confuse and scare you away from attempting to understand what the final European kingdom will actually be like. I threw this in so that you could at least get an idea of the various conclusions which can be reached. Don't let the diversity of opinions upset you. The important thing for us to do is WATCH and BE READY. I think that's what the Lord meant when he said "...*look at the fig tree and all the trees*". He wanted us to be sensitive to what would be going on among the nations in our day. He knew Satan would be trying his very best to keep his kingdom concealed during the build-up.

In any event, verse 13 says this final ten-horned beast will have *"one mind"* and *"will give their power and authority to the beast"*. That certainly ought to help us identify the regime once it gets here. The Common Market of today is well known for its dis-unity, not its unity. But this verse is very plain. They will one day have a leader who they believe in and to whom they will give their undivided attention and allegiance. That's what all Europe is waiting for — the leader who can bring them all together. He'll come. We can be sure of that for his forerunner is already here today. The current pope is very busy trying to get his 'church' together, as well as paving the way in

300

the politico-economic arena through Opus Dei. (The papacy has its own dual, temporal-religious aspects, too. You recall these were pictured and described to John in Revelation 13 as the False Prophet's *two horns*.)

THE LAMB - THE BEAST - THE HARLOT - THE WAR

14 "These will make war with the Lamb, and the Lamb will overcome them, for He is Lord of lords and King of kings; and those who are with Him are called, chosen, and faithful.
15 And he said to me, 'The waters which you saw, where the harlot sits, are peoples, multitudes, nations, and tongues.
16 And the ten horns which you saw on the beast, these will hate the harlot, make her desolate and naked, eat her flesh, and burn her with fire.
17 For God has put it into their hearts to fulfill His purpose, to have one purpose, and to give their kingdom to the beast, until the words of God are fulfilled.
18 And the woman whom you saw is that great city which reigns over the kings of the earth."

The most important part of Revelation is found here in this passage: **Jesus wins!** And we — the *"called, chosen and faithful"* — will share in His victory! Daniel also spoke of this time in reference to the destruction of the ten toes in Dan. 2:44:

"And in the days of these kings shall the God of heaven set up a kingdom, which shall never be destroyed; and the kingdom shall not be left to other people, but it shall break in pieces and consume all these kingdoms, and it shall stand for ever."

And referring to the ten horns he saw, Daniel said in Dan. 7:26:

"But the judgment shall sit, and they shall take away his dominion, to consume and to destroy it unto the end."

301

So, people of God, we do not have to worry. For no matter how tough the going gets, we will be victorious. Never forget that. We are with the OVERCOMER, the KING of kings. In their heyday, the anti-Christ and the kings of the coming European kingdom will seem indestructible but they will have only an "hour" (a brief time) with the *beast* to enjoy their seeming invincibility.

Verse 15 interprets for us that "waters" mean multitudes of people from all backgrounds and races. That's where the harlot sits. The Roman Catholic Church sits all over the world. In some nations she is the only 'state-approved' religion, particularly so in Spanish-speaking nations.

> Part of the meaning of the Roman Catholic Church's "harlotry" lies in the methods she uses to "christianize" the nations where she goes. She sends her 'apostles' out to the 'pagans', baptizing whole households, including babies. In this manner, the harlot is supposedly conveying sanctification upon all the peoples (i.e., the "waters") she touches. I presume this is what the papacy supposes is their mandate. This is nothing more than a gross perversion of the Biblical meaning of the **Great Commission.**

It's my conviction that Roman Catholicism is building an <u>earthly</u> kingdom. How does this stack up with the fact Jesus said His Kingdom was not of this world? It wasn't <u>then</u>. It isn't <u>now</u>. The real Church is not the Roman Church nor any combination of certain denominations — even the good ones. The Church is simply the sum total of born-again believers.

We know that the anti-Christ will ultimately claim personal godhood, as so many of his forerunners tried in ages past. The difference is, the final anti-Christ will have the full authority of Satan, none previously having achieved this 'honor'. When that happens, he will order the destruction of the harlot, believing he no longer needs her. Consequently, she will be made "*desolate*", "*naked*", her "*flesh*" will be "*eaten*", and she will be "*burned*" with fire, the Scripture says.

SUMMARY

In 1929, the 110 acres of Vatican City became a sovereign nation. It was the smallest nation on earth but the pope was given full sovereignty over it. We cannot ignore this dramatic and significant occurrence. Italy first established diplomatic relations with the Vatican. Today, many other nations have followed suit, now even our beloved United States.

The last verse of our current chapter under study, says *"the woman whom you saw is that great city which reigns over the kings of the earth."* I'm convinced this is a direct reference to Vatican City. Though technically a small nation, actually in the minds of those in power in the Roman Catholic heirarchy, I believe they see themselves as eventual heads over all nations. The *"harlot"* and the *"beast"* are the most awesome, "gruesome-twosome" of all times. But according to the Bible, even they shall come to their end. Praise God!

CHAPTER EIGHTEEN

THE FALL OF BABYLON THE GREAT

1 "And after these things I saw another angel coming down from heaven, having great authority, and the earth was illuminated with his glory.

2 And he cried mightily with a loud voice, saying, 'Babylon the great is fallen, is fallen, and has become a habitation of demons, a prison for every foul spirit, and a cage for every unclean and hated bird.

3 For all the nations have drunk of the wine of the wrath of her fornication, the kings of the earth have committed fornication with her, and the merchants of the earth have become rich through the abundance of her luxury.

4 And I heard another voice from heaven saying, 'Come out of her, my people, lest you share of her plagues.

5 For her sins have reached to heaven, and God has remembered her iniquities.

6 Render to her just as she rendered to you, and repay her double according to her works; in the cup which she has mixed, mix for her double.

7 As much as she has glorified herself and lived luxuriously, so much torment and sorrow give her; for she says in her heart, 'I sit as queen, and am no widow, and will not see sorrow.'

8 Therefore her plagues will come in one day — death, mourning, and famine. And she will be utterly burned with fire, for strong is the Lord God who judges her."

Revelation chapters 17 and 18 run together. We have noted that the final anti-Christ system will be double-sided: religious and temporal. Both will eventually fall and I think the duality aspect is brought out in verse 2 above by the double expression, *"is fallen, is fallen"*. The first *"is fallen"* refers to the harlot — the ecclesiastical structure of Roman Catholicism. Ironically, she falls at the hands of the anti-Christ who turns against Vatican City once he thinks the 'church' is no longer needed. (Rev. 17:16). The second "is *fallen*" refers to the politico-mercantile side of the final empire, which seems to be the more primary focus of this chapter.

In chapter 13 I spoke of the Opus Dei — the "work of God" organization — a group which likely represents the nuts-and-bolts of a global network designed to eventually have control of most of the world's commerce system. They are very secret today. Let's face it, if the objective is to control all "buying and selling", it makes good sense to keep things under cover until your 'machine' is in good working order. A design of this magnitude requires time and very careful planning. Remember, according to what *is* known, the training of Opus Dei members is both religious and temporal, with major emphasis on the latter. In the initial build-up (the first 3 1/2 years of the final 7 year period), the anti-Christ will need a prepared-people to work with. Since his ultimate plan is to reign over the masses, Opus-Dei-like organizations will fit perfectly into his strategy.

High-pressure commercialism is at the very core of humanism; and when all is said and done, humanism is at the root of all ungodliness. People have definite <u>needs,</u> but more important to consumerism is meeting people's obsessive <u>craves.</u> Whoever meets those demands at any given time will obviously exercise strong influence and control over the masses. I'm convinced this control will ultimately be in the hands of those in charge of the Holy Roman Empire. This may seem far-fetched right now. Many say "Well, it may come, but not in my lifetime." But I believe that most people living today will see it! Even now, you and I are already being prepared to accept the "Big Brother" concept as normal. Commodity-control is slipping away from the average person's influence. America (being one of God's primary "*witnesses*") will likely be the last nation to follow a true free-enterprise system. But even now we see it weakening every day.

Let me give you one, up-to-date example right out of my own life. I started writing today at 5 A.M., but first read yesterday's mail. One letter actually seemed appropriate and timely relative to this topic. Admittedly, the man was trying to sell me something but he made some very astute points. His reference was to the hundreds of large-scale optical chains on the drawing board of one major department store. According to him, this will eventually have a tremendous negative effect on me as a privately-practicing optometrist. He's right.

Actually this is not new, just another in a series of similar ventures which are already operating on a national scale. People are being duped with the brain-washing idea: "Equal Services at Lower Prices". The logic of these business movements goes something like this: "*We must meet modern demands and the needs of people with modern technology. Therefore, we need a new 'delivery system' to meet those demands.*" This kind of lingo sounds good but underneath is often a host of out-right lies and deception. What is really happening is the control is being removed from individuals working together for the common good of all and put in the hands of a few, far-away, money-hungry, corporate managers who really couldn't care less about helping people. Their purpose is to line their own pockets while also appeasing their stockholders who want to make money without working for it.

In just 32 years of professionalism, my income has changed from almost all coming directly from individuals at first, to approximately 80% covered by 'third party' systems today. Now, that may not startle you. But can you see the devastating potential this scenario could have if it runs its natural course to completion? We are being mentally prepared today to accept a system of "buying and selling" which will eventually be in the hands of others, exclusively! I don't know about you but the idea makes me shudder. The only hands I want to have total control over me is the Lord God of creation, not his adversary, the devil, whose business is 'big business' control.

I don't want to leave the impression that corporate structures and large business concerns are inherently evil. Some big business executives have sincere, good intentions relative to the their customers. Any business, small or large, is only as good as the character of the people in it. However, it's possible for something which begins with great motivation, even with a 'form of godliness' in it, to end up being Satan's stronghold. Indeed, we shall see later in this chapter that's exactly what eventually happens to most of the world's commercial industry. But Christians must be alerted to the insidious nature and the awesome power of the 'Commercial Beast'.

The root of this problem is right in our own individual tendencies towards greed. We are materialistic by nature; (i.e., our fallen nature). Most don't like to admit that that 'bent' is in us. The problem is a continual struggle for most of us. It is for this reason that the apostle Paul said, *"And having food and clothing, with these we shall be content. But those who desire to be rich fall into temptation and a snare, and into many foolish and harmful lusts which drown men in destruction and perdition."* 1 Tim. 6:8&9). Compare this language to the *"beast"* which goes into *"perdition"* as described in Rev. 17:8. *"The beast that you saw was, and is not, and will ascend out of the bottomless pit and go to perdition ..."*.

Here both Paul and John link lust-for-riches and material things to an eventual destination of death in hell. This kind of thirst eats away at all the human race — and, unfortunately, does not exclude Christians. Now, let's get back to Revelation 18 and note just how the whole scene will finally end.

Thus, *"Babylon The Great"*, in its last state, will be a combination of fallen-religion 'married' to the unified forces of a greedy, world-wide, politico-mercantile-social system. All of it will be under the control of the revived Roman Empire, which has at its head the *False Prophet* (including the papacy and all its subsidiaries) and the anti-Christ (the ruling temporal 'emperor'). Although the final image is not yet fully clear, things will soon come into focus — to the alert.

307

Now re-read verses 1 - 8. Verse 2 tells us when the two *"falls"* occur, this organization will have become the *"habitation of demons"*, *"foul spirits"* and *"unclean and hated birds"*. As the old saying goes, *'birds of a feather stick together'*. So, we should not be surprised to find *"demons"* (fallen angels) and *"unclean birds"* (unrepentant mankind) together in the same structure. Remember, Satan has his angelic heirarchy as well as certain human agencies all tied together to do his will. Getting full control of politics, commerce, etc., is necessary in order to be successful at tying the whole world together under one banner. So, at the top of the commercial ladder, we would expect to see many 'great' minds working together.

However, in verse 4 we see that there are also some Godly people within *"Babylon The Great"*. Note that God will say to them, *"Come out of her, my people, lest you share in her sins and lest you receive of her plagues."* Now, this can't refer to the rapture, as some say, for that will have already occurred prior to what we are now discussing. God's Wrath against the final *"Babylon"* comes at the <u>end</u> of the final seven year period. Nevertheless, we see here God calling his people out of this *"den of thieves"*.

Note: I don't wish to give anyone a spirit of fear but any true believer caught in any faction of what will eventually be a part of the anti-Christ system as described thus far, would do well to get out now! I feel we are rapidly approaching the time of our redemption and I believe there are better places for Christians to be than participating in an organization that is in process of becoming a *"habitation of demons"*.

(But, if you, dear brother or sister in Christ, are within the Catholic Church, and are becoming aware of its gross heretical teaching and practices, but feel your personal ministry is to remain and win lost souls to Christ, more power to you, my friends. Hang in there! But when the Lord tells you to come out — COME OUT!)

Verse 7 is very revealing. Here, it is obviously referring to the *"harlot"* aspect of the system, the adulterous "church". She says in her heart, *'I sit as queen, and am no widow'*... To understand this, we must see its logical base. Christ is not yet with His true Church, physically speaking. We await that now. The coming 'family reunion' of all believers joining Christ has been the hope of every Christian generation. Jesus is betrothed to us and will some day receive His Bride to Himself. Now hold on to that thought.

Next, note the *harlot* (the false church) described in this passage, says she is *"no widow"*. The Catholic Church has always given more emphasis to Jesus hanging on the cross (portraying death) than in the power of His resurrection. However, the fact does give a clue to help us understand this passage. Well, what does it mean when the *"harlot"* says she is a *"queen"* and *"no widow"?* I think it could have two explanations:

First, to be a *queen* infers the harlot will have achieved full religious authority, therefore she would not need a 'husband', most certainly not a dead one, i.e., referring to Jesus' death on the cross.

But there is a second possible explanation. *Babylon* saying she is no *"widow"* could be telling us she will then be 'married' to the alive 'other king' — the one Jesus predicted would *"come in his own name"* — the anti-Christ. (See John 5:43).

It may be that both explanations are correct.

Verse 8 tells us that God makes short work of destroying Babylon The Great. It comes in *"an hour"*. Again, it is doubtful that this means a literal hour. I think the emphasis here is on the brevity of time the *harlot* will be reigning as *"queen"* of all international, religious authority. It is also very difficult to say if God has in mind a particular place where the final "burning" occurs. One thinks of many world trade centers such as New York, Tokyo, Hong Kong, Paris, Mexico City, Rome, Brussels... It's hard to be dogmatic here. It could mean a certain city, or it could mean all of them combined. Knowing the absolute truth of this right now is really not all that important.

There are basically three parts in this chapter: Center-stage is *"Babylon The Great"*.

1. First is her fall, which was just discussed.
2. Next comes the world's view of her fall.
3. The final picture.

Let's now move on to Part 2.

THE WORLD MOURNS BABYLON'S FALL

9 "And the kings of the earth who have committed fornication and lived luxuriously with her will weep and lament for her, when they see the smoke of her burning,
10 standing at a distance for fear of her torment, saying, 'Alas, alas, that great city Babylon, that mighty city! For in one hour your judgment has come.'
11 And the merchants of the earth will weep and mourn over her, for no one buys their merchandise anymore:
12 merchandise of gold and silver, precious stones and pearls, fine linen and purple, silk and scarlet, every kind of citron wood, every kind of object of ivory, every kind of object of most precious wood, bronze, iron, and marble;
13 and cinnamon and incense, fragrant oil and frankincense, wine and oil, fine flour and wheat, cattle and sheep, horses and chariots, and bodies and souls of men.
14 And the fruit that your soul longed for has gone from you, and all the things which are rich and splendid have gone from you, and you shall find them no more at all.
15 The merchants of these things, who became rich by her, will stand at a distance for fear of her torment, weeping and wailing,
16 and saying, 'Alas, alas, that great city that was clothed in fine linen, purple, and scarlet, and adorned with gold, precious stones, and pearls!

17 'For in one hour such great riches have come to nothing.'
And every shipmaster, all who travel by ship, sailors, and as
many as trade on the sea, stood at a distance
18 and cried out when they saw the smoke of her burning,
saying, What is like this great city!'
19 And they threw dust on their heads and cried out,
weeping and wailing, and saying, "Alas, alas, that great city,
in which all who had ships on the sea became rich by her
wealth! For in one hour she is made desolate.
20 Rejoice over her, O heaven, and you holy apostles and
prophets, for God has avenged you on her."

That's quite a large portion of Scripture to consume at one time. However, you'll note it's just one, cohesive statement. In it is named virtually everything which can be bought and sold, including even the *"bodies and souls of men"*!

As already noted, today we are moving in the direction when all manufactured items will be at the disposal of one single organization. This has been fallen man's destiny since the tower of Babel — man's first Babylon. The *'Babylonish-Syndrome'* has been in man's complex from then until now. In the above verses, God is simply showing us the 'nth' degree of the tendency, here called *Babylon The Great*. There's really nothing all that new in the final Babylon. She's just more widespread and at last under one roof. Inspired by Satan. Built by man.

Three times in the above verses we hear the cry, *'Alas, alas',* followed by a comment that judgment will come quickly upon *Babylon*. This dual expression implies a two-sided personality of *Babylon The Great*.

Ships are mentioned several times here, making one think the 'home office' of this final regime is by the sea. This narrows the possibilities down a bit. Perhaps it will involve many port cities around the world, not just one. After all, most importation and exportation occurs at seaport cities. It's important to note in this passage that God is bringing this judgment. It is not merely a breakdown brought on by human conflict.

I think of my neighboring city, San Francisco, for example. To me, it's the most beautiful city in the world and I like visiting there just to take in the sights. And yet, every time I go anymore, I'm repulsed by the everywhere-evident, gross sinfulness. S. F. is America's capitol of the AIDS epidemic, brought about by hundreds of thousands of practicing sodomites. I'm reminded of the 'buying-and-selling' as I look at the numerous skyscrapers which house hundreds of home offices of mass merchandisers, most bent upon getting rich and delivering huge amounts of goods to feed the apetites of thirsty and greedy Americans. You can also see the 'spirit' of this in the beautifully-decorated and well-stocked stores.

Most of us are already far-past reasonable purchases of needed goods. Everyone wants more-more-more...of everything. It seems as if there is no end to how far man will go to create and meet the demands of selfish people. And nowhere is it more manifest than right here in my own backyard in the city by the bay — San Francisco. I can't help believing that this city pictures (if not indeed fulfills) the prophetic forecast given here in Revelation 18.

"REJOICE PROPHETS"

True prophets of God have always cried out against greediness. Particularly against those who perpetrate it, knowing their actions were responsible for devouring men's souls. The passage here confirms this. So, no wonder God says in verse 20, *"Rejoice over her, O heaven, and you holy apostles and prophets, for God has avenged you on her."* Christians, who yearn to see true repentance in the lost world around them, often don't get to see it actually accomplished. This has always been true, whether in the Christian era or during Old Testament days. Anointed people of God see the inherent evil underlying out-of-balance materialism. Jesus made the point abundantly clear when He said, *"No one can serve two masters;*

for either he will hate the one and love the other, or else he will hold to the one and despise the other. You cannot serve God and money." Matt. 6:24.

FINALITY OF BABYLON'S FALL

21 "And a mighty angel took up a stone like a great millstone and threw it into the sea, saying, 'Thus with violence the great city Babylon shall be thrown down, and shall not be found anymore.
22 And the sound of harpists, musicians, flutists, and trumpeters shall not be heard in you anymore. And no craftsman of any craft shall be found in you anymore. And the sound of a millstone shall not be heard in you anymore.
23 And the light of a lamp shall not shine in you anymore. And the voice of bridegroom and bride shall not be heard in you anymore. For your merchants were the great men of the earth, for by your sorcery all the nations were deceived.
24 And in her was found the blood of prophets and saints, and of all who were slain on the earth."

"MYSTERY BABYLON" covers a lot of territory. In real life and Biblically. First mentioned in chapter 14, her destruction was stated this way: *"is fallen, is fallen"*. The expression *"is fallen"* indicates past tense, and yet the next four chapters spell out the future, unfolding a long story of *how* she falls, building up to the climax described in the above 4 verses.

To demonstrate for John how the final *"hour"* would come, a *"mighty angel"* tossed a huge *"millstone"* in the sea, telling him the end of *Babylon* would come in like manner. What are we to get out of this? Think about it. If one were to literally throw a large stone into the ocean, the obvious thing that would first happen is a big splash, followed by disturbances in the surrounding waters. The stone would immediately sink, the waves would soon subside and things would quickly return to normal. Before long it would look as if nothing ever happened.

It appears that's the way it will be when God finally does away with the whole religious-temporal power structure which man (and Satan) have been putting together for centuries. God is very patient. However, in the end He will make dramatic, even violent, short work of Babylon's destruction.

NO CRAFTSMAN

Working men from all fields of endeavor have given their allegiance to "*MYSTERY BABYLON*". Man's skills to produce art-work or useful items eventually end up in the hands of merchandisers. There is nothing inherently evil about buying and selling, but unfortunately, underlying much of it is a foundation based on greed. The collective unification of all those who do these things for evil purposes is what's in view in Biblical "*Babylon The Great*". We see here the evil power that's behind the scenes, seducing and deceiving people who innocently give over the works of their hands to the evildoers. But God tells us in the above Scriptures that a day is coming (soon I believe) when all deception involving the fruits of man's labor will end. He will then separate (forever) honest providers from those who deceive them. What a great hope!

NO MUSICIANS

Music is a wonderful, universal language. Everybody loves some type of music. Music follows ryhthmic patterns, just as does the very nature of man. Even our heartbeat implies music. It's "in our blood". On the bad side, probably no medium has been used more than music to advance the cause of evil practices. You hear music at work, in the super-markets, in department stores, in your home, in your car, on the telephone when you're 'on hold', etc. Verse 22 says all this will end. This doesn't mean music shall end. But music designed to advance the "Babylonish-complex" shall someday end.

Surely God designed music. But man (with Satanic influence) has perverted it in many ways. That's what we see in the above passage. God will one day take away the Godly-gifted musician from "*Babylon*".

NO LAMP. NO BRIDEGROOM. NO BRIDE.

What does this mean? The terms are Biblically-defined for us. God's Word is a "*lamp unto our feet*", the Scriptures say. As the modern *tower* of *MYSTERY BABYLON* has been under construction, God's Word has always been right there in the middle of the process. God has been merciful to man in many ways but no way so great as the gift of His written message to lost mankind — the Holy Bible. It's still the "best seller". We must praise God for this!

Throughout history's turbulent struggles, God's Word has been there to draw men, to save men, to nourish men, and to give men hope. The Bible is man's greatest earthly asset. But the above Scripture says a day is coming when this will be removed from *Babylon*. No longer will there be this wonderful healing light in her which gives strength to those who grasp it. Unaware-*Babylon* has benefitted through Godly men who were nurtured by the 'light' of the lamp. But this too will end.

The "*bridegroom*" is, of course, a reference to Jesus Christ. He is THE CENTER of what we find in the "*lamp*" of God's Word. It is He Who upholds "*all things by the word of His power*" (Heb. 1:3). Think of that. Everything that *is,* is held together by the word of the Word that was made flesh, Jesus of Nazareth. He keeps all atoms and molecules functioning, even those in *MYSTERY BABYLON!* (This does not mean Jesus is the author of evil. He <u>allows</u> it; He doesn't <u>cause</u> it.)

Today, the administrator of God's action in this world is the Holy Spirit. He is the "*Restrainer*", the One who holds evil in check. He allows it to go only so far — as far as the sovereignty of God permits. Just as Babylon has benefitted from the other Godly manifestations within her, she has also gained from the presence of the *"bridegroom"* in her; in fact, moreso than any other. Of course, she, in her blindness, does not recognize this.

Jesus said there is no *"light"* in Satan; and yet he was a prime creation of God. No one created was more beautiful or more intelligent than he but wickedness was found in him. Since then, Satan has no real understanding of what God is building all around him. Such is the case with *MYSTERY BABYLON* and the *"bridegroom"*. She (*Babylon*) is a mighty fortress; she has *light* all around her, including the *"bridegroom"* Himself, and doesn't even know it! But, eventually this too will end.

The *"bride"* is the true Church. Jesus said He would build His Church and that the *"gates of hell would not prevail against it"*. There are many *"gates"* to hell. They are found in false philosophies, false religions, perverted Christianity, cults, etc. But no gate is so wide as *BABYLON*. Actually, it encompasses all the other *"gates"* listed above, plus some. *Babylon* sends out the invitation, "Come One, Come All!". But in spite of all the temptations Satan and Babylon put in front of potential believers, Jesus said, *"I will build My Church..."*. He has been doing it for nearly 2,000 years. And, in spite of the 'Babylonish fever', Jesus will victoriously complete His Church.

Of all the benefactors in her midst, *Babylon* has had none greater than the *"bride"* of Christ, His Church. Since I've already discussed Jesus as the *"bridegroom"* you are probably asking how I can say such a thing, knowing surely He is more valuable than we. Well, that's certainly true, spiritually speaking. But the *"bride"* is what's right out in the open. We are the physical, flesh-and-bones that Babylon sees. She can reach out and *touch* us. It is in this sense that we represent the *"body of Christ"*. We are that tangible outworking of God on earth, in the here-and-now. Babylon The Great has been greatly *"rewarded"* (undeservingly) by the *bride's* presence. Just by our being here, she gains in reputation. But, this too will end.

GODLY BLOOD IS IN BABYLON'S BODY!

Godly blood flows through *Babylon's* body. *"Preposterous!"*, you say! Well, I didn't say that. Verse 24 does: "*...in her was found the blood of prophets and saints...*". What does this mean? Well, throughout this last section I have pointed out several Godly features which have infiltrated *Babylon*. Verse 24 is merely giving us a picture of the sum-total of all the Godly influences which have been at the disposal of *Babylon*. Therefore, once she is "dead", within her body will be found the "*blood*" of various Godly people Babylon has 'eaten'. They will have sacrificed their lives for the sustenance of *Babylon's* life.

That sounds "gross" and cruel, but from God's long-range perspective, it has been His way of drawing others to Himself. In one way or another, God's people have always had to give their lives to assist in the building of His kingdom here on earth right among the evildoers. No where is this more evident than in the giving of His Own Son Jesus at Calvary.

God Himself is the ultimate sacrificer. Since true Godly people take on the very nature of God, it should not surprise us when we see Godly "*saints and prophets*" giving their lives to *Babylon*. In Jesus' day, Babylon was exemplified by the Roman Empire, which would take the very name of Jesus and use it to their own selfish-advantage throughout the whole Christian era. (Remember Constantine and all that transpired after that.) It will be similar in our day, as the modern Roman Empire continues its restoration; in its final stages many more Christians (*"saints and prophets"*) will again give their lives to *Babylon*. But, praise God, this will be the last one!

SUMMARY

Revelation 18, if it had a title, might be: "It's All Over But The Shouting!", which is true as we'll see in the next chapter.

In Glory, when we have complete and perfect understanding, "*MYSTERY BABYLON THE GREAT*" may actually mean more and be somewhat different than what I have conveyed. However, I think the main thoughts here are Scripturally accurate. Also, the added concepts seem to line up with both history and current events. Surely we can all agree that since the first *Babylon* (the tower of Babel) was destroyed, man has been in the process of building another. However, this one is of a more 'spiritual' nature which is being spread throughout the world rather than being localized as a single city.

As of now (1994), I'm convinced it's almost finished. And just as certain as the first Babel was destroyed, so also shall be the last one. Today, other than the written account, there is little (if any) trace of the real ancient tower of Babel. Likewise, one day there will not be a trace of modern Babylon The Great. All of man's efforts to build earthly kingdoms are heady and self-serving. But a day will come when Christ will put all things under His feet. Babylon The Great will be one of the last. "*Even so, Come, Lord Jesus!*"

CHAPTER NINETEEN

HEAVEN REJOICES

1 "And after these things I heard a loud voice of a great multitude in heaven, saying, 'Alleluia! Salvation and glory and honor and power to the Lord our God!
2 For true and righteous are His judgments, because He has judged the great harlot who corrupted the earth with her fornication; and He has avenged the blood of His servants at her hand.'
3 And again they said, 'Alleluia! And her smoke rises up forever and ever!'
4 And the twenty-four elders and the four living creatures fell down and worshiped God who sat on the throne, saying, 'Amen! Alleluia!'
5 And a voice came out of the throne, saying, 'Praise our God, all you His servants and you who fear Him, both small and great!'

There are many examples of responsive praises to God when He has done something special in behalf of His people. But the above verses must surely be the "Hallelujah Chorus" of them all! Everyone in heaven — the *'multitudes',* the *'four living creatures',* and the *'twenty-four elders'* — all join in exultation on this momentous occasion.

Then, a voice comes from the throne addressing all the *'servants'* and those who *'fear Him',* both *'small and great',* telling all of them to "Praise our God". This voice must be the Lord Jesus. Who else deserves to sit on the throne?

Remarkably, even in His Kingly position, Jesus is still showing His obedient nature. He is telling us that adoration is to be directed towards the One to Whom He prayed when He was here on the earth — the heavenly Father. That Jesus is <u>fully God</u> is unquestionable. But He personally tells us here there is something unique about the Father's <u>position</u> in heaven. The Father and Son are one but the Son is not the Father. Oh how worthy our Lord is! If only we could embrace just a little of His submissive spirit.

The praises shall ring out! What a day that will be! The amazing thing is *why* they are praising. It is because the "harlot" has been judged and executed. This says to me that the structure of *Babylon The Great* is a mighty big thing, obviously at the last encircling ALL evil practices.

In the final analysis of the "*harlot*", we must conclude that every resistance against godliness ultimately becomes a part of this mysterious *woman*. Therefore, we must not limit our thinking as we appraise *Babylon's* identity. It may seem I have done this very thing since I give so much attention to the last religious-temporal relationship — i.e., the Roman Catholic Church married to a unified-Europe. But, it must be remembered that what we see today in these circles, while already quite large and even with a bit of godliness still in it, is still in its formative stages. However, in the end, the organization will be on a much grander scale and the restrictions and control over mankind will be overwhelming.

In the last of the 'last days' many other 'churches' will likely have re-joined the 'mother of harlots' — Roman Catholicism. It is also noteworthy here to see that those in heaven seem to be getting a view of *MYSTERY BABYLON* in all its historical glories, extending far back to its commencement days, as well as observing the status of the harlot's last "*hour*".

THE BRIDE IS READY FOR MARRIAGE

6 "And I heard, as it were, the voice of a great multitude, as the sound of many waters and as the sound of mighty thunderings, saying, 'Alleluia'! For the Lord God Omnipotent reigns!

320

7 'Let us be glad and rejoice and give Him glory, for the marriage of the Lamb has come, and His wife has made herself ready.'
8 And to her was granted that she should be arrayed in fine linen, clean and bright, for the fine linen is the righeous acts of the saints.
9 And he said to me, "Write": 'Blessed are those who are called to the marriage supper of the Lamb!'" And he said to me, "These are the true sayings of God."
10 And I fell at his feet to worship him. And he said to me, 'See that you do not do that! I am your fellow servant, and of your brethren who have the testimony of Jesus. Worship God! For the testimony of Jesus is the spirit of prophecy."

From the time Jesus called His first disciples, continuing up to the present hour, all saints (Christians) have looked forward to this day with glad anticipation; the day when we would all gather together for the marriage feast — the wedding day of the *"Bride"* (all Christians) and the *"Bridegroom"* (Jesus).

It is humbling to read verse 8 and see that part of the beauty of our clothing results from our own righteous acts done in this world. (This is not referring to salvation, but to the good work which follows those that are truly saved.)

"Lord, help us to do good---NOW! Help us to be bold as we invite others to the marriage feast for You have called that "BLESSED"! Help us to help others. Give us hearts like the good Samaritan. And Lord, may we learn to be as the ones you seek: those who worship You in Spirit and in truth, in the here-and-now. Amen!"

It seems the apostle John had gotten so excited, he thought everything he was seeing was already accomplished. For a moment he must have forgotten this was a vision because he fell at the feet of the one telling him these things, presuming, it seems, that the angel was God Himself. John wanted to get in on this 'praise service'! Don't you just love this apostle? Thank you God, for John!

CHRIST ON A WHITE HORSE

11 "And I saw heaven opened, and behold, a white horse. And He who sat on him was called Faithful and True, and with righteousness He judges and makes war.
12 His eyes were like a flame of fire, and on His head were many crowns. And He had a name written that no one knew except Himself.
13 And He was clothed with a robe dipped in blood, and His name is called The Word of God.
14 And the armies in heaven, clothed in fine linen, white and clean, followed Him on white horses.
15 And out of His mouth goes a sharp sword, that with it He should smite the nations. And He Himself will rule them with a rod of iron. He Himself treads the winepress of the fierceness and wrath of Almighty God.
16 And He has on His robe and on His thigh a name written:

KING OF KINGS
AND LORD OF LORDS"

Little comment need be added to the plain message here. The few points I'll make should not be regarded as commensurate with the passage's import. Indeed, herein is described the crowning climax of the Christian hope — that we shall all one day join our Lord and Savior, Jesus Christ, Whom John refers to here as the "Faithful and True."

It's interesting to note that Jesus' robe will be *"dipped in blood"*. I believe this represents both His Own blood, as well as all the saints and prophets who have sacrificed their blood building God's Kingdom. Imagine that Jesus, the Son of the Living God, would give such honor and tribute to His own creation. More evidence of His graciousness, love, kindness and humility. Praise His Holy Name!

The "*armies*" in heaven would be the saints of all ages. The "*linen*" they wear, we recall from verse 8, is the result of their own righteous acts demonstrated while on earth. Just as Jesus will then have a unique name and wear a special robe, it seems the Christians will likewise be specifically-named and specially-arrayed. Now all this is not completely clear but one can't help speculating a little here.

Recall there was a white horse and rider discussed in chapter 6 under the Sixth Seal — Constantine The Great. He did great things in the name of Christianity but actually was a great perverter of the true faith.

But, thanks be to God, there will be another white horse and another Rider Who *can* be depended on! He is no fake. He bears no falsehood. There's no untruth in Him. His name is Jesus. In fact, one of His names is *Faithful* and *True*! His words are always right. They can be taken at face value — every time. When He speaks, God Almighty has said it. He is here called — The Word of God (verse 13).

This is great news, brothers and sisters in Christ! We have placed our confidence in the *Faithful and True One, The Word of God!* There's no other security like it in the whole universe. The apostle Peter put it like this: "*...for there is no other name under heaven given among men by which we must be saved.*" (Acts 4:12). Praise the Name of Jesus!

THE "OTHER" WHITE HORSES

I've read it many times but for some reason it never struck me so strong as it just did. The "*armies*" who follow Jesus, also ride white horses! What a sight that will be! It's awesome to contemplate. Ladies and gentlemen of The Faith, it is Biblically right and proper — for we are under command of our King—to walk humbly in this world. Humility, I think, is perhaps God's greatest Christian-character requirement during our earthly plight. But there is a flip side to this. James 4:10 says, "*Humble yourselves in the sight of the Lord and He WILL LIFT YOU UP.*"

Jesus put the same principle this way: "...*for everyone who exalts himself will be abased, and he who humbles himself WILL BE EXALTED.*" Matt. 23:12.

There is a fine line here for Christians to discern. We are not to humble ourselves for the *purpose* of being exalted; that's not the teaching. But, if we walk humbly in this world, God says in due course of His timing and at His discretion, we will be exalted. Those who ride the other "*white horses*" with Jesus as described in this passage confirms this understanding.

For some Christians, there are exaltations even in this life. I think God allows this to show us the principle does work — even here and now. But, prophetically speaking, there is a greater time coming when believers become a part of the "*armies in heaven, clothed in fine linen, and clean, followed Him on white horses.*"

There's an old song which says, "*O Lord I want to be in that number, when the saints go marching in...*". That's my hope and I hope it's yours. This is part of the final 'exaltation' God has prepared for those who humble themselves in this age, trusting Christ as their redeemer. Praise God for His plans and provisions he HAS executed, IS executing, and WILL yet execute for those He loves and saves.

THE ROD OF IRON

So, in this age, God expects Christians to be willing to assume low positions of honor. It may go "against the grain" at times, but God declares it righteous. But, when Christ reigns as Lord and King of the earth, things are going to be quite different. During His first advent, Jesus manifested His humility by riding into Jerusalem on the lowliest of animals — the donkey (a borrowed one at that). However, this will not be so when He makes His appearance at His second advent.

Verse 15 says He will "*smite*" the nations. The expression, "*sharp sword from His mouth*" is just another way of saying Jesus is "The Word of God". Jesus will be ruling the world by His spoken words when He is reigning physically as Lord and King of the earth. He will not be submissive then to any man or any earthly kingdom. That condition will be over and done with. A new day will have come. His 'exaltation' will have been perfected.

To make the point even more emphatic, the Scriptures say He "*Himself will rule them with a ROD OF IRON.*" What does this mean? In the next chapter, we shall see who will be here on earth under Christ's rule during the millennium. Whoever it is, this chapter says they shall be ruled sternly. (Note, I didn't say harshly. There's nothing wrong with firm rulership *if* the King is perfectly righteous and perfectly just.)

JESUS' NAME 'ON HIS THIGH'

The Bible identifies Jesus with many names. Another John saw was a name written "*on His thigh*" called, "*KING OF KINGS AND LORD OF LORDS*". The part I want to draw your attention to are the phrases "*OF KINGS*" and "*OF LORDS*". This refers to other people. To be a king, you must be ruler over something and someone. These "*kings*" and "*lords*" must refer to resurrected and glorified saints who will be reigning with Christ during the millennium.

But the main thing to understand is Who their King is. He is none other than the One who was first born in a stable in lowly Bethlehem, now exalted to the right hand of the heavenly Father, from where He presently reigns as our spiritual King. However, He will ultimately reign in the physical sense here on earth. Another song comes to mind: "*Glad day, O glorious day. Glad day, O glorious morning. That will be a glad reunion day.*"

Rejoice Christians, the King is coming!

THE BEAST AND HIS ARMIES DEFEATED

17 "And I saw an angel standing in the sun; and he cried with a loud voice, saying to all the birds that fly in the midst of heaven, "Come and gather together for the supper of the great God,
18 that you may eat the flesh of kings, the flesh of captains, the flesh of mighty men, the flesh of horses and of those who sit on them, and the flesh of all people, free and slave, both small and great.
19 And I saw the beast, the kings of the earth, and their armies, gathered together to make war against Him who sat on the horse and against His army.
20 And the beast was taken, and with him the false prophet who worked signs in his presence, by which he deceived those who had received the mark of the beast and those who worshiped his image. These two were cast alive into the lake of fire burning with brimstone.
21 And the rest were killed with the sword which proceeded out of the mouth of Him who sat on the horse. And all the birds were filled with their flesh."

One interpretation says the above Scriptures have already been fulfilled. They explain it as having taken place in the early centuries after Christ's ascension. Another view is that this is only a metaphorical picture, already accomplished by Christ's victory over evil "in the heavenlies". Both views avoid the obvious — that these verses clearly describe an end-time event.

We don't at this time know the names of these *"kings"*, the *"captains"* and the *"mighty men"* but we certainly know who their leaders are by title — the *"beast"* and the *"false prophet"*. *The* important thing is that all of them will be defeated by Christ, Who invites His followers to watch the 'battle'!

This final conflict is usally called the *"Battle of Armageddon"*. It will occur in the valley of Megiddo, where the anti-Christ and the False Prophet will have gathered their *"armies"* to fight Jesus and His armies. I don't think any of us know exactly how all this will work out but we do have specific information on part of it. In other Scriptures we've learned that a 200,000,000-man army will eventually invade the Middle East which surely must be a portion of this fulfillment. The rest will become more obvious as we approach the time of the event itself.

One must consider the recent conflict between Iraq (the modern name for ancient Babylon) and the USA. Another ruthless king has arisen to challenge where God chose to place His primary, two witnesses — Britain and America.   Just as God allowed Nebuchadnezzar and ancient Babylon to come against His people Israel in 606 B.C., He is again allowing another "Nebuchadnezzar" (Saddam Hussein) in our day to confront *spiritual* Israel.
It is likely for the same reason — apostasy. Our nations are unquestionably rooted in the Christian faith. But solid, Biblical teaching is on the wane in many of the mainline denominations. Outside the Church, the enemies of God among us are removing prayer, Bible reading and other Christian influences from public schools and other institutions. Be sure that God will not be mocked by this rejection of Him and the mandate these nations were given.

What's the main point here? I think there will never again be a significant period of peace on earth. I believe the Gulf War was merely the first in a series of battles which will lead up to the final one — Armageddon. The birth pains have begun.

However, when the final battle comes, it will be a no-contest situation. There won't be any great struggle from our side as has been typical of most of the wars in history. Christ the Lord will make quick work of it. Here's how Daniel saw it:

"And in the days of these kings shall the God of heaven set up a kingdom, which shall never be destroyed: and the kingdom shall not be left to other people, (i.e., no more "batons" to be passed on after this one) *but it shall break in pieces and consume all these kingdoms, and it shall stand forever. Forasmuch as thou sawest that the stone* (Christ)

was cut out of the mountain without hands, and that it brake in pieces the iron, the brass, the clay, the silver, and the gold; the great God hath made known to the king what shall come to pass hereafter: and the dream is certain, and the interpretation thereof sure." Daniel 2: 44 & 45.

Brothers and sisters, we can depend on the Lord Jesus Christ to do what He set out to do. He is that *"stone"* who will *"smite"* all the evil kingdoms in the final conflict. We have God's Word on it. Whatever the full scope and splendor is concerning the *"beast"*, the *"false prophet"*, and all their *"Captains"* and *"armies"*, the conclusion of the matter is plain in terms of who gets the final victory: they will be *"cast alive"* into the *"lake of fire burning with brimstone"*. And all the other evil people will be *"killed with the sword which proceeded out of the mouth of Him* (the Lord Jesus Christ) *who sat on the horse"*.

Our mandate today (as always) is to invite people to the *"wedding"*. Christians should not become complacent just because we already possess the great hope. Jesus didn't fall back while on His earthly ministry. He went the extra mile. So should we.

CHAPTER TWENTY

THE MILLENNIUM

1 "And I saw an angel coming down from heaven, having the key to the bottomless pit and a great chain in his hand. 2 And he laid hold of the dragon, that serpent of old, who is the devil and Satan, and bound him for a thousand years; 3 and he cast him into the bottomless pit, and shut him up, and set a seal on him, so that he should deceive the nations no more till the thousand years were finished. And after these things he must be released for a little while."

WHAT'S IN A NAME?

Words like *"abyss"* and *"bottomless pit"* are used several times in the Bible but nowhere have I found precisely what these terms mean. However, two things this passage tells us for sure: (1) **God has the key to it** and (2), **it will be Satan's abode for 1,000 years.**

Chapter 19 revealed the end of mankind's rebellion against God during this present age. We saw how God will destroy the evil forces and influences unrepentant-mankind will have had in progress. Now it's Satan's turn.

In this chapter, we see God sending an angel from heaven with a great chain in his hand with which he will bind Satan for a thousand years. Satan is the spiritual force behind all evil and wickedness. I find it interesting that John uses four names in verse 2 to describe him: the *dragon*, the *serpent of old*, the *devil*, and *Satan*. Obviously, God wants no misunderstanding who He's talking about here.

The Bible identifies God by many names also, such as *Jehovah, Elohim and LORD*. Each of these names implies certain characteristics about His nature — all good. Jesus has many names too: *Immanuel, Son of God, Son of Man, Son of righteousness, the Light of the world,* etc. The names are symbolic of Who He is and His character. Again, all good. And likewise, God's adversary, the primary rebel of all rebels, has several names and titles which are designed to tell us something of his character — all with evil implications.

Therefore, it is clear the Bible beautifully illustrates that the true nature and character of the primary, supernatural personalities who affect us is revealed by the very names God has given them, whether good or bad. *Satan, devil, dragon, serpent,* are all Biblically-related to wrongdoing. Even unbelievers use these terms to infer bad connotations. (But with every generation, the secular arena is making less-and-less of evil associated with the devil. It's common to hear people call someone a "little devil", etc., making light of these terms. They even name sporting teams that way, such as in my hometown where the athletic teams are called "Blue Devils".)

Of course, people who do such things manifest their ignorance of spiritual reality. It basically demonstrates their hard-hearted unawareness and/or unbelief of the Scriptures. To their own demise, if they continue in this direction, they may find themselves in the *"pit"* with the *"father"* of these terms.

"Satan" is the same person as the *"serpent of old"* who was in the garden tempting our great-grandparents, Adam and Eve. Since his fall, he has believed himself equal with God and he used the same philosophy on the first pair in the human race. Adam and Eve were fascinated with the idea of personal godhood and self-righteousness, which has ever since been woven into man's thinking, perpetuated by the serpent's lies and suggestions.

It may be hard to believe but this seemingly-eternal, ever-enlarging, snowball-like influence will end! God has a special 'melt-down' plan for Satan. According to the above Scriptures, a God-sent, angelic messenger will place him in the *bottomless pit* for 1000 years. How wonderful it will be when no outside evil spirit can have access to deceive the human spirit of man.

Some people do not believe in a coming, literal, 1000-year period when Christ reigns as King here on earth. They try to make this chapter say everything other than what it plainly does! The fact is, we shall see the term "1000 years" used six times in this chapter. As I look at this passage, I have no conclusion other than a straight-forward interpretation. And coming from me, that should be significant because as you well know by now, I always search for the Law-of-Double-Reference meanings. I see none here.

The term "millennium" is used quite broadly amongst Biblical interpreters, and some don't like it because the word doesn't appear in the Bible. I have no trouble with this fact because all millennium means when literally broken down is — 1,000 years. "Mille" means 1000; "nium" connotes years. (The word "rapture" doesn't appear in the Bible either but that doesn't mean the teaching is false.)

Verse 3 has a bit of a puzzle in it. It says, "*after these things* (i.e., the millennium) *Satan must be released for a little while*". Why do you suppose God will do that? Think about it. (More on this a little later).

THE SAINTS REIGN WITH CHRIST 1000 YEARS

4 *"And I saw thrones, and they sat on them, and judgment was given to them. And I saw the souls of those who had been beheaded for their witness to Jesus and for the word of God, who had not worshiped the beast or his image, and had not received his mark on their foreheads or on their hands. And they lived and reigned with Christ for a thousand years."*

This verse seems to say that the saints which go through the second half of the anti-Christ period are going to receive the position of Judgeship during the millennium. Recall the verse Rev. 14:13..., *"Blessed are the dead which die in the Lord from henceforth..."*; this was a reference to those who would become *"tribulation"* believers, but later losing their lives as Christian martyrs under the anti-Christ's rule. Our current verse under study must be referring to the same believers.

> I never cease being amazed at God's timing and involvment in everyday situations. Two years ago I had just examined a patient's eyes and for some reason he started telling me that *"by 1992 they want everybody using plastic credit cards"*. I had not heard this news report. (I have watched this movement for years, believing it would eventually lead to a full-scale, single card, monetary system.) Then I said to the man, *"You know that system can't work very well"*. *"Why not?"*, he asked. I responded, *"There are already tremendous abuses in the plastic-money, credit-card system — through theft, loss, telephone deception, etc. I believe the next phase will be to place an identification mark on each individual in an attempt to create an 'abuse-free' system"*. (Our conversation continued along those lines ending with him saying, *"They won't put a number on me!"*)

I do not accept one popular view which says the *"mark on the forehead"* pictures *mental yieldedness* and the *"mark on the hands"* symbolizes the giving of one's hands to evil endeavors. This could, of course, be a secondary meaning. But I'm convinced the marks of the beast will be quite literal. Furthermore, I believe it won't be long before the evildoers start suggesting its use. (A few weeks ago — late 1993 — I saw President Clinton on T.V. holding up the new 'Super Card' he wants to see put into effect relative to health care. The mark is on its way to reality.)

The beautiful thing to note in the Scripture above though is that there will be saints who refuse (as my patient vowed) to accept the mark on their bodies. Some will not only refuse the mark, proving their allegiance to God and their defiance of anti-Christ, they will even give their lives rather than receive it. The results of their sacrifice? Exaltation to the position of rendering judgments during the millennium! I suppose God's reckoning is that a previously-martyred saint makes one particularly suited to become a judge. This is a wonderful example of God's trustworthiness to stand behind His Word.

"Therefore humble yourselves under the mighty hand of God, that He may exalt you in due time,..." 1 Peter 5:6.

God's Word is true and dependable. Hang on to it with all you've got, believers. Praise the matchless name of Jesus!

THE FIRST RESURRECTION & THE SECOND DEATH

5 "But the rest of the dead did not live again until the thousand years were finished. This is the first resurrection."
6 "Blessed and holy is he who has part in the first resurrection. Over such the second death has no power, but they will be priests of God and of Christ, and will reign with Him a thousand years."

This is an appropriate point to give an accounting of the eventual destiny of the spirits (the undying part) of all men. We need to answer questions like, "Who will be on earth during the millennium?" and "What is the meaning of the first resurrection and the second death?". I think a lot of people are confused about exactly what happens when they die. I don't mean to be unkind but what many say sounds more like a fairytale than what the Bible teaches. I'm no different, for I too once held views far removed from what I've learned in the Scriptures. I want to be as accurate as possible so let's tackle the above questions, step-by-step.

First of all, let's recall where we are right now in our study:

1. The Church will have been raptured, so the spirits of those saints are with Christ.
2. The spirits of the dead, Old-Testament believers are also in heaven.

333

3. All spirits of dead unbelievers are being held in 'hades' to await their final judgment from God; John refers to these as the *"rest of the dead"* who will not *"live again until the thousand years are finished"*.

So, we are talking about <u>everyone</u> who has died. Some are with Christ waiting to return to *"...reign with Him a thousand years"* on this earth, the others are unbelievers who remain dead until the "Great White Throne Judgement". (More on that later.)

Verse 6 says those who come with Christ are *"blessed and holy"*. The blessedness results simply by being a Christian. These will be *"priests of God"* in Christ's earthly Kingdom. The *"second death"*, means eternal hell. It is referred to as "second" because there was already a physical death. The *"second death"* follows the millennium and the *"first resurrection"* saints will be unaffected by this second-phase resurrection; i.e., when the *"rest of the dead"* are raised up for their final judgment.

Above, I talked about everyone who had died a physical death, some believers, some unbelievers. However, only the believers will take part in that *"first resurrection"*. The Bible says resurrected saints *reign* with Christ. We have already noted that to reign implies authority and rulership. The question is, over what and whom? Surely they won't be reigning over each other for their sinful nature will be gone. At that time, all believing, resurrected people will have glorified, immortal bodies similar to Jesus after His resurrection here 2,000 years ago. Therefore, they won't need to be disciplined by other resurrected saints. They will probably be under command (like angels today) but not disciplined in any ordinary sense, for they will then have unwavering allegiance to Christ, their Lord. The only remaining possibility is this — **first-resurrection saints reign over ordinary human beings!** Where did these ordinary citizens come from? Are they sinners? Can they have children and other practices just like today?

Before the millennium starts, Christ will have stopped the war conflicts by the *"brightness of His coming"*. But not every person on earth will have been destroyed. I'm convinced these are the people who will be subject to Christ and His followers during His earthly Kingdom age. I'm also convinced that a major portion of them will be ancestorally-rooted in Abraham.

(Actually, the millennium could begin with a relatively small number of people, but that will change rather fast because God will have renewed the earth and long-life expectancy will have been re-established.)

RESURRECTED SAINTS & "NORMAL" HUMANS TOGETHER?

There are some real interesting prophecies in Isaiah which have never come to pass. For a beautiful picture of millennial conditions, read Isaiah 11, 65 and 66. To give you an idea of what you'll find, note these amazing predictions by the ancient prophet of God:

"There shall be no more thence an infant of days, nor an old man that hath not filled his days: For the child shall die an hundred years old: But the sinner being an hundred years old shall be accursed." Is. 65:20.

Folks, history has never seen this. Who can even imagine a one hundred year old child? The idea seems ludicrous to our present way of thinking. This can mean only one thing: God will have restored this earth to its pre-flood condition. Modern, Godly scientists have given much attention to what the earth and the sky was probably like prior to Noah's day. Their general consensus goes something like this: Much of the water we see covering two thirds of our planet now, was once out in space! It existed there as a thick layer of vapor which enveloped the earth. This 'water-canopy' provided ideal living conditions here underneath it, acting much like a terrarium.

335

(Here's how a terrarium works: It's usually a round-shaped, clear, plastic bowl, into which moist soil is placed. This is an ideal kind of environment for the growth of plant life. If it's well sealed with just the right amount of water in it, very little new watering is necessary. The moisture feeds the root system, some also rising up through vaporization to create an 'atmosphere' within the container which then condenses and falls gently on the external leaves of the plant-life to nourish them; finally, it returns to the soil and then the cycle repeats, etc.)

This little, man-made hothouse is believed to be a miniature replica of God's original design of planet earth. Note the similarities of water conditions on the earth prior to the flood as described in Genesis 2:5&6:

"...for the Lord God had not caused it to rain upon the earth, and there was not a man to till the ground. But there went up a mist from the earth, (like the terrarium) and watered the whole face of the ground."

However, the above conditions were not good for plant life only; man likewise benefitted from this. Indeed, God created it for man! He lived much longer then (up to 960 years) — even after his fallen nature guaranteed he would die some day. (I once did a Bible study on chronology. Starting at Noah's life, I checked his age at death, then his ancestors, and noted that only a few generations passed before man's life expectancy became the same as it is today — roughly seventy.)

But almost 3,000 years ago we see the prophet Isaiah, speaking in the name of the Lord, said a time would come when this would all change, even children living to age 100! The obvious implication is that most people would live for centuries. But it's very important to note some will still die, in spite of the beautifully restored earth.

Now if you have followed my steps through the Scriptures you'll see that one can arrive at only one conclusion: during the millennium there will be two kinds of persons living together:

1. "Normal" humans and,
2. "Glorified" saints.

Each group will have its own function.

Because of better living conditions brought about by the restored earth, ordinary people will have good health and, consequentially, long life expectancy. I believe these will re-populate the earth to far greater numbers than we can now even conceive. Today's vast polar regions and deserts will most likely be changed to ideal, habitational land. Archaelogical digs have uncovered all kinds of evidences showing that today's wastelands were once lush and green. (If this seems confusing to you, just remember, no rainfall was needed prior to the flood. When the "water canopy" is back in place, there will once again be a perfect balance of the moisture and the temperature underneath it — even at the poles and today's deserts!)

I think the resurrected saints will be similar (in function, not looks) to the way angels are today — neither marrying or reproducing. They will look like humans, just as Jesus did after His resurrection, but no ordinary blood will flow through their bodies. It won't be needed. A different form of life than blood will be sustaining them — God's glorious, "spiritual blood", if you will. The Bible is relatively quiet on this subject. The apostle John said, "*...it has not yet been revealed what we shall be, but we know that when He is revealed, we shall be like Him, for we shall see Him as He is*". (1 John 3:2). What a wonderful hope Christians have to anticipate. I don't know about you but this excites me. As "joint heirs" in Christ's Kingdom, our assignment will then be to assist in rulership throughout the planet, reigning over "normal" humanity for one thousand years. Praise God!

THAT OLD DEVIL IS OUT AGAIN!

7 "And when the thousand years have expired, Satan will be released from his prison
8 and will go out to deceive the nations which are in the four corners of the earth, Gog and Magog, to gather them together to battle, whose number is as the sand of the sea."

Now these two verses help substantiate the interpretation I just explained, that there will be two **kinds** of beings walking about on this earth some day. Surely no one can deny that the Scriptures clearly reveal that Christian-age believers will be raised from the dead (see verses 5 & 6 above): Those will be in the FIRST RESURRECTION. Two facts are known:

1. They can **no longer die** and,
2. they will one day be on this earth — **reigning**.

But also, the Scriptures teach that during the same period there will be people here who **live** and **die**. These can't be the ones who *reign* for they can never die again.

Look again at verse 3. Recall when Satan was placed in the *"bottomless pit"* at the beginning of the millennium, John said he would later be *"released for a little while"*. Then verses 4 - 6 addresses the millennium itself. But at the end of the 1000 years, verse 7 says Satan will be released again just as John had earlier predicted. And once loosed, what do we see Satan doing? The same thing he's always done — deceiving people.

The questions are, *"who is Satan tempting?"* and *"can he deceive a resurrected saint?"* No, that's impossible! Why so? Because of the promise in verse 6 which says the *"second death"* has no power over resurrected saints. They will be like the holy angels of our present day and age, completely obedient to God and His ways. They will have a perfected new nature which Satan can't tempt to rebel against God. And yet we see above

338

that Satan is able to *"deceive the nations"* and *"gather them to battle, whose number is as the sand of the sea"*. This is no small group, folks! Since this can't be those who have reigned with Christ, we are left with only this alternative: They are an army of rebellious, sinful humans. Where will these come from?

REBELS IN THE KING'S COURT?

Surely the question must be in your mind, *"How could anyone possibly be tempted to go against Christ after living directly under His Holy ordinances and perfectly-rendered judgements?"* Remember, that's the way it will be in the millennium. We've already seen that Christ will rule 'normal' humans with a *"rod of iron"*. But we must remember, just because Satan will have been *'tied'* during the thousand year reign of Jesus' as King of the earth, in no way reduces unregenerate-man's sinful nature. Thus, although Satan won't be around as a tempter, man's own rebellious condition will be to rise to its own full measure in the millennium, <u>uninfluenced by evil spirits</u>.

Now, no one is sure exactly how things will be during the millennium but let me make the following suggestions:

Imagine yourself commencing the millennium as an ordinary human being. The earth will be a renewed paradise, a wonderful place to raise families, to build homes, cities, etc. You, along with all other ordinary people, will take part in this, but all the time under the guidance and watchful eyes of Christ and the joint-heirs of His Kingdom. Now, many people will appreciate these wonderful things and will gladly submit to the Godly-ruling authorities. The Bible indicates these will occasionally "go up" to Jerusalem to worship the King of Kings and Lord of Lords. It will be a time when belief of ordinary people will be based on both faith and by sight, as was the case when Jesus was here the first time. But in the future period, Christ will be reigning as Lord and King.

Some will become "saved" during those days, and not all that differently than the disciples of Jesus were at His first advent. Question: Will this be a 'better' salvation than now and will those living then be more fortunate than us? I think Jesus said no! Do you recall the situation with Thomas when he wouldn't accept the report of the other disciples who had seen Jesus alive? He demanded to see and touch Him himself. Later, Jesus allowed Thomas' wish but said, "...*Thomas, because you have seen Me, you have believed. Blessed are those who have not seen and yet have believed.*" Jn. 20:29. True, Thomas did then fall on his knees and worship Jesus. But, the point is, just seeing Jesus during the millennium, or a resurrected joint-heir of His, will not automatically insure one will exercise genuine, saving belief. Not everyone who saw Jesus during His first Advent became believers, did they?

Now think about this: human blood flowed through Jesus' veins before. He could hurt. Even die. But at times He manifested some of the same kind of power then as He will in the Kingdom age, and yet many people scorned Him! Does that not almost seem ridiculous? Project yourself as an unsaved person back then into the very presence of Christ. You would not automatically become a believer just because you saw Him render a perfect judgement or miracle in front of your eyes. In fact, if the occasion called for a rebuke against you, you would likely resent Him for it even though you might know it was a just cause! Also, you would probably have a grudge against His close associates (the disciples) who represented His ways.

In the Kingdom age, I don't think it will be much different (spiritually) than it was before. Only in the millennium it will be greatly expanded in magnitude with Jesus and the glorified saints in power and ruling. The Scriptures make clear that certain resurrected saints who were formerly martyred will act as judges then. Just as Thomas worshiped Jesus when he saw Him, some will believe and submit to the Godly authorities and thereby enjoy all the fruits of peace and joy just like believers today, only theirs will be in an environment better than ours is now. Thus, in principle, things will be quite the same as today. The bottom line is that in order to have the joy and peace of God requires <u>belief</u> regardless of surrounding conditions.

So, since it really isn't hard to imagine that man can still rebel even when living in the presence of the Lord, it shouldn't surprise us that he will quite willingly listen to Satan when he is again released. After all, a fallen man in the Kingdom Age, who continues in his unbelief, will be saying in response to Satan's deception, *"That's what I've been wanting to do all along. I just haven't had sufficient 'inspiration' and determination to go to war against this Christ and His 'undying gang' who have placed unreasonable demands* (His 'rules of righteousness') *on me and my kin. Let's 'go for it' men, and see if they are really all that indestructible."* And so it will go. God will once again allow Satan a free hand to raise up another army of wicked unbelievers to come against Christ and His Kingdom.

One final thought here on verses 7 and 8: it may be that those who remain alive at the end of the Tribulation will all be believers but do not go into the millennium immortalized. This being the case, everyone entering the millennium would be believers! Some glorified, some not — but all believers. So, where do those come from who Satan gathers to rebel against Christ and His Kingdom at the end of the millennium? At the beginning of the millennium there will be children survivors of the Tribulation and pregnant women. These little ones will have fallen natures just like any other human being living at any other time since Adam and Eve.

To me, this understanding helps remove some of the veil of millennial conditions. The young ones who go into the millennium will have no personal recollection of former things, only what their parents and others <u>tell</u> them. They will not think it extraordinary that there is a King ruling the entire world, nor that He has a host of followers and assistants 'like' Him. Therefore there is no reason to assume these children will automatically grow up to be believers. Their hearts will be as potentially wicked as ours today.

> (Christ in you or in me today, via the Holy Spirit, is just as real now as it will be then, spiritually speaking. The only difference then will be that sin-proneness will be completely gone in our new, incorruptible state. But this will not be the case with the "normal" people. Thus, many will hate us because of the difference.)

You may be wondering where I would get such thoughts. I think Jesus may have alluded to this when He was discussing the final Tribulation in Matthew 24. He referred to mothers when He said, *"But woe to those who are pregnant and to those with nursing babies in those days!"* Matt. 24:19. If we view this verse in the literal sense only, one would conclude Jesus was simply talking about personal problems mothers will encounter during the Tribulation. I don't mean to imply Jesus is not showing sensitivity to the personal sorrows of mothers with small children of that time but I think there's more here than that.

What I want to underscore on this point is the fact that when the word *"woe"* is used prophetically (as Matthew 24 most certainly is), it usually alludes to something with broadscaled implications. For example, we saw *"three woes"* earlier in our study and all had to do with world-wide conflicts. Now what I'm suggesting is the possibility that Jesus, while speaking about the problems of pregnant women and mothers with young children during the closing hours of this age, was also looking into the far, far distant future (the LODR), seeing that there would be offspring from these babies which would rise up against Him again at the end of the millennium.

You see, in Jesus' mind (if my guess here is correct), He saw the anti-Christ system which would come against Him at the end of the present age, as being very similar, even a spiritual-continuum, to what Satan would eventually inspire into the minds of some of the offspring of these expectant

Tribulation mothers. In any event, whoever they are and wherever they come from, let's now look at the outcome of those who choose to be "rebels in the King's Court" after Satan is loosed.

GOD'S JUSTICE

9 "And they came up on the breadth of the earth and surrounded the camp of the saints and the beloved city. And fire came down from God out of heaven and devoured them. 10 And the devil, who deceived them, was cast into the lake of fire and brimstone where the beast and the false prophet are. And they will be tormented day and night forever and ever."

Mere <u>assent</u> to facts is not synonymous with <u>belief</u>. The above Scripture is really plain talk, folks! The knowledge of God has been around a long time. Preachers, evangelists and lay Christians have been telling the Gospel story for 2,000 years, and yet the masses continue to sin and rebel against God and His prophetically-perfect Word. Unbelief will also continue throughout the millennium; even with Christ and His Bride (resurrected saints) as living proof that God's Word is true and just. There will be many under Satan's inspiration who resist and come against Jesus and His followers on the last day.

But, look at the above verses again. When the armies come, not one earthly weapon will be necessary to stop the invaders. God will take care of this one — Personally. The rebels will be "devoured" with God-sent fire.

This is it, folks! From then on there will be no more human resistance against God. The battle is over. God's victory is completed. The 'sin-curtain' falls at this final act. Fallen man will have lost in his seemingly-endless desire to be his own god.

That's what it has been all about, friends. Ever since the serpent suggested to Adam and Eve they could be like gods, this same lie has been perpetuated throughout the history of

343

mankind. It was a lie in the beginning. It is a lie today. But THE LIE will come to its end, along with the LIARS, and both will lie with the *serpent* where they belong. Verse 10 gives us the answer where that will be, as they are *"cast into the lake of fire and brimstone where the beast and false prophet are. And they will be tormented day and night forever and ever."*

Since we have come to the end of all rebellion, one might assume this would be a good place to end this book. I would agree, but the Bible doesn't end here, so I can't either.

THE GREAT WHITE THRONE JUDGMENT

11 "And I saw a great white throne and Him who sat on it, from whose face the earth and the heaven fled away. And there was found no place for them.
12 And I saw the dead, small and great, standing before God, and books were opened. And another book was opened, which is the Book of Life. And the dead were judged according to their works, by the things which were written in the books.
13 And the sea gave up the dead who were in it, and Death and Hades delivered up the dead who were in them. And they were judged, each one according to his works.
14 And death and Hades were cast into the lake of fire. This is the second death.
15 And anyone not found written in the Book of Life was cast into the lake of fire."

We must differentiate the "Judgement Seat of Christ" (which will have already occurred a thousand years earlier) from the Great White Throne Judgement (GWTJ) we see described here in these verses. You recall verse 5 said the "rest of the dead" (the unsaved) remained so until after the millennium. These

344

too will someday be raised up, along with all who die during the millennium (some believers, some not), to face the GWTJ of God when all shall hear the final verdicts upon all mankind — commonly called JUDGEMENT DAY.

There will be different kinds of books which will be opened. I presume some books reveal God's perfect Holy Ordinances as well as an account of each person's record of life here on earth. I believe we will see a book of God's own personal 'translation' of the Bible. (I would not suppose God's Bible to be all that different from what we already have. But it will be untarnished, given exactly as it was first uttered thousands of years ago by the Holy Spirit to the prophets-of-old.)

There will be a Book of Life which will have all the names of the saved in it. These will include all the resurrected saints who served with Christ during the millennium as well as the "normal" people who become believers during that period. I believe when true faith is exercised in the propitiatory work of Jesus Christ at Calvary, one's name is immediately written down in this special record book. This will be written with 'indelible ink', folks. I say this because we learned in verse 6 that the *"second death"* would have *"no power"* upon the glorified saints who enter Christ's Kingdom to reign with Him. So, these can't possibly face any kind of potential condemnation at the GWTJ.

JUDGED BY WORKS?

Verse 13 is a bit troublesome for us salvation-by-faith-alone believers, isn't it? For it says each one at the GWTJ will be judged *"according to his works"*. What does this mean?

Unbelievers have always loved to ask Christians these kinds of questions: *"What happens to the African native who never hears the Gospel? Does God send him to hell? How could he become a believer? He never had a chance!"*, and so on. It may come as a surprise to you but God has dealt specifically with these questions in Romans 1 and 2. Study the chapters carefully. In essence, it says God knows the heart of everyone.

345

Therefore, He has no trouble in knowing whether they would have come to Him if they had heard the Gospel. What this means is that God, at times, does some of His own soul-harvesting!

Some people (like the African in the jungle), never having heard the Gospel, live out their lives dictated by their inner spirit which has believed all it knew about truth. Their actions reflect this inner belief and these *"works"* become self-evident of what's going on inside. What then can we conclude other than they will have done the best they could with what they had and will be judged accordingly?

Just because God has been so generous to us "born-again" believers saved in a 'normal' manner, does not annul God's right to Personally join in the salvation process, <u>without our help</u>. How dare we limit God's calling and choosing to only our part in sending out the Word! Our efforts are an important portion of God's overall strategy — not the sum total of it.

This thinking may mess up some readers' theology, and/or alter your confidence in my credibility. If so, I have a question for you: How do you deal with this statement? *"They were judged, each one <u>according to his works</u>."*

Now most of you know that the Bible clearly teaches we are saved through no merit of our own. *"For by grace you have been saved through faith, and that not of yourselves; it is the gift of God, NOT OF WORKS, lest anyone should boast."* Eph. 2:8. This verse makes plain that salvation can never be by a man's *"works"* and yet Rev. 20:12 says that the *"dead were judged according to their works..."*. And we know some of these in Revelation 20 who *are* judged by their *"works"* will be saved, for in verse 15 we find this: *"Anyone not found written in the Book of Life was cast into the lake of fire".* To say *"Anyone not found written",* unmistakeably implies that some names <u>were found</u> written in the book. Therefore, since we know there can be no contradiction here, we must conclude the *"works"* of Rev. 20:13 embraces more than a mere, literal interpretation would allow.

346

Some theologians say all Rev. 20:12 means is that since no man's "*works*" are good enough for salvation, each and every one of these who stand before God at the GWTJ will be sent to hell. If this is so, why should there even be a mention here of the "Book of Life" which contains the names of the saved? Is it merely to let them know their name isn't in the book?!

I believe God (or a representative of His) will be reading some names of people who will go into eternity with Him which you and I had nothing to do with saving. The apostle Paul was likely alluding to these when he wrote, "*...these although not having the law, are a law to themselves, who show the work of the law written in their hearts, their conscience also bearing witness, and between themselves their thoughts accusing or else excusing them in the day when God will judge the secrets of men by Jesus Christ,...*" (Romans 2:14-16).

Some people are troubled by this line of reasoning, saying it reduces the motivation for Christian evangelization. They ask, **"Why does God need the Church at all?"** Such a question reflects nothing but pride.

Please realize I believe God has purposed to save some through you and I only. That is, if it wern't for the Gospel proclamation, some people wouldn't be saved, period. It is in this way that we become partakers in His Kingdom-building process. With pride put aside, we should be <u>en</u>couraged, not <u>dis</u>couraged, by the above analysis of how God will deal at Judgement Day with those who never heard the Gospel via the Great Commission of the Church. As I see it, the central thrust of Romans 2:14-16 is that *God* is the ultimate, fair Judge.

Since the day I decided these are not merely <u>my</u> ideas, but really just a correct understanding of God's truth, it has given me a new inner peace and confidence, as well as a new appreciation of the almightiness of God. The concept also helps me to see what I really am — a servant "in His vineyard". I've thought on this subject many, many times and no matter how I have approached it, I always come up with this undeniable conclusion: the viewpoint that salvation is effectual only through the Church's influence, forces a spiritual paralysis upon God's sovereignty to act when no man is around. So, understanding that God will also reap some souls without my help lets me know He is working while I am working. I like that — and shall now leave it at that.

EVEN DEATH AND 'HADES' ARE REMOVED

Hades is supposed by most expositors to be that place where the souls of unbelievers go to await the GWTJ. I agree. Of course, from Adam until the end, all face physical death (Exception: the saints raptured alive). But, at Judgement Day, God will even send both Hades and death to eternal destruction! Verse 14 calls this the "second death", which, we recall, has no power over those who participate in the first resurrection.

Since we don't have much Biblical evidence of what exactly will transpire at the GWTJ, there is room for variation and speculation. And, in spite of the fact I spent quite a bit of time on it, I think we shouldn't overburden ourselves too much in this area. Our main focal point should be on the *first resurrection* because here we have a more sure word of promise for those participating in it. Also, concentrating our efforts here should increase our fervency to get the Gospel out and see as many saved as possible. It is here we find our guarantee that the *second death* will have no effect. So, let's be about it, Christian friends!

CHAPTER TWENTY ONE

I said at the beginning that this book would mainly be concentrated on Revelation 6 - 20. But also included was the text of the first five chapters, basically without commentary, as we shall now do with chapters 21 and 22.

ALL THINGS MADE NEW

1 "And I saw a new heaven and a new earth, for the first heaven and the first earth had passed away. And there was no more sea.
2 And I, John, saw the holy city, New Jerusalem, coming down from God out of heaven, prepared as a bride adorned for her husband.
3 And I heard a loud voice out of heaven saying, 'Behold, the tabernacle of God is with men, and He shall dwell with them, and they shall dwell with them, and they shall be His people, and God Himself shall be with them and be their God.
4 And God shall wipe away every tear from their eyes; there shall be no more death, nor sorrow, nor crying; and there shall be no more pain, for the former things have passed away.
5 And He who sat on the throne said, 'Behold, I am making all things new.' And He said to me, 'Write, for these words are true and faithful.'
6 And He said to me, 'It is done'! I am the Alpha and the Omega, the Beginning and the End. I will give of the fountain of the water of life freely to him who thirsts.
7 He who overcomes shall inherit all things, and I will be his God and he shall be My son.

8 'But the cowardly and unbelieving and abominable and murderers and sexually immoral and sorcerers and idolaters and all liars shall have their part in the lake which burns with fire and brimstone, which is the second death."

THE NEW JERUSALEM

9 "And one of the seven angels who had the seven bowls filled with the seven last plagues came to me and talked with me, saying, 'Come! I will show you the bride, the Lamb's wife.'

10 And he carried me away in the Spirit to a great and high mountain, and showed me the great city, the holy Jerusalem, descending out of heaven from God,

11 having the glory of God. And her light was like a most precious stone, like a jasper stone, clear as crystal.

12 And she had a great and high wall, and had twelve gates, and twelve angels at the gates, and names written on them, which are the names of the twelve tribes of the children of Israel:

13 three gates on the east, three gates on the north, three gates on the south, and three gates on the west.

14 And the wall of the city had twelve foundations, and on them were the names of the twelve apostles of the Lamb.

15 And he who talked with me had a golden reed to measure the city, its gates, and its wall.

16 And the city is laid out as a square, and its length is as great as its breadth. And he measured the city with the reed: twelve thousand furlongs. Its length, breadth and height are equal.

17 And he measured its wall: one hundred and forty-four cubits, according to the measure of a man, that is, of an angel.

18 And the construction of its wall was of jasper; and the city was pure gold, like clear glass.

19 And the foundations of the wall of the city were adorned with all kinds of precious stones: the first foundation was jasper, the second sapphire, the third chalcedony, the fourth emerald,
20 the fifth sardonyx, the sixth sardius, the seventh chrysolite, the eighth beryl, the ninth topaz, the tenth chrysoprase, the eleventh jacinth, and the twelfth amethyst.
21 And the twelve gates were twelve pearls: each individual gate was of one pearl. And the street of the city was pure gold, like transparent glass."

THE GLORY OF THE NEW JERUSALEM

22 "And I saw no temple in it, for the Lord God Almighty and the Lamb are its temple.
23 And the city had no need of the sun or of the moon to shine in it, for the glory of God illuminated it, and the Lamb is its light.
24 And the nations of those who are saved shall walk in its light, and the kings of the earth bring their glory and honor into it.
25 And its gates shall not be shut at all by day, for there shall be no night there.
26 And they shall bring the glory and the honor of the nations into it.
27 And there shall by no means enter it anything that defiles, or causes an abomination or a lie, but only those who are written in the Lamb's Book of Life."

When you are down-and-out and feel the need for spiritual encouragement, as most of us do occasionally, read this chapter a few times. Thinking on the things God has prepared for those who love and expect Him will lift your spirit. There is no better medicine for the weary soul in today's sin-laden world than to meditate on God's promises that will someday belong to His Own in a new, sin-free world. Praise His Holy Name!

351

CHAPTER TWENTY TWO

THE RIVER OF LIFE

"1 And he showed me a pure river of water of life, clear as crystal, proceding out of the throne of God and of the Lamb.
2 In the middle of its street, and on either side of the river, was the tree of life, which bore twelve fruits, yielding its fruit every month. And the leaves of the tree were for the healing of the nations.
3 And there shall be no more curse, but the throne of God and of the Lamb shall be in it, and His servants shall serve Him.
4 And they shall see His face, and His name shall be on their foreheads.
5 And there shall be no night there; they need no lamp nor light of the sun, for the Lord God gives them light. And they shall reign forever and ever."

THE TIME IS NEAR

6 "And he said to me, 'These words are faithful and true.' And the Lord God of the holy prophets sent His angel to show His servants the things which must shortly take place.
7 "BEHOLD, I AM COMING QUICKLY! BLESSED IS HE WHO KEEPS THE WORDS OF THE PROPHECY OF THIS BOOK."
8 And I, John, saw and heard these things. And when I had heard and seen, I fell down to worship before the feet of the angel who showed me these things.
9 Then he said to me, 'See that you do not do that. For I am your fellow servant, and of your brethren the prophets, and of those who keep the words of this book. Worship God.'

10   And he said to me, 'Do not seal the words of the prophecy of this book, for the time is at hand.
11   He who is unjust, let him be unjust still; he who is filthy, let him be filthy still; he who is righteous, let him be righteous still; he who is holy, let him be holy still."

JESUS TESTIFIES TO THE CHURCHES

12   "AND BEHOLD, I AM COMING QUICKLY, AND MY REWARD IS WITH ME, TO GIVE TO EACH ONE ACCORDING TO HIS WORK.
13   I AM THE ALPHA AND THE OMEGA, THE BEGINNING AND THE END, THE FIRST AND THE LAST."
14   Blessed are those who do His commandments, that they may have the right to the tree of life, and may enter in through the gates into the city.
15   But outside are dogs and sorcerers and sexually immoral and murderers and idolators, and whoever loves and practices a lie.
16   "I, JESUS, HAVE SENT MY ANGEL TO TESTIFY TO YOU THESE THINGS IN THE CHURCHES. I AM THE ROOT AND THE OFFSPRING OF DAVID, THE BRIGHT AND MORNING STAR."
17   And the Spirit and the bride say, "Come!" And let him who hears say, "Come!" And let him who thirsts come. And whoever desires, let him take the water of life freely."

A WARNING

18   "For I testify to everyone who hears the words of the prophecy of this book: if anyone adds to these things, God will add to him the plagues that are written in this book.

19 And if anyone takes away from the words of the book of this prophecy, God will take away his part from the Book of Life, from the holy city, and from the things which are written in this book."

I AM COMING QUICKLY

20 "He who testifies to these things says, "SURELY I AM COMING QUICKLY." Amen. Even so, come, Lord Jesus. 21 The grace of our Lord Jesus Christ be with you all. Amen."

As I read the inspired words of John concerning the "*adding*" or "*taking away*" of the words of this prophecy, my spine tingles a little as I realize that I have just written a commentary on the book! With this thought in mind, let me urge you to let God's Word be true. After you have read this — or any other commentary on Holy Scriptures — you should then go back to the Holy Bible, read it thoroughly, meditatively, prayerfully, seeking the Holy Spirit's guidance as you go. His Word will still be standing when all commentaries fall by the wayside.

Whether you accept the overall thesis in my book is perhaps not really all that important. But if you have been challenged sufficiently to do your own prophetic studies, then I shall be satisfied believing this work was not altogether fruitless.

At this point you must again be thinking this book ought to end here. Some who have read this remaining section said they found this part more interesting to them than the main body of my book! You be the judge.

On the next few pages are charts which give an outline of the "Tribulation" and "Wrath" periods as already described. Take some time with these, reflecting on all you have already read. These charts present, as I see it, the whole prophetic spectrum at a glance.

CHARTS

Chart # 1 gives a pictorial outline of the 'Tribulation'. As pointed out in this study, this refers to a specific time-span dating from some point after Jesus' ascension and continues up to the rapture of the Church. Following this, there will be a literal 1260-day Tribulation period beginning at the death of the national "*two witnesses*" — the United States and Great Britain (Canada today being the main remnant of the 'British factor').

As you know, most writers concentrate solely on the literal side of this coin. But the chief emphasis of my book has been that we understand there is a 1260 year time-span of "witnessing" to be done through the Church within Great Britain and the United States. As I have repeatedly indicated, we don't know the exact "*day and hour*" when the national aspect of prophecy ends but all indications are that we are fast-approaching that time.

The *Wrath of God* period depicted on Chart # 1 is out of proportion (size-wise) relative to the reign of the anti-Christ but the space was needed in order to get the Seven Vials indicated on the chart. By simply looking at the chart, one gets the impression the dispensation of the Vials will last as long as the long-range aspect of the Trumpets. This is not true. We don't know exactly how long the Wrath of God period lasts, but it seems to be very short, perhaps taking only a matter of days. Immediately following this period will be the beginning of Christ's reign on earth during the millennium.

The second chart is a blow-up of the small seven year end-time period indicated by the narrow regions where the heavy line crosses between the rapture of the Church and the reign of the anti-Christ on Chart # 1. Everything to the left of the heavy vertical line on Chart 2 represents the 3 1/2 year build-up ("man of lawlessness" period) of the anti-Christ's reign. It begins at the time of the defeat of the two national

355

"witnesses", the USA and Canada. Everything to the right of the heavy line (Chart 2) represents the actual reigning period of the anti-Christ, more commonly known as THE GREAT TRIBULATION. During this period (after the Church will have been removed), the 144,000 Israelites which have been set-aside will be used in a supernatural way of world-wide evangelization. The Rapture is indicated by the upward-sweeping arror at the mid-point of the final seven year period.

HOW TO READ THE CHARTS

Charts are often misleading or misinterpreted. So let me take a little more time to further explain mine:

1. Read Chart 1 from bottom up and Chart 2 from left to right with page turned sideways.

2. As you progress up (or left-right), time advances beginning from the crucifixion of Jesus Christ, going up to the beginning of the millennium at the top of Chart 1 (or extreme right on Chart 2).

3. On Chart 1, at the heavy dark line, the 3 1/2 year build-up of the anti-Christ (on the bottom side of the line) is condensed into a small area and all of this period is then expanded out for you on the left half (with book turned) of Chart 2. Then, the 3 1/2-year reigning period of the anti-Christ (his heyday) is just above the heavy dark line of Chart 1, again expanded on Chart 2.

4. As you know, I've discussed the Law of Double Reference throughout the text. In line with this concept, think of Chart 1 like this: from Constantine up to the death of the *two witnesses* comprises the long-range Tribulation. After the witnesses are destroyed, there will

then be a repeat of the same pattern of the Seals and Trumpets, only then the time period will be a brief 3 1/2 years. Thus, to see this clearer and more broadly, I've telescoped it separately on Chart 2.

Likewise then, the actual reigning 3 1/2 years, when anti-Christ reaches the climax of his wicked rulership, is again expanded out for easier viewing above the heavy line on Chart 2 (or to the right if you are holding the book sideways).

5. The millennium begins at the top of Chart 1 and at the extreme right of Chart 2.

Keeping these thoughts in mind, now look over the charts carefully.

357

MILLENNIUM

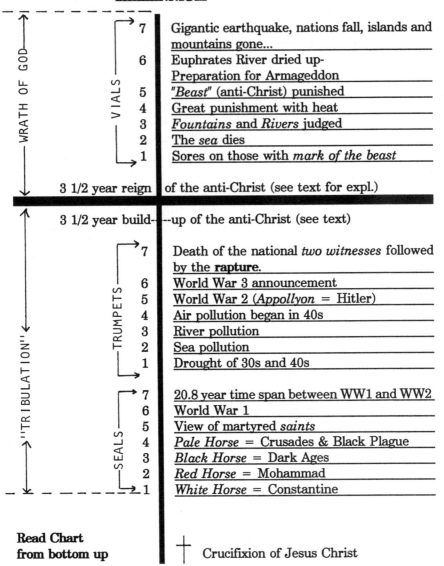

WRATH OF GOD	**VIALS** 7	Gigantic earthquake, nations fall, islands and mountains gone...
	6	Euphrates River dried up- Preparation for Armageddon
	5	*"Beast"* (anti-Christ) punished
	4	Great punishment with heat
	3	*Fountains* and *Rivers* judged
	2	The *sea* dies
	1	Sores on those with *mark of the beast*

3 1/2 year reign of the anti-Christ (see text for expl.)

3 1/2 year build--up of the anti-Christ (see text)

"TRIBULATION"	**TRUMPETS** 7	Death of the national *two witnesses* followed by the **rapture.**
	6	World War 3 announcement
	5	World War 2 (*Appollyon* = Hitler)
	4	Air pollution began in 40s
	3	River pollution
	2	Sea pollution
	1	Drought of 30s and 40s
	SEALS 7	20.8 year time span between WW1 and WW2
	6	World War 1
	5	View of martyred *saints*
	4	*Pale Horse* = Crusades & Black Plague
	3	*Black Horse* = Dark Ages
	2	*Red Horse* = Mohammad
	1	*White Horse* = Constantine

Read Chart from bottom up   † Crucifixion of Jesus Christ

REMEMBER: The whole theme of this book has been to present a picture of prophecy of long-range proportions. Chart 1 here depicts that. However, the short-range, literal seven-year reign of anti-Christ (i.e., prophecy as understood by practically all other writers on the subject) is included here also — by the area just above and just below the heavy horizontal line. This portion is broadened out on Chart 2.

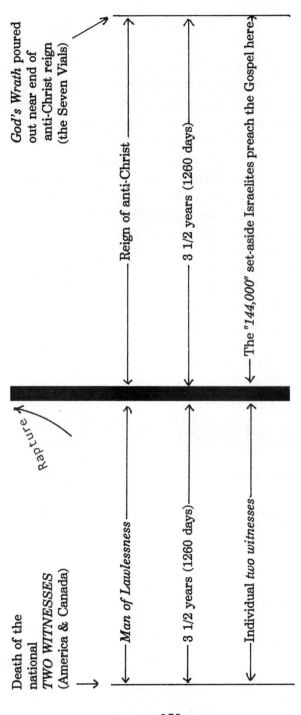

MILLENNIUM

God's Wrath poured out near end of anti-Christ reign (the Seven Vials)

Reign of anti-Christ

3 1/2 years (1260 days)

The "144,000" set-aside Israelites preach the Gospel here

Death of the national *TWO WITNESSES* (America & Canada)

Rapture

Man of Lawlessness

3 1/2 years (1260 days)

Individual *two witnesses*

Chart 2 expands and explains that section of Chart 1 that speaks of the build-up and reign of the anti-Christ. During this 7 year period, there may very well be a recapitulation of the entire longitudinal *Tribulation.* For example: The original White Horse was Constantine and the Roman Empire. On the short scale we will likely see new life returned to the regime he started. Similarly, Mohammad's empire (the Red Horse) will rise again to oppose the modern day Roman empire (today's EEC). The other Seals and Trumpets would follow this same pattern. (Of course, the whole text of my book must be read carefully to fully grasp what the charts portray.)

CHAPTER TWENTY THREE

The book of Daniel cannot be left out of any serious study on Biblical prophecy. However, for brevity sake, I shall make reference only to certain passages which have long-range application involving prophecy up to and including our day. What Daniel packed into 12 brief chapters is quite phenomenal. While most of what he said related specifically to certain individuals and kingdoms of ancient times, the predictions also had Law-of-Double-Reference connotations. That being the case, you know I've got to comment on the book.

Some Christians actually object to those of us who relate the numbers of Daniel and Revelation to history. This is a very strange reaction for surely the Holy Spirit inspired Daniel to record all those numbers for someone's benefit — in my opinion, ours. In fact, that it is for our day is even implied by Daniel himself. Daniel once asked: (See Dan. 12:6).

"How long shall it be to the end of these wonders?"

And again in verse 8 he asked:

"What shall be the end of these things?"

Then Daniel gets his answer from the Lord in verse 9:

"Go thy way, Daniel: For the words are closed up and sealed <u>till</u> the time of the end."

We saw in Revelation that John was not to seal up his book and some expositors say this also means Daniel's book became unsealed at that time. I don't think so. The command in Daniel 12:9 is clear. The facts are that some of Daniel's "secrets" were not to be understood *"till the time of the end"*. Now does the *"time of the end"* refer to the day the apostle John wrote or, does it not simply mean what it says — *"the time of the end"*? (Paradoxically, those who object — i.e., those who see Daniel's book as "unsealed" at John's day — call themselves literalists!)

Jesus' disciples asked Him about the sign of His return and of the *"end of the age"* (Matthew 24:3) and His answer clearly relates to the last of the *"last days"*. He made references to conditions which would be prevailing on the earth during the very moments of His coming. Neither did He give them some kind of vague answer insinuating the *"end"* meant all the days from His ascension up till His return, (which is the teaching of some).

God made it quite clear He would Personally clear up the mysteries Daniel inquired about when He said in verse 10:

"Many shall be purified, and made white, and tried: But the wicked shall do wickedly: and none of the wicked shall understand: But the wise shall understand."

In other words, God would someday open certain eyes to Daniel's questions about the *"time of the end"*. This would not be plain to the *"wicked"* (unbelievers) but the *"wise"* (believers) would know. Wisdom is a gift from God. It comes at His discretion, at His timing and is given to whom He chooses.

I think the people who are upset by those of us who see prophetic significance in Biblical numbers and Scriptures which contain allegory is because (1), they personally have difficulty seeing and understanding allegory in the first place (whether it comes through numbers or words) and (2), they are aware of others out of the past who (allegorizing) made certain predictions based on these same passages — which DIDN'T come true. Most of those were cults and their errors have had the effect of steering Christians away from numbers and allegory. Sometimes lack-of-understanding and sometimes over-reaction to Satan's scare-tactics produces skepticism.

361

Now, don't get me wrong. I love these skeptical men — in the Lord. But I also feel the necessity not to be intimidated by their convictions. Therefore, I must take the plunge into this "no man's land". Remember, one of the characteristics of the final anti-Christ (as given right here in Daniel 7:25) is to: "...*think to change times and laws...*". In other words, it is Satan who tries to confuse us. We must never forget that he often sends his counterfeit prophets in advance of God's army in an attempt to discredit them when they come with God's correct understanding. This has the effect of deviating God's people away from the truth. Satan knows this. He's been in "Sunday School" a long time now. So, there's nothing new here. Satan is following the same old procedure he always has.

In spite of the fearless attitude I may have unintentionally conveyed, I want you to realize I do not at all consider my observations as perfect knowledge. But I have to believe I've discovered something of value here because of the amazing consistency among the FOUR prophecies we'll study.

Each of the four specific prophecies I shall talk about will reveal a long span of years, beginning at a certain time and place, in association with a specific person, and ending at some pertinent time in the future. Now, right off, some will think I'm trying to set the exact date of the Lord's return. I'm not. Jesus said that would be impossible. (See Matthew 24:36). However, I'm convinced God has set the prophecies in motion and given adequate information so that we may <u>approximate</u> the time. Jesus — Who was the One that said we couldn't know the exact "day and hour" — also gave a detailed discourse on the highlights of the world scene just prior to His coming, making clear that He wanted us to know the general time of His return.

Actually, even if we knew for sure what the Biblical numbers meant, we still couldn't calculate fulfillment dates with certainty because of the inaccuracies in our calendar systems. As already noted, even Jesus' Own birth date is in dispute, varying from 2 to 8 B.C. among reputable scholars (5 B.C. being my

362

presumption, you'll recall). Surely, in His sovereignty, God has allowed these variations. He could have let us maintain unquestionable records if that had been His desire. But He obviously had specific reasons for doing it the way He has. However, just because we don't have absolutely precise information on exact dates, we don't want to over-react to the other extreme either — paying no heed to what God *has* given us to work with. My guess is that on all these evaluations to be discussed, we are off no more than five or six years at the most.

As for the purpose of numerics, I suspect it may be God's way of reaching a certain 'kind' of personality. Like it or not, folks, there are people who are more inclined to numbers than they are words! So, let's be generous, just as our heavenly Father is. Let's 'allow' God the space to reach into some of these areas where our usual testimonies seem to have little effect. The case of doubting-Thomas is again applicable here. Although He rebuked him (mildly), Jesus did honor Thomas' request to see His scars. Why do you think Jesus showed him? I believe it's because God is:

"...not willing that any should perish, but that all should come to repentance." (2 Peter 3:9).

PROPHECY # ONE

The first prophecy to which I'd like to give attention is from Daniel 4. Daniel had miraculously recalled king Nebuchadnezzar's dream he had forgotten. Then Daniel proceeded to also interpret the dream for him. Nebuchadnezzar was to be driven out of his own kingdom (the Babylonian) to live like an animal in the wilderness as indicated in verses 31 & 32:

"While the word was in the king's mouth, there fell a voice from heaven, saying, O king Nebuchadnezzar, to thee it is

363

spoken: The kingdom is departed from thee. And they shall drive thee from men, and thy dwelling shall be with the beasts of the field: They shall make thee to eat grass as oxen, and <u>seven times</u> shall pass over thee, until thou know that the most high ruleth in the kingdom of men, and giveth it to whomsoever He will."

The following verses (33 - 37) show Nebuchadnezzar did indeed go and live with *"the beasts of the field"*, after which he praised and extolled the king of heaven saying, *"...those that walk in pride He is able to abase."*   So, the prophecy of Nebuchadnezzar's dream was fulfilled according to Daniel's interpretation.

It is important to note how long 'Neb' was in the wilderness. He was there *"seven times"*. We remember from our Revelation study that *"3 1/2 times"* is equal to 1260 days.   We also determined that in certain prophecies this is talking about "prophetic days", which means years. If *3 1/2 times = 1260 days,* then *7 times = 2520 days.*   Now the old king was with the *"beasts"* for *seven "times"*, which, literally-interpreted, means 7 Hebrew years. (Remember, 2,520 days = 7 Hebrew years).

So, Nebuchadnezzar was out of his mind for seven years (2,520 days), after which he returned to normal and then praised the true God of heaven. I'm convinced (by the Law of Double Reference) what happened to 'Neb' personally was a prophetic picture of several future kingdoms, beginning with his and ending with the final anti-Christ kingdom.

In fact, I will go so far as to say I think this is the underlying reason God allowed Nebuchadnezzar's predicament! Let me show you what I mean. Recall in our Revelation 17 study that John saw a certain number of empires which would come before God's kingdom would finally be established? Now note the clear parallel between what happened to 'Neb' as an individual and what has occurred on a grander scale of mankind's kingdoms on the whole. Neb's craziness in the wilderness for 2520 literal-days was a portrayal of all fallen-mankind's craziness in the "wilderness" for 2520 prophetic-days (years).

This is a beautiful picture of the Law of Double Reference. If we are to make any real, prophetic-sense (other than the typical generalizations most make of this) of the links between the books of Daniel and Revelation, we've got to get more specific. Let me do that now.

In our Revelation study we saw that the apocalyptic Scripture references set Babylon as the first in a string of certain earthly empires. Most historians give a beginning date of 606 B.C. as when Babylon took Israel into captivity, holding them then for seventy years. Now, Israel has always been God's prophetic "time-clock". Therefore, I think it is reasonable to take the year of their captivity as the signficant beginning date of this particular prophecy. Following through on that thought one day, here's what was discovered:

$$
\begin{array}{r}
2,520 \\
- 606 \\
\hline
1,914 \\
+ 4 \\
\hline
= 1,918 \text{ A.D.}
\end{array}
$$

(The reason for the addition of the four years, you recall, is due to the calendar error. I'm assuming Jesus' birth as 5 B.C.).

What do we know about the year 1918 that might be of prophetic significance? That's the year WW1 ended! Since we are looking for something which would relate to national Israel here, the question arises, "can we find anything of pertinence in this regard?" We sure can!

Near the end of WW1, Great Britain drove the Turks out of Israel (the nation 'Neb' held captive; the same nation God dispersed for 2,000 years from their land; the same *"fig-tree"* nation Jesus told us to watch at the end of the age, etc.,). It was this British action that set the stage for the Balfour Declaration which allowed Jews to once again purchase land in their ancient homeland.

Now let's try to make some sense of all these facts. I believe World War One was a battle which marked a special time-spot of gigantic prophetic significance, call it a breaking up of the old order. It was the beginning of the *time of the end.* It is no little thing that the conflict was world-wide. Modern man tends to think of such conflicts as commonplace but a war of this magnitude had never occurred before in all history!

We have determined there 'just happens' to be a 2,520 year time-span separating Nebuchaddezzar's day (606 B.C.) and the year which saw the beginning of the re-establishment in our day of Israel, God's prophetic-time-clock nation. Remember now, this is the same literal number of days (2520) that Nebuchaddezzar spent in the wilderness. We see again how God used a literal-day situation as a prophetic scenario which would later have a long-range counterpart.

And look at this: counting forward 30 years from 1918, we come to 1948. Do you know the Biblical inference of the number 30? It means *maturity.* (Ex: Jesus began His ministry at age 30.) And what was important about 1948? That was the very year Israel was once again established as a real nation.

Another important number which relates here is 70, the number of a generation. Counting forward 70 years from 1918 brings us to 1988. And if we count backwards 2,520 from 1988, we come to 536 B.C. which, according to Reese's Chronological Bible, was the coincidental year of the end of Israel's captivity in Babylon! Can you accept all these dates and times involving Israel are but mere-chance occurrences? Not me.

Recall from our Revelation study of chapter 18, that spiritual Babylon (Babylon The Great) would eventually reach a point when the "bride" and the "Bridegroom" would no longer be in her (which has reference to the Rapture and the marriage feast). Well, just as surely as there finally came a time for

366

national Israel to be released from national Babylon in 536 A.D., a time will come for 'spiritual Israel' — Christ's "bride", the Church — to likewise be released from 'spiritual Babylon'. I'm not predicting a specific year this will occur but there is too much fulfilled prophecy and parallelism here, both in words and numbers, to not realize the Christian age is fast-approaching a climactic state. Jesus said the Father alone knows the exact "day and hour" of the end but the stage seems to now be set. The fog is lifting. And, there is yet more proof.

> Let me again comment on the recent war in the Middle East. Iraq is the modern name for Babylon. And just as in days of old, her purpose was to destroy national Israel. Oil, the Palestinian issue and all the rest, are but surface problems associated with the deeper, spiritual conflict which still lingers in the hearts and minds of those possessing the 'Nebuchadnezzar-complex'. Saddam Hussein is possessed by this drive. The Gulf War illustrates the Mohammadan-uprising forecasted earlier in this book. (Remember, much of the information here was written long before this war. The first draft of this book was finished in 1979. It has been edited several times since then including this final version now in 1994.)

PROPHECY # TWO

The next prophecy I want to comment on also seems to have a double application. It comes from Daniel 5 and concerns another Babylon king. He had seen a hand writing on a wall which said:

"And this is the writing that was written; mene, mene, tekel, upharsin." (Daniel 5:25).

As we've seen, distant prophecies are often found hidden in the time it took for some particular, short-range prophecy to take place. Using the Law of Double Reference, one takes the number of those literal days and assumes they have a yearly meaning also. (This assumption is not mere speculation. The text itself usually includes implications of long-range applicability.) But here in Daniel 5, we find the 'mysterious' numbers hidden another way. The words *mene, mene, tekel* and *upharsin* are Aramaic weights. (This particular segment of Daniel was written in Aramaic in the original writings — not Hebrew.)

It is strange (though not unusual) that God would not only reveal such a profound truth to an ungodly king, but also that it would be given in such an odd manner. Just imagine the actual situation: the king (Belshazzar) had thrown a great party and had demanded his princes to bring the beautiful things his grandfather Nebuchadnezzar had stolen from Israel. They were eating and drinking and having a grand-ole-time when, all of a sudden, king Belshazzar sees this hand (no body mind you, just a hand!) writing out words on a wall. Now that would get anybody's attention! Here's how Belshazzar responded:

"Then the king's countenance was changed, and his thoughts troubled him, so that the joints of his loins were loosed, and his knees smote one against another." (Daniel 5:6).

This verse always makes me smile. It says God has a great sense of humor. But there is a very serious revelation here too. Following in his grandfather's footsteps, Belshazzar calls on Daniel to interpret the vision. Daniel comes and says:

"This is the interpretation of the thing: Mene: God hath numbered thy kingdom, and finished it. Tekel: Thou art weighed in the balances, and art found wanting. Peres: Thy kingdom is divided, and given to the Medes and Persians." (verses 26 - 28)

Now this interpretation had application for both Belshazzar as an individual and his kingdom as a whole. For Belshazzar it meant he would die that night; it also meant his kingdom would later be taken by the Medes and the Persians. Both happened.

368

At the time, Daniel limited his verbal interpretation to these two short-range events. But notice this very important little detail in Daniel's explanation: Belshazzar had also seen a word called upharsin — Aramaic. But when Daniel interpreted it he changed this word (and only this word), to "peres" — a Hebrew word! Now why did he do that? Was this a mere slip of the pen? A mistranslation? Or, was it designed as a clue for us? I think the latter. Let's follow Daniel's suggestion and change Belshazzar's vision of all the Aramaic weights to Hebrew:

MENE	=	MINAH
MENE	=	MINAH
TEKEL	=	SHEKEL
UPHARSIN	=	PERES

Minah, shekel and peres are Jewish weights. Now the lowest, useful Jewish weight was the "gerah". Let's convert all the larger weights into the common gerah and see what we've got:

MINAH	=	1000 GERAHS
MINAH	=	1000 GERAHS
SHEKEL	=	20 GERAHS
UPHARSIN	=	500 GERAHS
TOTAL	=	2520 GERAHS

Look at the interesting number that "pops up" again! The very same number which was earlier associated with Belshazzar's grandaddy, Nebuchadnezzar. In "Neb's" case, we saw the prophecy logically related to the end of age, specifically, I think, to the document which allowed Israel to begin the re-establishment of their nation (1918). To arrive at that we simply started with the Babylonian captivity and counted forward 2520 years. In Belshazzar's case though, the ancient date of significance is his own death, (see verse 30) which history has recorded as 539 B.C.

369

(It is quite reasonable for us to make this assumption because Belshazzar's death is what set the stage for the commencement of the next empire, the Medo-Persian).

Following the pattern, let's count forward 2520 years from Belshazzar's death and see where it ends:

$$2520$$
$$- \ \ 539$$
$$1981$$
$$+ \ \ \ \ \ 4$$

$$= \ 1985 \ \text{A.D.}$$

I'm uncertain as to exactly what was supposed to have happened in 1985 insofar as fulfilled prophecy is concerned. It is interesting to note, however, that Iran (modern name for Persia) was at war with Iraq (modern name for Babylon) from about 1982 until the mid-80s. Was this conflict perhaps but another indicator of the end of this age?

Think about this: 2520 years ago the Persians fought Babylon and killed king Belshazzar — and now, 2520 years later, Persia (Iran) has once again been battling with Babylon (Iraq). And remember, the mysterious handwriting had related to the old king that his days were "numbered", and that written message had contained in it a secret number which just happened to be 2520, the number of years separating the ancient war from today's Gulf conflicts! Again I ask, do you believe all this is just chance-coincidence? No way. This is fulfilled prophecy.

THE SACRED CUBIT

With consideration given to the fact that Daniel's 'mystery' here involved a certain measuring system of his day, I find it interesting that in this very hour America is undergoing a change of our system of weights and measures. There is a big push from within and without, to get us away from the old tried-

and-true British system, into the European metric system. I have worked with metrics in practical situations for 30+ years (essentially all optometric measurements are based on it), so I'm probably more acquainted with the system than the average American citizen. From many practical considerations, the metric concepts are not an improvement. It may be man's best, admittedly appealing in some situations, but I'm convinced God 'consigned' earth with a better measuring system.

Yes, you heard me right. I believe God actually gave a special measuring system to certain, ancient men of God. It is based on the Sacred Cubit. Let me give you a brief rundown: First of all, the Sacred Cubit is distinctly different from the common cubit of 18 inches. Without going into all the background, the Sacred Cubit was probably used in the building of Noah's Ark, the Tabernacle in the Wilderness, Solomon's Temple, the Ark of the Covenant and, of all things, the Great Pyramid of Giza in Cairo, Egypt.

The Sacred Cubit is about 25 inches long and it was broken down into 25 equal parts, one part being the Sacred Inch. An amazing fact to me was to learn that the Sacred Inch just happens to be almost exactly equal to our English inch.

My own tests and observations indicate that the human body seems to be designed around it! The length of human fingers, the thumbspan, the handbreadth, the average length of the forearm, and much more, seem to have a definite relationship to the English system when average comparisons are made.

Now, let me show you another astounding fact: The polar radius of the earth, as recently determined from the orbits of artificial Earth satellites, is 3,949.89 miles. Dividing this figure by 10,000,000 equals 25.027 British inches, which is the precise length of the Sacred Cubit to three decimal places! This means the radius of the earth is 10,000,000 Sacred Cubits. Why is this so astounding? Well, first note the perfect round number. Secondly, this degree of accuracy of measurement was not realized by modern man until 1958. Thirdly, this exactness was obviously known by <u>someone</u> 5,000 years ago.

You mathematicians will notice that in terms of 'significant numbers' the British inch is the same as the sacred inch. In other words, there are 25.03 British inches in 25 sacred inches, or 1 SACRED CUBIT. For all practical purposes then, the British inch is the same as the sacred inch! The amazing thing about this is that so few people seem to know anything about it. I discovered it only 14 years ago. I was surprised to learn that there is actually a great deal of literature available on it.

Surely such accurate measurements in ancient times could have been known only by God. And being the loving God He is, He has revealed something of His perfect nature in this very beautiful manner. I mean, after all, God made the earth so it should not surprise us to learn that He would have no problem in knowing (and sharing with us) a system which would be most accurate to use in working within His creation. But man has abused God's laws — all God's laws — including those physical laws designed for ordinary life here on this planet.

Through ignorance and unbelief, Europe, for the most part, has already thrown God's measuring systems away. Today, America is in the process of doing the same thing. Fallen-man is tossing out God's spiritual-yardstick, the Bible, which was God's way of 'measuring' us, godly-wise and morally-wise. And we're also now dumping God's physical yard-stick measuring system, the British System, which was obviously based on the God-given Sacred Cubit System. So what does all this mean?

Folks, mankind is being "...*weighed in the balances*," and is being "...*found wanting.*" Unregenerate man always thinks he has a better idea. He wants the easy way out. Since the building of the tower of Babel he has continued his search to do his own thing, in his own way — without God. Yielding the English measuring system and joining the ranks of the general mediocrity is but one of many ways we demonstrate unbelief. I like the old system. It feels right in my hands. I sense its correctness in my heart. And I hate to see it go.

PROPHECY # THREE

Most apocalyptic-Scripture interpreters agree that Alexander The Great is prophesied in Daniel 8. In verse 5 he is represented as a "he-goat".

"And as I was considering, behold, an he-goat came from the west on the face of the whole earth, and touched not the ground: And the goat had a notable horn between his eyes."

In verse 8 we are told:

"...when he was strong, the great horn was broken:..."

This refers to the early death of Alexander. He died at age 33. Now for further validation that this king was in fact Alexander the Great, look at verse 21:

"And the rough goat is the king of Grecia: And the great horn that is between his eyes is the first king."

Now, once again we find one of those mystery numbers. Note how cleverly Daniel worked it into the Scriptures: (Actually, it was the Holy Spirit's work.)

"Then I heard one saint speaking, and another saint said unto that certain saint which spake, 'How long shall be the vision concerning the daily sacrifice, and the transgression of desolation, to give both the sanctuary and the host to be trodden under foot?' And he said unto me, 'unto two thousand and three hundred days: Then shall the sanctuary be cleansed.'" (Daniel 8:13 & 14)

This topic intrigued me so much a few years ago I wrote a tract on it. Earlier I had given a certain pastor a copy of one of my first drafts of the manuscript you are now reading. He had rejected much my overall presentation but after reading the tract on Alexander he later said to me, *"Lance, this is really good!"* (I guess a smaller "bite" of my overall concept was "digestible" but not the whole thing at once! That was hard for me to accept at the time but I'm learning it's a normal process when men have already made up their minds about something. But, since it reached my pastor friend, I'll share with you the same information I wrote in the tract.)

ALEXANDER THE GREAT

One of the most influential men to have ever lived, ancient or modern, would have to be Alexander The Great. Much has been written about him and most encyclopedias will give you a fairly good picture of the man and his accomplishments.

Briefly, Alexander built one of the ancient-world's largest empires, stretching from the Mediterranean Sea to India. He did this in eleven years, ending in early death at age 33 in 323 B.C. Since his life and accomplishments were just 'peaking out', most humanists would probably say his was a very untimely death. Actually, just the opposite is true. My main purpose here is to neither praise nor degrade Alexander The Great. I merely want to report about him with the same attitude as the Scriptures portray: a powerful ruler who became head of one of the most prominent ancient empires.

In 1981, when I first wrote about this, I became aware of seven occurrences that year which, directly and/or indirectly, involved the great historical figure, Alexander The Great.

1. In the December issue of Time magazine, one of the books reviewed was called "Funeral Games" by Mary Renault, which mainly emphasized Alexander The Great.
2. In the same issue was an advertisement about an exhibition going on in America at that time called "The Search For Alexander".

374

3. Bookstores everywhere were featuring a book by that title.

4. That summer (1981), I took my daughter and one of her friend's to Carmel for a vacation. While the girls shopped in the novelty stores, I browsed around and became somewhat startled by the fact that seemingly half the items bore a picture of a one-horned animal — sometimes a goat! It was the "fad" of that year.

5. Also that summer (in fact, right at the exact time I was studying Daniel 8 and doing this research on Alexander), I was shocked one morning as I sipped my coffee and read the morning newspaper. Right there on the front page staring me in the face, was a picture of a real-life, one-horned, shaggy white goat! I am not kidding!
The article explained how a couple had discovered an ancient technique for breeding such an animal. I'm not vouching on the authenticity of this. However, the animal made the 6:00 o'clock television news that same night and after that he was a regular 'show-goat' at Africa-Marineworld near San Francisco. Another thing which got my attention that day was the pet's name: he was called LANCELOT — my own, childhood nickname! Folks, when God wants to get our attention He sometimes works it in, in strange and mysterious ways!

6. On January 1, 1981 of that same year, modern Greece (the modern remnant of Alexander's empire) became the 10th member of the Common Market. (More on this fact later.)

7. About the same time, another newspaper article which I had earlier clipped out and saved, came to my mind. It was a report of a recent archealogical discovery. They had found artifacts of a place where ancient Olympic Games had been held in Greece. The point of interest? They approximated the date the place was last active as 2300 years ago! (Remember this number.)

THE ANALYSIS

I think it is important for you to realize that the above seven things happened almost simultaneously and, amazingly, during this very writing. I didn't engineer any of it. I merely observed it. Daniel 8 was the central focus of my attention in my on-going prophecy study at that time, which I also didn't plan. It just worked out that way. I had started my study of prophecy in 1978 and in the summer of 1981, I had, in God's providential timing and control of things, arrived at the pertinent passage in Daniel at that strategic point in time.

Suppose *you* were a prophetically-inclined individual and these facts came your way at the same time: a book about Alexander which suddenly hits the market in 1981, + an ongoing, worldwide exhibition of recently-discovered Alexandrian artifacts, + other books suddenly appearing on the scene on the Search for Alexander, + novelty shops filled with pictures of one-horned animals, + a real, one-horned shaggy-goat is bred with your nickname, + Greece becomes the 10th member of the EEC and finally — super + — the discovery of a 2300 year old Grecian-Olympic-Games arena. Also, imagine that all these realities developed in the same year. How would *you* handle those facts?

You need one more piece of the puzzle to see how it all fits together. The Scripture in Daniel 8 says that the truth of God would be trodden under foot for a period of 2300 *'EVENINGS-MORNINGS'*, after which would come a restoration. It doesn't say 2300 "*days*" in the original. Your version may say "days" (as my quotation from the King James above) but if you look it up in the NAS you'll see "*evenings and mornings*". Although this is better, it still isn't quite accurate because no "and" appears in the original language. *Evenings-mornings* would be a closer English rendering of the

376

original language, the dash conveying some kind of link between the "*evenings*" and the "*mornings*".

I wondered why Daniel would give so much careful attention to this point. I had read[11] that in those days (i.e., Daniel's day) that people often used an expression similar to our word "*evening*" when they wanted to make reference to the darker portion of the year — the fall-winter season; and "*morning*" to that portion of the year which has more daylight hours — spring-summer. When the two terms are put together like this —— *evening-morning* —— the result is a rather obvious connotation of a one-year cycle! Now, with that background, all of a sudden a whole new picture emerges from this passage. The obvious inference is that 2300 "evenings-mornings" means **2300 years!**

To prove that this is a correct interpretation, note how it was explained to Daniel:

"*And the vision of the evenings and mornings which has been told is true; but keep the vision secret, for IT PERTAINS TO MANY DAYS IN THE FUTURE.*" (Dan. 8:26).

If the one explaining Daniel's vision had only meant 2300 literal days, surely he wouldn't have used this kind of language. (That this definitely "pertains to the time of the end", see also Daniel 8:17). The phrase "*many days in the future*" provides the key to understanding that this Scripture refers to a long, long time ahead. We also get more exact information by realizing the facts behind the little-known, "*evenings-mornings*" expression.

But even if one agrees that the far distant future is in view here, the question remains, "where does one start counting and what is supposed to happen at the end of the 2300 years?"

---

[11]"Flee To The Mountains" by R. E. Dunlop

I approached this with the same logic as I did in Belshazzar's case — the leader's death. As I said earlier, Alexander died in 323 B.C. (i.e., when the *notable horn* was *'broken'*). Now we are beginning to see why God has allowed this date to be so well recorded for us (i.e., everybody seems to agree on this one, Bible scholars and secular-historians alike). So, back again to the same little formula:

$$
\begin{array}{r}
2300 \\
-323 \\
\hline
1977 \\
+\ 4 \\
\hline
=\ \mathbf{1981} \quad !!!
\end{array}
$$

Well, what do you know? We arrive at yet another date which ended in our era! But that brings up another question: what was supposed to happen in 1981? Obviously the main thing concerned Greece becoming the 10th member of the EEC, having been offically recognized **January 1, 1981**. Another point I observed was the fact that this date completed exactly **23 years** of the EEC since its inception. Was this perhaps God's way of providing a double emphasis relative to the <u>2300</u> years? Folks, God deals in the affairs of men in very real, recognizable and recordable ways.

What's the prophetic significance of becoming the 10th member of the EEC? Just this. In the preceding chapter (7), Daniel describes this very organization. He explains it as a ten-horned beast which will arise at the end of the age. And from this group will later rise its final king who will link them in one accord. This will be a 'resurrection' of the Roman Empire over which will reside the greatest empire-ruler to have ever come on the scene — Alexander having been one of the greatest forerunners. (We have already covered much of this in Revelation. Daniel 7 and 8 are the Old-Testament counterpart.)

Now the main point to see here is that THE TEN must be in place before we can expect the *"man of sin"* (as Paul calls him) to come. He will come from the <u>eleventh</u> horn. He is <u>not</u> one of THE TEN. What we must understand though is that when Greece became the tenth (fulfilling the prophecy of the *"notable horn"* of Daniel 8), the stage was set for the final anti-Christ picture to unfold. Quite obviously the "TEN" had to come first before an eleventh could arise. What I'm saying folks is that the prophecies of Daniel 7 and 8 are RIGHT NOW almost complete.

One final word on "Prophecy # 3": Daniel 8:14 says:

"And he said to me, 'For two thousand three hundred days; then the sanctuary shall be cleansed.'

This 2300-year prophecy is not predicting the end of time; I believe the intended meaning is that the end of the 2300 *"evenings-mornings"* prophecy signals the soon-to-follow Kingdom of Christ. Only Christ can *"cleanse"* the sanctuary and it won't be done until His second coming.

Therefore, we have now seen three prophecies, none of which spell out the actual date of the end, but each provides its own unique part of the overall puzzle of the times and conditions JUST PRIOR to the end. This, I believe, is what Jesus meant when He said:

"...Behold the fig tree (Israel), *and all the trees* (other pertinent nations of prophetic importance); *as soon as they put forth leaves, you see it and know for yourselves that the summer is now near. Even so you, too, when you see these things happening, recognize that the kingdom of God is near."* Luke 21:29-31.

PROPHECY # 4

DANIEL 12: THE 1290 AND 1335 "DAYS" AND THE 'ABOMINATION OF DESOLATION'

Insofar as chronology is concerned, the main essence of this chapter is found in verses 11 and 12:

"And from the time that the daily sacrifice shall be taken away, and the abomination that maketh desolate set up, there shall be a thousand two hundred ninety days.
Blessed is he that waiteth, and cometh to the thousand three hundred and five and thirty days."

Most prophecy 'experts' teach these 1290 and 1335 days start from the mid-way point of the final 7-year period. They believe that (1) the *'abomination that maketh desolate'* refers to the anti-Christ and (2) the *"time that the daily sacrifice"* being taken away refers to the anti-Christ having put a stop to the then re-established Jewish custom of animal sacrifices. This may eventually be true but at this time (1994), as usual, I believe the Historical aspect must first take priority over the Futuristic.

Now, let's put all the Biblical references to the *"abomination of desolation"* together for easy comparison:

1. *"When ye therefore shall see the abomination of desolation, spoken of by Daniel the prophet, stand in the holy place, ..."* Matt. 24:15.
2. *"But when ye shall see the abomination of desolation, spoken of by Daniel the prophet, standing where it ought not, ..."* Mark 13:14.
3. *"And arms shall stand on his part, and they shall pollute the sanctuary of strength, and shall take away the daily sacrifice, and they shall place the abomination that maketh desolate."* Dan. 11:31.

380

4. *"And from the time that the daily sacrifice shall be taken away, and the abomination that maketh desolate set up, there shall be a thousand two hundred and ninety days."* Dan. 12:11.

In the Mark 13 passage we saw that Judea was to *"flee into the mountains"* when they saw the *"abomination of desolation"*. In our Revelation study I shared my belief that the *"abomination"* was a reference to the Mohammadan Dome of the Rock, and the "fleeing into the mountains" referred to Israel's "flight" into the many nations during the Christian era.

Now note the slight variations in the way the different authors made reference to the *"abomination of desolation"*: One said it *"stands";* another called it an *"it"*, still another said it was *"placed"* and finally that it was *"set up"*. An unbiased, straight-forward interpretation of these words leads to only one logical conclusion — a <u>BUILDING</u> was in mind. The anti-Christ system may very well be the futuristic side of this coin but we must search out the more obvious meaning first.

As pointed out earlier, the dome on the Mohammadan mosque in Jerusalem was completed in 691 A.D. Now let's assume the Daniel and Gospel references are speaking of this as the <u>Historical</u> *"abomination of desolation"* (not to preclude the later Futuristic application). If this is true, 691 A.D. would seem to be the feasible beginning date of this prophecy. Let's also assume that the 1290 and the 1335 *"days"* are 'prophetic days' (i.e., years). Thus, to arrive at the distant-end of the prophecies we merely add these numbers to the year 691 A.D. (No 4 year correction need be made here for the calendar errors occurred prior to 691 A.D.)

Date # 1	Date # 2
691 A.D. (mosque finished)	691 A.D.
+1290	+1335
= 1981 A.D.	= 2026 A.D.

THE INTERPRETATION

The first and most obvious observation is that the 1290 *"days"* end the same year as Prophecy # 3 did, although starting from a completely different date and based on completely different concepts! That alone is striking. The thing common to chapters 8 and 12 is that they both refer to the time of anti-Christ when much wickedness occurs, which is to be followed by a period of righteousness.

With regards to Prophecy # 4, verse 10 says concerning the end of the 1290 days:

"Many will be purged, purified and refined; but the wicked will act wickedly, and none of the wicked will understand, but those who have insight will understand."

Again Daniel had sought to know the meaning of these numbers and how they applied to the coming events. He was told:

"...Go your way, Daniel, for these words are concealed up until the end time." Daniel 12:9.

O.K., suppose the end of the 1290 *"days"* of Daniel 12 is intended to be coincident with the end of the 2300 *"evenings-mornings"* of Daniel 8, why were the 1335 *"days"* mentioned in the same passage? As I've studied other views on this subject, I've learned this one gives everybody problems. It doesn't "fit" perfectly into my Historical concepts either but neither do the Futurists handle it very well. However, as you might guess, I do have a perspective on it.

Let's look at the verse again:

"How blessed is he who keeps waiting and attains to the 1335 days!" Dan. 12:12.

Looking back at the above mathematics, we see that counting forward 1335 *"days"* from 691 A.D. will bring us to the year 2026. Is there anything we presently know of which might be predictable to occur that year? After all, if the anti-Christ and his government is soon to come, the 1,335 prophetic days would take us into the millennium!

I'm not sure about this but there is a very significant anniversary coming up in 2026 A.D. It will be precisely **2,000** years since the year Jesus started His earthly ministry during His first advent! How did I get this?

Jesus' age: (see Luke 3:23)	30 years
Jesus' assumed birth year (5 B.C.)	-4 years
	= 26 A.D.
	+2000 years
Brings us to the year:	2026 A.D.

In making this computation, I have followed the same assumptions used throughout the book, that Jesus' birth was 5 B.C. As a reminder, there is no "0" year so one must add (or subtract as the case may be) 4 years. If this is the God-intended meaning of this passage, then the numerical aspect of the Scripture would indeed be fulfilled in the year 2026 A.D.

But there's another significant point here. Looking again at verse 12, we see that Daniel was told, "...*BLESSED is he who keeps waiting and attains to the 1335 days!*" Why would this *"he"* be so "*BLESSED*" by "*waiting and attaining*"? Is it not a fair appraisal to guess that this "*he*" refers to anyone who goes into the millennium with Christ? What a blessing to "*wait*" for; what a blessed reality to "*attain*"! Therefore, it could refer to (1) Christians or (2) bloodline Jews who go into the Kingdom under Christ's rule. In either case, this "*he*" (or she) could most-appropriately be called "*blessed*".

So, although I can't be dogmatic about this evaluation, it certainly brings life to the mysterious 1335 "days", doesn't it? If I could be so bold, it could even be God's answer as revealed in verse 9 which says that "*...these words are sealed up until the end time*", the "*seal*" perhaps being broken right now.

SUMMARY

We have examined four prophecies in the book of Daniel. The first one, associated with Nebuchadnezzar, had a number which related to time, 'hidden' by a term called "*seven times*" which we learned means 2520 "*days*". The second number, also 2520, was discovered to be Aramaic weights, but which, again, had time associated with it. The third mysterious number was 2300, which the prophet referred to as "*evenings-mornings*". Then fourthly, we saw in combo, 1290 and 1335 "*days*".

Now the incredible facts are that each of these prophecies in its original context was found to be associated with a particular empire, person or place, all of which have been dated by both secular and Biblical historians through God's providential control. Simply counting forward from a particular event described in each of the Scripture passages, we discovered that every one of the predictions had a "deadline" year which contained some particular event that seemed to meet the requirements demanded by each prophecy. Equally interesting, and even more importantly, these prophecies — while starting as much as 13 centuries apart — all end in our era!!!

In a nutshell, all I have done was to consider each situation, count forward the number of years as stipulated in the text, note the year of destination, and then look at modern, well-known facts which seem to relate to what Daniel was talking about. You also need to know I did not attempt to force certain events into the prophecy. These things came to my attention in amazing ways, which would in itself require a small book to explain them all.

Now I've perhaps introduced several new ideas to you, but if you'll take the time to go back through the book, I think you'll agree that my approach has been both logical and straight-forward. We must balance the Historical and Futuristic perspectives of Biblical prophecy. In my opinion, neither viewpoint makes altogether good sense without the other. It is my hope and prayer that this effort will at least be a significant reminder to Christians that God is a prophetic *God of the Ages,* not just of the last few moments right before the end. Indeed, understanding the Historical, with its own end clearly a part of the whole, is what allows us to get a better view of when the Futuristic begins. If I may one last time borrow the apostle John's closing comment from Revelation:

"Even so, Come Lord Jesus!"

BIBLIOGRAPHY

The primary reference source for this book was, of course, the Holy Bible. The King James Version and/or the New King James Version were used throughout the text.

The footnotes of other references are listed below indicating the page numbers where the particular quotations can be found:

1. "Commentary On The Whole Bible" by Jamieson, Fausset, & Brown. Pub. by ZONDERVAN. Page xv.

2. "The 100" by Michael H. Hart. Pub. by HART. Page 17.

3. A letter from Jacque Cousteau. Page 59.

4. "Operation World" by Patrick Johnstone. Pub. by WEC. "Let The Earth Hear" by Paul E. Freed. Pub. by NELSON. Page 119.

5. THE HISTORY OF ENGLAND by Jarold J. Shultz. Pub. by BARNES & NOBLE. Page 120.

6. "Days Of Praise" by Henry Morris. Pub. by INSTITUTE FOR CREATION RESEARCH. Page 126.

7. "The Light And The Glory" by Peter Marshall and David Manuel. Pub. by REVELL. Page 130.

8. "Apocalypse When" by Ed Moore. Pub. by CHRISTCHURCH PUBLICATIONS. Page 156.

9. "TIME Magazine". Pub. by TIME Inc. Issue June 11, 1984. Page 256.

10. "INSIGHT Magazine". Pub. by NEWS WORLD COMMUNICATIONS Inc. Issue November 16, 1987. Page 256.

11. "Flee To The Mountains" by Reginald E. Dunlop. Page 377.